SharePoint
CHEAP
THRILLS

Ira Fuchs

ihf
PUBLISHING

SharePoint Cheap Thrills

Published By
IHF Publishing
Forest Hills, NY 11375

Copyright ©2013 by IHF Publishing
Forest Hills, New York

ISBN 978-0-615-84032-1

Book design & layout by Mark Hogan
markhogandesign.com

Acknowledgements:

I am grateful for my tenure at Microsoft where
I have had the opportunity to work with and
think about SharePoint a lot, which in turn has
made this book possible. I would also like to
thank my manager at Microsoft, Adam Beacher,
for being supportive and enthusiastic about
all of my endeavors. Everyone should have the
good fortune to work for someone like Adam.

To my family – Jean Citarella, Chloe and
Adam Fuchs, and Jackson our cat; thank you for
letting me use your pictures in this book,
and for being my favorite people in the world.

Also by Ira Fuchs:

Enterprise Application Development in SharePoint 2010 – Creating an End-to-End Application without Code

The book takes the reader through the complete process of creating a sophisticated application using declarative development

 tools and methodologies. All of the application functionality is implemented using rule logic, information sets, and attribute settings.

This book is valuable to anyone who has an interest and stake in SharePoint application development. People who are not conventional programmers will be very comfortable with the no-code approach of the book, while developers who primarily work in code will be pleased to discover the efficiencies, power and control that the declarative development capabilities of SharePoint provides them.

Contents

Introduction

In my first book, **Enterprise Application Development in SharePoint 2010 - Creating an End-to-End Application without Code**, my objective was to demonstrate the viability of SharePoint as a platform for creating scalable, distributed applications incorporating complex business logic, identity-driven behavior, and information from external systems. It was also my intent to showcase the value and virtues of SharePoint's rule and configuration based development paradigm: it is easy-to-use and understand; and the application components created in SharePoint are readily extensible, self-documenting and reusable. Neither of these claims can be made for code based development platforms.

However, because I chose a sophisticated reference application to make my case with, the reader in turn had to work through a comprehensive development process in order to obtain the full value of the book. The consequence of which was to limit the audience for the book to those people who were seriously invested in being SharePoint developers.

In this book my objectives are the same but I wanted to make the information and knowledge accessible to a much broader audience, and make it easier to negotiate and absorb. To this purpose, I have devised a thematic approach and named the book after it: "SharePoint Cheap Thrills". Each of the book's chapters describes how to implement a truly useful, real-world productivity solution based on SharePoint, in just hours. The cost to master the information presented in each chapter is "cheap": a very modest investment of time and effort. The payback however, in terms of the usefulness and applicability of the resulting solution is hugely "thrilling". Hence, "SharePoint Cheap Thrills"; getting something of substantial value for a nominal cost — a true bargain.

This is not merely a compilation of tips and tricks. The solutions that I have focused on address highly identifiable, common real-world needs that are typically not being met effectively. The fact that SharePoint provides the tools and functionality to address so many requirements is a testament to its robust capabilities. But many of SharePoint's most powerful and valuable features are not well understood, and consequently are under-utilized and under-appreciated. Hopefully, this book will go a long way to rectifying that imbalance and as a result people will take greater advantage of the more leveraged features and functions of SharePoint.

I learned a lot by writing this book. I hope that your experience reading it is equally as enlightening and gratifying. Please feel free to let me know what you think about the book. My email address is ira@ihfpublishing and you can also find me on Linked-In.

What You Need To Create the Solutions in this Book

To create all of the Solutions in this book you need to be working with SharePoint 2010 and Share-Point Designer 2010. If you are working with SharePoint 2013, either the On-Line or On-Premise version, you will need to use SharePoint Designer 2013. SharePoint Designer 2010 will not work with SharePoint 2013. One SharePoint Designer 2010 feature, Design editing mode, for manipulating List, Library and Data Views, is no longer available in SharePoint Designer 2013. The Solution described in Chapter 7 - "How to Create Custom Designed SharePoint Site Templates without Having to Modify SharePoint Master Pages, HTML Code or Style Sheets!" is entirely dependent on using Design editing mode in SharePoint Designer. Consequently the Solution cannot be implemented in SharePoint 2013. Some Solution features described in other chapters are also dependent on using Design edit mode but you can still implement the overall Solution without these features. This dependency is identified In each chapter where SharePoint Designer Design edit mode is utilized.

In the second half of Chapter 3 - "How to Set Up a Flexible and Scalable System for Distributing and Updating Contact Information in Outlook Using SharePoint Contact Lists and SharePoint External Content Types" an External Content Type is created in SharePoint Designer from an SQL database. The sample SQL database used is available for download on the Codeplex.com site at http://msftdb-prodsamples.codeplex.com/releases/view/93587. However you will also need to have access to an instance of SQL Server to execute this part of the Solution, which in most organizations requires the assistance of a Database Administrator.

Chapter 4 - "How to Efficiently Import Large Information Sets from Excel and Customize the Presenta-tion of Information Using View Styles and the Identity of the User" requires the Microsoft Office Excel application in any version from 2007 up.

Chapter 5 - "Using InfoPath Web Part Forms to Present Information Effectively and Enhance the Way SharePoint Pages Look" requires the InfoPath client application and InfoPath Form Services running on a SharePoint Server Farm. InfoPath Form Services is an Enterprise Feature requiring ECAL licenses.

Typographical Conventions Used in the Book

There is a lot of detailed information and procedures described in this book. In order to keep the procedural narrative from getting confusing the following typographical conventions are used.

Italicized text in the *Arial Narrow* typeface is used to identify proper nouns, such as *SharePoint*, and also to identify an object, artifact, feature or function that is the focus of an action such as:

> Return to the top *Term Group* to add the *Term Sets* for "Audience" and "Organization".

Text within "quotation marks" identifies a literal string that should be entered somewhere as illustrated in the line directly above.

Bold text is used to indicate an Illustration or on the word "Note" to call attention to something important. ***Bold and italicized*** text in the body of a paragraph is also used to call attention to something important.

How to Create a Great Scheduling and Resource Reservation System Using SharePoint Calendars

Every organization needs a flexible and scalable system for reserving and scheduling shared resources such as conference/meeting rooms and audio/visual equipment; or in a completely different context, the dining room seating or tennis court reservations in a club. Well guess what — both *SharePoint 2010* and *SharePoint 2013* provide great capabilities for this type of application. So why isn't that well known? Because the calendar features that enable these functions are hidden away like buried treasure. So let's get started setting up and configuring our Resource Reservation and Scheduling System. The steps involved in doing this are:

1. Activate the *Group Work Lists Feature*
2. Create the *Resource Groups* and *Resources*
3. Create Resource Reservation Events
4. Create a Reservation Approval Workflow

Activate the Group Work Lists Feature

The first thing we need to do is activate the *Group Work List Feature*. Go to the *Site Settings* page for the site where you want to activate this Feature as shown in **Illustration 1** below. Under *Site Actions* click on *Manage site features*.

Illustration 1

The *Features* page will display as shown in **Illustration 2** below.

Click the *Activate* button for the *Group Work Lists* Feature.

Illustration 2

Next, create a new calendar list and go to its *List Settings* page. Click on the *Title, description and navigation* settings link which will bring you to the *General Settings* page as shown in **Illustration 3** below. In the *Group Calendar Options* section click on the *Yes* radio button for *Use this Calendar for Resource Reservations* and click the *Save* button.

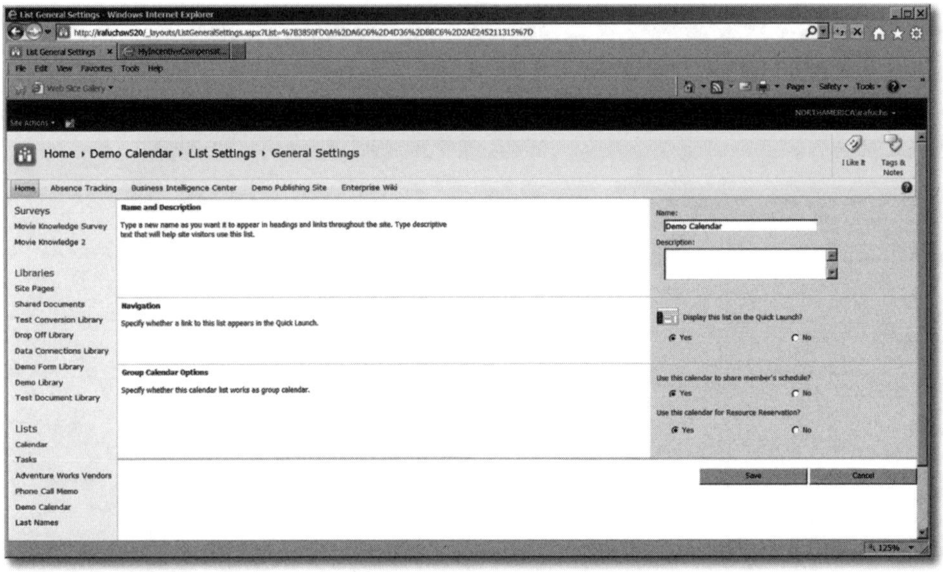

Illustration 3

When you return to the calendar and click on the *Events Ribbon* button you will now see the additional *New Event* options for *Schedule and Reservations and Reservations,* as well as the controls for adding people and resources to these events as shown in **Illustration 4** below.

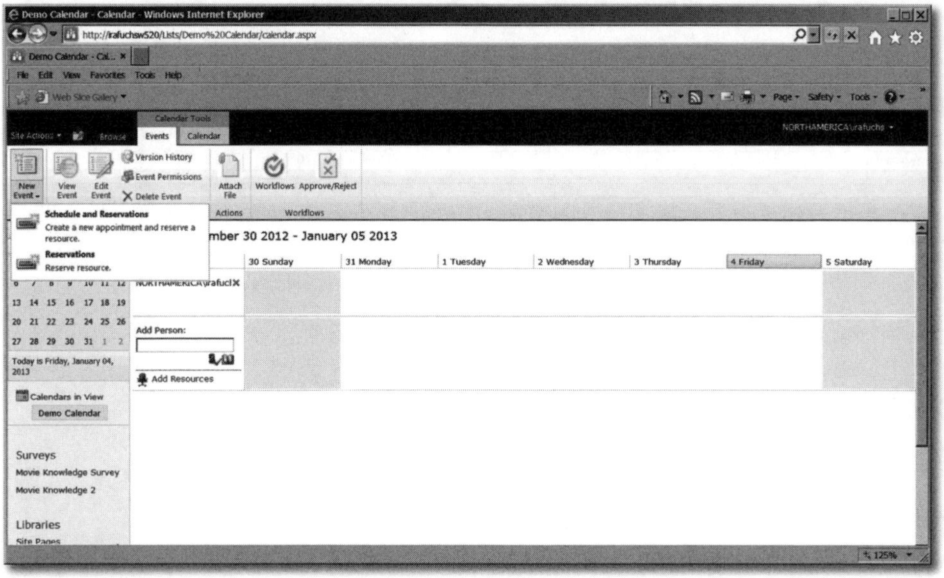

Illustration 4

Now click on the *Calendar Ribbon* button and you will see that the *Ribbon* now has additional button options for *People, Resources, Day Group* and *Week Group* as shown in **Illustration 5** below. When you select *Day Group* or *Week Group* on the *Ribbon* the options to add people and resources to events will display.

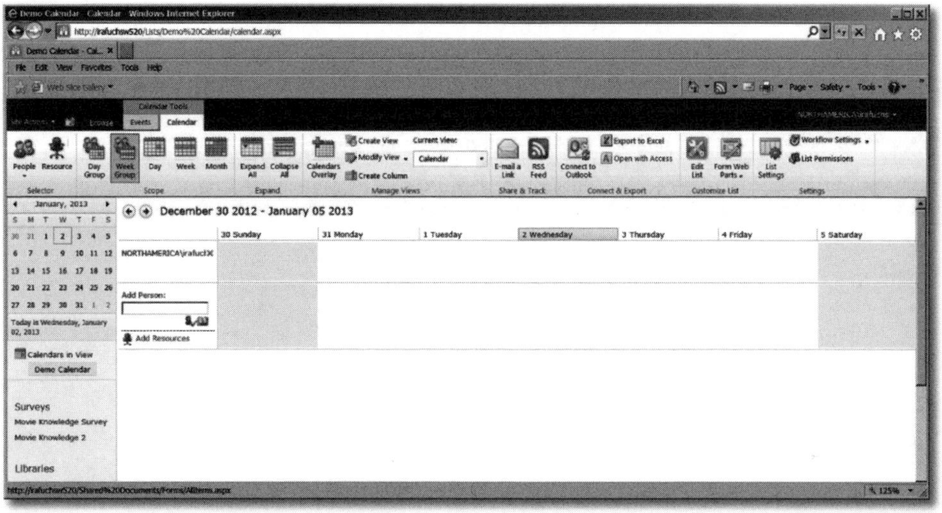

Illustration 5

In addition to these extended calendar features a *Resources* list was created when the *Group Work Lists Feature* was activated. Go to the *View All Site Content* page under *Site Settings*. Under *Lists* you will see the *Resources* list item. Click on it to go to the *Resources* list page as shown in **Illustration 6** below.

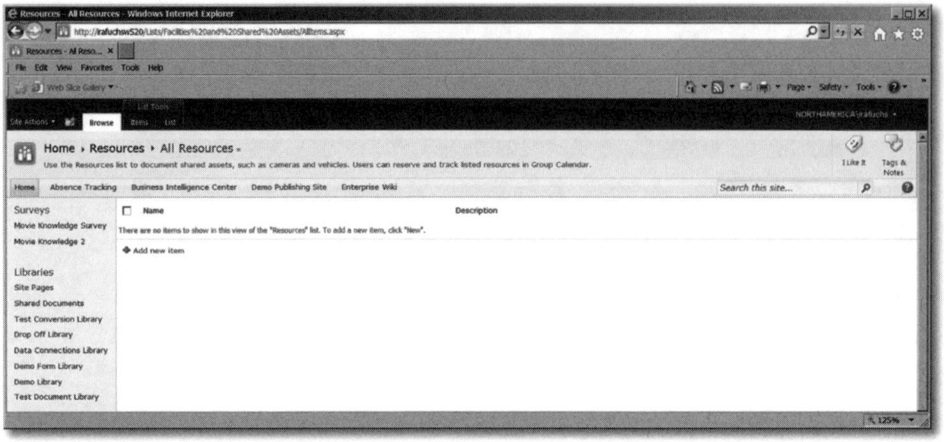

Illustration 6

How SharePoint Content Types Enable this Advanced Calendaring Functionality.

Content Types are the DNA of *SharePoint*. Practically everything in *SharePoint* is defined as a *Content Type* from which all other *SharePoint* artifacts are created and assembled into components. A *Content Type* is the abstract representation of a *SharePoint* artifact combined with its respective property settings. A *Content Type* is conceptually analogous to an XML schema that defines the content, structure and attributes of an object or function and is used to generate an actual usable instance of the object or function. A *Content Type* can also be copied and extended to create its derivatives. In *SharePoint, Content Types* can also have behavior; you can bind *Policies* and workflows to them. **Illustration 7** below displays the *Content Types* that were automatically created when the *Group Work Lists* Feature was activated.

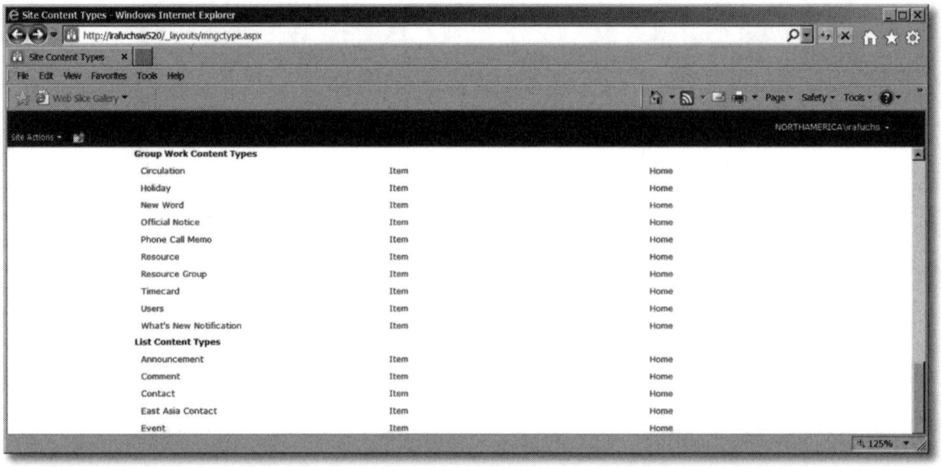

Illustration 7

Illustration 8 below shows the *Settings* page for the *Reservations Content Type.*

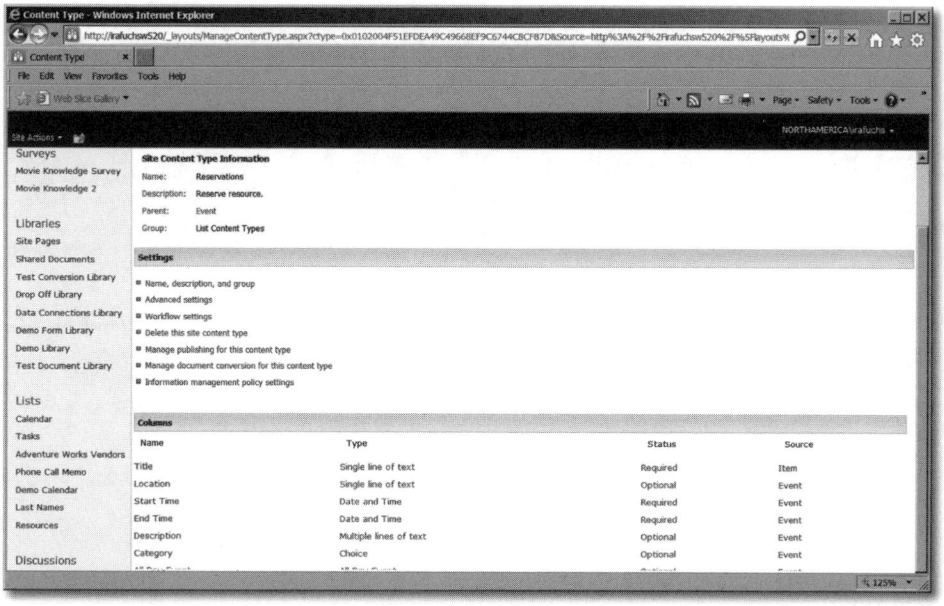

Illustration 8

Illustration 9 below shows the *List Settings* page for the *Demo Calendar* with the *Content Types* that were instantiated for the calendar when the *Resource Reservation* setting was turned on in the *Title, description and navigation* page.

Illustration 9

Illustration 10 below shows the *Settings* page for the *Schedule and Reservations Content Type* for the calendar. Note that this *Content Type* is a copy of the master *Content Type* in the *Site Collection Content Type Gallery* and it has been extended with additional columns. This also was done automatically when the *Group Work Lists Feature* was activated and the *Resource Reservation* setting turned on for the calendar.

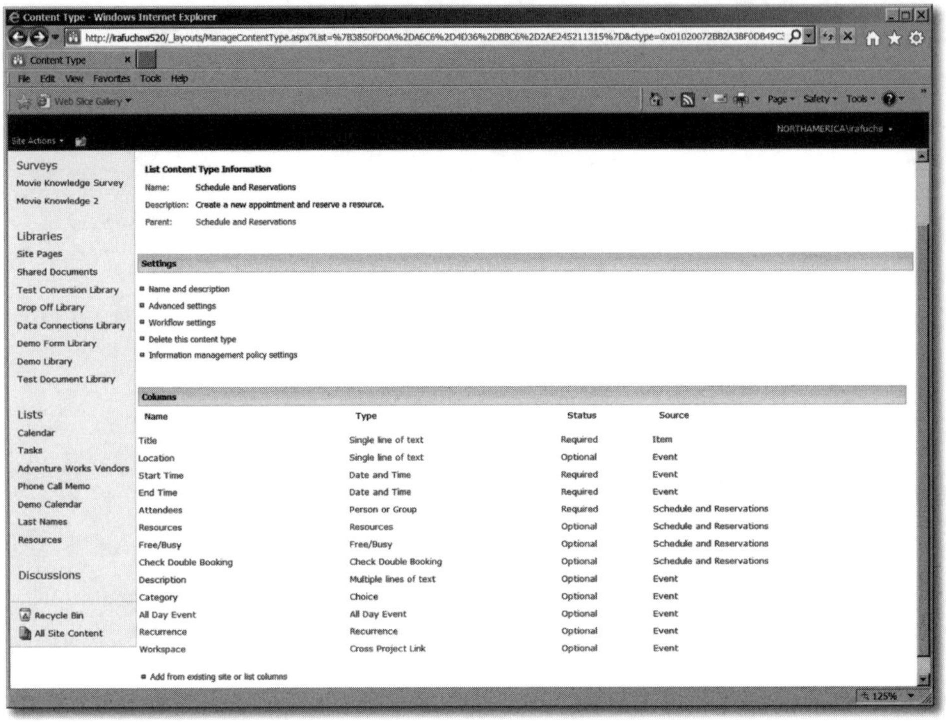

Illustration 10

Creating Resource Groups and Resources

The next step is to define and organize the resources you want to manage. It's worth making an effort to think about how you want to organize your resources because this will impact the end-user's experience of using the system.

A *Resource Group* allows you to create *Resource Categories* that logically organize resources that belong together. An example of this is organizing meeting rooms by building and floor. Alternatively you might want to organize meeting rooms by the number of people they can accommodate. In an entirely different context you could readily use this resource reservation system to manage the booking of courts in a tennis facility.

For this exercise we will create two meeting rooms and two event room resources and then assign them to two *Resource Groups*: *Second Floor Conference Rooms* and *Second Floor Event Rooms*. Go to the *Resources* list that was created; select *Items* on the Ribbon and under *New Item* select *Resource*. The *Resources – New Item* dialogue screen will display as shown in **Illustration 11** at right.

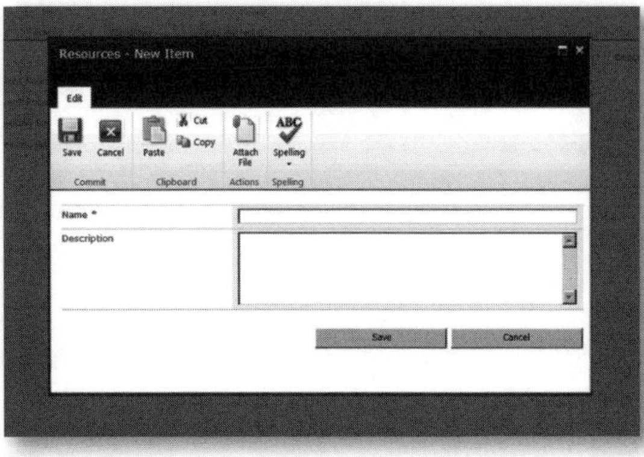

Illustration 11

Create the following four items: *Second Floor Meeting Room 1*, *Second Floor Meeting Room 2*, *Second Floor Event Room 1* and *Second Floor Event Room 2*. After you have done this, select *Resource Group* under the *New Item Ribbon* tab. The *Resources – New Item* dialogue screen will display. Enter *Second Floor Meeting Rooms* for the Name and add the two meeting room resources as shown in **Illustration 12** at right. Repeat this step for the *Second Floor Event Rooms Resource Group*.

> **Note** – if you try to create a *Resource Group* without adding *Resources* you will get an error when you save. You have to create *Resources* that are applicable to the *Resource Group* first.

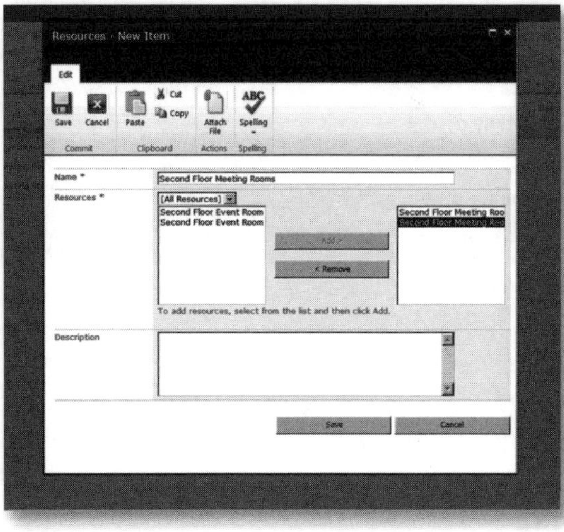

Illustration 12

Working with Resource Reservation Events

Now let's return to the calendar and see how resource reservations work. Click on the *Events* tab on the *Ribbon*. Under the *New Event* tab select *Reservations*. The *New Item Reservation* dialogue screen will display as shown in **Illustrations 13 and 14** on the next page. Enter a Title for your reservation and pick a date and time duration. Note that *All Resources* is the default option for *Resources* and consequently all resources will be displayed in the selection box. Clicking on the drop-down selection button will display the two *Resource Groups* that you created and selecting either one will display only the items for that group. Select the *Second Floor Meeting Room 1* for this reservation.

Illustration 13

Illustration 14

Note that one of the nice features of the reservation system is the ability to click on the *Check Double Booking* button to determine if the resource requested has already been booked for that date and time as shown in **Illustration 15** on the next page. This way it is not necessary to check the availability of a resource ahead of time and it prevents wasting time and effort in booking a resource that is already reserved. You also have the ability to book resources for an all-day event or on a recurring basis.

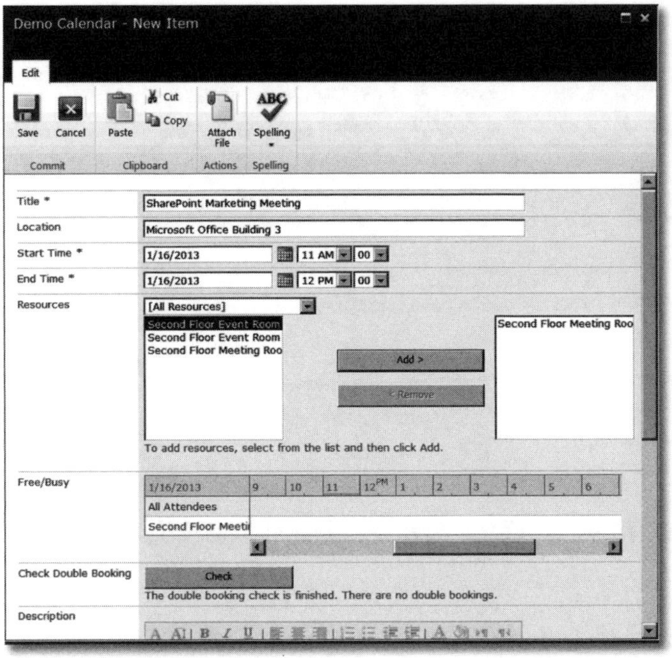

Illustration 15

Now add another *Reservation* for a different start and end time but on the same day, and select *Second Floor Meeting Room 2* for the requested resource.

> **Note** – creating a *Reservation* event does not give you the opportunity to add people to the event. To be able to do this you must have turned on the *Use this Calendar to share a member's schedule* radio button on the *Title, description and navigation* page for the *Calendar List Settings*. If you have not already turned it on, we will do so shortly. But first we will examine the behavior of just resource reservations on the calendar.

Now click on the *Calendar tab* on the *Ribbon* to display the calendar functions and select the date that the two resource reservations were made for. As you can see in **Illustration 16** on the next page, no reservations are displayed on the calendar. This is because the calendar does not offer a default display of the reservations that have been made. Instead you select the resources you want to check on by clicking on the *Add Resources* button and the calendar will then display the reservations for that resource.

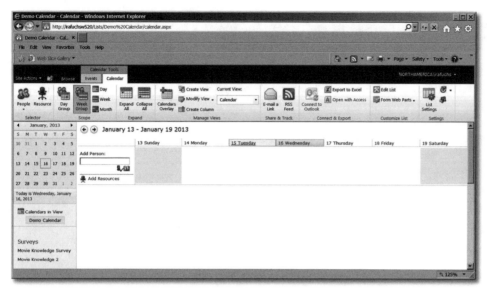

Illustration 16

Click on the *Add Resources* link to display the *Select Resources and Resource Groups* dialogue screen as shown in **Illustration 17** below. Select the *Second Floor Meeting Rooms* Resource Group and click the *Add* button, then the *OK* button.

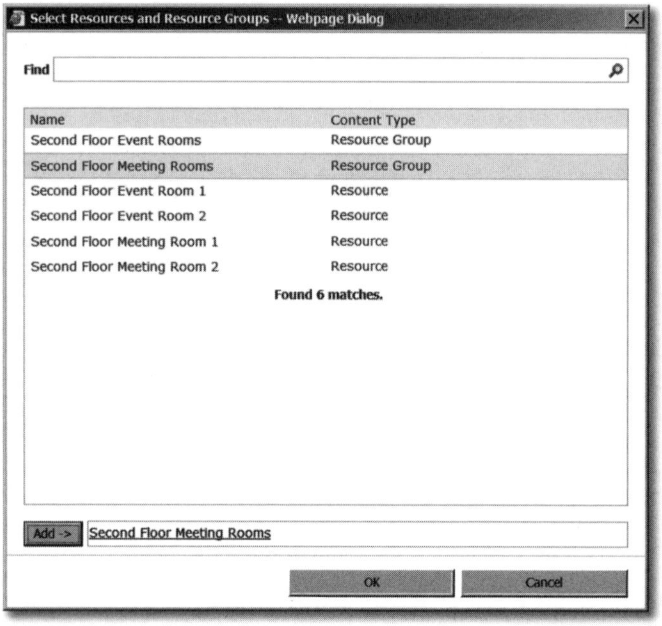

Illustration 17

The calendar will now display a column on the left with a row for each of the *Resources* in the *Resource Group* for which there is a reservation as shown in **Illustration 18** below. This is why it is important to carefully organize *Resources* into *Resource Groups*.

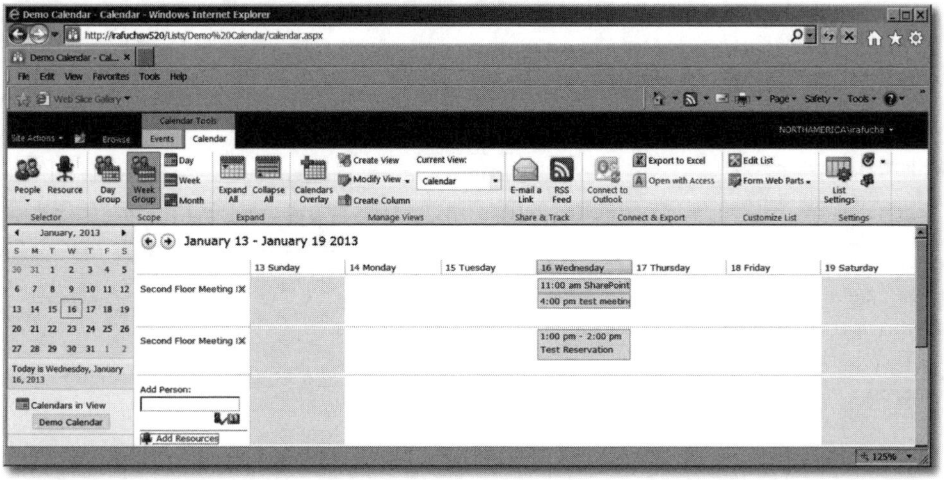

Illustration 18

Click on the *X* to the right of each *Resource* in the calendar to remove them. Now click on the *Add Resources* link to display the *Select Resources and Resource Groups* dialogue screen and select the *Second Floor Meeting Room 1 Resource* and click the *Add* button, then the *OK* button. The calendar will now display just that one *Resource* as shown in **Illustration 19** below.

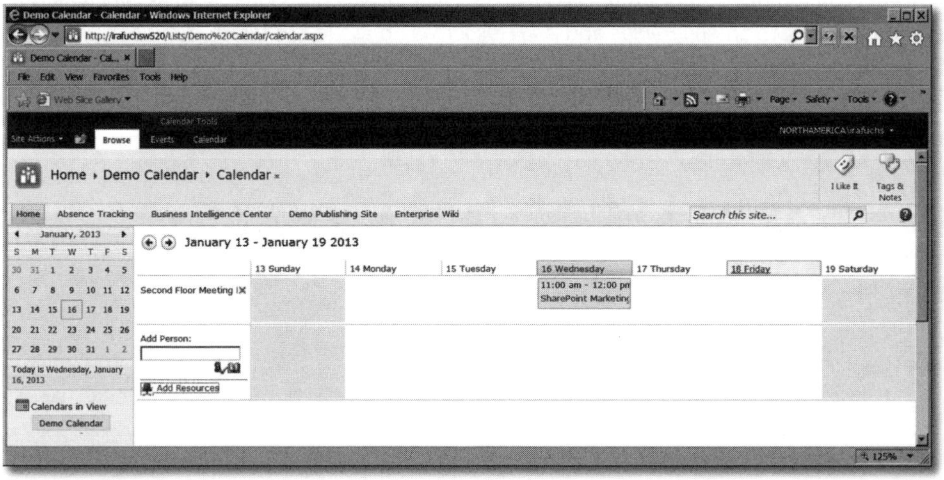

Illustration 19

If you haven't already done so go to the *List Settings* page and click on the *Title, description and navigation* page link. On that page click on the *Use this Calendar to share a member's schedule radio button* to enable this functionality.

Creating Appointments with Resources

Now let's create an *Appointment* event with a *Resource*. Click on the *Events* Tab on the *Ribbon* and select that option from the *New Event* drop-down selection. The *New Item* dialogue screen will display as shown in **Illustration 20** at right. In this screen there is now a *People Picker* control for selecting the attendees and a *Free/Busy* display control for determining the availability of attendees for the event time and adjacent times. We will review where this *Free/Busy* information is coming from shortly.

Illustration 20

Add attendees and pick a *Resource* to create an appointment and save it. Note that by default the creator of the event is an attendee. Click on the *Calendar Ribbon* tab. Now click on the *Week Group Ribbon* button. Note that there is both an *Add Person* and *Add Resources* option in the first column of the calendar as shown in **Illustration 21** below.

Illustration 21

Now click on the *Week Ribbon* button. The *Add Person* and *Add Resources* options no longer display. This is the standard calendar view where the hours of the day are the default focus as shown in **Illustration 22** below.

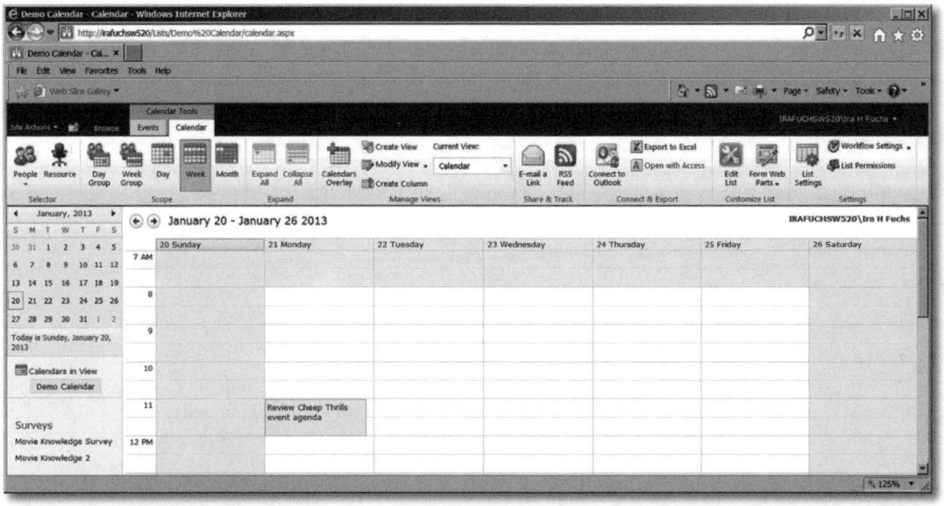

Illustration 22

Now click on the *Week Group Ribbon* button and the focus of the calendar changes to both the *Attendees* and the *Resources*. Enter one of the attendees for the event you just created and you will see that they are now displayed in the first column of the calendar and the event displays in its corresponding day. Click on *Add Resources* and select *Second Floor Meeting Room 2*. The attendees and the resources are displayed in the first column and their respective events are displayed in the columns for the days. Note that the same event is repeatedly displayed for each attendee and resource as shown in **Illustration 23** below. With this calendar focus you can track all the events for a day, week or month for any given individual or resource.

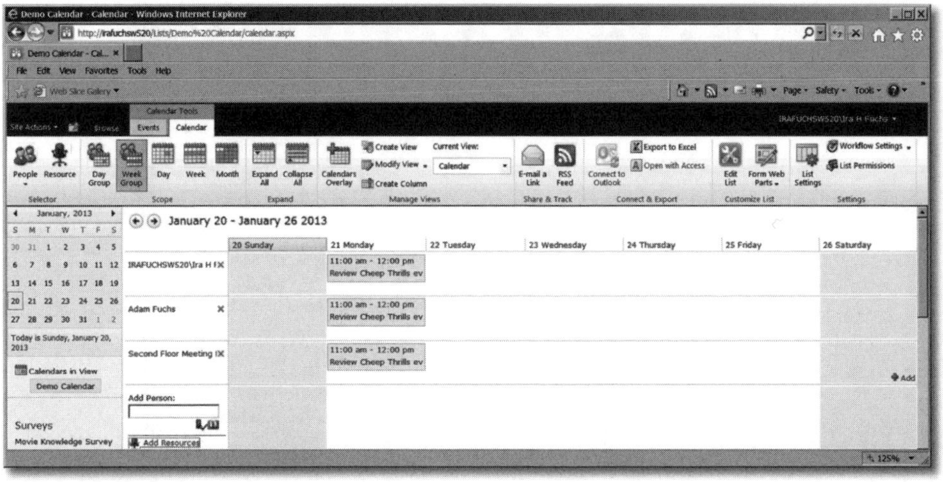

Illustration 23

Calendar Overlays

The *Free/Busy* capability that is available when you create an appointment is based on the *Calendar Overlay* function. Click on the *Calendar Overlays Ribbon* button as shown in **Illustration 23** above. The *Calendar Overlay Settings* page will display as shown in **Illustration 24** below. Here you can add up to ten calendars that can be overlaid together or displayed with the *Free/Busy* function. Click on the *New Calendar* link.

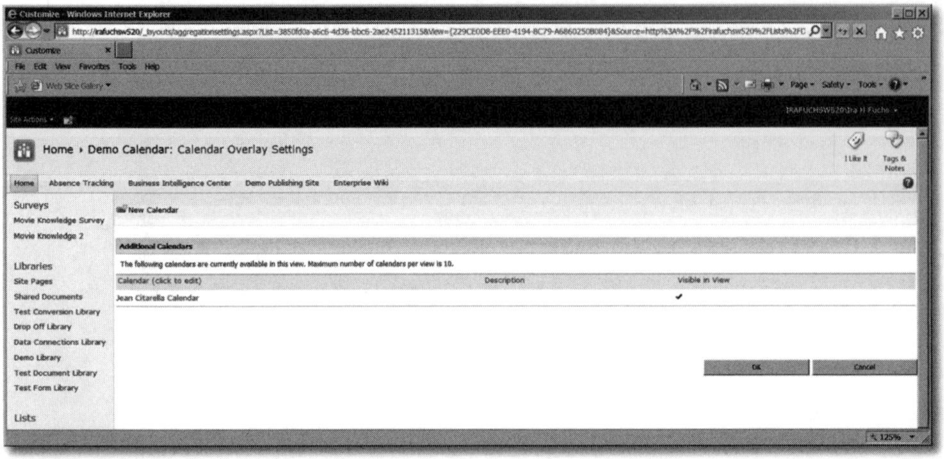

Illustration 24

The *Customize Calendar* screen will display. This is where you can point to an ***existing*** *SharePoint* or *Exchange* calendar as shown in **Illustrations 25** below **and 26** on the next page. When you select a *SharePoint* calendar you can provide the URL of the site and then select the calendar that you want from the list drop-down selection, and then further select a specific View of the calendar. Alternatively you can provide the direct URL address of the calendar.

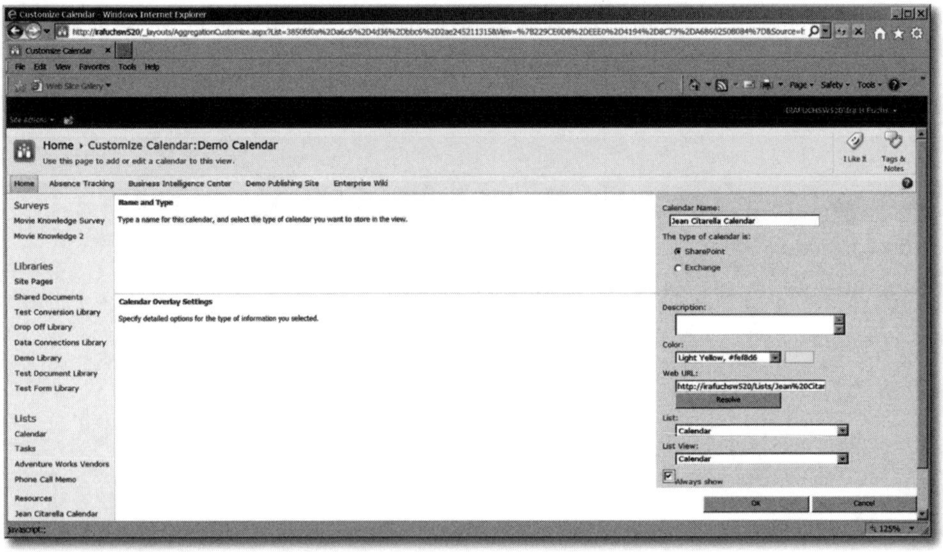

Illustration 25

If you select an *Exchange* calendar you can click the *Find* button and *SharePoint* will automatically obtain the *Outlook Web Access URL* as well as the *Exchange Web Service URL* if your organization is using *Exchange* for its mail server. For each overlay calendar you can select a different color.

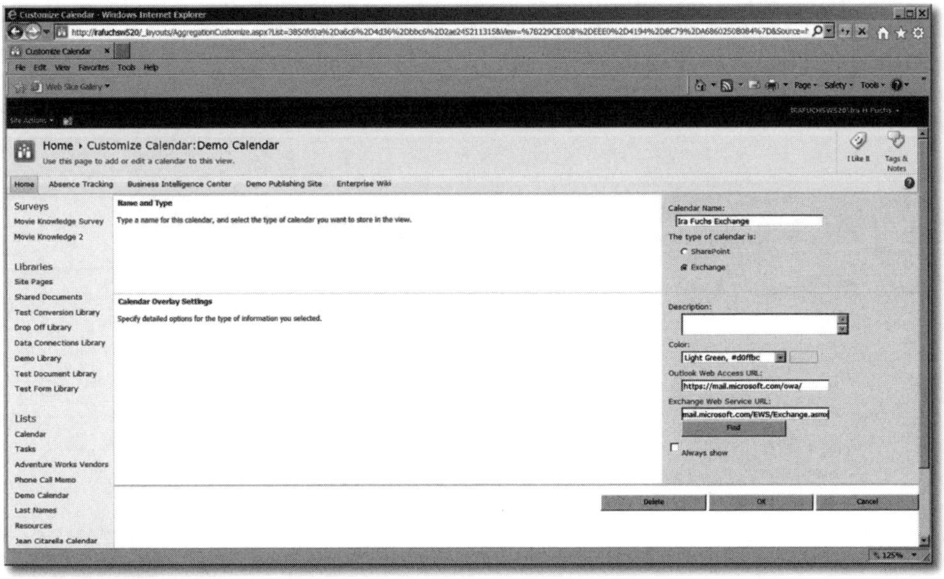

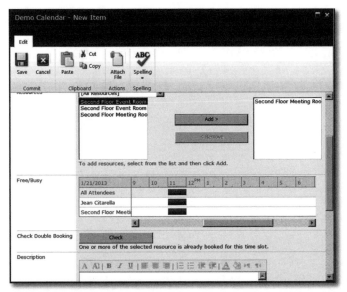

Illustration 26

Now if you create another appointment for the same time with the same attendees and/or resources you will see a *Busy* bar for that duration and if you click the *Check Double Booking* button an error message will display as shown in **Illustration 27** below.

Illustration 27

Additional Calendar Views

One of the really nice things about calendars in *SharePoint* is that they are just specialized lists, and as such all of the *SharePoint* list functions and features are available for use in your application. Creating specific list Views of resources and/or people is one of the flexible functions that make a *SharePoint* based *Scheduling and Resource Reservation* application highly useful. **Illustration 28** below shows the ease in which to access or create multiple different Views of the calendar and the respective events it contains.

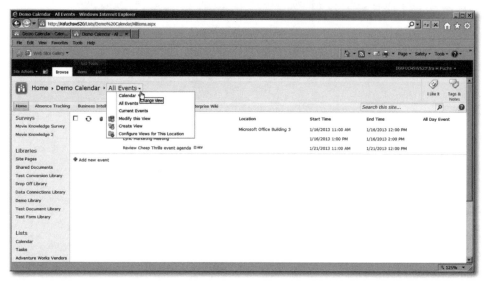

Illustration 28

Illustration 29 below shows the *Create View* page for the Calendar list and the various View options available.

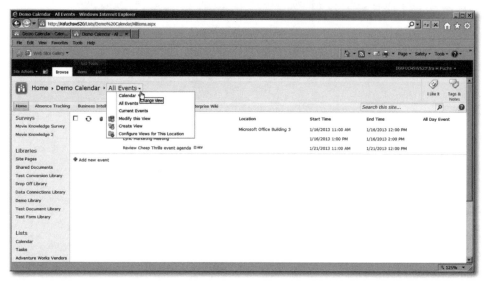

Illustration 29

Creating a SharePoint Designer Workflow to Generate Email Notifications of Scheduling Events

So now we have this very versatile application; but wait, there is something that is just not quite complete about it – it doesn't generate an email notification of a scheduling event! Well not to fear, that is easily remedied by a *SharePoint Designer* workflow. So let's get to work and create one.

Open *SharePoint Designer* and open the site that contains the calendar that you have created for this application and then click on *Workflows* in the *Navigation* pane as shown in **Illustration 30** below.

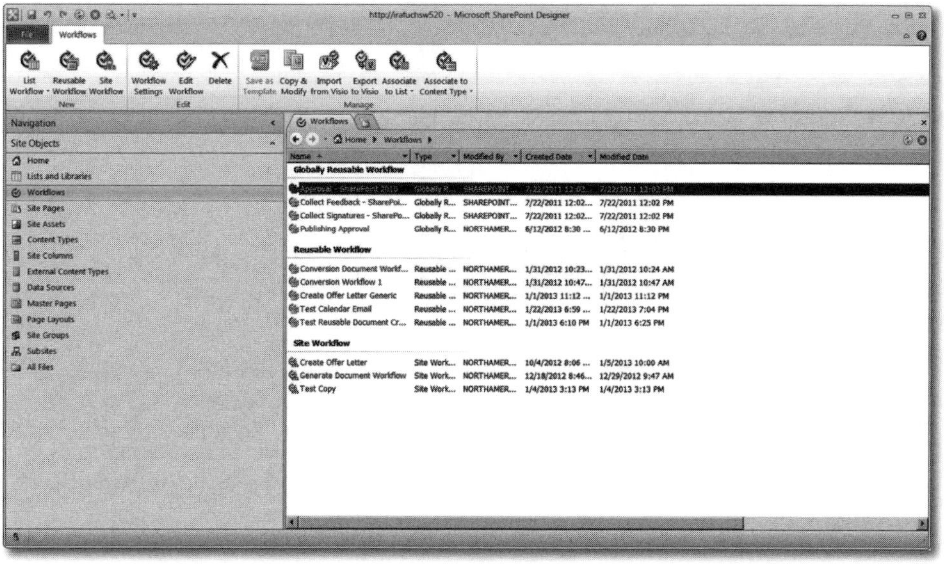

Illustration 30

Now click on the *Reusable Workflow* button on the *Ribbon* menu. We are going to use a *Reusable Workflow* for three reasons:

One, there is a very good chance that multiple calendars with the *Scheduling and Resource Reservation* functions enabled will be instantiated in an organization. As such you want to create the workflow once and then simply associate the workflow with each new instance of the calendar. By using a *Reusable Workflow* you can do that.

Two, when you create a *Reusable Workflow* you can base it on a specific *Content Type*, which in turn provides your workflow with all the relevant metadata (column information) that you will need to build your workflow.

Three, when a workflow is based on a *Content Type*, *SharePoint Designer* automatically manages the workflow correlation to the "Current Item"; the Current Item being the object of the workflow process. In this case the workflow object is the creation or modification of a calendar event. Neither the developer of the workflow, nor the end user submitting the form need to do anything to relate the new workflow to the unique calendar event.

The *Create Reusable Workflow* dialogue screen will display as shown in **Illustration 31** below. Give the workflow a name and select the *Schedule and Reservations Content Type* from the drop-down selection box.

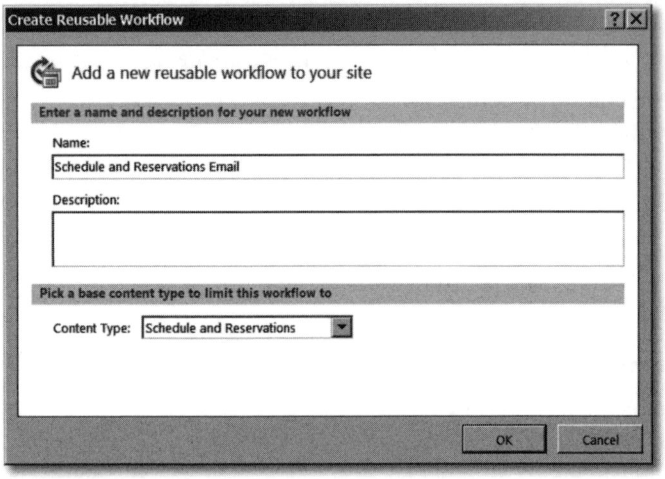

Illustration 31

The *SharePoint Designer* workflow editor will display with a blank *Step 1*. Place your cursor in *Step 1* and from the *Actions Ribbon* button drop-down selector, pick *Send an Email*. The *Email these users* action will be inserted as shown in **Illustration 32** below.

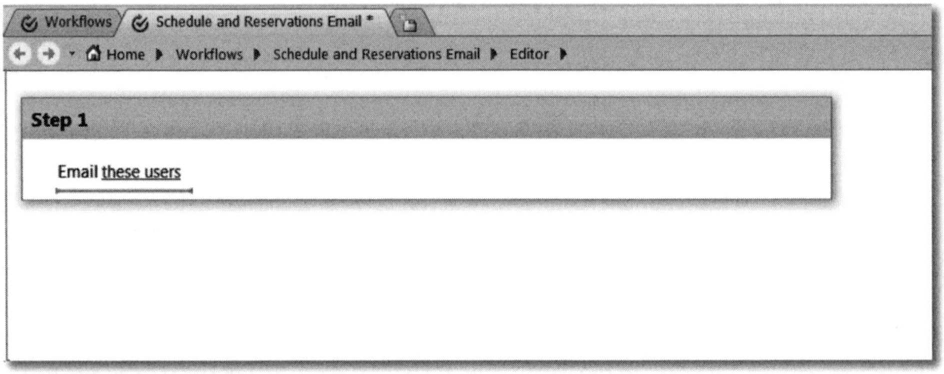

Illustration 32

Now click on *these users*. The *Define E-mail Message* workflow template will display as shown in **Illustration 33** below:

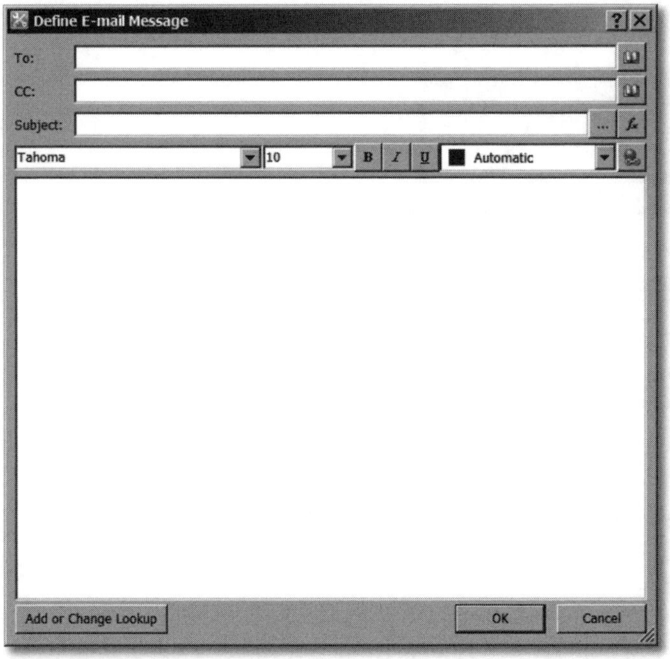

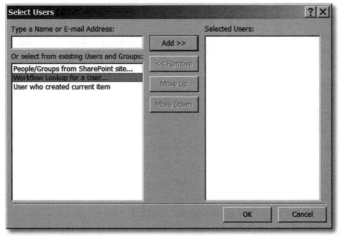

Illustration 33

Click on the look-up button to the right of the *To:* box. The *Select Users* dialogue screen will display as shown in **Illustration 34** below.

Illustration 34

With the *Workflow Lookup for a User* selection highlighted click the *Add* button. The *Lookup for Person or Group* dialogue screen will display as shown in **Illustration 35** below. Leave the default *Current Item* value for the *Data source*. From the drop-down selection box for *Field from source*, select *Participants*. From the drop-down selection box for *Return field as*, select *Email Addresses, Semicolon Delimited*.

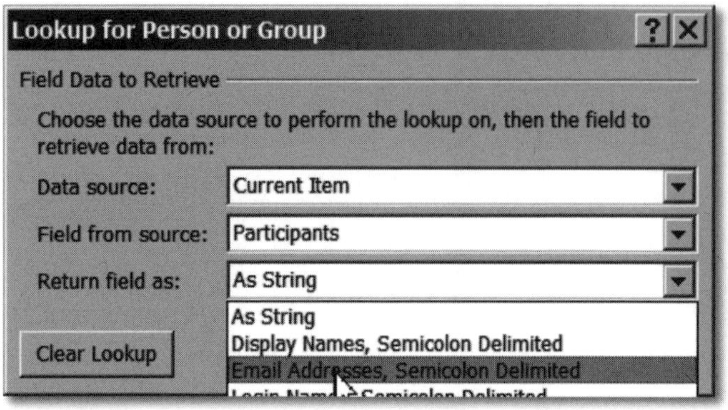

Illustration 35

> **Note** – The *Field from source* value that displays for the *Current Item* is *Participants*. However this field is **not** one of the metadata columns defined for the *Schedule and Reservation Content Type*. The metadata column defined for the people picker function is *Attendees*. The workflow will generate an email to the people selected as the *Participants* so this is not an issue that poses an execution problem. If you create this workflow template based on the actual calendar list, *Attendees* will be displayed but not *Participants*.

For the *Subject:* field, again click on the look-up button to the right of the *Subject:* box. The *Lookup for String* dialogue screen will display as shown in **Illustration 36** below. Leave the default *Current Item* value for the *Data source*. From the drop-down selection box for *Field from source*, select *Title*. The *Return field as:* will return *As String* and be greyed out.

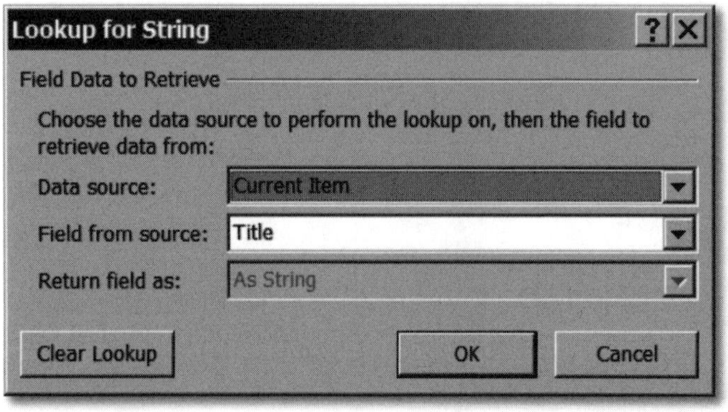

Illustration 36

You can also add information to the body of the email about the scheduling and/or reservation event. Clicking on the *Add or Change Lookup* button on the bottom of the *Define E-mail Message* template allows you to select any of the *Current Item* fields, such as *Created By, Start Time, End Time* etc. This can be seen in **Illustration 37** below.

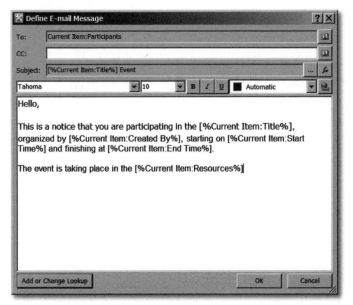

Illustration 37

Clicking *OK* on the *Define E-mail Message* template will return you to the workflow editor. You might want to capture information about the execution of the workflow actions in the *Workflow History* list. You can do this with the *Log to History List* action. Again you can lookup up information for the *Current Item*, variables and parameters, workflow context or other data sources. The *Log to History List* action can be seen in **Illustration 38** below.

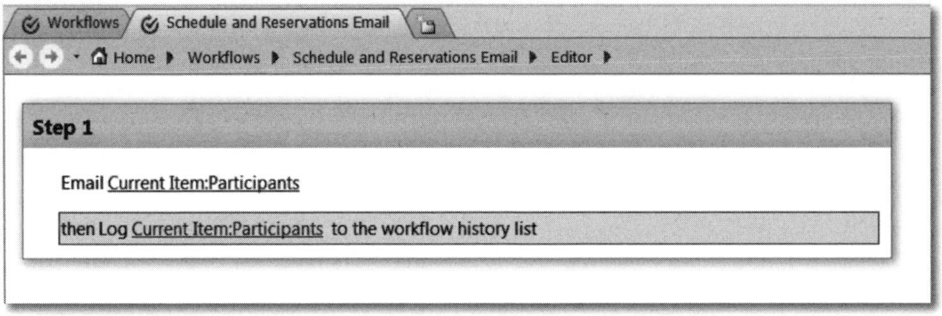

Illustration 38

You are now finished composing the workflow. Save it and publish it by clicking on the *Publish Ribbon* button.

Now you must associate the workflow to a list or *Content Type*. We are going to associate the workflow to the calendar list we have created. Click on the *Associate to List Ribbon* button. Any list to which the *Schedules and Reservation Content Type* has been added will display under the *Associate to List Ribbon* button as shown in **Illustration 39** below. Select the calendar name that you are working with.

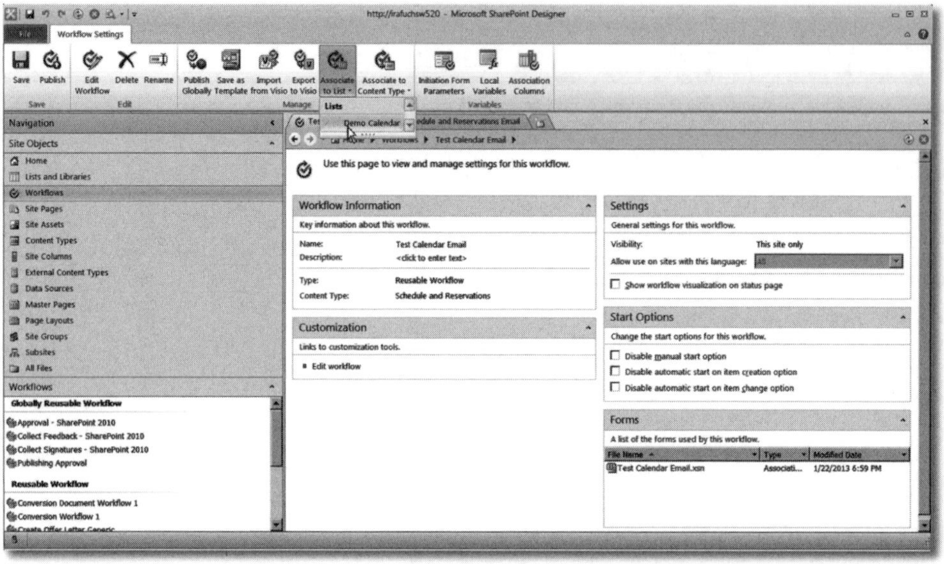

Illustration 39

The *SharePoint Add a Workflow* page (go to *Calendar List Settings,* click on *Workflow Settings,* and then *Add a workflow)* will display as shown in **Illustration 40** on the next page. Click on the *Content Type* drop-down selection list and choose the *Schedule and Reservations Content Type*. The *Workflow* template selection directly below will now become active and you will see the *Schedules and Reservation* workflow (or whatever name you gave the workflow) is available.

Now you must enter a unique name for the ***instance of the workflow template*** that will be instantiated for this calendar list.

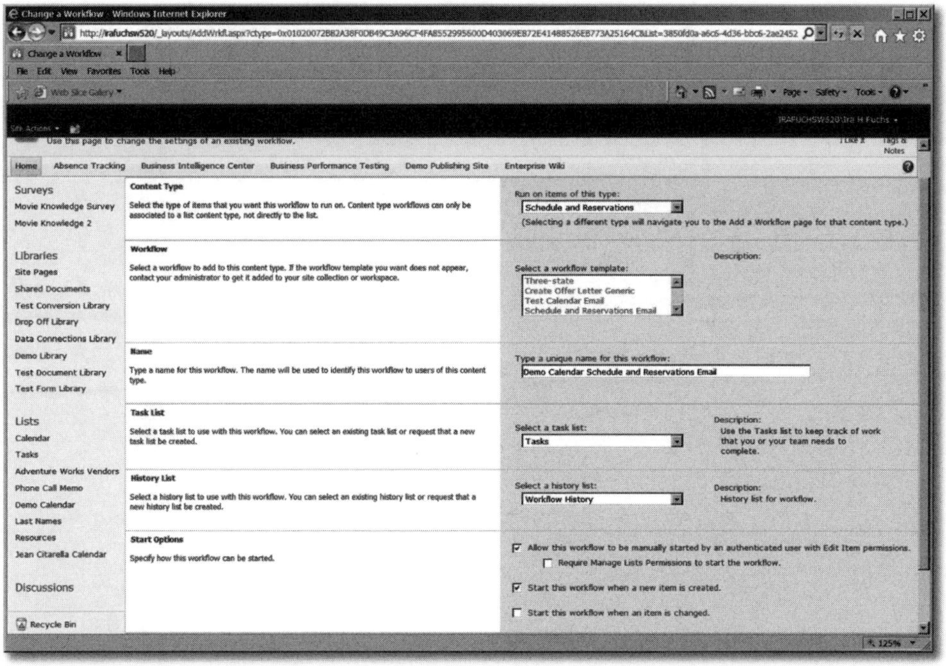

Illustration 40

On this page you can also specify the Start Options for the workflow. The default setting is *Allow the workflow to be manually stared by an authenticated user with Edit Item permissions.* Also click on the *checkbox* for *Start the workflow when a new item is created,* so that the email is generated automatically whenever a *Schedule and Reservation* event is created.

> **Note** – you would **not** want to also select the *Start this workflow when an item is changed* option simply because the message that was inserted in the body of the email would not be relevant to a change. What you can do is make a copy of this workflow, modify the message in the body of the email, associate the new workflow to the same calendar list and *Content Type,* select the *Start this workflow when an item is changed* option, and deselect the *Start the workflow when a new item* is created option.

Clicking *OK* on the *Add a Workflow* page will bring you back to the *Workflow Settings* page for the calendar list and you will see that a new instance of the *Schedules and Reservations* workflow is now bound to the calendar as shown in **Illustration 41** on the next page.

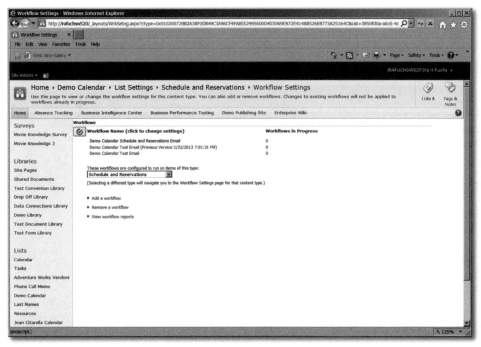

Illustration 41

Now let's try it out! On the calendar create a *Schedule and Reservation* event. Within a couple of minutes you should receive a notification email like the one shown in **Illustration 42** below.

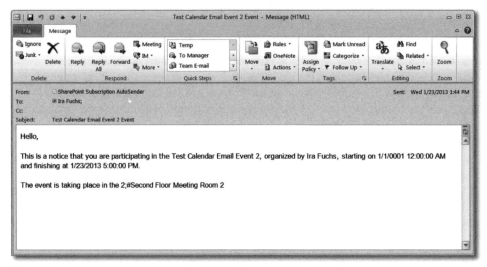

Illustration 42

Congratulations on creating a great Resource Reservation and Scheduling application!

Document Creation Automation Using SharePoint Designer Workflows

In this chapter we are going to investigate the capabilities of *SharePoint Designer* workflows to auto-mate document creation; that is, the automated creation of documents based on templates that will have information inserted into them by the workflow. There are numerous use cases and automation scenarios for this type of functionality and *SharePoint Designer* workflows provide an easy and versatile way to accomplish this automation without requiring any code.

The use case for our example is the generation of a job *Offer Letter* to a prospective hire. The typical manual process would be to open a *Word* template and enter the required information in the body of the document. In our automation scenario the process works as follows:

A user clicks on a link to start the workflow as shown in **Illustration 1** below:

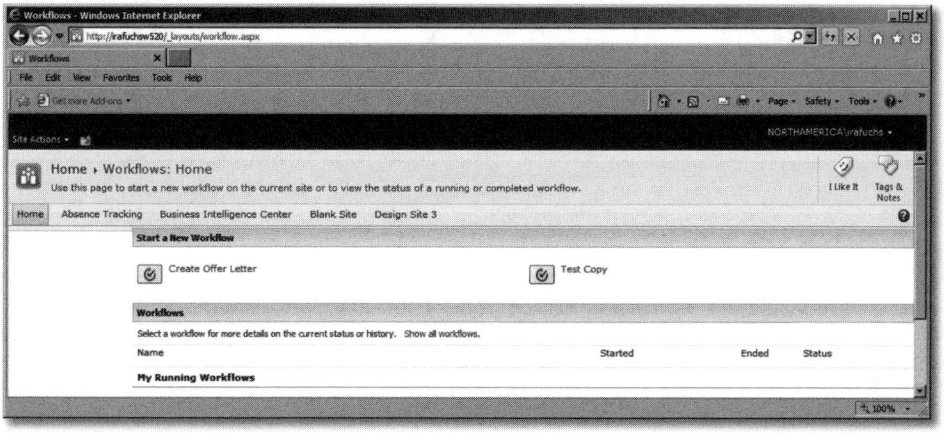

Illustration 1

The workflow will begin by presenting the user with a form as shown in **Illustration 2** below. The information entered here will be inserted into the document and used in other workflow actions, such as sending an email to people informing them that the document has been created.

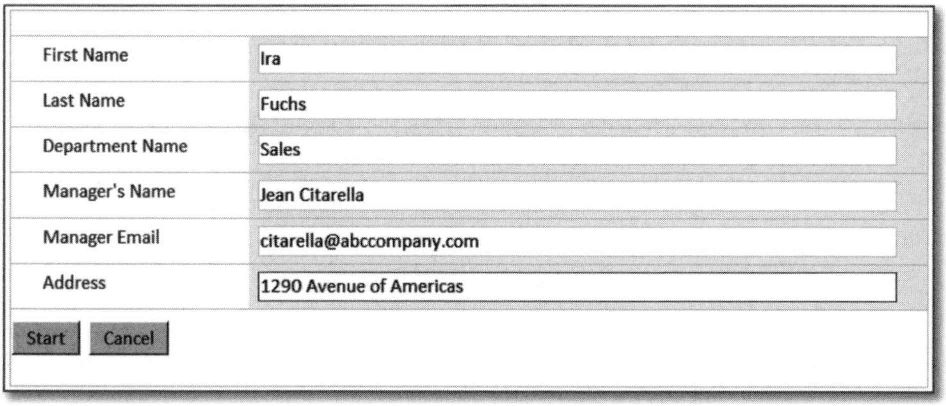

Illustration 2

Illustration 3 below shows the Library where the document was created. The information entered into the form also populates the column metadata for each document created.

Name	First Name	Last Name	Address	Country/Region	Modified By	Manager's Name
Offer Letter Sales	Jack	Schwartz			IRAFUCHSWS20\Ira H Fuchs	Ira Fuchs
Offer Letter FinanceCunningham	Bill	Cunningham	1291 Avenue of Americas		IRAFUCHSWS20\Ira H Fuchs	Jean Citarella
Offer Letter Sales SupportHoffman	Bill	Hoffman	1290 Avenue of Americas		IRAFUCHSWS20\Ira H Fuchs	Ira Fuchs
Offer Letter SalesFuchs	Ira	Fuchs	1290 Avenue of Americas		NORTHAMERICA\irafuchs	Jean Citarella

Illustration 3

Illustration 4 below shows the document created by the workflow with the embedded information that was captured from the workflow initiation form. The highlighted address indicates the presence of a *Quick Part Document Property* for the *Address* field with the value from the form that has been automatically embedded in the document by the workflow.

Microsoft¶
¶
Official·Offer·Letter¶
¶
Ira·Fuchs¶
1290·Avenue·of·Americas¶
¶
The·position·is·part·of·the:·Sales·-Department¶
Your·Manager's·name·is·Jean·Citarella¶
¶

Illustration 4

Steps for Building this Application

The following are the steps involved in creating this workflow application:

1) Create the *Content Type* for the *Offer Letter* and its requisite *Site Columns* and associate an actual document to the *Content Type Document Template*.

2) Configure a Document Library to support *Content Types* and add the *Offer Letter Content Type* to that Library.

3) Edit the *Content Type Document Template* **in that Library** to include the *Quick Part Document Property* fields for the information that will be auto-populated.

4) Update the document associated with the *Master Offer Letter Content Type* with the one that includes the *Quick Part Document Property* fields.

5) Create the document creation workflow.

6) Testing the workflow.

Creating the Content Type for the Offer Letter and its requisite Site Columns and associated document

Content Types and *Site Columns* are *Site Collection* objects and the *Galleries* for both are found on the *Site Settings Page* for the *Site Collection* as shown in **Illustration 5** below:

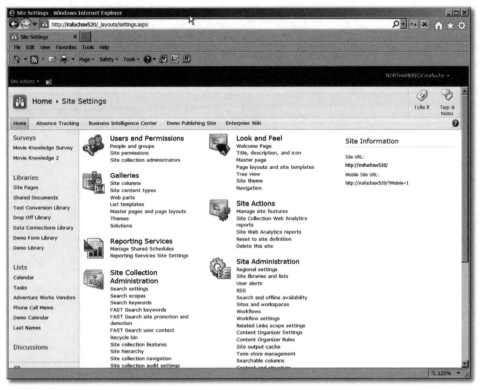

Illustration 5

A *Content Type* must be created using *Site Columns*, not ordinary column metadata; so before we create the *Content Type* we need to ascertain that *Site Columns* suitable for our needs already exist or we need to create them. For our example we need the following column fields:

> *First Name*
> *Last Name*
> *Department Name*
> *Address*
> *Manager's Name*
> *Manager's Email*

In the *Site Column Gallery* you will find *Site Columns* for *Address, Company, E-mail* and *First Name,* and *Manager's Name* in the *Core Content and Calendar Columns* category which you can use. In addition you need to create the *Department Name Site Column.* Create this as a *Single line of text.*

With all the necessary *Site Columns* available you can now create the *Offer Letter Content Type*. Click on the *Site Content Types* link under *Galleries* and then click the *Create* icon link at the top. You will be presented with the *New Site Content Type* dialogue screen as shown in **Illustration 6** below.

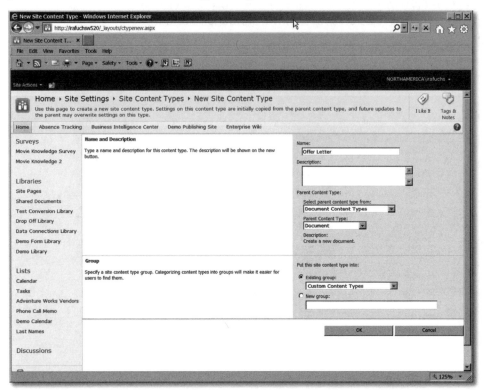

Illustration 6

Enter *Offer Letter* for the *Name*, select *Document Content Types* from the drop-down control, then select *Document* as the *Parent Content Type*. For the *Group* where the *Offer Letter Content Type* will be placed select *Custom Content Types* from the drop-down control. Click *OK*. You will be presented with the *Settings* page of the *Offer Letter Content Type* as shown in **Illustration 7** on the next page.

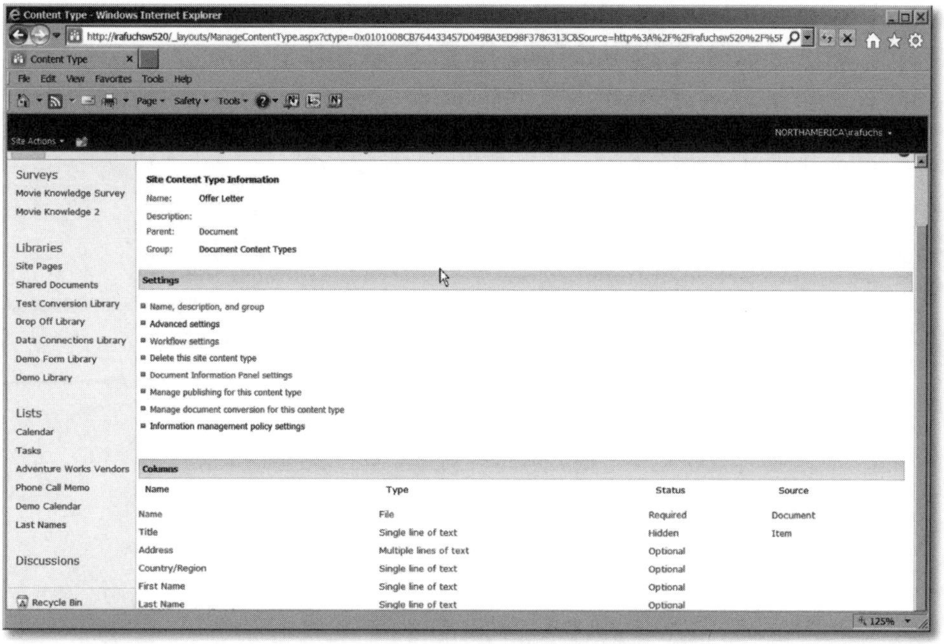

Illustration 7

In the *Columns* area you will click on *Add from existing site columns* to add the *Site Columns* described earlier. After you have done this click the *Advanced* settings link in the *Settings* area. You will be presented with the screen shown in **Illustration 8** below:

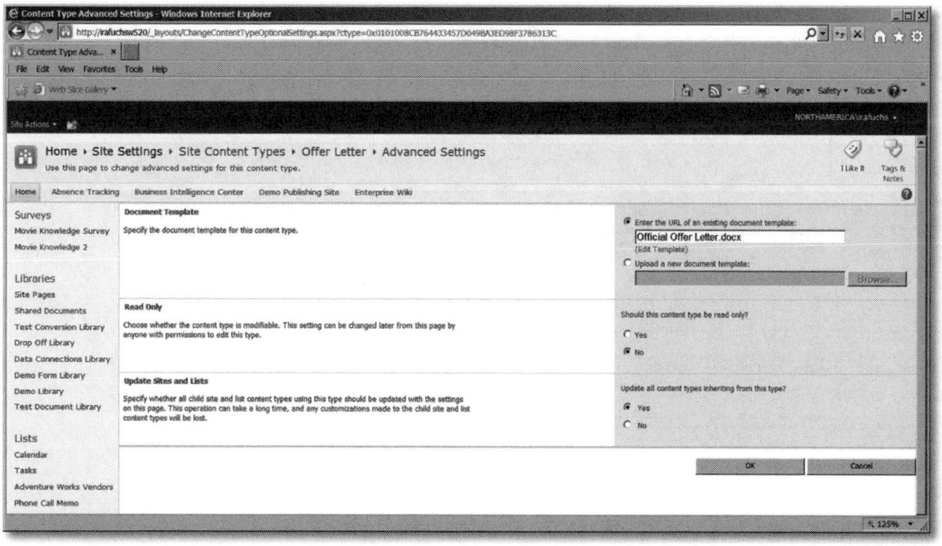

Illustration 8

Here you can upload a *Word docx* document (***but not a* template dotx** file) that contains the content of the *Offer Letter*. This completes the first part of the development process.

Configuring a Document Library to support Content Types and Adding the Offer Letter Content Type to that Library.

The next step is to create a new *Document Library* or configure an existing *Document Library* to support *Content Types*. **Illustration 9** below shows the *Library Settings* page for a *Document Library*. Click on the *Advanced Settings* option under *General Settings*.

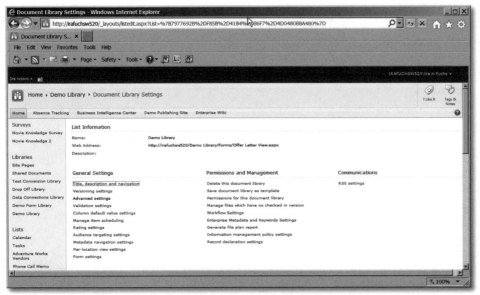

Illustration 9

On the *Advanced Settings* page select the *Yes* radio button under *Allow management of Content Types?* as shown in **Illustration 10** below:

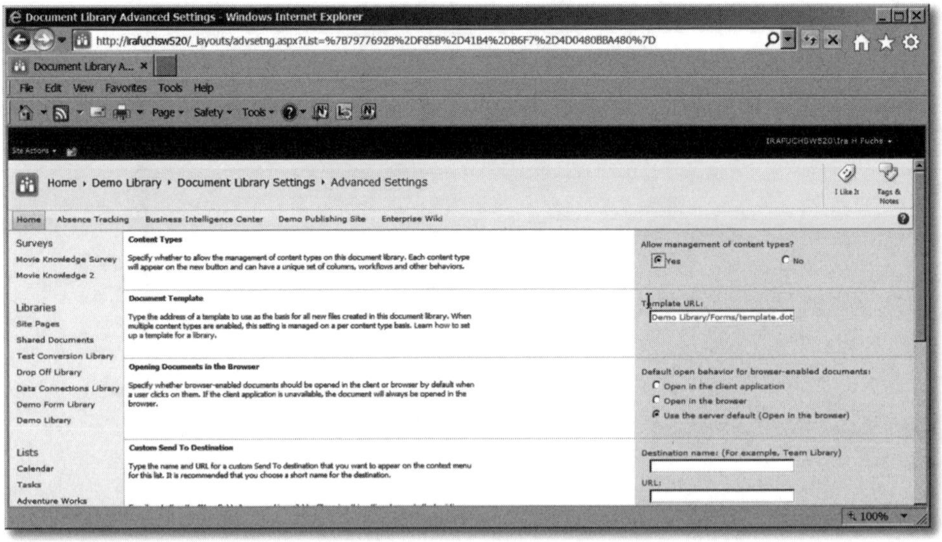

Illustration 10

The *Library Settings* page will now display a new *Content Types* section as shown in **Illustration 11** below:

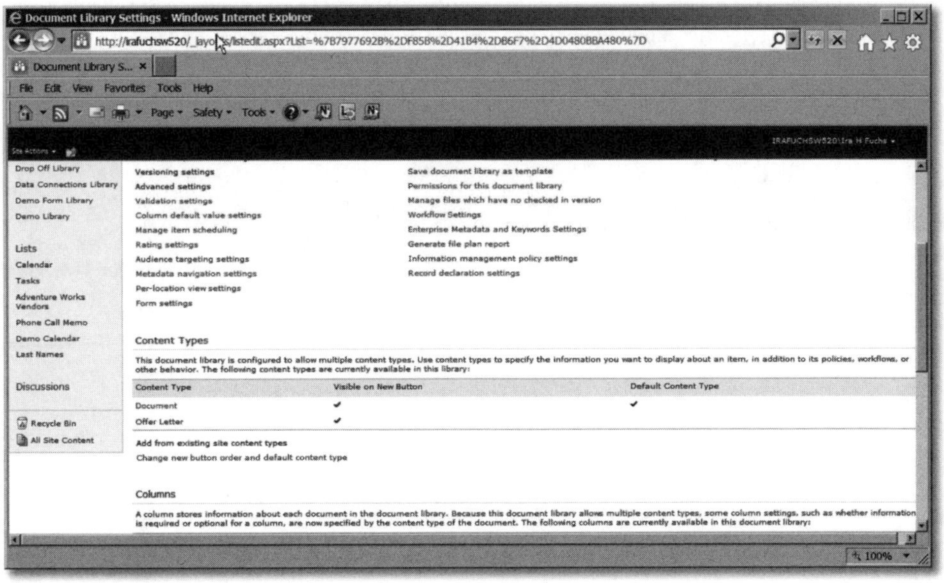

Illustration 11

Click on the *Add from existing site Content Types* option to display the dialogue screen shown in **Illustration 12** below where you can add the *Offer Letter Content Type* to the *Document Library* by selecting it from the drop-down list of available *Content Types*.

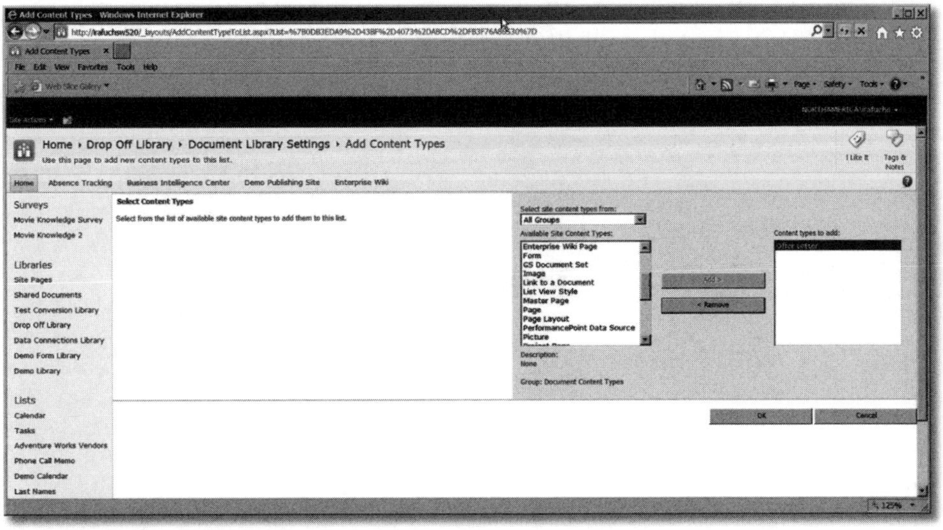

Illustration 12

Clicking on the *Offer Letter Content Type* that now displays in the *Content Types* section of the *Document Library Settings* page will bring up a *Settings* page for the **unique instance** of the *Offer Letter Content Type* that was instantiated for this specific *Document Library*. This is shown in **Illustration 13** below.

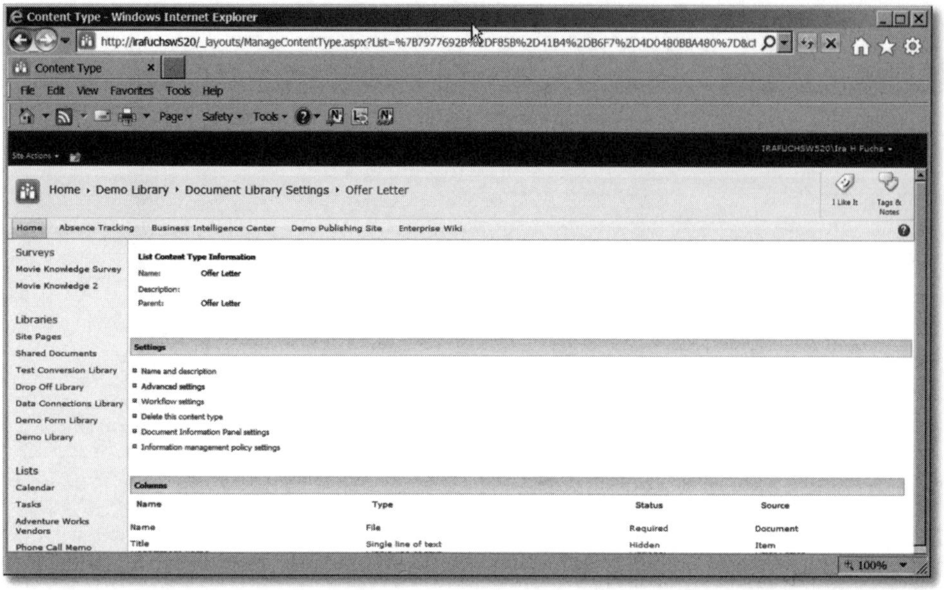

Illustration 13

Clicking on *Advanced Settings* will display an *Advanced Settings* page as shown in **Illustration 14** below that is identical to the original *Offer Letter Content Type* that we created in the *Content Type Gallery* of the *Site Collection*. Note however that when we edit the *Word* template for this *Document Library* instance of the *Offer Letter Content Type* **we are editing a copy** of the original *Word* document that was uploaded earlier. Click on the *Edit Template* option.

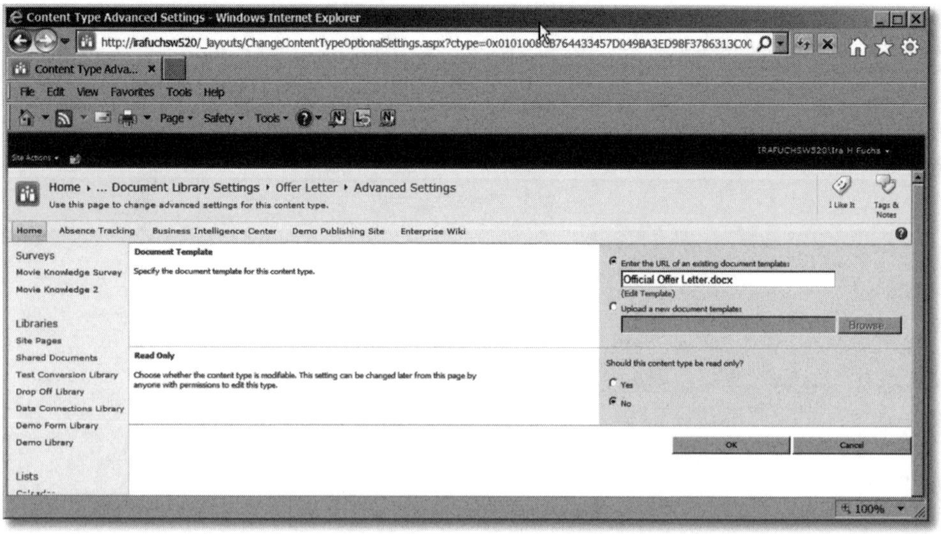

Illustration 14

Edit the Content Type Document Template to include the Quick Part Document Property fields for the information that will be auto-populated.

A copy of the original *Word* document that was uploaded for the original *Offer Letter Content Type* will open as shown in **Illustration 15** below.

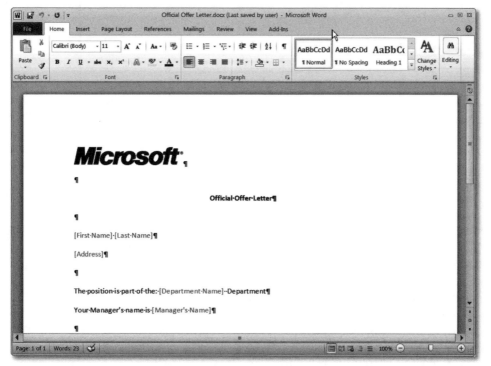

Illustration 15

> **Note —** you will not see the *Quick Parts Document Properties* fields already in the document as shown above. You will add these now.

Click on the *Insert* tab of the *Ribbon*. The *Quick Parts* option will display in the *Text* area. Select the *Document Property* option which will display a fly-out selection of generic document property tags as well as tags for the *Site Columns* that we used when creating the *Offer Letter Content Type* as shown in **Illustration 16** on the next page.

Place your cursor anywhere in the document and select the tag for the columns that define the *Offer Letter Content Type* such as *First Name, Last Name, Address,* etc. These tags serve as the placeholders for the actual information that will be inserted into the template from the information entered in the *workflow initiation form* when the workflow starts.

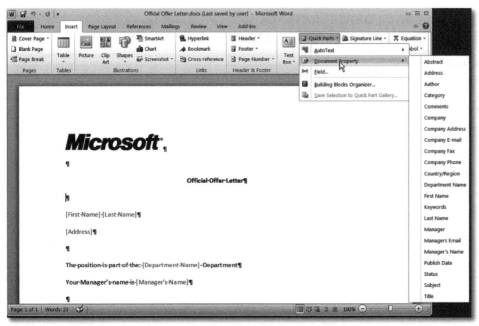

Illustration 16

After you save the document as the *Library Offer Letter Content Type* template, save a copy of this document to your computer as well. Now return to the *Advanced Settings* page of the *Offer Letter Content Type* in the *Content Type Gallery* as shown in **Illustration 17** below. Click on the *Upload a new document template* in the *Document Template* section and upload this document. The original template did not have the *Content Type* metadata embedded in the body of the document using the *Quick Part Document Properties*, which it will have now. Now whenever the *Offer Letter Content Type* is instantiated in any *Document Library* the template will be capable of embedding the values from the workflow initiation form.

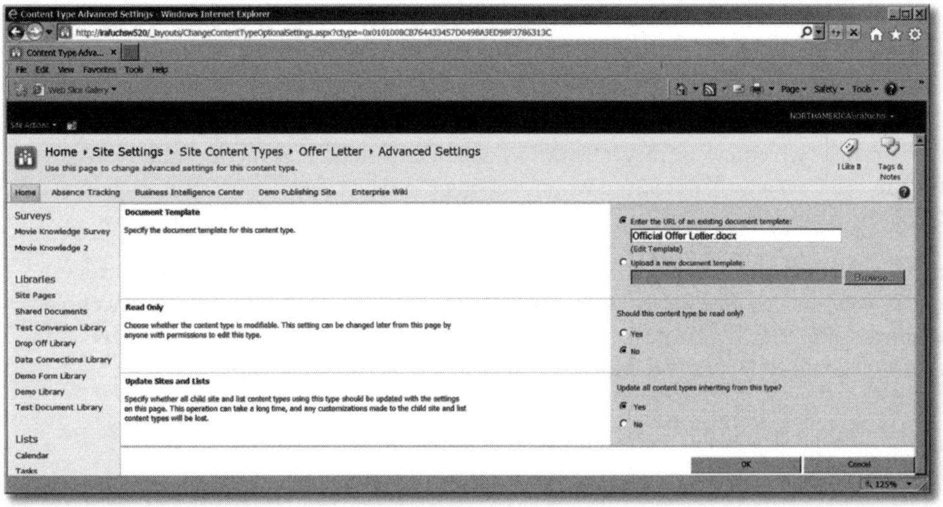

Illustration 17

Creating the SharePoint Designer Workflow for Generating an Instance of the Offer Letter Content Type.

The next step is creating the document generation workflow in *SharePoint Designer*. For this type of application we can use either a *Site workflow* or a *Reusable workflow* based on a Content Type. In this case we will use a *Site workflow*, which can be started from the *View All Site Content* page in *SharePoint* as shown in the very first illustration in this chapter.

Open *SharePoint Designer* and connect to the site where you want to create the workflow. Once connected, click on *Workflows* on the *Site Objects Navigation* pane, as shown in **Illustration 18** below.

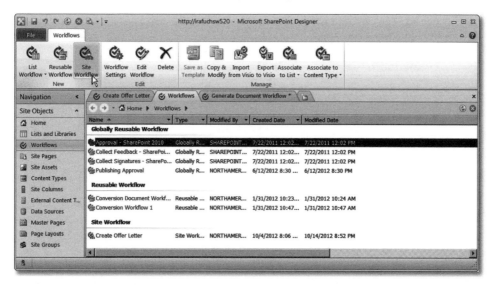

Illustration 18

Click on the *Site Workflows Ribbon* button and give the workflow a name and optional description. The *SharePoint Designer* workflow editor will display a blank *Step 1* as shown in **Illustration 19** below.

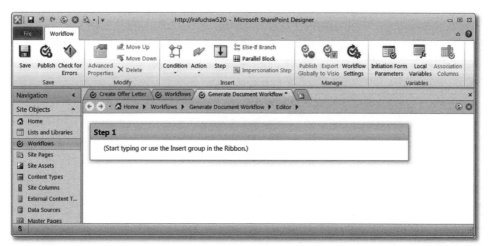

Illustration 19

Place your cursor in *Step 1* directly under "Start typing". From the *Action Ribbon* drop-down selection list pick the *Create List Item* option. Your workflow will like **Illustration 20** below.

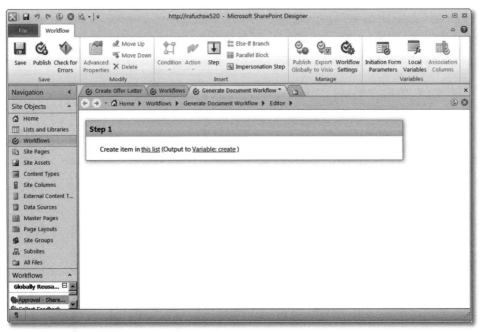

Illustration 20

Now click on the *Initiation Form Parameters Ribbon* button. When the user starts the workflow they will be presented with the form shown in **Illustration 2** on **page 27** where they can input the values that will be embedded in the document when it is generated. The *Initiation Form Parameters* dialogue screen is where we define the form fields and values that the user will be prompted for. Click the *Add* button to create the following parameters as single lines of text: *First Name, Last Name, Department Name, Manager's Email,* and *Address*. The completed dialogue will look like **Illustration 21** below.

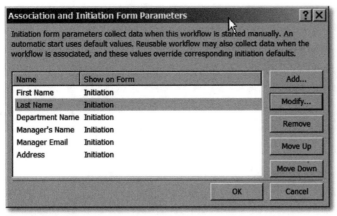

Illustration 21

Now click on *this list* in the action statement of the workflow. The *Create New List Item* dialogue screen will display. Select the name of the Library you are working with (*Demo Library* here) from the drop down selection box. The *Create New List Item* dialogue screen is where you define the type of item that will be created with the fields and respective values for that item. The default fields that will display are the *Content Type ID* and *Path and Name* as shown in **Illustration 22 below left**. Select the *Content Type ID* field and click the *Modify* button. The *Value Assignment* dialogue screen will display as shown in **Illustration 22 below right**. Click on the *To this value* drop-down selection arrow and select *Offer Letter* (or whatever *Content Type* name you used).

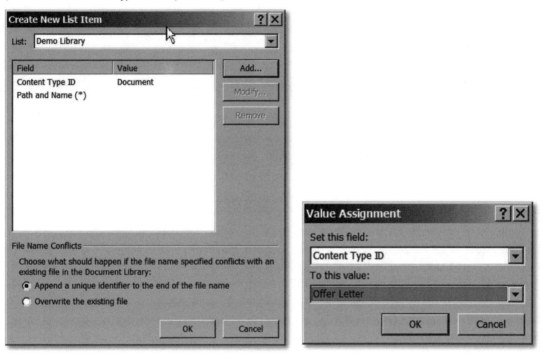

Illustration 22

Click *OK*. Now click on the *Add* button to display an empty *Value Assignment* dialogue screen. In the *Set this field* drop-down selection box, select *Department Name*. The fields that will display here are the columns defined for the *Offer Letter Content Type*. Now click on the *formula* button of the *To this value* drop-down selection box. The *Lookup for Single line of text* dialogue screen will display as shown in **Illustration 23 below left**. For the *Data source* drop-down selection box select *Workflow Variables and Parameters*. For the *Field from source* drop-down selection select *Parameter:Department Name*. For the *Return field as* selection select *As String*. The completed dialogue screen will look like **Illustration 23 right below**.

Illustration 23

Repeat this step for the other fields defined for the *Offer Letter: First Name, Last Name, Address* etc.

The fields of the *Workflow Variables and Parameters* come from the *Initiation Form Parameters* that we created earlier. What we are doing in this step is instructing the workflow to capture the values for the fields entered in the workflow initiation form and write those values to the corresponding fields of the *Offer Letter Content Type* in the target Library.

Once you have added all of the fields and values in the *Create New List Item* dialogue box select the *Path and Name* field and click the *Modify* button to display the *Value Assignment* dialogue screen as shown in **Illustration 24** below.

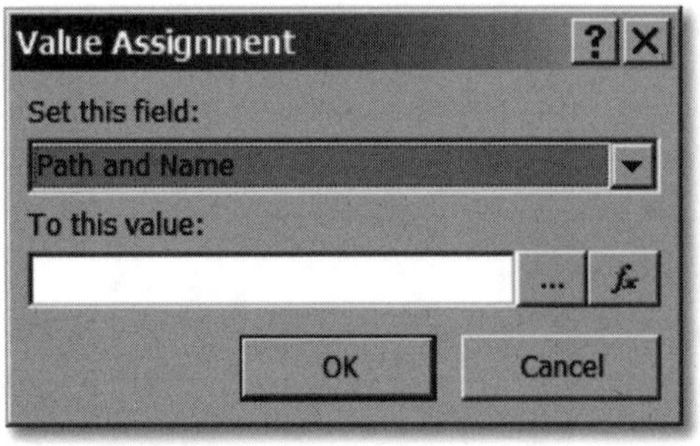

Illustration 24

Click on the *String Builder* button (with the …) for the *To this value* selection box to display the *String Builder* screen as shown in **Illustration 25 below left**. This is where we define how each document created will be named. Enter the text "Offer Letter" (or whatever you would like to use to name each document instance), then click on the *Add or Change* Lookup button, which will display the *Lookup for String* dialogue screen as shown in **Illustration 25 below right**.

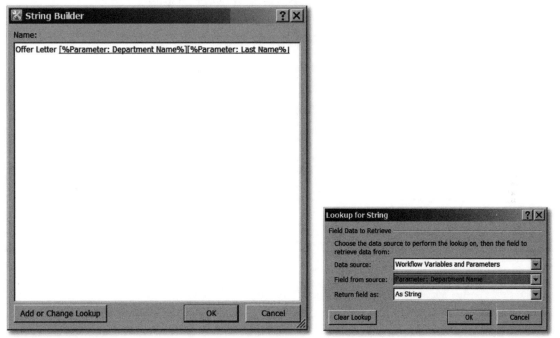

Illustration 25

Select the *Workflow Variables and Parameters* for the *Data source* and *Parameter: Department Name* as the *Field from source* value. Repeat this step to add the *Parameter:Last Name* value. Now when each instance of the *Offer Letter* is generated it will have a concatenated name of "Offer Letter Department Name value Last Name value".

You are now finished with the first part of this workflow. Save the workflow and click the *Publish* button to publish it. You can now test the published workflow on the site where you published it.

Augmenting the Workflow to Send an Email and Copy the Generated Document

After the workflow has generated the document you may wish to send an email to one or more people notifying them of this event and you may also want to copy the document to another location. The completed workflow for these additional two actions would like **Illustration 26** below.

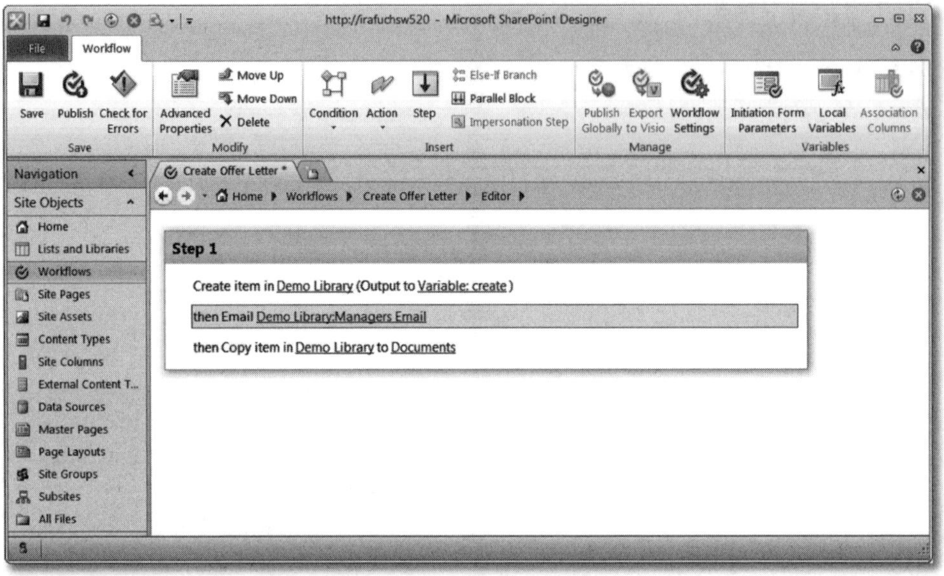

Illustration 26

Place your cursor under the *Create item* action in the workflow and from the *Action Ribbon* button select *Send an Email*. The action will be displayed in the workflow editor as shown in **Illustration 27** below.

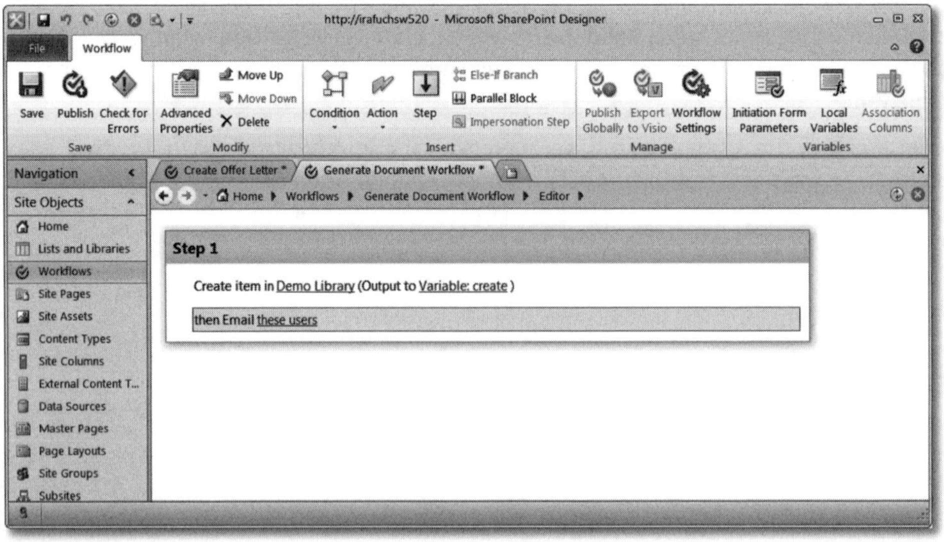

Illustration 27

Click on *these users* to display the *Define E-Mail Message* template as shown in **Illustration 28** below.

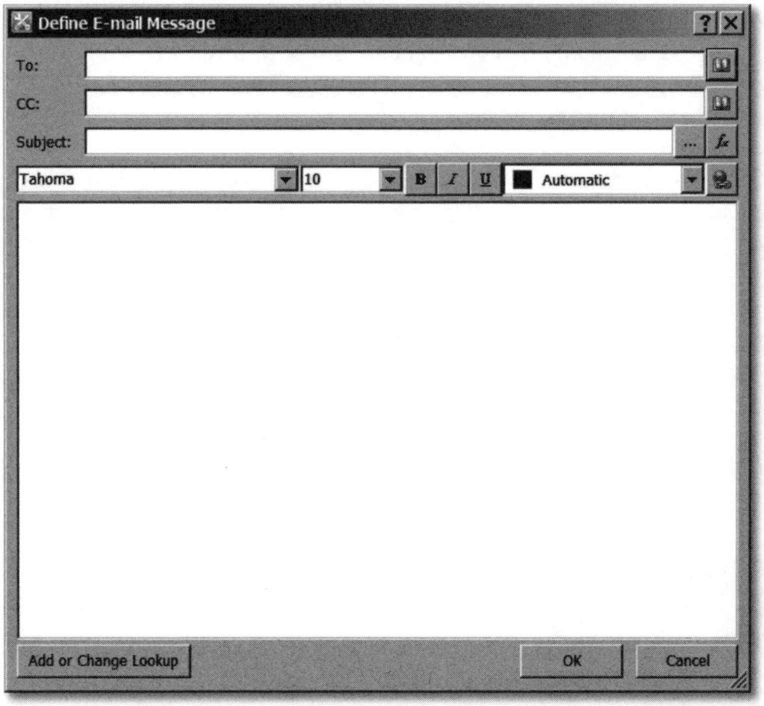

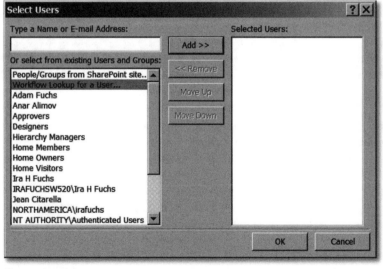

Illustration 28

Click on the Look-up button to the right of the *To* line in the *Define E-mail Message* template. The *Select Users* dialogue screen will display as shown in **Illustration 29** below:

Illustration 29

From the selection box on the left pick W*orkflow lookup for a User*. This will open the *Lookup for Person or Group* dialogue screen as shown in **Illustration 30 below left**. From the *Data source* drop-down selection box pick *Demo Library*. From the *Field from source* drop-down selection box pick *Managers Email*. Note that the *Managers Email* is a metadata column that was defined for the *Offer Letter Content Type*. Because the *Offer Letter Content Type* was instantiated in the *Demo Library* the fields for the *Offer Letter Content Type* will also be accessible from within a workflow.

What we need to do now is identify the *Manager's Email* value for the specific *Offer Letter* document created by this workflow. If we had created this workflow as a reusable workflow based on the *Offer Letter Content Type* the *SharePoint Designer* workflow editor would automatically provide us with the "Current Item" context for the document being created, that is, a built-in correlation mechanism for identifying the unique item that has been instantiated by the workflow. Since we created the workflow as a *Site workflow* we need to manually define this correlation mechanism, which was the reason for using a *Site workflow* in this example. In the *Field* drop-down selection box in the *Find the List Item* section pick the *ID* field. Now click on the *formula* button to the right of the *Value* drop-down selection box. The *Lookup for Integer* dialogue screen shown in **Illustration 30 below right** will display. For the *Data source* select *Workflow Variables and Parameters*. For the *Field from source* select *Variable:create* and leave the *Item ID* value for the *Return field as* selection.

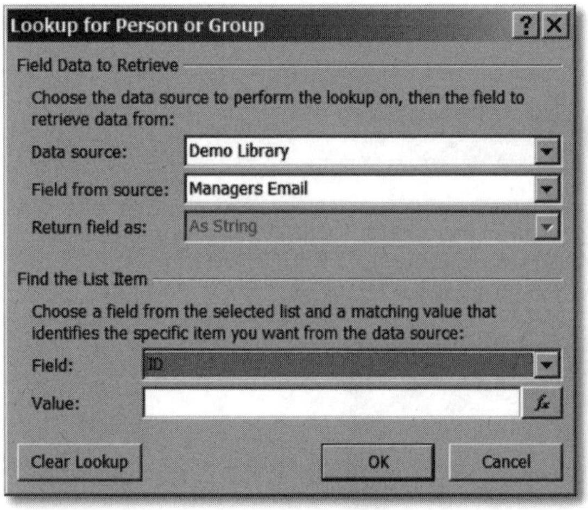

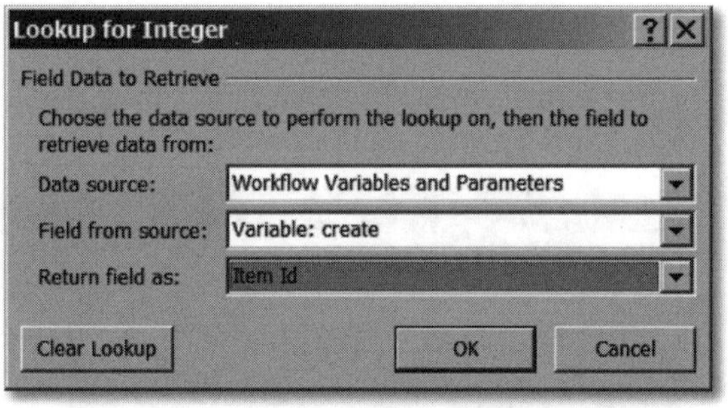

Illustration 30

What we have done in this procedure is to identify the *Managers Email* value for the document created in the *Demo Library* whose unique item *ID* matches the value of the *ID* written to the *Variable:create* by the workflow. Where and when was this *Variable:create ID* value generated? It was automatically generated by the *Create List Item* action. If you click on the *Local Variables Ribbon* button the *Workflow Local Variables* dialogue screen will display as shown in **Illustration 31 below left**, and you will see that there is a variable named "create" that is a *List Item Id Type*. If you select the *create* variable and click the *Modify* button you will see the drop-down selection box for the Type as shown in **Illustration 31 below right**.

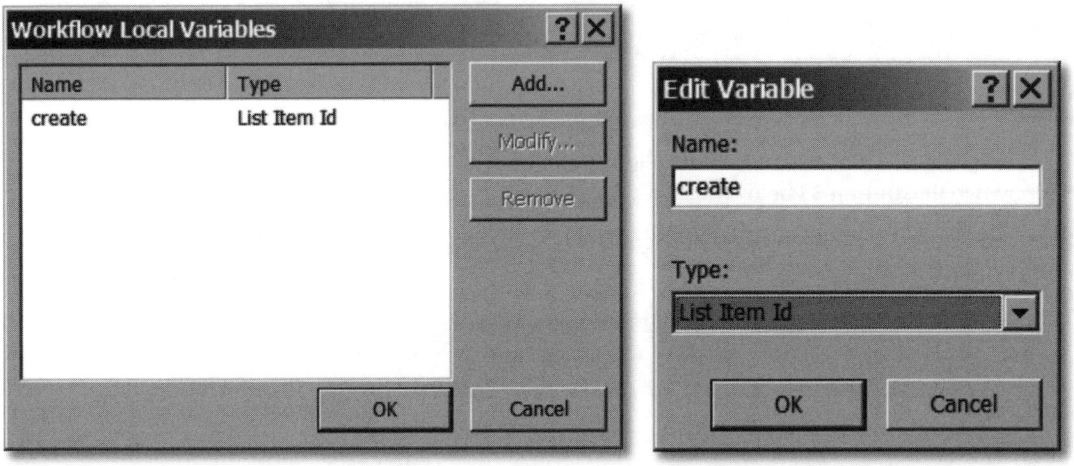

Illustration 31

When the workflow *Create List Item* action runs it generates a unique *ID* for the new item and the *ID* value is written to the *create* variable. By matching the *ID* of the document in the *Demo Library* with the value of the *ID* in the workflow variable we are creating the correlation mechanism that identifies the unique instance of the document that we want to capture the *Managers Email* value from. We will use the same correlation mechanism to identify a Link to the document and copy it.

Note, that the warning in **Illustration 32** on the next page will display when you click the *OK* button on a Lookup dialogue screen. This warning is displayed because the workflow editor cannot validate that the *Variable:create* is an exact match for the *ID* found in the *Document Library*. However, because the *ID* generated for the Library item and the value written to the create variable was executed simultaneously by the same workflow action we can have a high level of confidence that the correlation will identify a unique item.

Illustration 32

The next thing we want to do is embed a link in the body of the email to the newly created document, as shown in **Illustration 33** below.

Note the text "Link: [%Demo Library:Encoded Absolute URL%]" is present for reference purposes only, it provides no functional use.

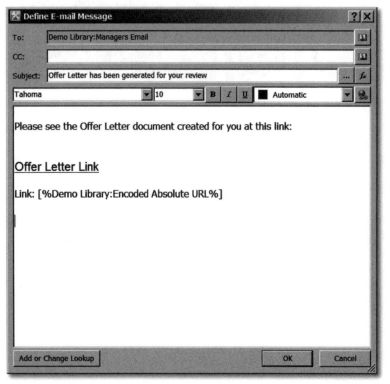

Illustration 33

Place your cursor anywhere in the body of the email message and click the *Hyperlink* button to the right of the typeface settings. The *Edit Hyperlink* dialogue screen will display as shown in **Illustration 34** below.

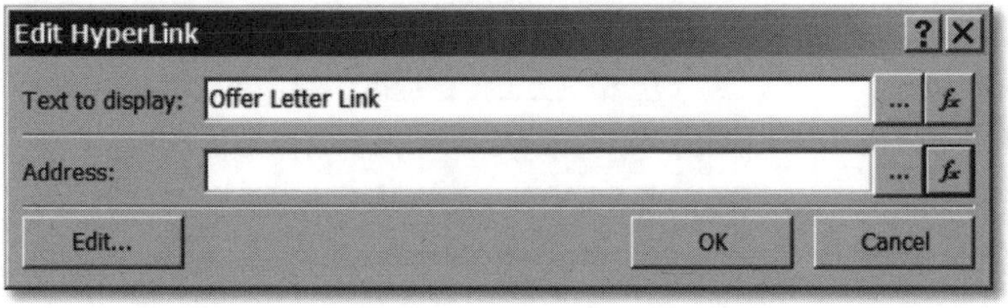

Edit HyperLink

Text to display:	Offer Letter Link
Address:	

Edit...   OK   Cancel

Illustration 34

Enter the hyperlinked text that you wish to display, then click on the *formula* button to the right of the *Address* box. The *Lookup for String* dialogue screen will display as shown in **Illustration 35 below left**. For the *Data source* select the name of the Library where the document was created. For the *Field from source* value select *Encoded Absolute URL*. Once again you will have to establish a correlation mechanism to identify the unique instance of the document that you want. You will use the same technique of matching the *ID* for the item in the *Document Library* with the *ID* written to the *create* variable described above and shown in **Illustration 35 below right**.

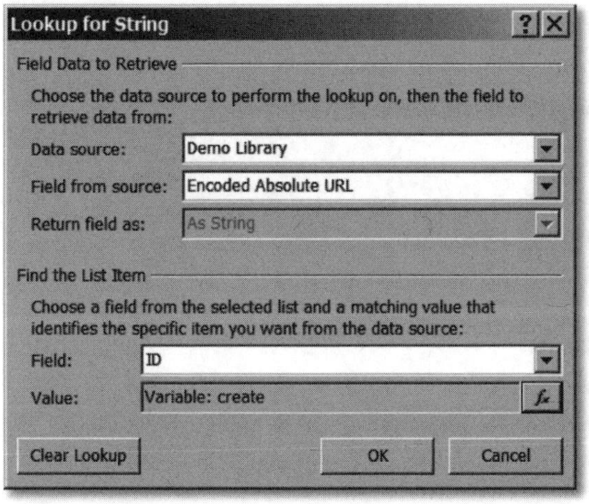

Lookup for String

Field Data to Retrieve

Choose the data source to perform the lookup on, then the field to retrieve data from:

Data source:	Demo Library
Field from source:	Encoded Absolute URL
Return field as:	As String

Find the List Item

Choose a field from the selected list and a matching value that identifies the specific item you want from the data source:

Field:	ID
Value:	Variable: create

Clear Lookup   OK   Cancel

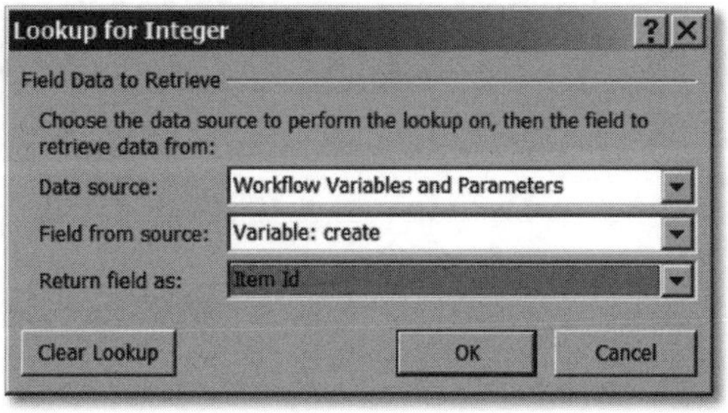

Lookup for Integer

Field Data to Retrieve

Choose the data source to perform the lookup on, then the field to retrieve data from:

Data source:	Workflow Variables and Parameters
Field from source:	Variable: create
Return field as:	Item Id

Clear Lookup   OK   Cancel

Illustration 35

The last action in our workflow is *Copy List item*, for the purposes of copying the newly created document to another Library. Click on the first *this list* in the action statement and select the Library that the document was created in the *Choose List Item* drop-down box as shown in **Illustration 36** at right. To identify the unique document use the same matching *ID* correlation mechanism. Select any Library to copy the document to.

Illustration 36

Now *Save* and *Publish* the workflow by clicking on their respective buttons on the *Ribbon*.

Before you can test the workflow you need to configure the Library where the document will be copied to support the same document *Content Type*, which is the *Offer Letter Content Type* in this exercise. In your copy-to Library repeat the steps itemized on **pages 32 and 33**.

Testing the Workflow

Go to the *All Site Content* page and click on *Site Workflows* to go to the *Workflows: Home* page as shown in **Illustration 37** below. Click on the workflow name that you used to start the workflow.

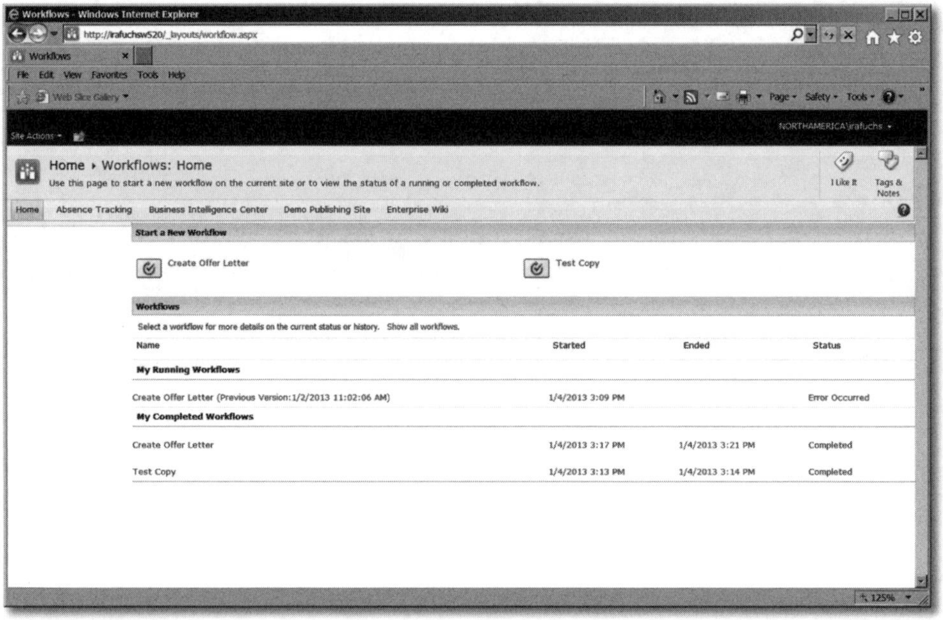

Illustration 37

The workflow *Initiation Form* will open where you enter the fields that will populate the document.

After you have entered this information click the *Start* button to execute the workflow. After the workflow runs you will find that the *Offer Letter* has been successfully created with the *Quick Part* property fields populated with the values you entered in the *Initiation Form*.

However, the workflow *Status* will indicate that an *Error Occurred* as shown in **Illustration 37** above. Clicking on the *Error Occurred* message will bring you to the *Workflow Status* page for the workflow as shown in **Illustration 38** below, where the *Workflow History* section will provide you with additional information about the errors. Unfortunately, this information is for all intents and purposes useless.

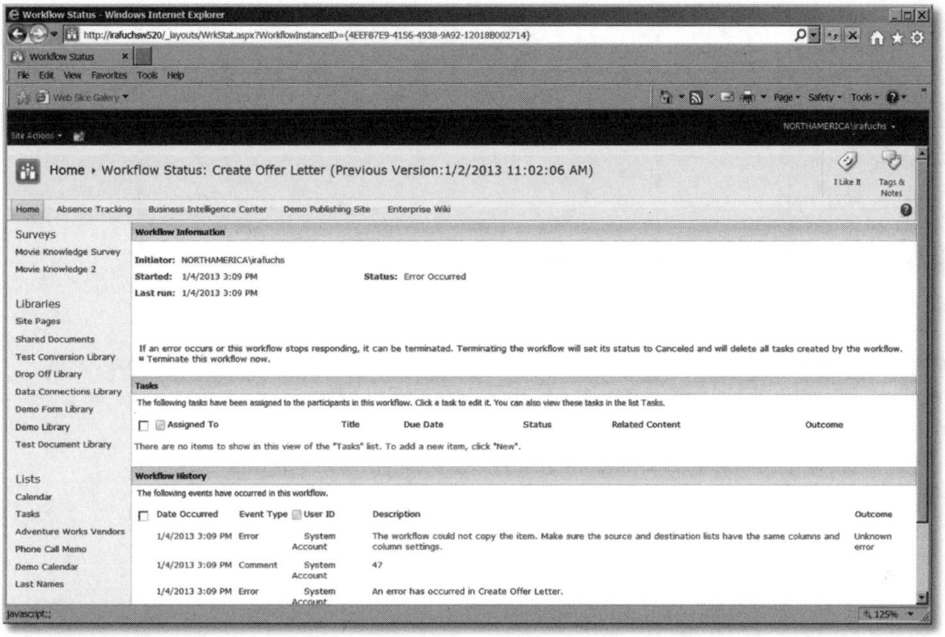

Illustration 38

> **Note** — if your *SharePoint Server* is not configured to send email than the workflow will have failed in the execution of the second action (*Send an Email*) and the last action (*Copy List Item*) will also not execute.

If your *SharePoint Server* (or *SharePoint* dev/test environment) is configured to send email both actions *will still fail* however for another reason: The *Copy List Item* action will fail because the *Copy List Item* action is fired before the document is completely created, and the workflow is trying to copy the document before the document is fully created. The workaround for this problem is to add a *Pause for Duration* action directly after the initial *Create List Item* action in the workflow as shown in **Illustration 39** on the next page*. This persists the workflow and gives *SharePoint* enough time to finish creating the document. A two minute pause will be sufficient for the workflow timer job to recognize the presence of the document. You can also move the Send an Email action after the *Copy List Item* action.

*Thank you to Cosmin Barsan of the SharePoint Product Group who identified the problem and provided the fix!

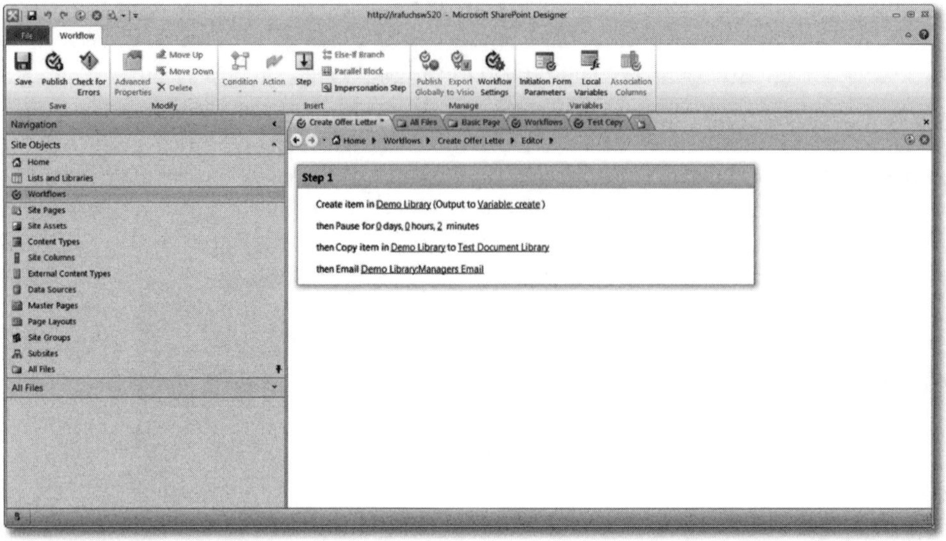

Illustration 39

Save and *Publish* your workflow again and test it. It should execute just fine. Congratulations, you have completed an automated document generation workflow! Enjoy!

How to Set Up a Flexible and Scalable System for Distributing and Updating Contact Information in Outlook Using SharePoint Contact Lists and SharePoint External Content Types

A common process found in any organization is the generation of contact information that needs to be made available to numerous people. The generation of sales leads; publishing and updating an organization's membership directory; or simply capturing LinkedIn contacts are typical use case scenarios representing this type of activity. The medium of distribution is usually an *Excel* spreadsheet or a *PDF* document. However, what most users really want to do with this information is bring it into their *Outlook Contacts* data store where they can then use it in the flexible ways that *Outlook* enables. To do this each person must individually go through the time consuming, manual process of re-entering the information into *Outlook*. However, once it is in *Outlook* it is isolated and static, and any updates require additional manual effort.

In this chapter we are going to demonstrate two methods for automating and optimizing the process of capturing contact information using *SharePoint* and effortlessly making it available to *Outlook* for any number of people. In addition, this methodology provides an equally valuable additional benefit: the contact information is editable from both *Outlook* and *SharePoint*, and any changes are reflected automatically in both places, because we are working from one shared data source. Furthermore, if a *SharePoint External Content Type* List is used, which is a dynamic connection between *SharePoint* and an external data source such as *SQL Server*, then changes to the external data source will also update the *Outlook* contact information and vice versa. It is fully bi-directional.

Creating a SharePoint Contact List, Importing Information from an Excel Spreadsheet, and Connecting the Contact List to Outlook.

So let's get started with the first method. Click on *Site Actions* from within any *SharePoint* site and select *More Options*. The *Create* dialogue screen will display as shown in **Illustration 1** on the next page. Select the *Contacts* List; give it a name and click the *Create* button.

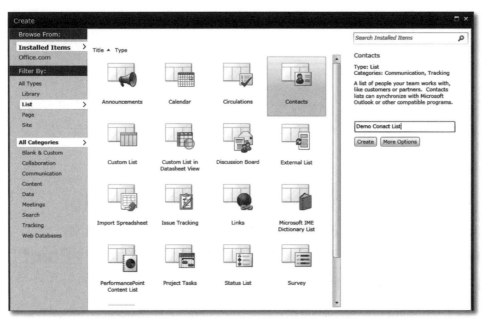

Illustration 1

The *Contacts List* will be created as shown in **Illustration 2** below, and behaves just like any other *SharePoint* List. However, the *Contacts List* provides one very specific capability that is not available from a generic *Custom List*: when you click on the *Connect to Outlook Ribbon* button on the *List Tools* tab, also shown in **Illustration 2** below, it will connect to *Outlook* and create a *Contact group* with the same name as the List and will display the List items as *Outlook* contacts! The contact items from the List will function and behave just like any other *Outlook* contact items, and if your organization uses *Microsoft Lync Server*, you will be able to make telephone calls from the items as well.

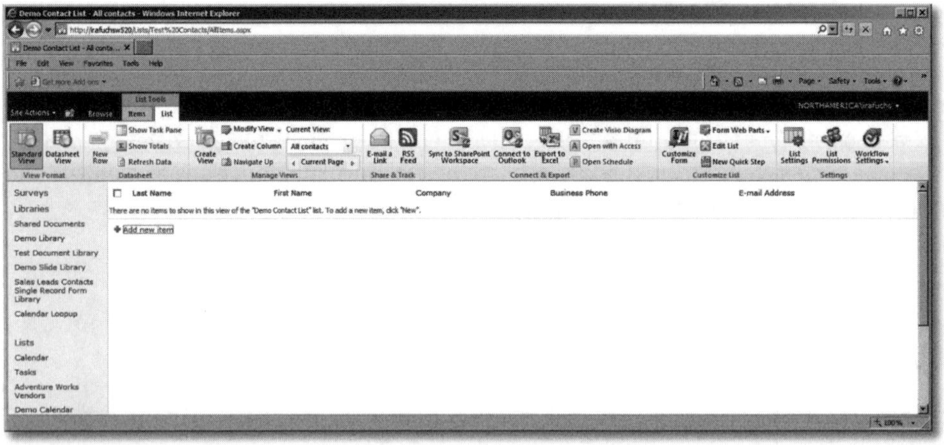

Illustration 2

Note that the default *All contacts* View displays just the columns for *Last Name, First Name, Company, Business Phone* and *E-mail Address* but if you click the *Add new item* button or the *Edit item* button the List form will contain additional fields, all of which map to the *Outlook* contact fields as shown in **Illustration 3** below.

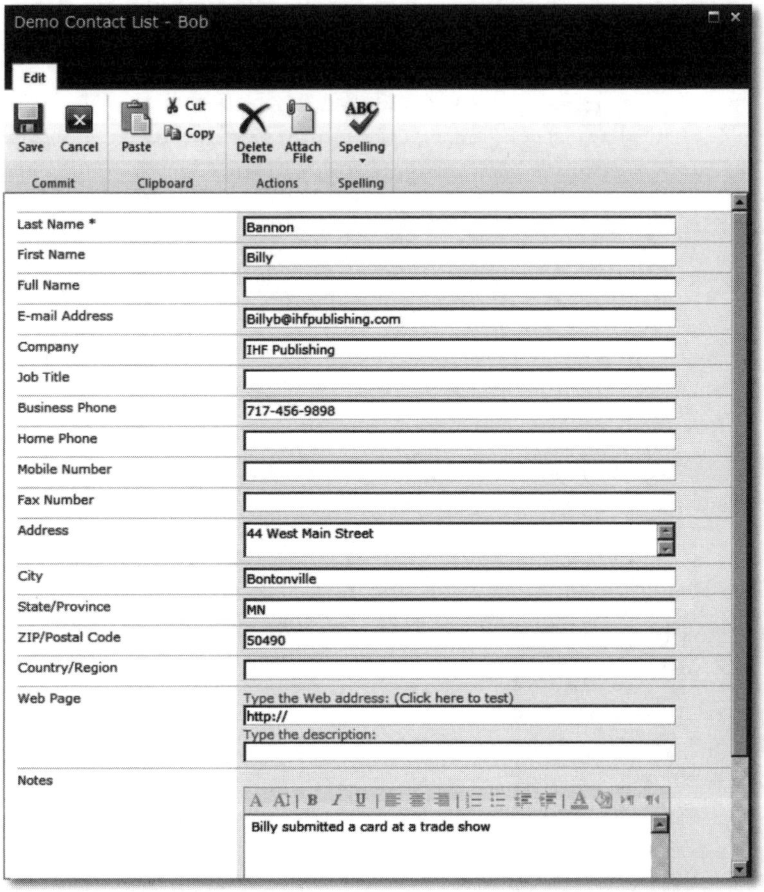

Illustration 3

Add a List item and save it. If you are using *Lync* there will be a telephone icon next to the phone number. If you click on the email address *Outlook* will create a new email to the addressee. The *Contacts List* is generated from the *Contacts Content Type* using the corresponding *Site Column* definitions. The List implements the actionable functionality for the applicable information.

Make sure your *Outlook* application is open and click on the *Connect to Outlook Ribbon* button on the *List Tools* section as shown in **Illustration 4** below.

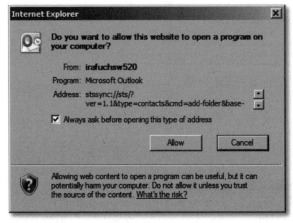

Illustration 4

The security dialogue screen shown in **Illustration 5** below will display. Click the *Allow* button.

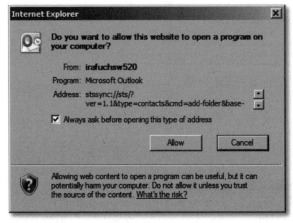

Illustration 5

Now go to *Outlook* and under *My Contacts* in the *Navigation* pane you will see a contact group with the same name as the *Contacts List* and the record that you added as shown in **Illustration 6** below.

Illustration 6

Double click on the contact item to open its property screen as shown in **Illustration 7** below. Note that all the information that you entered in the List form is present.

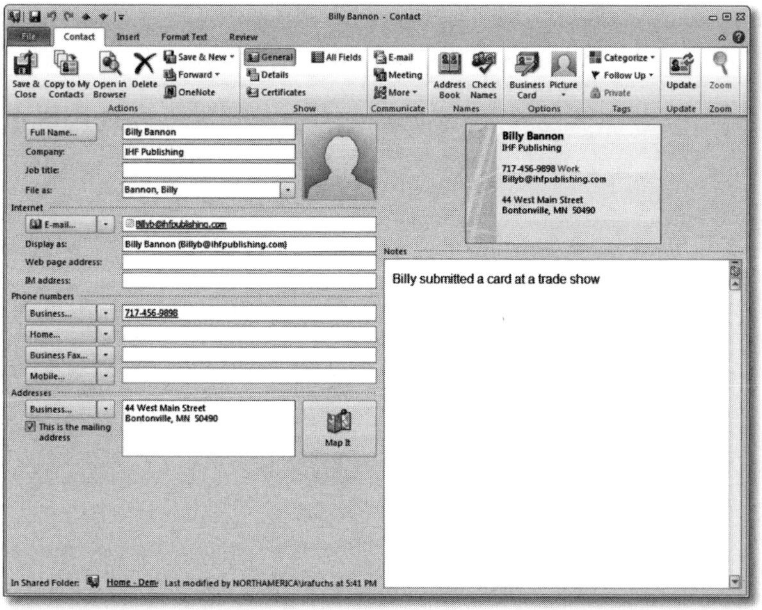

Illustration 7

In *Outlook* create a new contact record in the *Outlook* contact group for the List and return to your SharePoint *Contacts List* and refresh it. The new contact that you just created in *Outlook* will be displayed in the List as shown in **Illustration 8** below.

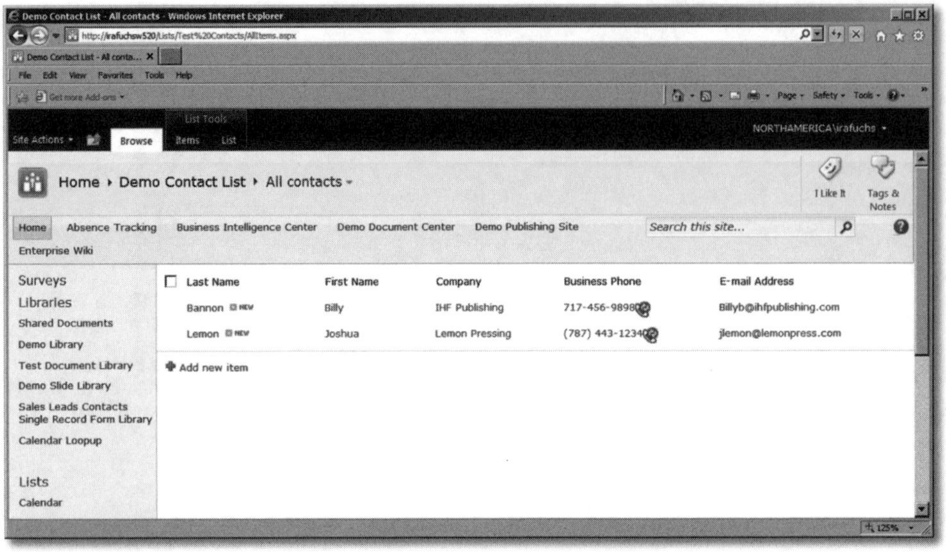

Illustration 8

Select the new contact and click *Edit* item. The edit form for the contact item will open as shown in **Illustration 9** below.

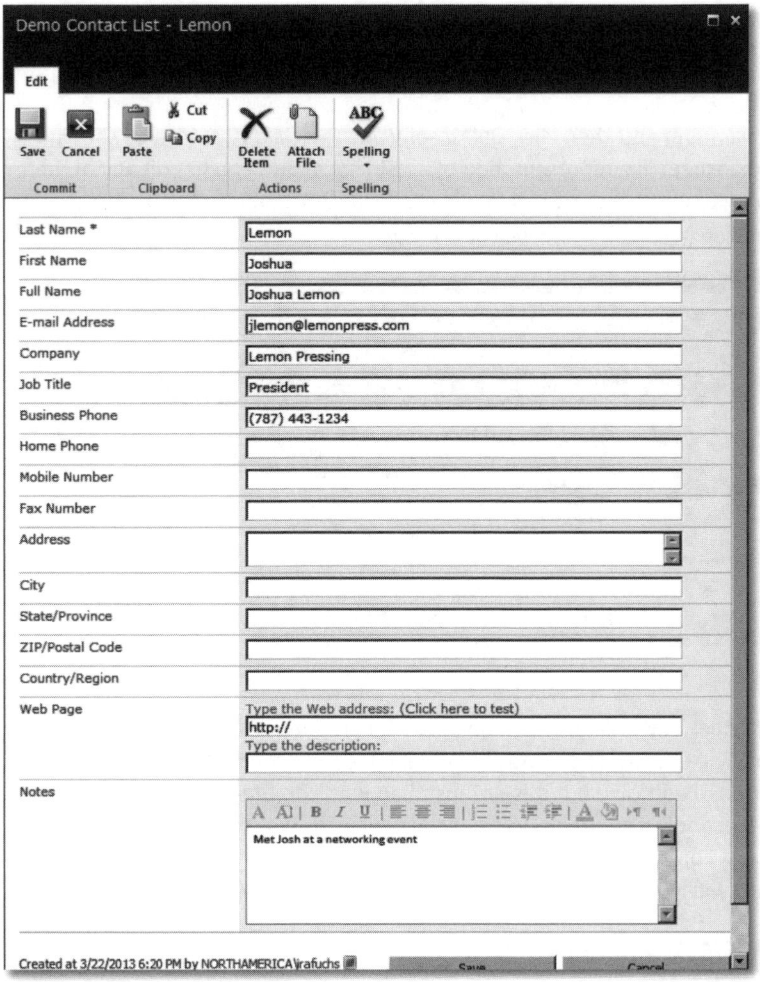

Illustration 9

Note that all the information entered in *Outlook* is present. Change or add any information in the record and click the *Save* button. Return to the contact group in *Outlook* and inspect the record to see that the modifications are there.

So far, so good; but it gets better! Most contact information is generated and distributed using *Excel* spreadsheets. What we will demonstrate now is the ability to simply copy rows of contact information from an *Excel* spreadsheet and paste them directly into the *SharePoint Contact List*, where they will then immediately be accessible through *Outlook*.

The first step in doing this is to structure the columns in the spreadsheet so that their order is identical to the order of the columns in the *SharePoint Contact List*. You can do this any number of ways. If there is more useful information in the spreadsheet that you would like to incorporate into the List you can add columns to the List and/or create multiple List views. If there is information in the spreadsheet that you don't want to use you can delete, move or hide those columns. The important thing is that the columns in the SharePoint List View and the spreadsheet are in the same sequence.

Click on the *List* tab of the *Ribbon* menu and then click *Datasheet View*. The *Datasheet View* as shown in **Illustration 10** below is a spreadsheet like representation of a List that allows you to edit any of the information in-line without having to open each record in edit mode. In *Datasheet View* you can also add or delete multiple rows of information (records), which we will do now.

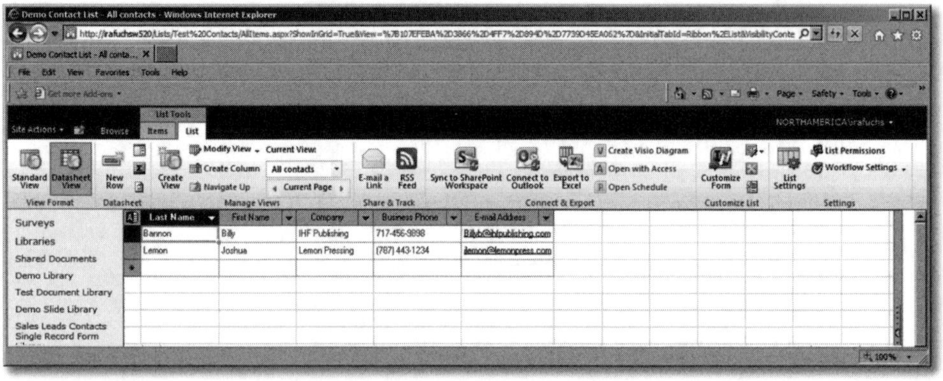

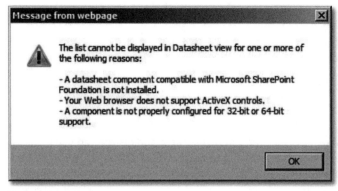

Illustration 10

> **Important Note** – The *Datasheet View* will not work on a user's computer if the datasheet component is not installed. The datasheet component is installed with the *Microsoft Office Professional* 2003, 2007, or 2010 editions; but it is **not** installed with the **Standard** or **Student editions** of these versions. Secondly, the user's browser must also **allow** *Active X* controls to run within it. If the datasheet component is not installed and/or *Active X* controls are not enabled in the browser, you will get the error message shown in **Illustration 11** below.

Illustration 11

In *Excel* create a simple spreadsheet with the same five columns and in the same order as the *Contacts List* default view (*Last Name, First Name, Company, Business Phone, Email Address*). Create four or five rows of sample information with content in each cell as shown in **Illustration 12** below.

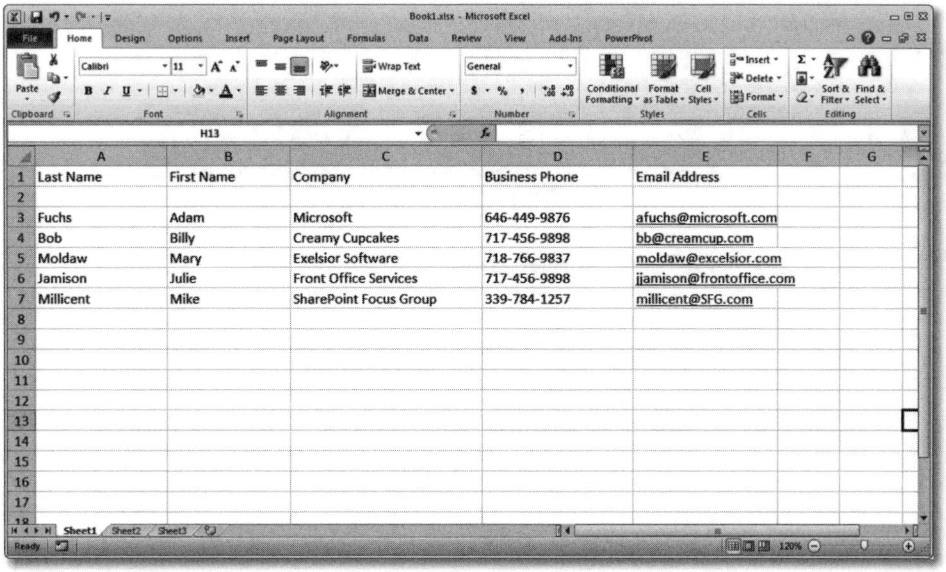

Illustration 12

After you have created these rows of information select them with your cursor; that is, select the range of cells from cell A:3 to cell E:7 as shown in **Illustration 13** below.

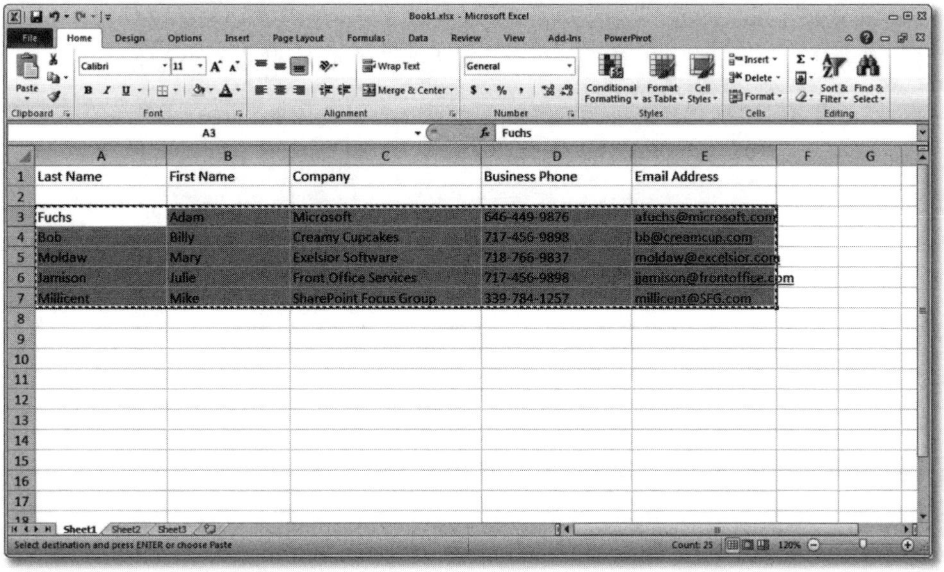

Illustration 13

With your cursor placed within the range of cells right-click and select *Copy.* Now in the datasheet view of the contacts list, place your cursor in the first column of the third row (the empty row with the * to the left of the first column), right-click and select *Paste.* The records from the spreadsheet are now copied to the *Contact List* as shown in **Illustration 14** below.

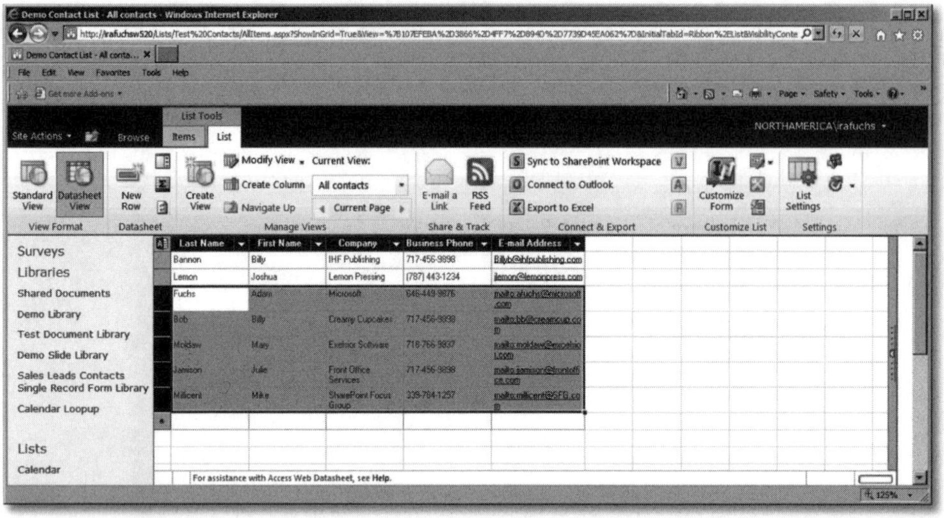

Illustration 14

Click on the *Standard View* button on the *Ribbon* menu to see the records in this view as shown in **Illustration 15** below.

Illustration 15

Using this simple technique you can copy and paste tens of thousands of rows of information in minutes! Once in the *SharePoint Contacts List* it will show up in the *Outlook* group immediately.

Important Note – deleting contacts in *Outlook* will delete the items in the *SharePoint Contacts List* as well. If multiple people are connecting to and using this information you probably do not want people to be able to delete items from the List. There is a way that you can allow people to delete a contact so that it will be deleted from their *Outlook* contacts group but will remain in the *SharePoint Contacts List*. This is accomplished by declaring all or selected items in the *Contacts List* as "Records". When a List or Library item is "declared a record" it can no longer be edited or deleted from the List or Library until it is "undeclared a record".

There are two ways to declare records in any List or Library. The first way is to automatically make all the items in the List records. This is accomplished by going into *Library Settings*, clicking on the *Record settings* option in the *Permissions and Management* section, and then checking the *Automatically declare items as records when they are added to this List* check box, as shown in **Illustration 16** below. When you use this method however you will no longer be able to edit any of the items in the List, either directly from *SharePoint* or from within *Outlook*. Essentially the entire List becomes read-only.

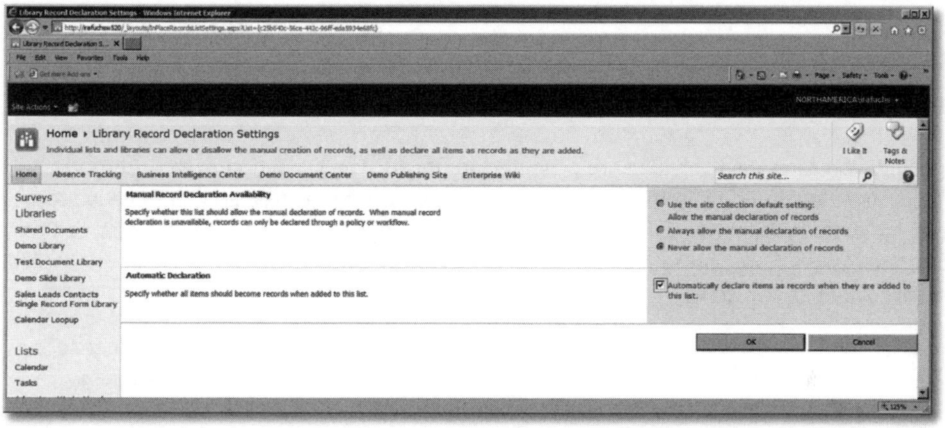

Illustration 16

The contacts can now be deleted from any person's *Outlook* contact group but the actual item will not be deleted from the *SharePoint Contacts List*. The significant limitation of using this Library setting is that you cannot edit the items either, from within *SharePoint* or *Outlook*. In *Outlook* you can modify the fields but after you save the changes they will not actually be saved. In *SharePoint* you can open the item in edit mode but you will get an error message when you attempt to save the item. Furthermore, you cannot undeclare individual items. This method is only viable for those use cases where the contact items need to be accessible to multiple people and no editing of the items is acceptable.

The second method is to selectively declare records by choosing one or more List items in the *Standard View* and clicking the *Declare Record* button on the *Ribbon* from the *List Tools* tab as shown in **Illustration 17** below.

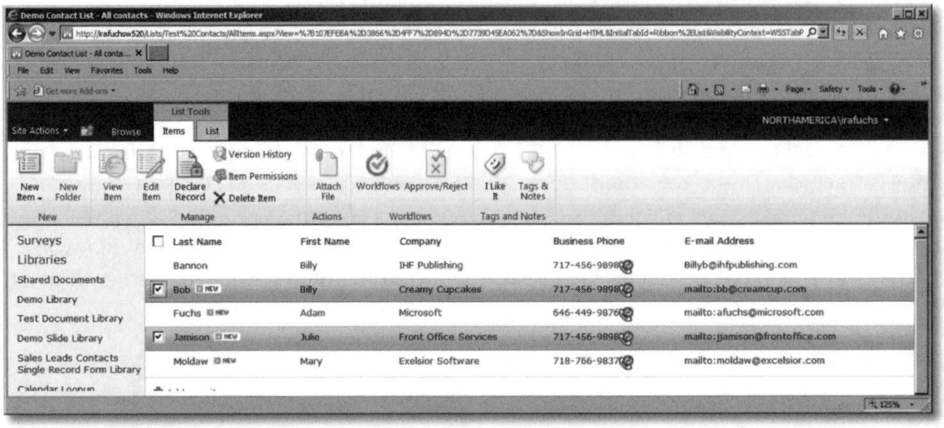

Illustration 17

With this capability you can selectively declare or undeclare items. The limitation of this method is that while you can select multiple items and declare or undeclare them at once, you still have to select each one individually from the List in the *Standard View*. Unfortunately you cannot execute this function in *Datasheet View* where you can Shift-click on one record, scroll down to a subsequent record and automatically select all the items.

If you want to know which items have been declared as records you can go to the *Settings* page for any View and select the *Declared Record* column to display it that View as shown in **Illustration 18** below.

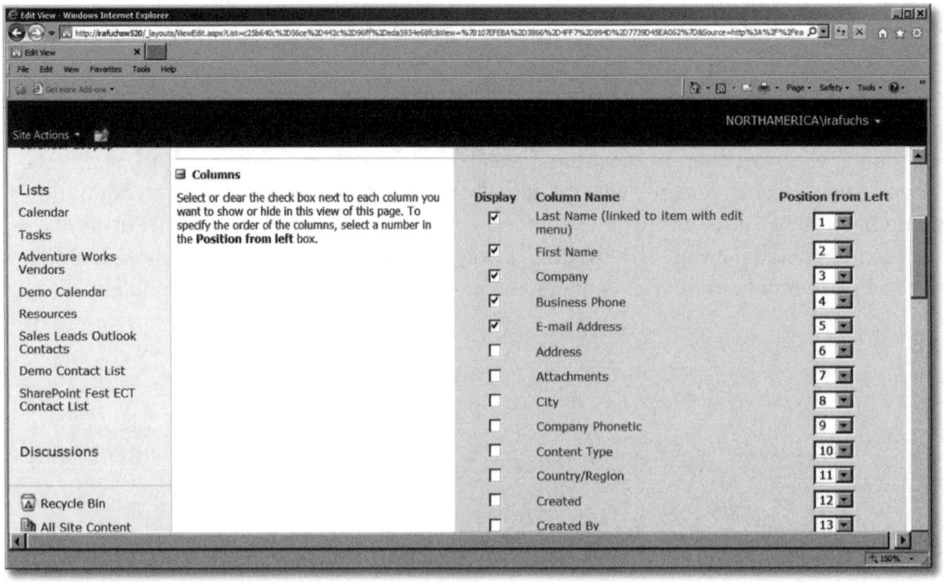

Illustration 18

Illustration 19 below shows the *Contacts List* with the *Declared Record* column displayed.

Illustration 19

Lastly, if you want to undeclare an item as a record, right-click on the item and from the drop-down menu select *Compliance Details* to display the *Compliance Details* dialogue screen as shown in **Illustration 20** below. Click the *Undeclare record* link to the right of *Record Status*.

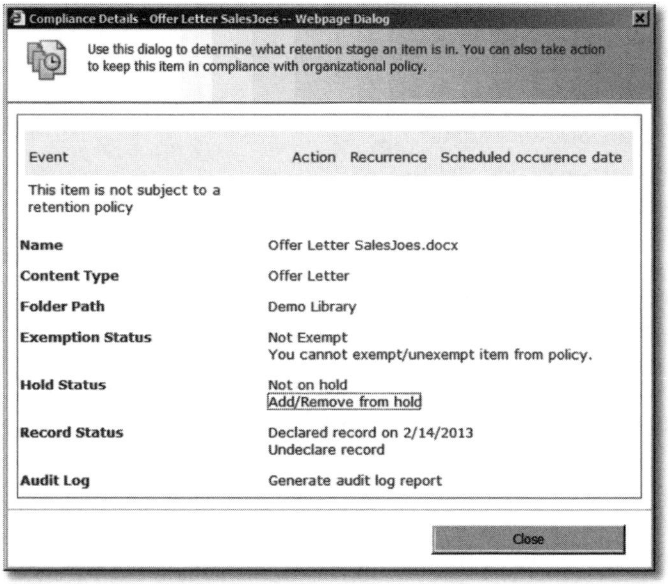

Illustration 20

Declaring items as Records is obviously a less than optimal workaround to preventing contacts from being deleted from a List when it is deleted within *Outlook*. What we will see in the next part of this chapter is that using *External Contact Types* mapped to *Office Contact Properties* provides a more flexible and elegant solution to managing the operations executed on contact List items by multiple people.

SharePoint Business Connectivity Services (BCS) enables you to declaratively model external systems so that you can expose the information and operations of external data sources for use in *SharePoint* and also make that information available to *Outlook* and *Microsoft Word*. *SharePoint Designer* provides a Wizard-like tool to connect with external systems that in turn identifies the information sets that can be accessed; enables the operations that can be executed on the information sets; and exposes the information as a List within *SharePoint*. In addition you can map the fields in the information set to *Office* data types for use in *Outlook* and *Word*. An *External Content Type (ECT)* is the representation of the external data source in *SharePoint* defined by the information set and the operations that can used with that information set.

So let's get started creating our *ECT* in *SharePoint Designer*.

> **Note** – The implementation of this functionality requires that the contact information be loaded into an *SQL Server* database. In this exercise we use the *AdventureWorks* sample databases, which are available for download on the Codeplex.com site at http://msftdbprodsamples.codeplex.com/releases/view/93587. You can download the database samples that are applicable to the version of *SQL Server* that you are running. You will then need to restore the database to an instance of *SQL Server*. To this purpose you may need the cooperation of the database administrator (commonly known as a *DBA*) in your IT department to get this done; and then make the database available to you. It's a nominal effort that is worth doing, because as you will see, the payback in productivity for many people will be huge!

The steps that we will take to implement this *SharePoint* functionality are as follows:

- Create and name the *External Content Type*.
- Create a data source connection to the *SQL Server* database.
- Specify the operations (Create, Read, Update and Delete) that we will allow people to execute on the *ECT*.
- Select the fields in the data source that we want to expose through *SharePoint*.
- Map the selected fields to their respective *Office* contact properties.
- Create a *SharePoint* List for the *ECT* and an *InfoPath* List form.
- Configure *Object Permissions* for the *ECT* in *SharePoint Central Administration*
- Connect the *SharePoint ECT* List to *Outlook* to display the records as contacts.

Create and Name the External Content Type

Open *SharePoint Designer* and connect to the site where you want to create the *ECT*. Click on *External Content Types* on the *Navigation Site Objects* pane as shown in **Illustration 21** below. The main information section will be empty if you have not as yet created any *External Content Types*.

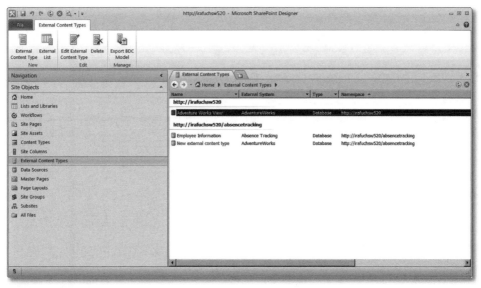

Illustration 21

Click on the N*ew External Content Type* button on the *Ribbon*. The *External Content Type Summary Page* will display as shown in **Illustration 22** below.

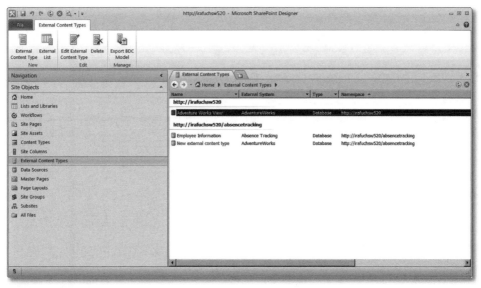

Illustration 22

Change the *Name and Display Name* to "Sales Leads Outlook Contacts". In the drop-down selection box for *Office Item Type* select *Contact*. Now click on the *Click here to discover external data sources and define operations* link either in the *External Content Type Information* section or the *External Content Type Operations* section. The *Operation Designer* screen will be displayed as shown in **Illustration 23** below.

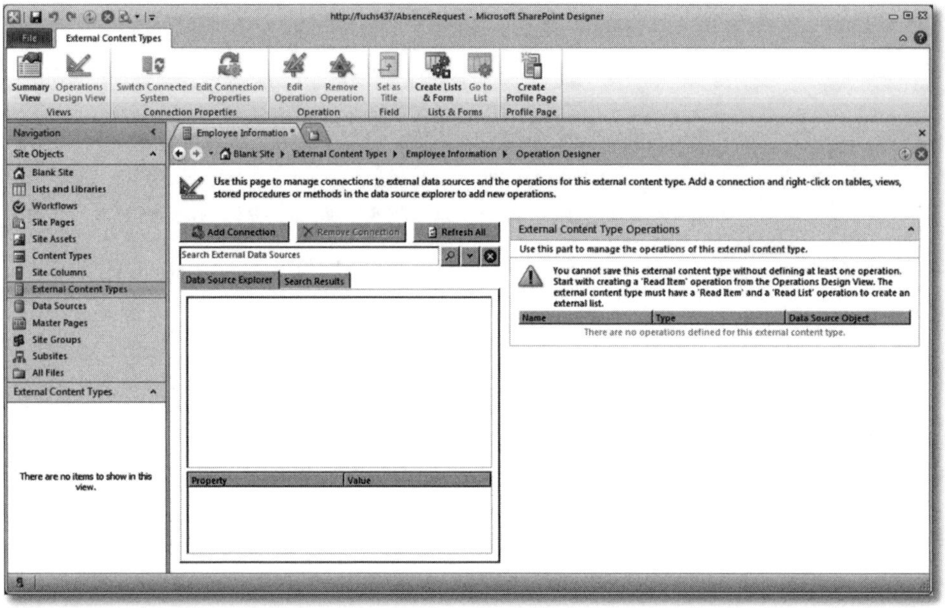

Illustration 23

Creating the External Data Source Connection

This page contains the *Data Source Explorer* section and *External Content Type Operations* section. This is where we will create a connection to a data source, in this case to an *SQL Server* database named *AdventureWorks* that contains sample tables and views that can be used for testing.

> **Note** — The *AdventureWorks* sample databases are available for download from the *Codeplex.com* site at http://msftdbprodsamples.codeplex.com/releases/view/93587, as shown in **Illustration 24** on the next page. You can download the database samples that are applicable to the version of *SQL Server* you are running.

Illustration 24

Click on the *Add Connection* button. The *External Data Source Type Selection* dialogue box will display as shown in **Illustration 25** at right.

Illustration 25

Choose *SQL Server* and click *OK*. The *SQL Server Connection* dialogue box will appear as shown in **Illustration 26** at right. Enter the name of your Database Server and the Database Name which will be "AdventureWorks" if you are using this sample database. Leave the default *Connect with User's Identity* radio button value.

> **Note** — Your Database Administrator will have restored this sample database to an *SQL Server* instance and set your credentials so that you can connect to the AdventureWorks database in this step.

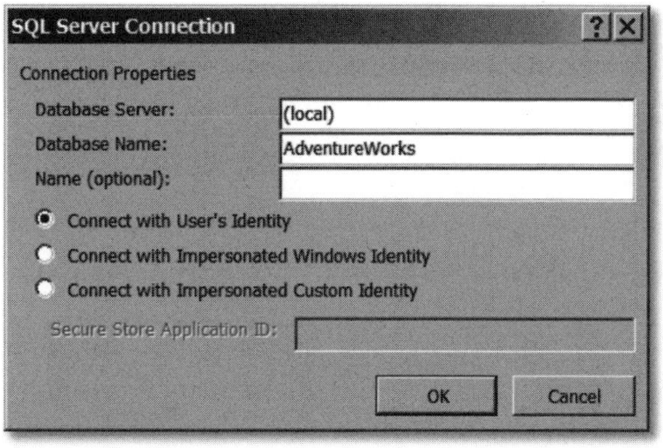

Illustration 26

When the connection is made the *AdventureWorks* database will be displayed in the *Data Source Explorer* panel as shown in **Illustration 27** below. If other data sources were previously created they will be displayed as well.

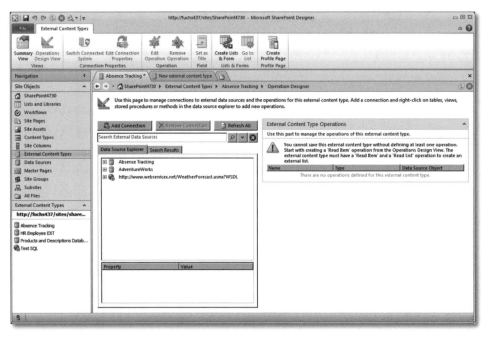

Illustration 27

Expand the *AdventureWorks* database icon in the *Data Source Explorer* to view the Tables, Views and Routines that are exposed. Clicking on the *Tables* or *Views* folder will reveal the database columns for each table or view as shown in **Illustration 28** below.

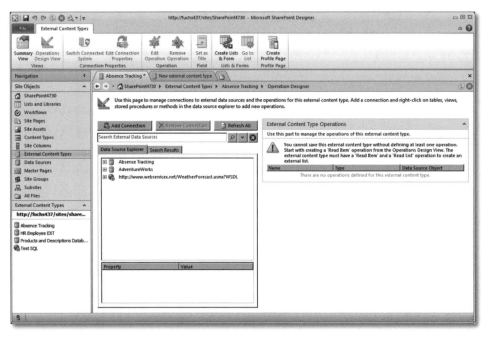

Illustration 28

Creating the External Content Type Operations

The next step is to create the operations that can be executed on the information in the tables or views and choose what information to make available through the *ECT*. These operations are the standard Create, Update and Delete (CRUD) functions available in most applications. Right-click on any table or view and the following options will be displayed, as shown in **Illustration 29** below:

- Create All Operations
- New Read Item Operation
- New Read List Operation
- New Create Operation
- New Update Operation
- New Delete Operation
- New Association

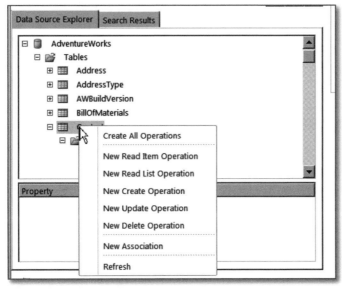

Illustration 29

The *SharePoint Designer External Content Type* creation tool is decidedly granular about what information you can expose and what you can do with that information. The following is a description of the Operation choices:

Create All Operations – Choosing this option will initiate a Wizard that will create and configure all of the Operations below.

New Read Item Operation – Choosing this option will initiate a Wizard that will allow the ECT List Form to access and display a single record from the data source.

New Read List Operation – Choosing this option will initiate a Wizard that will create a data set from the data source that will display as a SharePoint List. This Operation is prerequisite requirement of creating an External Content Type List and Form.

New Create Operation – Choosing this option will initiate a Wizard that will allow a user to create a new record in the data source using the underlying InfoPath form for the ECT List. This is a new write-back capability of BCS.

New Update Operation – Choosing this option will initiate a Wizard that will allow a user to update one or more data source fields with a new value from an ECT List view or from the underlying InfoPath form for the ECT List. This is a new write-back capability of BCS.

New Delete Operation – Choosing this option will initiate a Wizard that will allow a user to delete an entire record. This can be accomplished by deleting a row in an ECT List view or as an item displayed in the underlying InfoPath form for the ECT List. This is a new write-back capability of BCS.

New Association – Choosing this option will initiate a Wizard that is used to link two tables in the same database.

For the *Sales Leads Outlook Contacts ECT* we will *Create All Operations* on the *vIndividualCustomer* View in the *AdventureWorks* database.

Note – A View in a database is a virtual table comprised of fields from multiple tables that have been joined. Since and ECT can be created from a View we are able to access information that exists in multiple tables all at once.

Right-click on the *vIndividualCustomer* View icon in the *Data Source Explorer* and click on *Create All Operations*. The *Operation Properties* Wizard screen will display as shown in **Illustration 30** below.

All operations	? X

Operation Properties
Parameters
Filter Parameters

Operation Properties
This wizard will create all operations required to create, read, update, delete, and query data for this external content type. You will be able to select the columns you want to expose and define parameters. The names of the operations will be:

Create
Read Item
Update
Delete
Read List

Errors and Warnings

To configure Parameters, click Next.

< Back   Next >   Finish   Cancel

Illustration 30

Click on the *Next* button to display the *Parameters Configuration* page of the wizard as shown in **Illustration 31** below. Four section panels are displayed: the *Wizard steps*, the *Data Source Elements*, the *Element Properties* and *Errors and Warnings*.

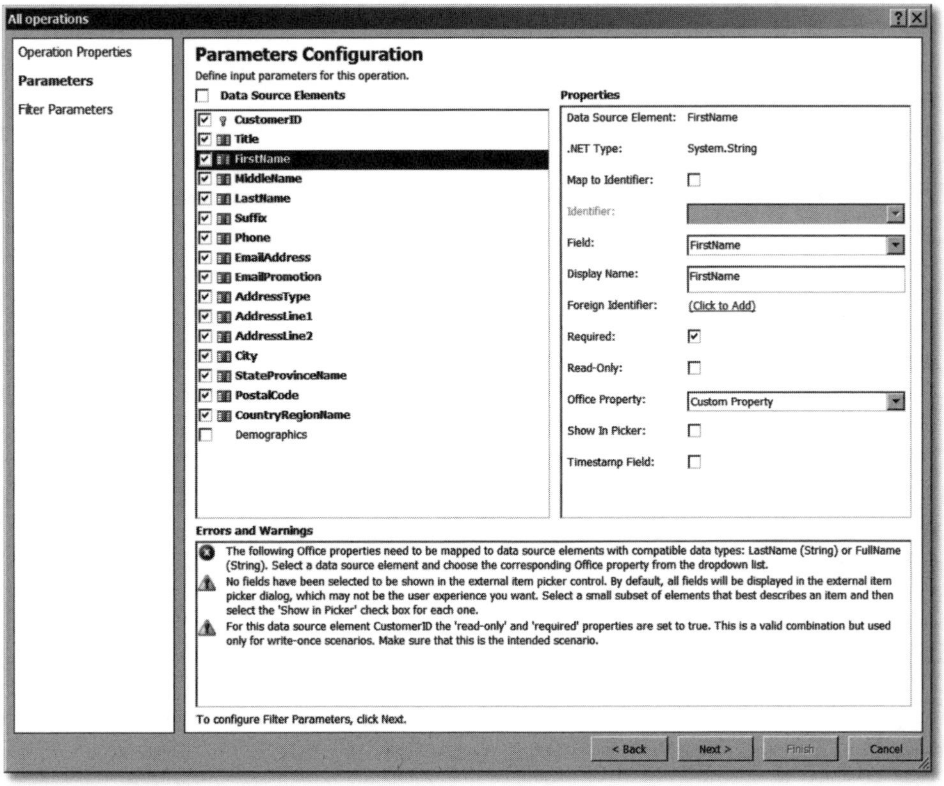

Illustration 31

On this Wizard step we can choose the fields from the database table that we want to use in the *External Content Type* and configure settings and properties for the fields. The *Data Source Elements* section displays the available fields from the database table. All fields from the data source are selected for inclusion in the *External Content Type* by default but any field that is not required can be de-selected and omitted from the *External Content Type* record definition. The Wizard accesses the properties defined for these fields in the *SQL database* and makes sure that any of the choices in this step do not invalidate those properties. For example, if we de-select any of the fields that were set to not nullable (i.e. required) such as the First Name, the Wizard would display an error message in the *Errors and Warnings* panel. An error message is displayed for every instance of an error condition.

Depending upon the operations and the data source fields selected the *Properties* panel will display different property settings. The following is a description of these property items:

Data Source Element – The name of the field in the data source

.NET Type – The data type assigned to the field in the data source

Map to Identifier check box – Used to specify which field will be used as the key (indexed) fields in the External Content Type. At least one field must be specified as the Identifier, typically the same key field defined in the database, such as the *ContactID*. You can create multiple key fields by selecting a field in the *Data Source Elements* panel, clicking *Map to Identifier.* The *ECT Identifier* by default will be the same field specified in the database.

Identifier – When a *Data Source Element* is checked to *Map to Identifier* a corresponding *ECT* field must be identified.

Field – The default mapping of the data source field name to the *ECT* column name.

Display Name – If you would like to use a friendly or different name for the ECT column it can be specified here. For example, instead of FirstName as the default *ECT* column name, you can make the Display Name for the column "First Name".

Office Property – Options for mapping an *ECT* field to Office metadata definitions will be displayed in this drop-down List if an Office Item Type (Appointment, Contact, Task or Post) was set for the *ECT* on the *External Content Type Information* tab of the *Summary Page*. We set this mapping earlier to Contact and it is this mapping that will allow the ECT information exposed in *SharePoint* to be used by *Outlook*.

Required – A check box setting used in the *Create Read List Operation* to indicate that the field is required. If this property was set in the data source it will be checked here.

Read Only – A check box setting used in the *Create Read List Operation*. This setting allows you to make the ECT field read only.

Show in Picker – A check box setting used in the *Create Read List Operation* that will bind this field to a picker control in the ECT List form.

Time Stamp Field – A check box setting used in the *Create Read List Operation* to time stamp this field.

Foreign Identifier – Used to link two database tables in an Association.

The first thing we want to do on the *Parameters Configuration* screen is de-select the fields that we won't need in the *ECT*. De-select *MiddleName*, and *Demographics*. Note if you try to de-select any of the other fields you will get an error in the *Errors and Warnings* section indicating that these are not nullable.

The second thing we will do on the *Parameters Configuration* screen is change the *Display Name* values for the fields so that FirstName will display as First Name.

The last and most important thing to do is map each of the fields in the *Data Source Elements* to an *Office Property* field. This is the mechanism that will allow the *ECT* to display in *Outlook* as a contact record. Select the *Title* field and from the *Office Property* drop-down selection box select *Title* as shown in **Illustration 32** at right.

Do this for all the fields. Note that once you have mapped the *LastName* field to its corresponding Office Property field the error message in the *Errors and Warnings* section will disappear.

Now click the *Next* button to go to the *Filter Parameters Configuration* page of the *ECT Wizard* as shown in **Illustration 33** below.

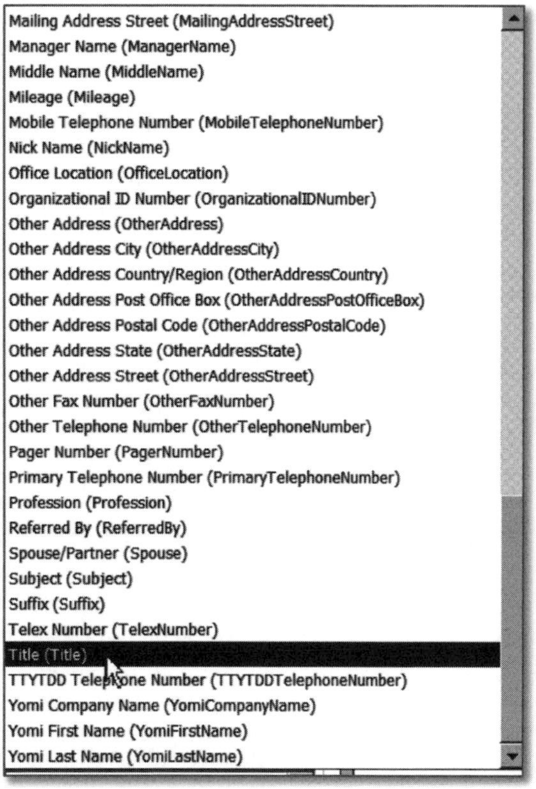
Mailing Address Street (MailingAddressStreet)
Manager Name (ManagerName)
Middle Name (MiddleName)
Mileage (Mileage)
Mobile Telephone Number (MobileTelephoneNumber)
Nick Name (NickName)
Office Location (OfficeLocation)
Organizational ID Number (OrganizationalIDNumber)
Other Address (OtherAddress)
Other Address City (OtherAddressCity)
Other Address Country/Region (OtherAddressCountry)
Other Address Post Office Box (OtherAddressPostOfficeBox)
Other Address Postal Code (OtherAddressPostalCode)
Other Address State (OtherAddressState)
Other Address Street (OtherAddressStreet)
Other Fax Number (OtherFaxNumber)
Other Telephone Number (OtherTelephoneNumber)
Pager Number (PagerNumber)
Primary Telephone Number (PrimaryTelephoneNumber)
Profession (Profession)
Referred By (ReferredBy)
Spouse/Partner (Spouse)
Subject (Subject)
Suffix (Suffix)
Telex Number (TelexNumber)
Title (Title)
TTYTDD Telephone Number (TTYTDDTelephoneNumber)
Yomi Company Name (YomiCompanyName)
Yomi First Name (YomiFirstName)
Yomi Last Name (YomiLastName)

Illustration 32

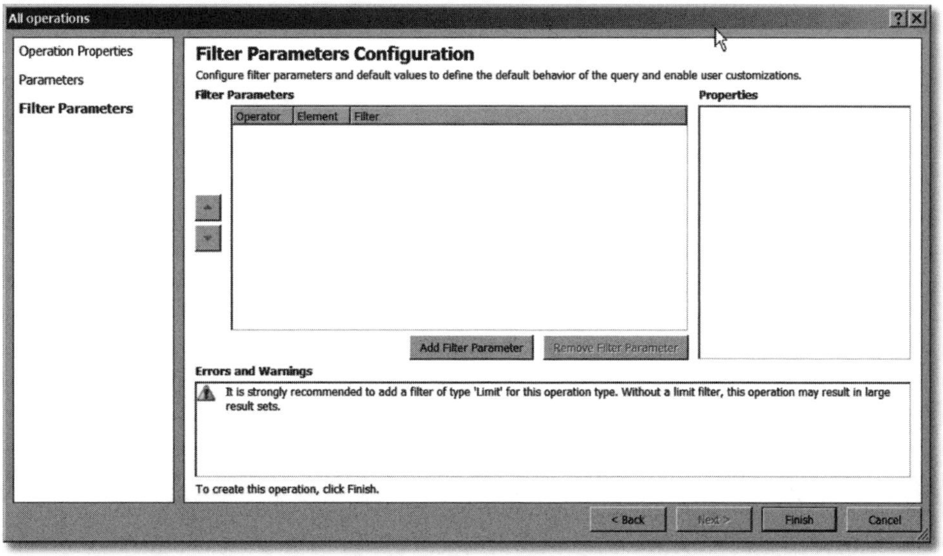
All operations
Operation Properties
Parameters
Filter Parameters
Filter Parameters Configuration
Configure filter parameters and default values to define the default behavior of the query and enable user customizations.
Filter Parameters
Properties
Operator
Element
Filter
Add Filter Parameter
Remove Filter Parameter
Errors and Warnings
It is strongly recommended to add a filter of type 'Limit' for this operation type. Without a limit filter, this operation may result in large result sets.
To create this operation, click Finish.
< Back
Next >
Finish
Cancel

Illustration 33

Click the *Add Filter Parameter button*. By default the first field (*CustomerID*) in the data source will display in the *Filter Parameters* panel. Click the *Click to Add* link for *Filter* in the *Properties* panel. The *Filter Configuration* dialogue box will display as shown in **Illustration 34** below.

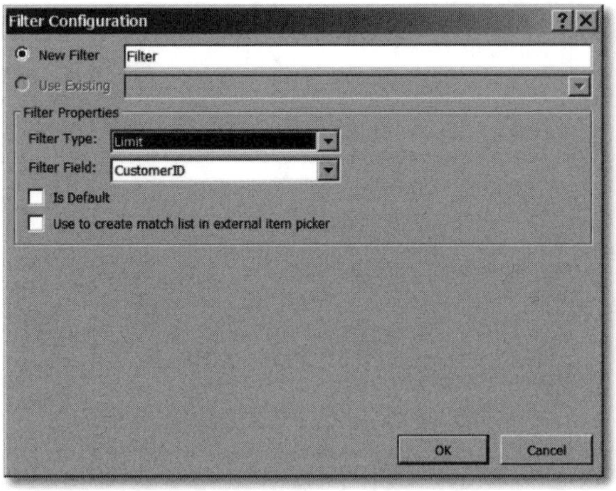

Illustration 34

Select the *Limit* for the *Filter Type* and *CustomerId* for the *Filter Field*. Click *OK*. In the *Default Value* drop-down selection box enter a numeric value that will specify the number of rows the *ECT* List will return on a page, as shown in **Illustration 35** below.

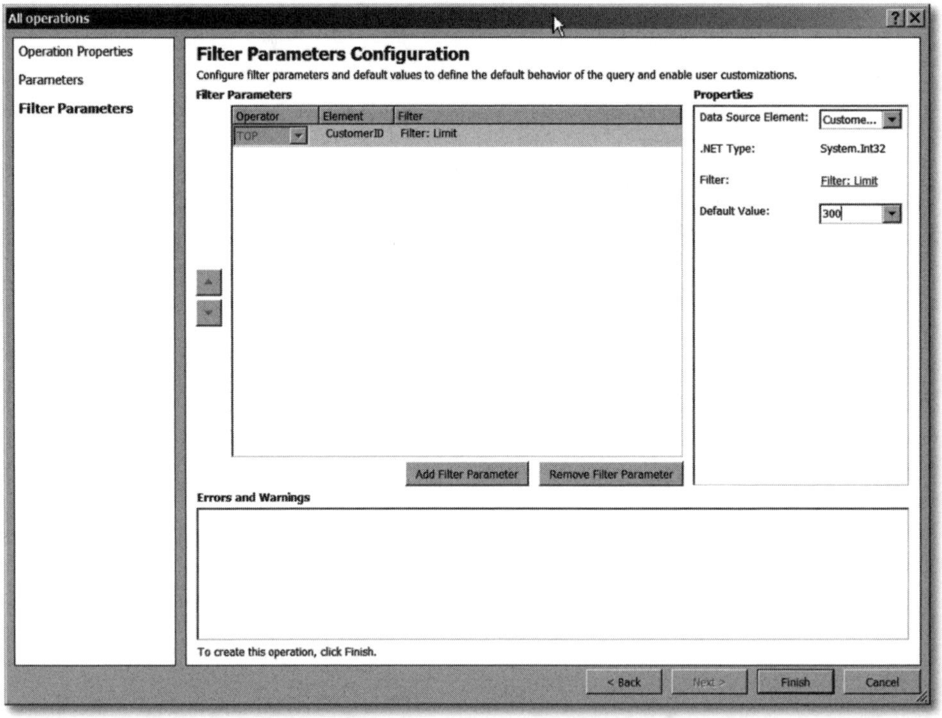

Illustration 35

Click the *Finish* button. We have completed the step of creating the *Sales Leads Outlook Contacts ECT* operations. If you return to the *Summary Page* by clicking on the *Summary View* Ribbon button you will now see all the operations displayed in the *External Content Type Operations* section as shown in **Illustration 36** below:

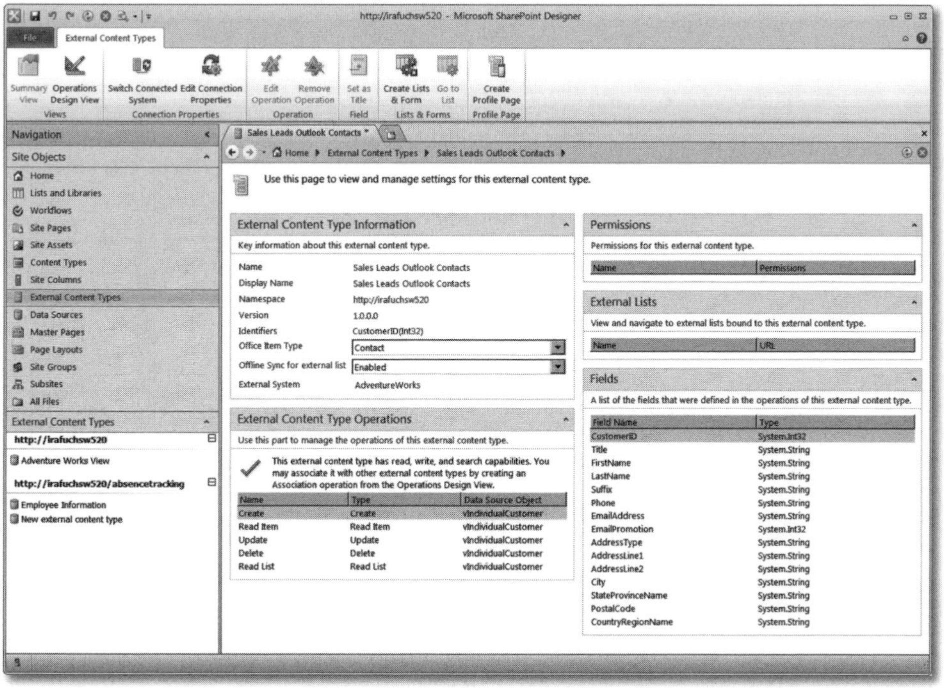

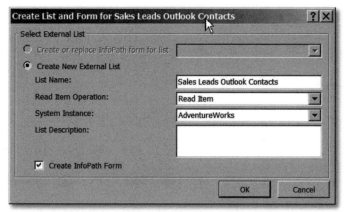

Illustration 36

Creating the ECT List and Form

The next step is to create the *ECT List* and Form for this *ECT*. Click on the *Create Lists & Form* button on the *Ribbon*. The *Create List and Form* dialogue screen will display as shown in **Illustration 37** below:

Illustration 37

The *radio button* for *Create New External List* will be displayed. Enter a List Name and check the *Create InfoPath Form* check box. Note that you can create multiple external Lists for an *ECT*. Click the *OK* button. *SharePoint Designer* will now generate an *External List* for the ECT. Click on the *Lists and Libraries* icon in the *SharePoint Designer Navigation* pane and you will see the *Sales Leads Outlook Contacts* List under the *External Lists* group as shown in **Illustration 38** below.

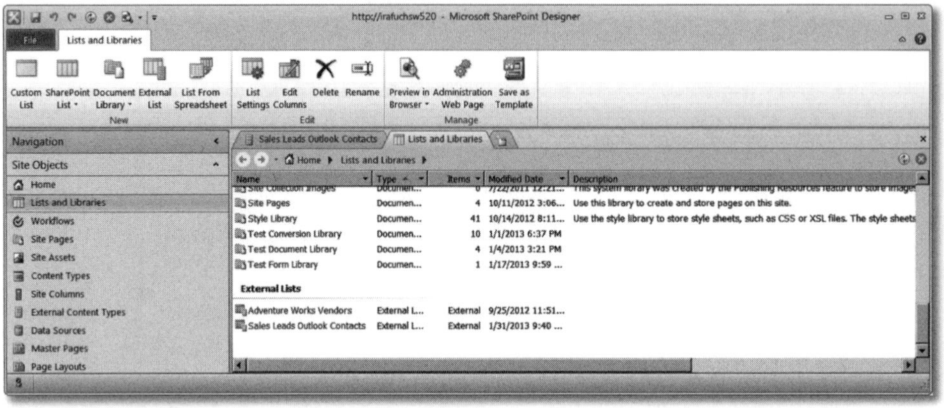

Illustration 38

If you click on the *Sales Leads Outlook Contacts* List item, *SharePoint Designer* will open the *Summary Page* for the List as shown in **Illustration 39** below.

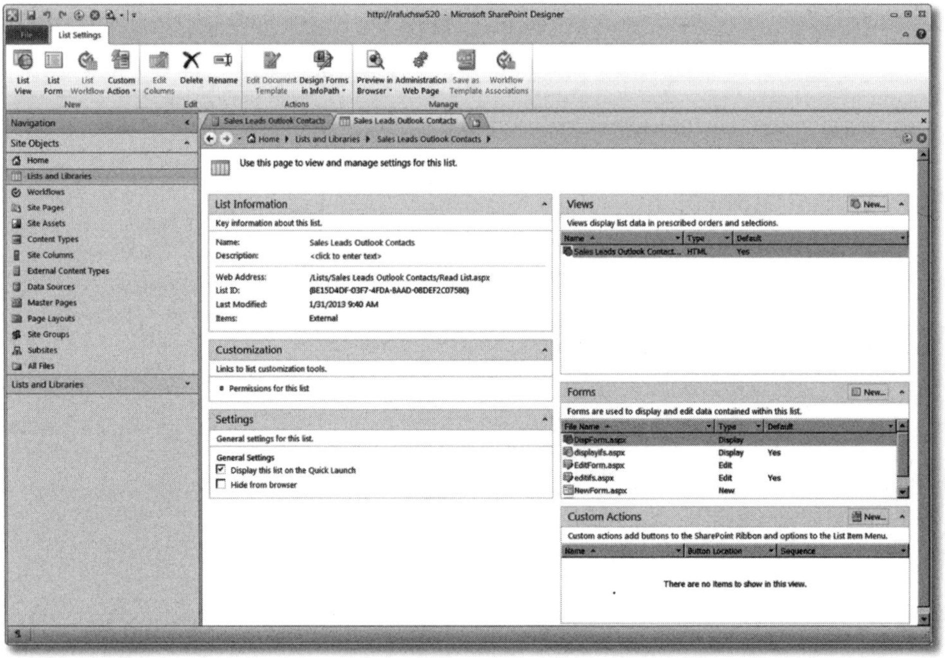

Illustration 39

From the *List Summary Page* you can set the permissions for the List, create custom actions and view and modify the underlying *InfoPath* List form.

Return to the *Summary Page* for the *Sales Leads Outlook Contacts ECT*. You will now see all the fields Listed in the *Fields* tab as shown in **Illustration 40** below.

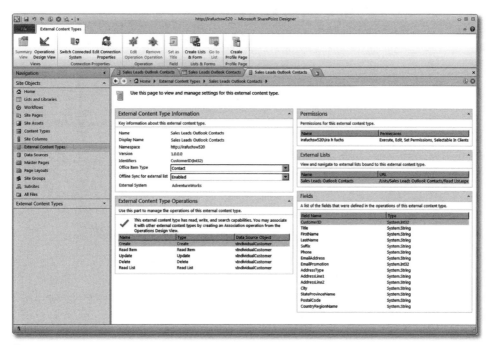

Illustration 40

Configure Object Permissions for the ECT in SharePoint Central Administration.

The *External List* that we just created from the *Sales Leads Outlook Contacts ECT* will not be accessible to a user until they are granted permissions to access the *External Content Type*. Accessing the *ECT* information from within *SharePoint* requires a ***separate ECT permission setting process*** than just providing permissions to access the List itself. Without the *ECT* permissions the following screen message, as shown in **Illustration 41** on the next page will be displayed when a user accesses the *Sales Leads Outlook Contacts* List.

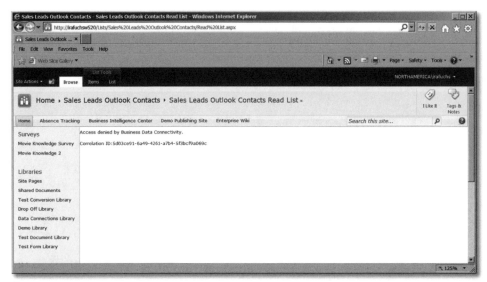

Illustration 41

Note— Permissions to access the *ECT* are set in the *Secure Store Service* of *SharePoint Central Administration* and the Users and Groups that the permission is granted to **can only be Active Directory Users and Groups, not SharePoint Users or Groups**.

In a production environment the procedure described below is done by the *SharePoint* farm administrator. From the *Central Administration* main page click on *Manage service applications* in the *Application Management* section. The *Service Applications* page will display as shown in **Illustration 42** below.

Illustration 42

Click *Business Data Connectivity Services* to display the *External Content Types* that have been created. *ECT's* are farm level objects and are accessible from any *Site Collection* in the farm. From the drop-down List of the Views tab on the *Ribbon* make sure that *External Content Types* are selected. The *Sales Leads Outlook Contacts ECT* will be displayed as shown in **Illustration 43** below.

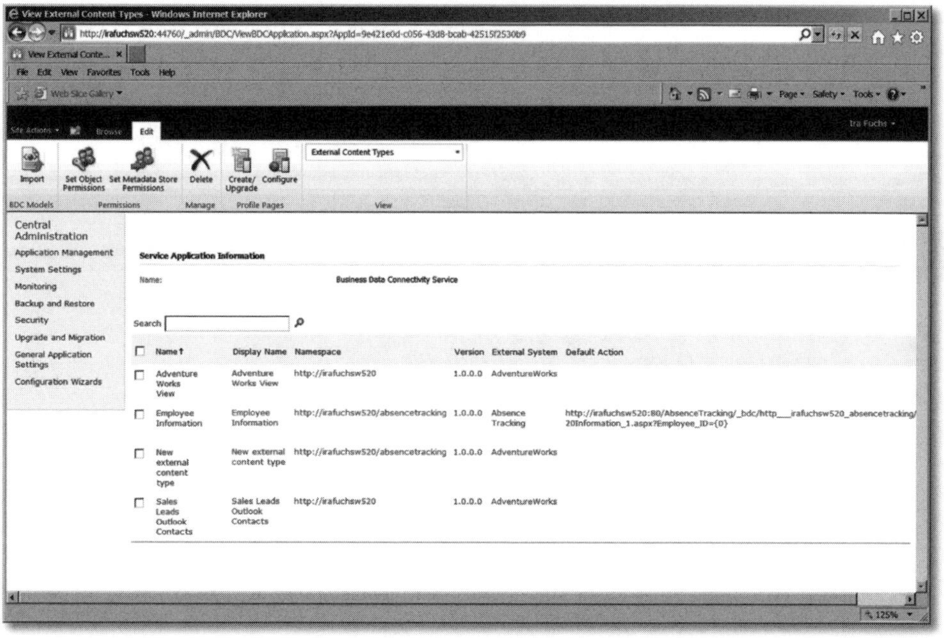

Illustration 43

Select the *Sales Leads Outlook Contacts ECT* by checking its checkbox. Now click the *Set Object Permissions* button on the *Ribbon*. The *Set Object Permissions* dialogue screen will display as shown in **Illustration 44** below.

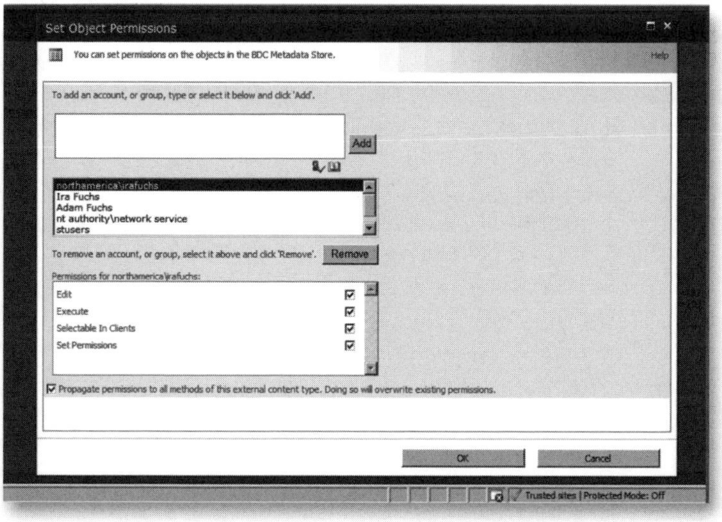

Illustration 44

Use the *People Picker* control to add the Users and/or Groups who are entitled to have access to this information, including your own user account. For each User or Group select all the permissions in the Permissions List and click *OK*.

Now go to the *Sales Leads Outlook Contacts* List in *SharePoint*. The *ECT* records will display as a List as shown in **Illustration 45** below. *ECT* Lists behave like any other *SharePoint* List – you can create and modify views and you can modify the *InfoPath* List form for working with each item.

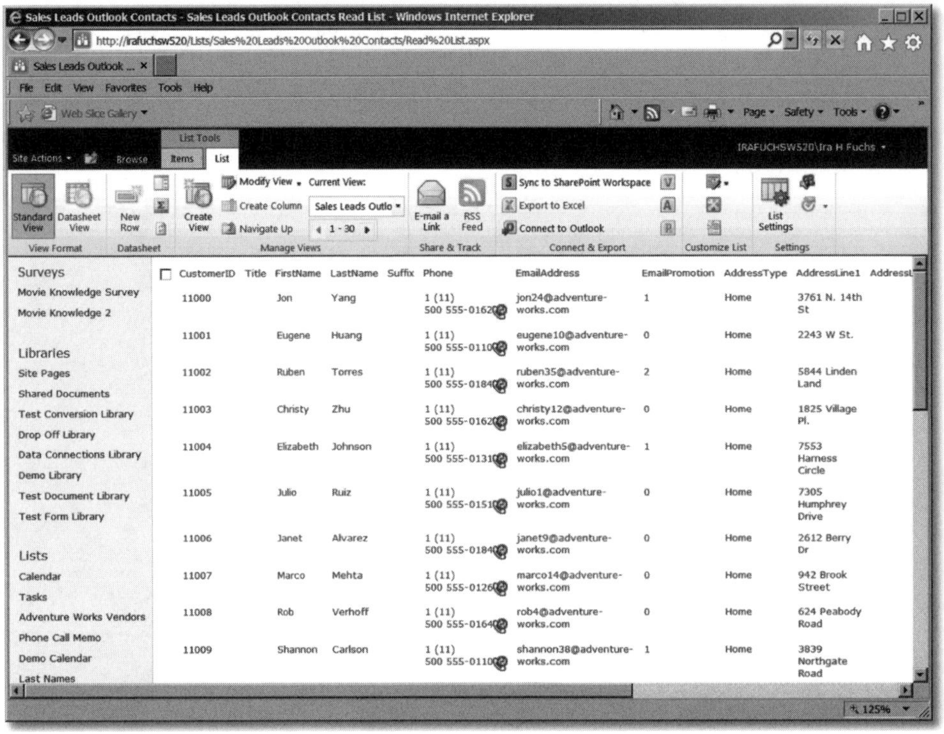

Illustration 45

Now let's do the magic of connecting this List to *Outlook* and bring this information into it as contacts.

> **Note** — Make sure *Microsoft Outlook* is open when you proceed with the following step.

Click on the *List* button from the main *Ribbon* menu and then click on the *Connect to Outlook* button. The *Microsoft Office Customization Installer* application will start and complete as shown in **Illustration 46** below.

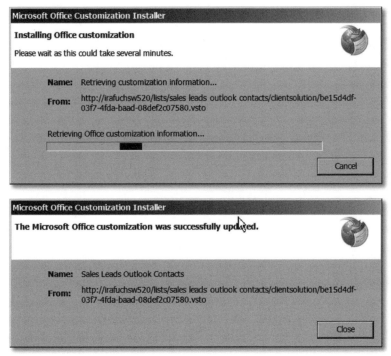

Illustration 46

Your *Outlook Navigation* panel should contain a new *SharePoint External Lists* item group as shown in **Illustration 47** below.

Illustration 47

Now click on *Contacts* on the *Navigation* pane to display your contact groups. You should see a new group named *Home – Sales Leads Outlook Contacts*. Click on this contact group and the records from the *ECT* will display as *Business Cards* as shown in **Illustration 48** below.

Illustration 48

Click on any of the other three display options in the *Current View Ribbon* section to change the view of the contacts. The List view is shown in **Illustration 49** below.

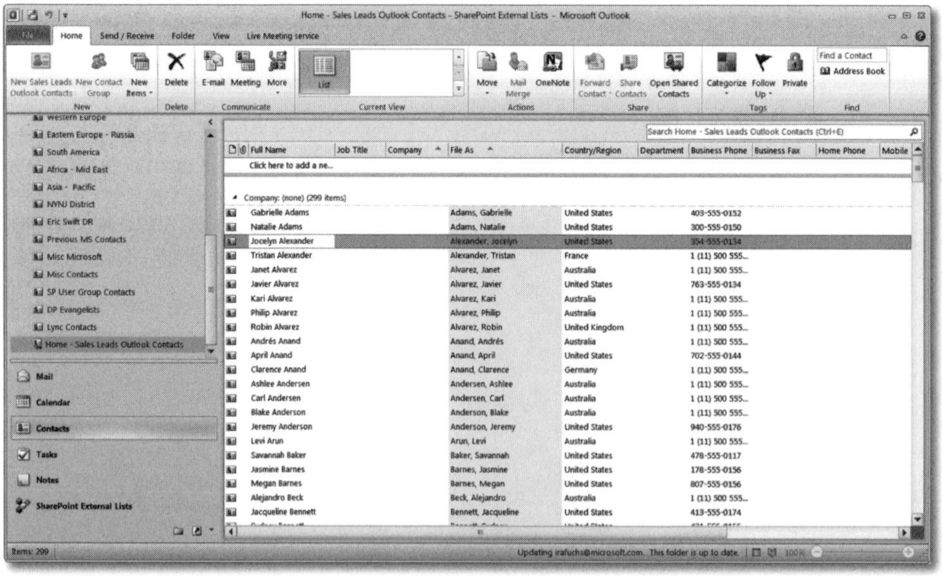

Illustration 49

Note that **not** all the fields in the *SharePoint ECT* List are displaying for the contacts in *Outlook*. This is because *Outlook* does not display all the fields by default. To add the other fields right-click on the *field column header* and select *Field Chooser,* which will display as shown in **Illustration 50** at right. You can then drag the additional fields that you want onto the field column header and rearrange them.

Illustration 50

The *ECT* contact records in *Outlook* behave like any other contact items. If you right-click on any contact the *Outlook* drop-down menu options will display as shown in **Illustration 51** below. You can execute all the communication functions available from *Outlook* and *Lync* if it is being used.

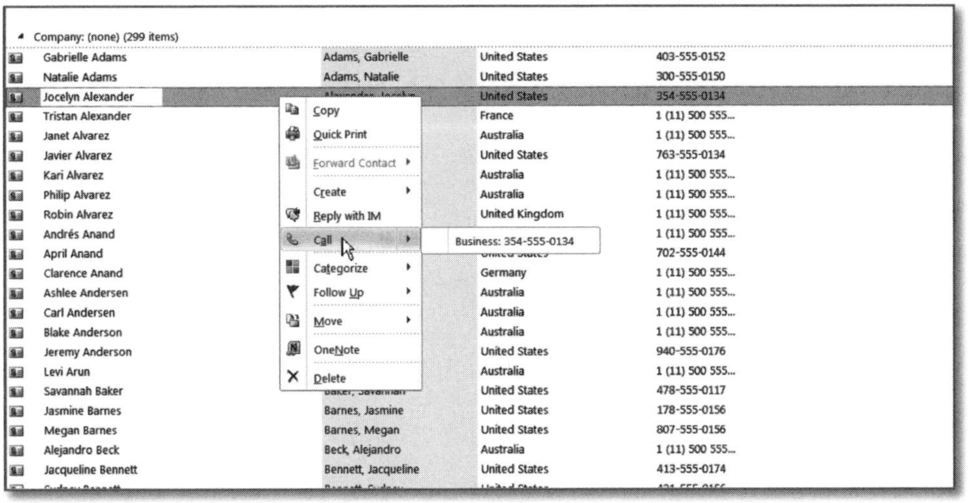

Illustration 51

You can also double-click on any contact and open the contact details screen as shown in **Illustration 52** below, where you can add additional information.

> **Note** – any additional information added to the contact details screen will **only** be added to the *Outlook* contacts data store for each user. It will not update the *SharePoint ECT* List.

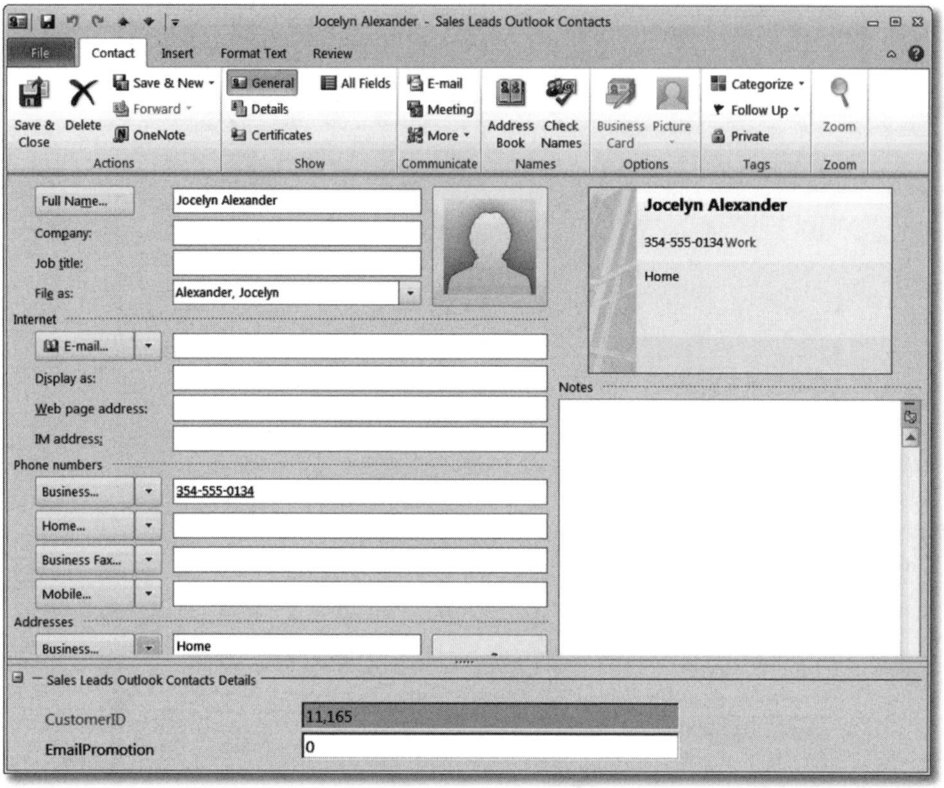

Illustration 52

Congratulations! You have now taken advantage of a real benefit of *SharePoint ECT* functionality to address a real-world contact information requirement.

How to Efficiently Import Large Information Sets from Excel and Customize the Presentation of Information Using View Styles and the Identity of the User

As is often the case, large amounts of information are typically generated and distributed using *Excel* spreadsheets for consumption by end-users. While this works well for people who regularly use *Excel* to view or manipulate tabular information, making large information sets available to people as a *SharePoint* List becomes a more appealing distribution method when a) the *Excel* application is not available, b) the end-user is only interested in or should only see a subset of the information, and c) it is a better experience for the user to see and use the information in a non-tabular format.

In this chapter we will examine *SharePoint* facilities for efficiently bringing *Excel* spreadsheet information into a *SharePoint* List that is comprised of numerous rows and columns. We will also demonstrate *SharePoint* capabilities for presenting that information in non-tabular ways, as well as presenting information relevant to the user based on their identity.

In the previous chapter we demonstrated copying and pasting information from an *Excel* spreadsheet into a Contacts List template. Before we executed the copy and paste function we had to make sure that the spreadsheet columns identically corresponded to the List column order. While this is easy to accomplish when there are just a small number of columns, the effort to do this can become very time consuming when there are a large number of columns to work with.

Consider the sample spreadsheet shown in **Illustration 1** below, for which only a portion of its columns are displayed.

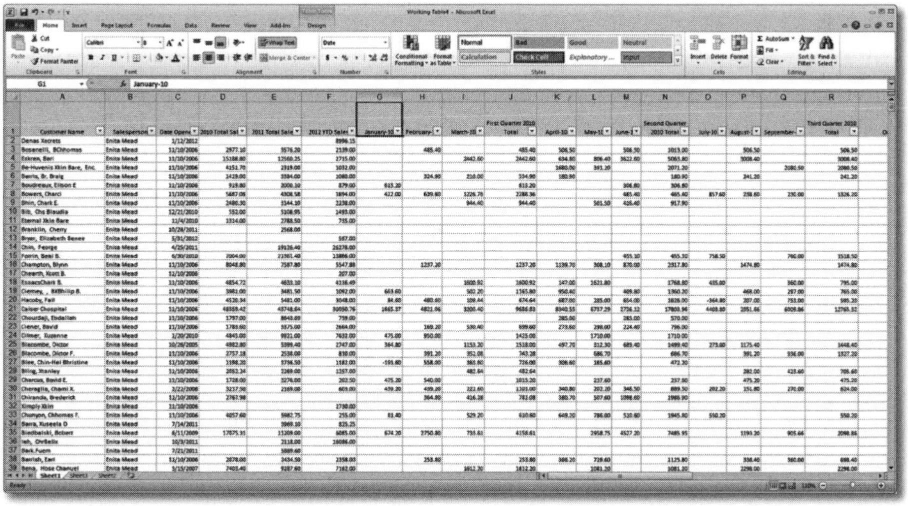

Illustration 1

There are approximately two dozen columns in the spreadsheet (and over two thousand rows) and they are ordered so as to provide multiple timeframe reference comparisons. While this column order supports the primary purpose of the report, alternative presentations of this information would be useful in supporting different but equally useful purposes. Furthermore, when published as a spreadsheet the dataset typically contains information relevant and applicable to multiple people but also exposes subsets of the information to people for whom it is not applicable. In most situations this should be avoided and only the information that is relevant and pertinent to any given person should be available to them. We will demonstrate a highly useful technique for revealing information based on the identity of the user.

The first method of importing spreadsheet information into a *SharePoint* List is to use the *SharePoint Import Spreadsheet List* template. To access this List template select *More Options* or *View All Site Content* from the *Site Actions* drop-down menu and then click *Create*. Select *List* from the navigation menu to display the various List template options. You may have to scroll down to show the *Import Spreadsheet* template as shown in **Illustration 2** below.

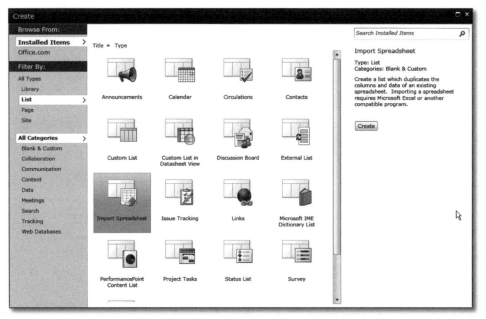

Illustration 2

As a best practice for importing a spreadsheet using this template you should first format you spreadsheet as a table. While it is not necessary to do so it does make the process easier and you will have to do it for the second import method we will review, which is to generate the *SharePoint* List directly from *Excel*.

The *Format as a Table* option is available from the *Design Table Tools* tab on the *Excel Ribbon* menu as shown in **Illustration 3** on the next page. It does not matter which table design pattern you choose; the important format change is creating column headings that can be filtered. The spreadsheet shown in **Illustration 3** was already formatted as a table and you can see the column headings.

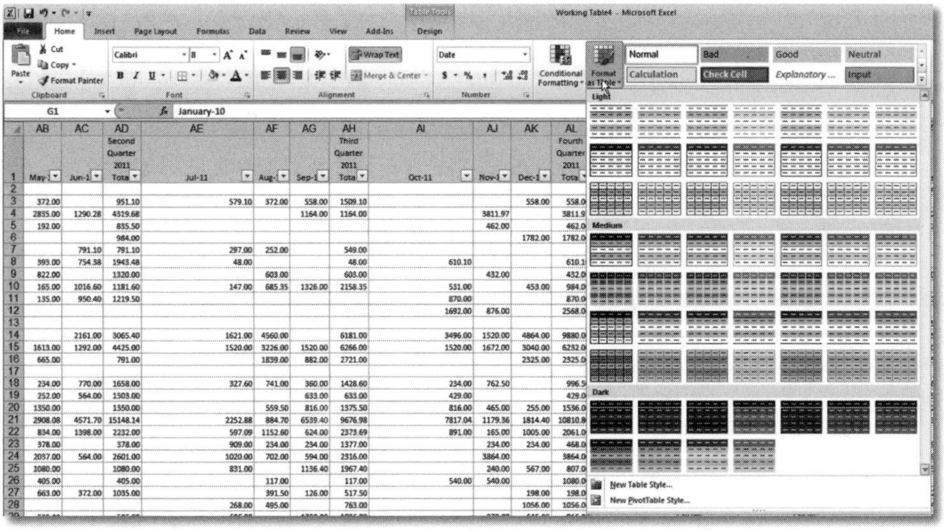

Illustration 3

After you have formatted your spreadsheet as a table return to *SharePoint.* Click on the *Import Spread-sheet List* template from the *Create* dialogue screen. A screen will *be* presented where you will enter a name for the List and then browse to the location where the spreadsheet is saved. Click the *Import* button after you have entered this information. The targeted *Excel* spreadsheet will open (if it isn't already open) and you will be presented with an *Import to Windows SharePoint Services List* dialogue screen as shown in **Illustration 4** below.

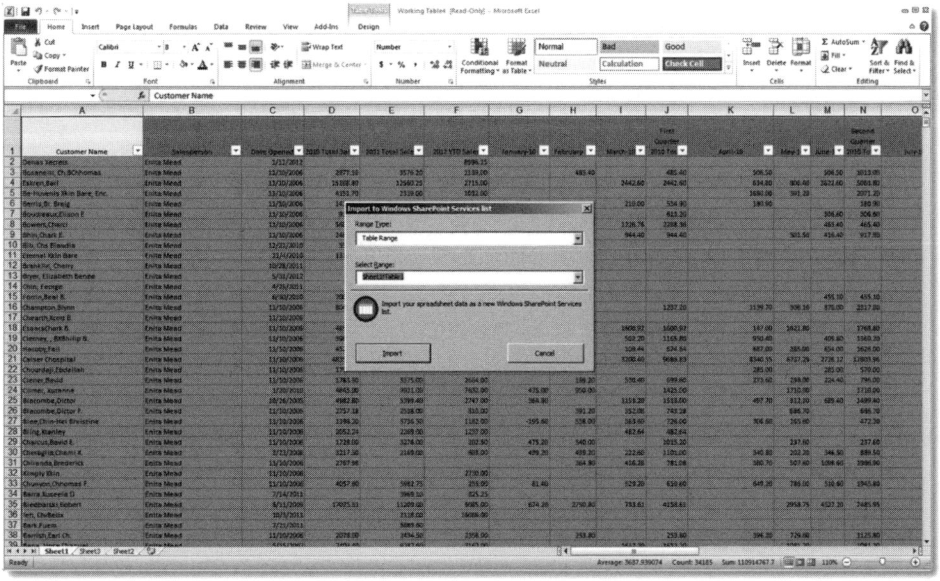

Illustration 4

There are three options for the *Range Type* – *Range of Cells, Table Range* or *Named Range* as shown in **Illustration 5 below left**. When you pick the *Table Range* option the entire spreadsheet will automatically be selected as shown in **Illustration 4** above and **Illustration 5 below right**. If you selected the *Range of Cells* option you would have to manually select a range of cells, including a row that would serve as the column heading.

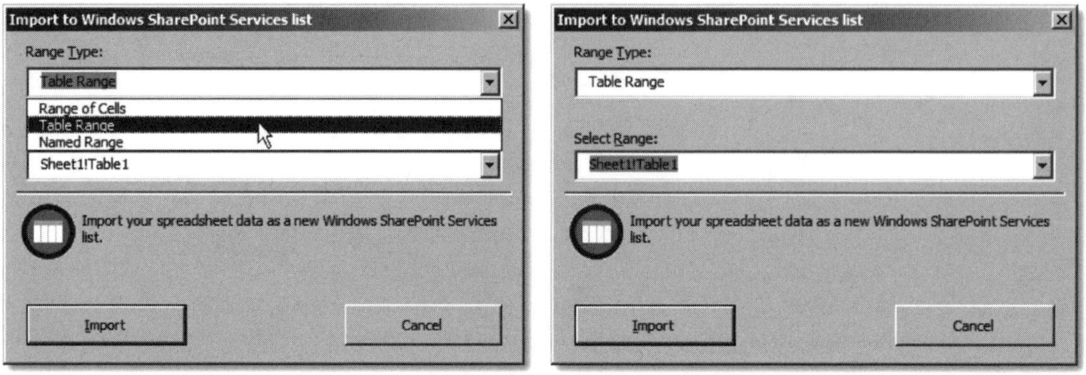

Illustration 5

If you are importing a large number of rows it will take a few minutes for the process to complete. Once completed, you will be presented with the new populated *SharePoint* List as shown in **Illustration 6** below.

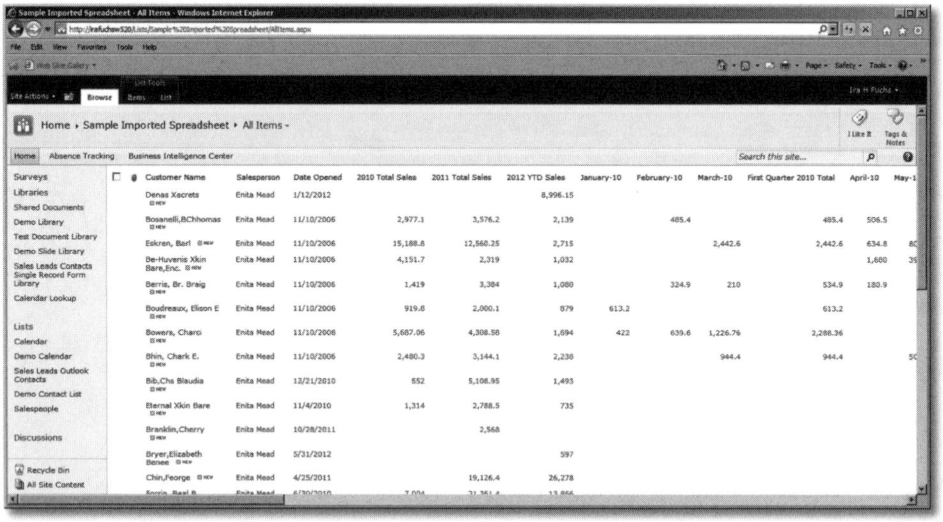

Illustration 6

The first thing that you might notice is that as a direct reproduction of the *Excel* spreadsheet column order the *SharePoint* List does not provide a useful or friendly user interface to the information. There are too many columns to navigate easily and the column headings do not remain displayed as you scroll down. While the default column width is automatically set for 255 characters the actual display appears to be much less with text wrapping on two lines. You may have also noticed that only thirty rows are displayed on each screen and you have to use the paging function at the top of the List menu or at the bottom of the screen. All of which is provides a less than optimal user experience of the information. It is also probable that many of the columns in the spreadsheet may not be necessary in the context of a *SharePoint* List or are not in an order that is useful. The reason that we did not restructure the spreadsheet in *Excel* is because deleting, copying and hiding columns of data in *Excel* isn't always easy and efficient, especially when there are a large number of columns.

However, now that the information is in a *SharePoint* List we actually do have some tools and methods that are easy-to-use and efficient to restructure and present the information; as well as make it available only to the people who should see it. So our first order of business is to examine the various options for rendering the information in the List selectively. Assuming that we want to keep all the columns that were imported our first tool of choice for restructuring the information in the List is the ability to create and modify Views of the List information. To access the View options click on the *List* tab of the *Ribbon* menu. Click on the *Modify View* button to display the *Edit View* page for the *All Items View* as shown in **Illustration 7** below. From here you can choose which fields to display and in what order, as well as a variety of other display settings. We will return to the *Edit View* page later when we create new Views.

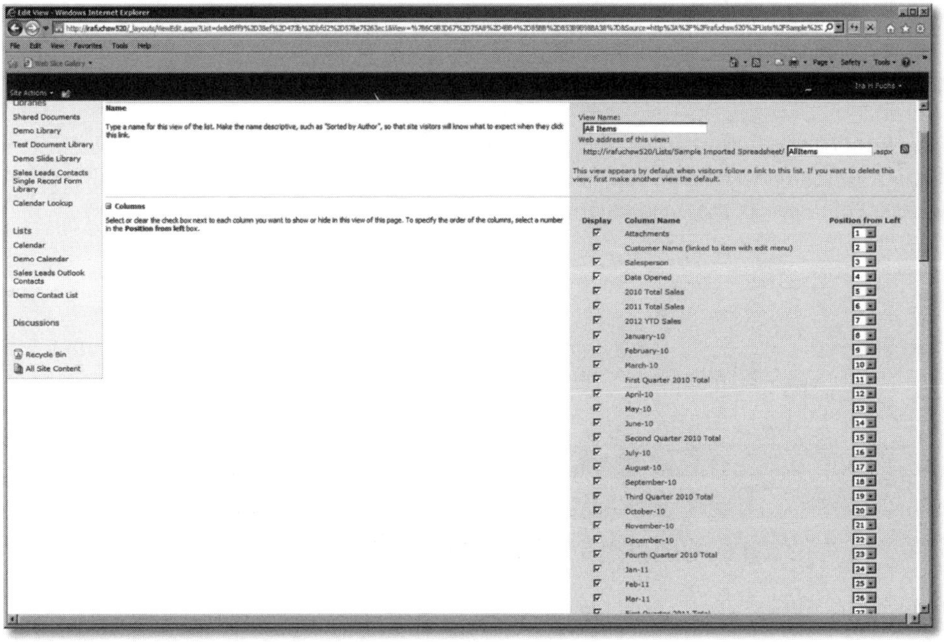

Illustration 7

Presently, we are going to make the assumption that the columns reporting results for individual months are not necessary for our purposes and we will want to remove them. To this purpose we will employ *SharePoint Designer*. Open *SharePoint Designer* and connect to the site where you created the List. Click on the *Lists and Libraries* from the *Navigation Site Objects* pane and select the List you created. The *Summary Page* for the List will display as shown in **Illustration 8** below.

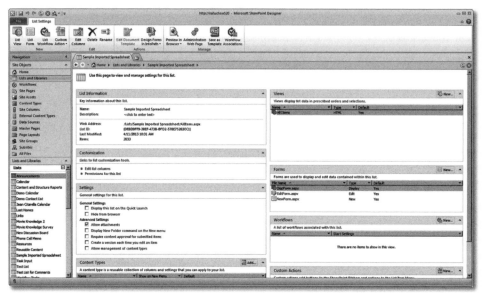

Illustration 8

Now click on the *Edit Columns* button on the *Ribbon* menu. You will see all the columns displayed in their original order. You can now hold down your *Control-key* and click on each of the individual month columns to select all of them, as shown in **Illustration 9** below, and then delete them.

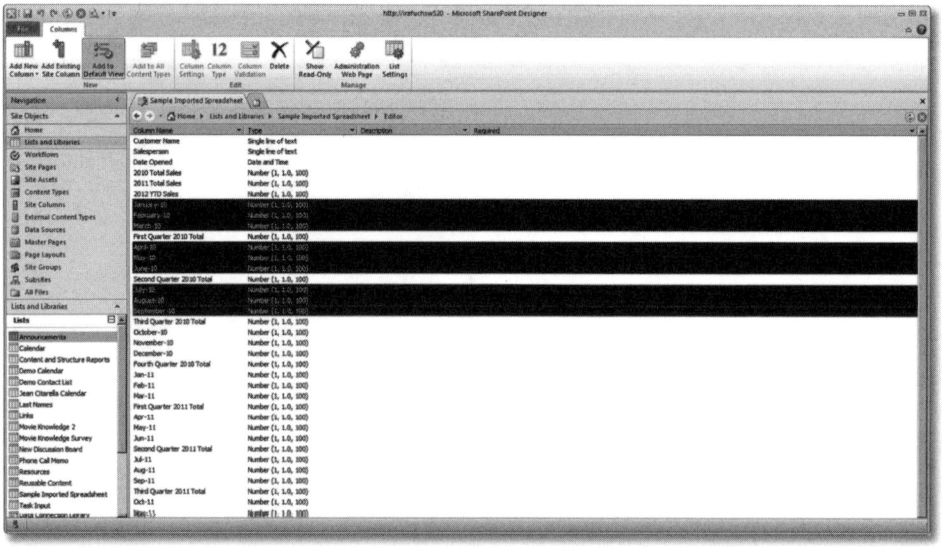

Illustration 9

While you could have deleted these columns before importing them, it is quicker and easier to do it this way, and efficiency is one of the things we want to achieve when we do things like this. From the *File* menu click *Save*. Now return to the List in *SharePoint* and refresh the page. The deleted columns are no longer there as shown in **Illustration 10** below.

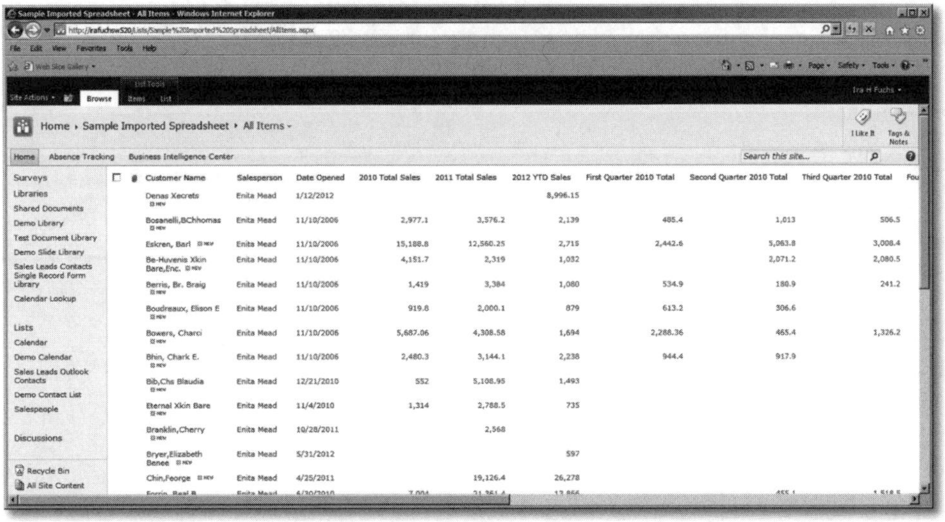

Illustration 10

For this type of financial reporting information the default *SharePoint* List format is still far from useful and useable. So let's do something to make it useful and useable. Click on the *List Ribbon* menu item and then click *Create View*. From the *Create View* page select the *Standard View* option. The *Create View* settings page will display as shown in **Illustration 11** below. For the *View* name enter "Pane View"

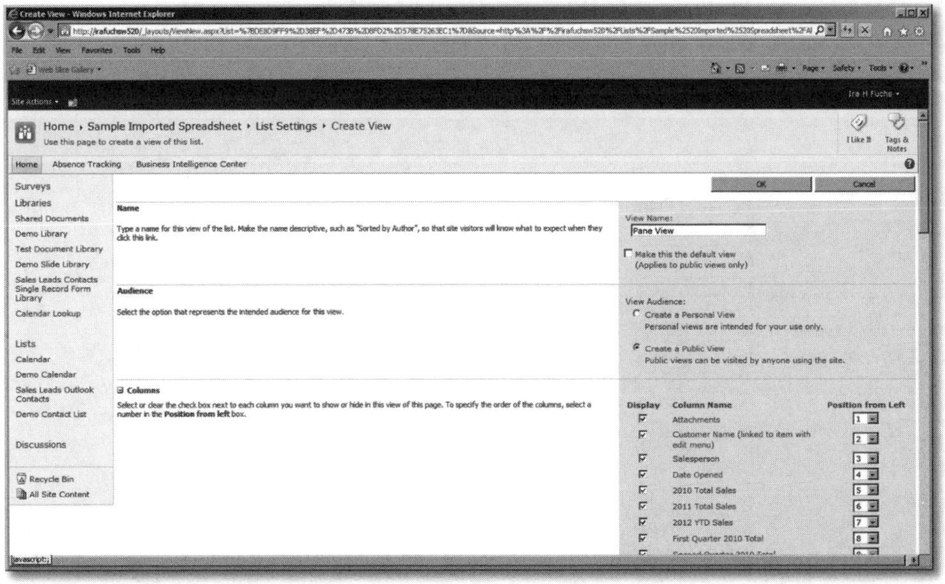

Illustration 11

Now scroll down the page and click on the *Style* link to display the available View styles. Select the *Preview Pane* option as shown in **Illustration 12** below. Now click the *OK* button.

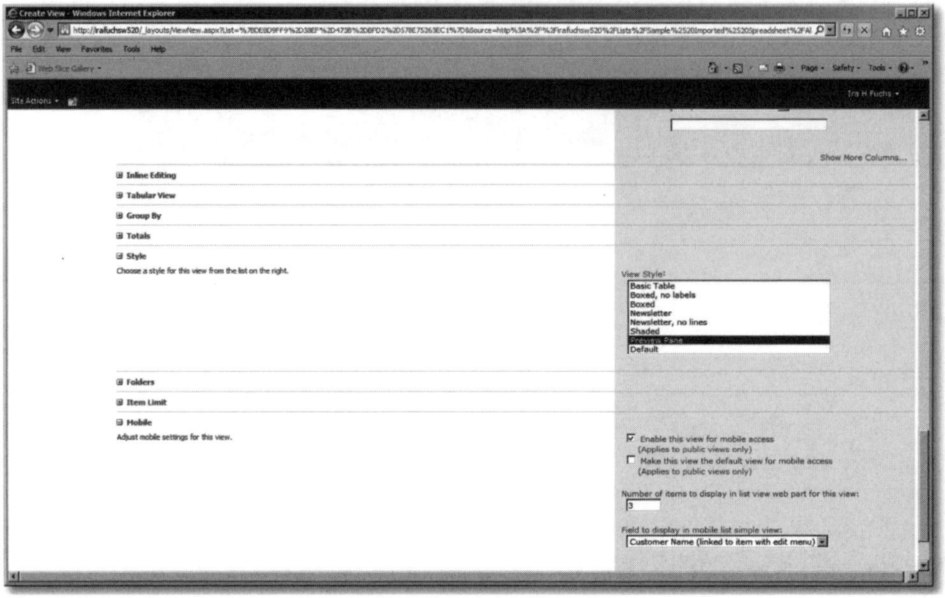

Illustration 12

The new *Pane View* will display as shown in **Illustration 13** below. Hover over any of the names on the left column and the respective reporting details for each name will display in the right pane. Now this has some real potential as a means of presenting information in *SharePoint* in a valuable and useful way!

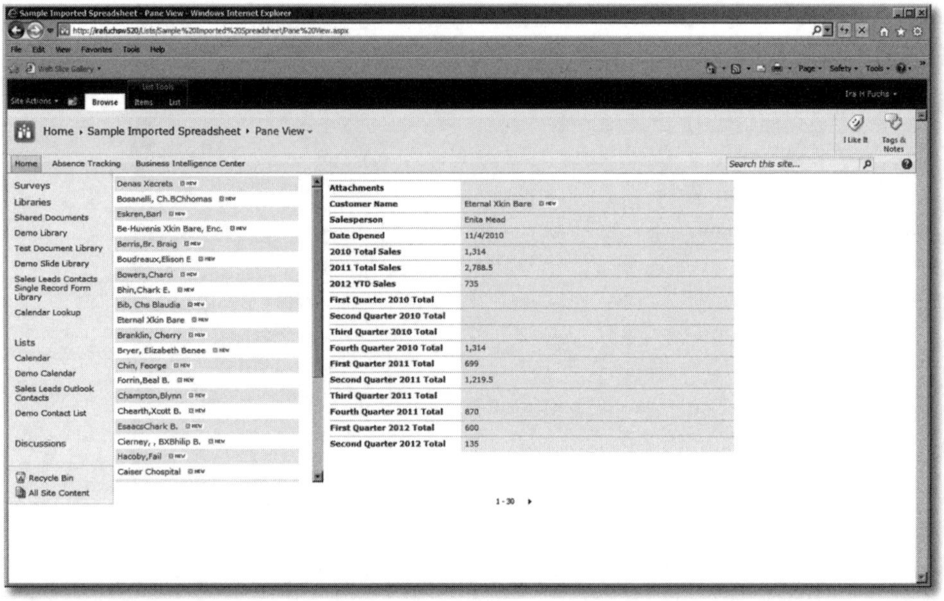

Illustration 13

The column on the left will scroll 30 names at a time, which is the default value. Go back to the *Edit View Settings* page for the *Pane View* and scroll down to the *Item Limit* option. Click on it and enter 100 for the value as shown in **Illustration 14** below and then click the *OK* button.

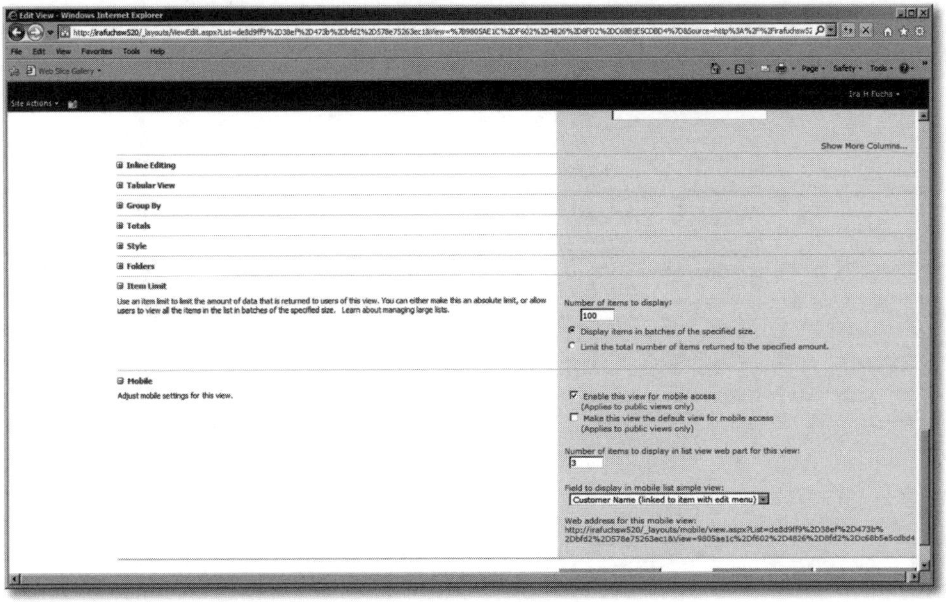

Illustration 14

Now you can scroll 100 names at a time. Now let's apply an alphabetic sort order to the names in the left column. On the *Edit View Settings* page select *Customer Name* as the value for the *First sort by the column* sort option as shown in **Illustration 15** below. You can add a secondary sort value as well.

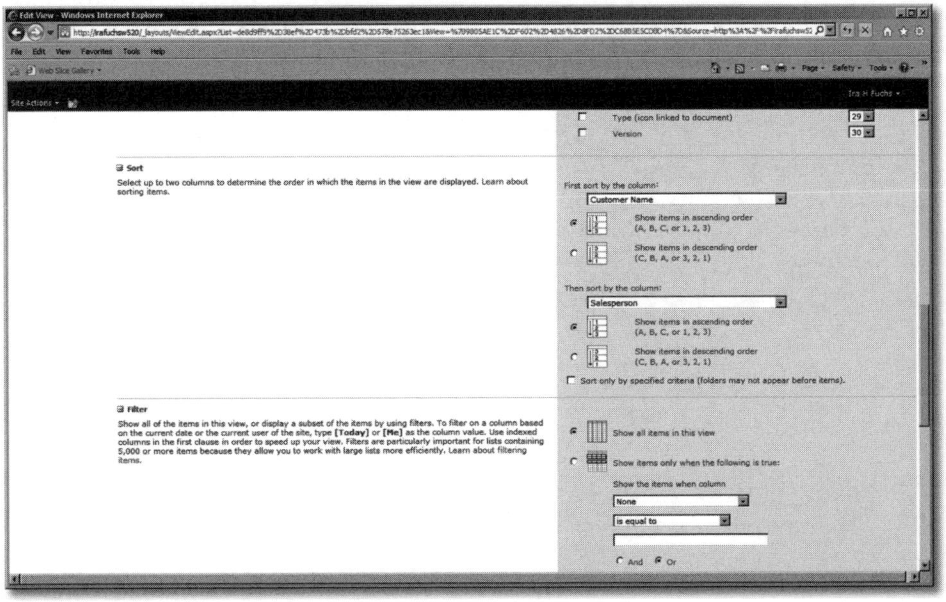

Illustration 15

Return to the *Pane View* to see that the names are now indeed sorted in alphabetical order as shown in **Illustration 16** below.

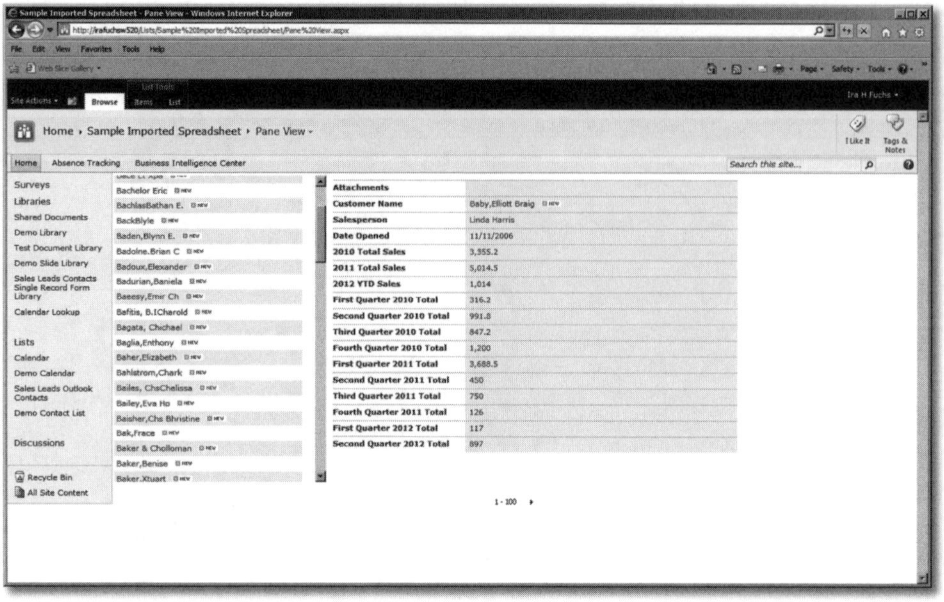

Illustration 16

With just a few steps, literally in minutes, it is possible to take large and complex sets of information from an *Excel* spreadsheet and convert it into a format that is highly accessible and resides in Share-Point. Now let's examine the second method of bringing *Excel* spreadsheet information into *SharePoint*

The second method of importing *Excel* spreadsheet information into a *SharePoint* List is to use the *Export Table to SharePoint List* function directly from *Excel*. This function is displayed on the *Ribbon* menu when you select the *Table Tools – Design* tab as shown in **Illustration 17** below.

Illustration 17

As with the first method of importing *Excel* spreadsheet informaiton into *SharePoint* you must format the sheet as a Table, as we did earlier. Click on the *Export Table to SharePoint List* button to display the *Step 1* dialogue screen as shown in **Illustration 18** at right.

Export Table to SharePoint List - Step 1 of 2

Where do you want to publish your table?

Address: http://irafuchsw520

☐ Create a read-only connection to the new SharePoint list

Provide a name and description for your table.

Name: Sample Spreadsheet Import 2

Description:

| Help | Cancel | Back | Next | Finish |

Illustration 18

Enter the URL address of the *SharePoint* site where you want to create the List and give it a name; then click the *Next* button to start the List creation process. Depending on the number of rows and columns this may take a little while. The dialogue screen for *Step 2* will display as shown in **Illustration 19** at right.

Export Table to SharePoint List - Step 2 of 2

To publish to a SharePoint list, Excel must force columns to use certain recognized data types. All cells with individual formulas will be converted to values.

Verify that each of the columns listed below is associated with the correct data type. If a column is associated with an incorrect data type, click Cancel and confirm that the key cell can be converted to the correct type.

Column	Data Type	Key Cell
Customer Name	Text (single line)	
Salesperson	Text (single line)	
Customer ID	Text (single line)	
State	Text (single line)	
Date Opened	Date	
2010 Total Sales	Text (single line)	F16
2011 Total Sales	Number	
2012 YTD Sales	Number	
January-10	Number	

| Help | Cancel | Back | Next | Finish |

Illustration 19

What this dialogue screen shows is how the column data in the spreadsheet will be mapped to a *SharePoint Data Type* for the corresponding columns. If one or more *Key Cells* are identified (e.g. $F:16) this means that the *Data Type* for the information in that cell is not consistent with the *Data Type* for the rest of the cells found in that column as shown in **Illustration 20** at right where the letters"abc" are in a column cell that should contain numeric data.

E	F	G
Date Opened ▼	2010 Total Sales ▼	2011 Total Sales ▼
1/12/2012		
11/10/2006	2977.10	3576.20
11/10/2006	15188.80	12560.25
11/10/2006	4151.70	2319.00
11/10/2006	1419.00	3384.00
11/10/2006	919.80	2000.10
11/10/2006	5687.06	4308.58
11/10/2006	2480.30	3144.10
12/21/2010	552.00	5108.95
11/4/2010	1314.00	2788.50
10/28/2011		2568.00
5/31/2012		
4/25/2011		19126.40
6/30/2010	7004.00	21361.40
11/10/2006	abc	7587.80
11/10/2006		

Illustration 20

When this happens processing will not continue. You must *Cancel* the export and correct the *Data Type* entry in each of the identified cells. If there are no *Key Cell* errors identified click the *Finish* button; within a few minutes the *SharePoint* List will be created as shown in **Illustration 21** below.

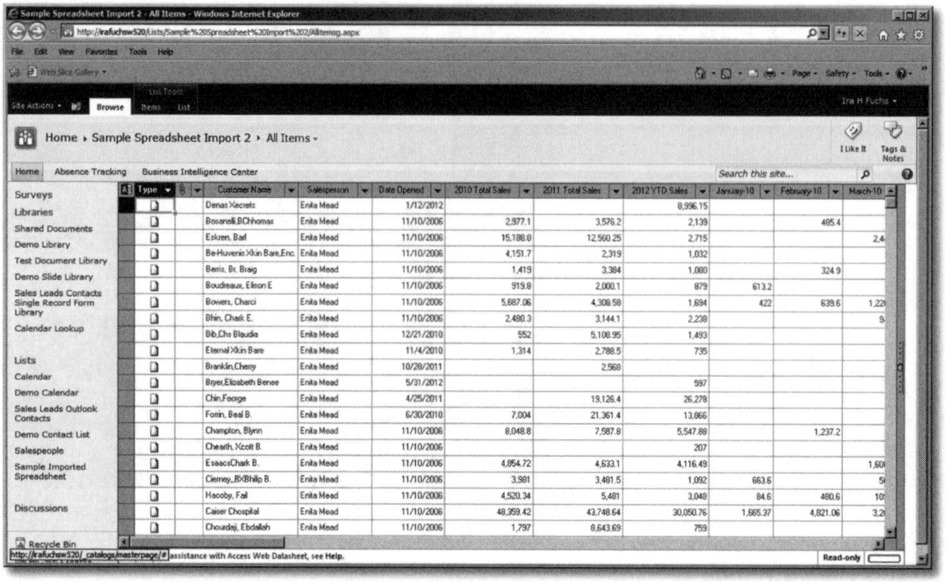

Illustration 21

Note however that the default *All Items View* for the newly created List is a *Datasheet View*, the *Access* tabular display functionality in *SharePoint*. You must first explicitly create another *Standard View* (and optionally designate it as the default view) before you can make use of the *Style* settings to reformat the presentation as we did earlier.

Selectively Displaying Information Based on the Identity of the User

Returning to the *Pane View* of our imported List, what we want to do now is display only those accounts that are assigned to a given salesperson when that salesperson accesses this View. That is, when Ira Fuchs goes to the *Pane View* for this List he will only have access to and see the accounts assigned to him.

To implement this user identity driven scenario we will add two Web Parts to the *Pane View*: the *Current User Web Part*, and a *List Web Part* for a custom List that contains two fields: the Salesperson Name and the Salesperson Alias.

Every List and Library View is simply a Web Part page containing a Web Part for that specific List. You can see this by clicking *Edit Page* under *Site Actions* for any List or Library View as shown in **Illustration 22** below.

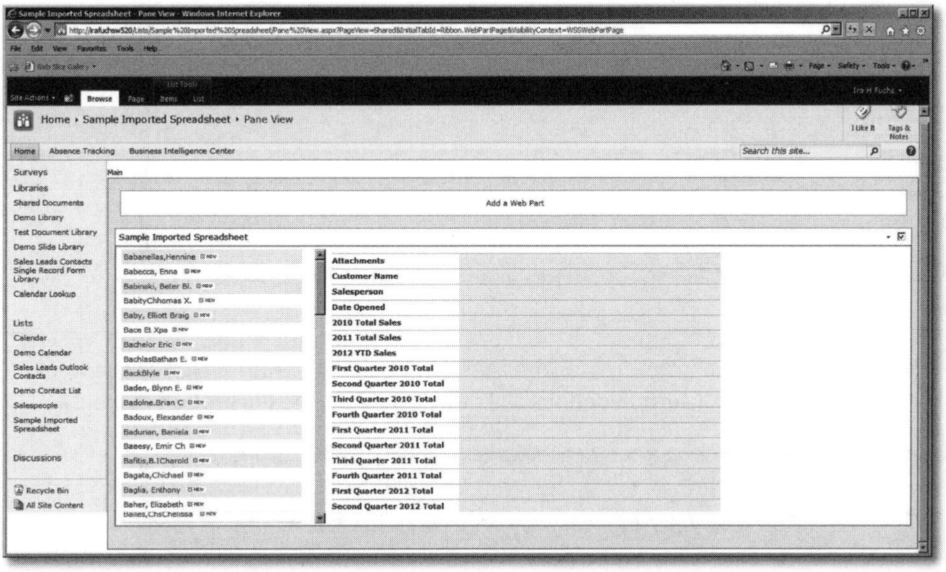

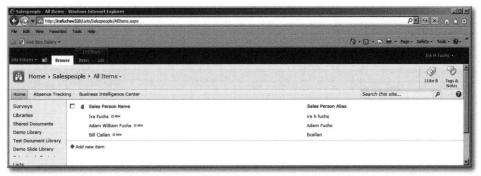

Illustration 22

Furthermore you can add other Web Parts onto the Page and have them communicate with each other, which is what we will be doing shortly. But first, create a custom List that contains two fields – Salesperson Name and Salesperson Alias, as shown in **Illustration 23** below. Populate this List with two records of actual *SharePoint* users; that is two individuals who have Username Alias's in the *User Profile Service*. These will be our test names.

Illustration 23

Next, edit four of the records in your imported records List to change the Salesperson's names to the test names you just created, in two records each. As shown in **Illustration 24** below two records now show Ira Fuchs as the Salesperson and two records have Adam William Fuchs as the Salesperson.

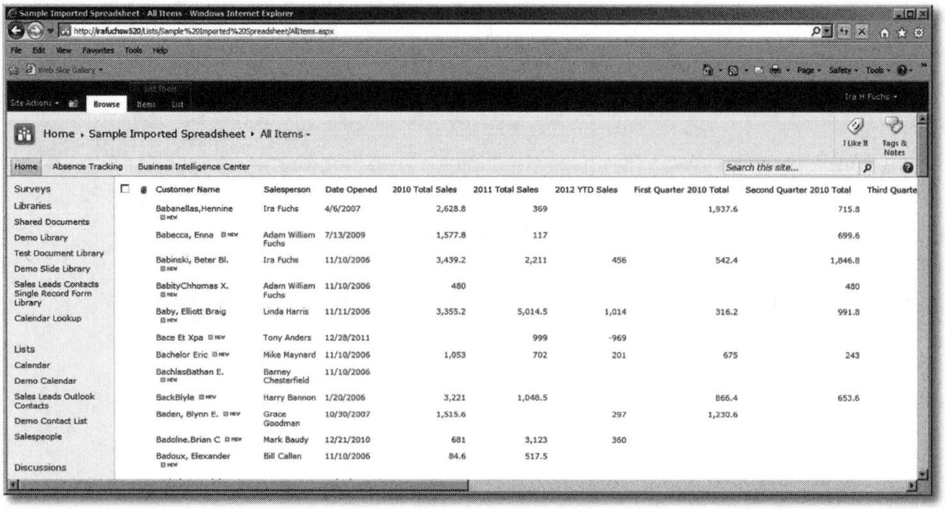

Illustration 24

Return to the *Pane View* and click *Edit Page* from *Site Actions*. Click the *Add a Web Part* link in the web part zone at the top. The Web Part insertion options will display as shown in **Illustration 25** below.

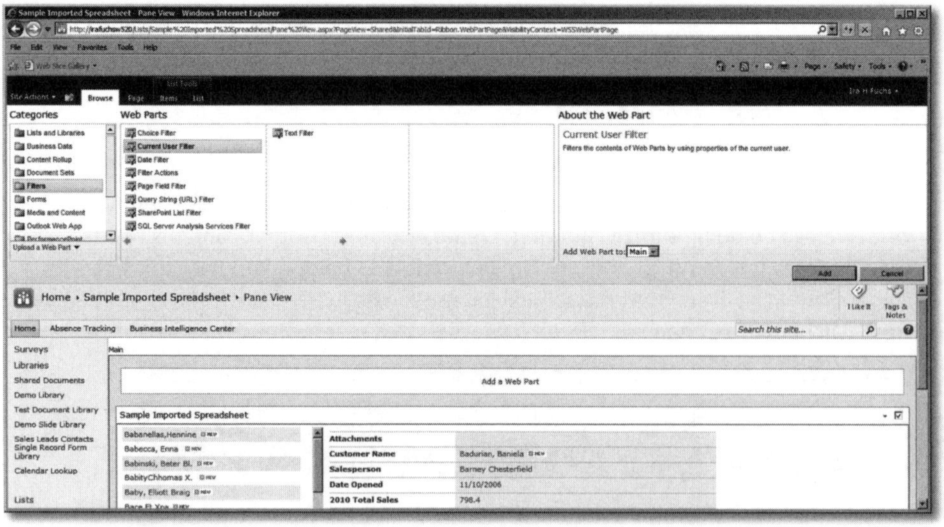

Illustration 25

From the *Categories* pane on the left select *Filters*. The various Filter web part options will display in the Web Parts pane. Select the *Current User Filter* and click the *Add* button. The *Current User Filter* Web Part will be inserted in the Web Part Zone as shown in **Illustration 26** below.

Main

Add a Web Part

🖳 Current User Filter

⚠ ⊞ This filter is not connected.
🔷 ⊞ This is a context filter.

Sample Imported Spreadsheet		· ☑

Babanellas,Hennine ⊟ NEW	**Attachments**	Sample Imported Spreadsheet
Babecca, Enna ⊟ NEW	**Customer Name**	Bachelor Eric ⊟ NEW
Babinski, Beter Bl. ⊟ NEW	**Salesperson**	Mike Maynard
BabityChhomas X. ⊟ NEW	**Date Opened**	11/10/2006
Baby, Elliott Braig ⊟ NEW	**2010 Total Sales**	1,053
Bace Et Xpa ⊟ NEW	**2011 Total Sales**	702
Bachelor Eric ⊟ NEW	**2012 YTD Sales**	201
BachlasBathan E. ⊟ NEW	**First Quarter 2010 Total**	675
BackBlyle ⊟ NEW	**Second Quarter 2010 Total**	243
Baden, Blynn E. ⊟ NEW	**Third Quarter 2010 Total**	135
Badolne.Brian C ⊟ NEW	**Fourth Quarter 2010 Total**	
Badoux, Elexander ⊟ NEW		

Illustration 26

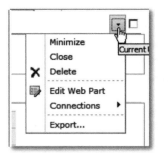

Illustration 27

Click on the drop-down menu *icon* on the right side of the Web Part as shown in **Illustration 27** at left and select *Edit Web Part*.

◀ Current User Filter   ✕

Filter   ⌃

Learn about filter web parts
Filter Name
Current User   *

Select value to provide
  ⦿ Current user name
     Example: irafuchsw520\ira h fuchs
  ○ SharePoint profile value for current
     user
     ⌄ *

➕ Advanced Filter Options

Illustration 28

The *Edit Web Part Pane* will display as shown in **Illustration 28** at left. The *Current User Filter* Web Part is hidden; it does not visually display on any Page that it is embedded on. Its purpose is to use the *SharePoint username* of the current user to access and store an attribute value from the *SharePoint User Profile Service* that it will then pass to another web part on the page. By default, the *Current User Filter* stores the fully qualified user-name, i.e. "computername\irafuchs". However this string will not match an Alias's unqualified literal value, i.e. "irafuchs".

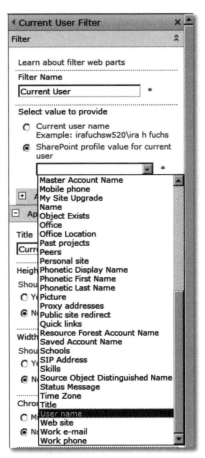

Illustration 29

Select the *radio button* for *SharePoint profile value for current user*. The drop-down selection box will display the various *User Profile Service* attributes that may or may not be populated in your *SharePoint* deployment. Scroll down and select *User name* as shown in **Illustration 29** at left. This will capture the unqualified value of the username Alias.

If the username (Alias) was one of the column values in the imported spreadsheet List we could connect the *Current User Filter* directly to the List in order to filter it. However this is not the case. We only have the Salesperson name; hence we created the *Salespeople List* to provide the mapping of the Salesperson name to their username Alias.

What we will do next is place a Web Part on the Page for the *Salespeople List* and connect it to the *Current User Filter*. We will pass the username value from the *Current User Filter* Web Part to the *Salespeople List* Web Part in order to filter it to obtain the value of the logged-in Salesperson name. We will then connect the *Salespeople List* Web Part to the imported spread-sheet List and pass the Salesperson name value to filter the imported spreadsheet List by the Salesperson name, and thus display only those records for the current logged-in user.

Important Note – This is a simple and elegant method for filtering the information in any List or Library by the identity of the logged-in user, and it can be used with any View. The technique augments List and Library permissions and it will work with External Content Type Lists as either the source or target List. Consequently it is a practical best practice to create and maintain these identity mapping Lists. Often this information can be generated from *Active Directory* or from another database/directory service. Furthermore, as we will see later, these Lists can be hidden, and used to filter identity on any List or Library using a variation of the method described here. Note also, that while this sample spreadsheet contains over 2000 records, there is a many to one relationship between accounts and sales people, so there are only about a dozen sales people records required. This is typical and consequently the overhead of creating and maintaining these identity mapping Lists are nominal relative to the value. Also, the same identity mapping List can be used repeatedly.

Once again click on the *Add a Web Part* link in the *Web Part Zone* at the top of the Page. From the *Categories* pane select *Lists and Libraries*. You will most likely have to scroll horizontally in the Web Parts pane to get to the *Salespeople List*. Select it and click the *Add* button. The *Salespeople Web Part* will be added to the page as shown in **Illustration 30** on the next page.

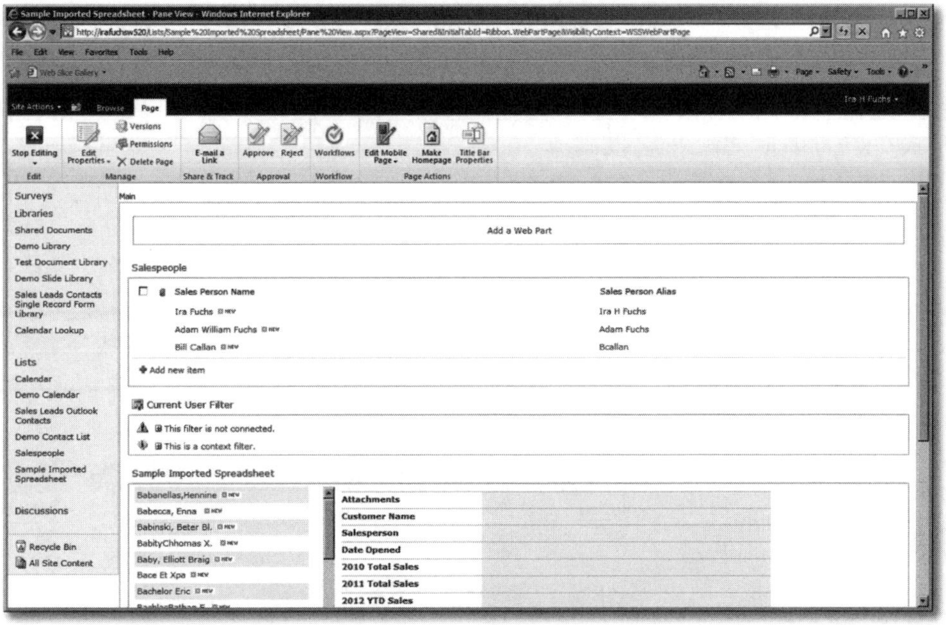

Illustration 30

Now click on the drop-down menu *icon* on the right side of the *Current User Filter* Web Part as shown in **Illustration 31** at left and select *Connections*.

Illustration 31

The drop-down options *Send Filter Values To* or *Send Default Value To* will display; select *Send Filter Values To*. The drop-down options for the two Web Parts on the Page will display as shown in **Illustration 32** below. Select the *Salespeople* Web Part.

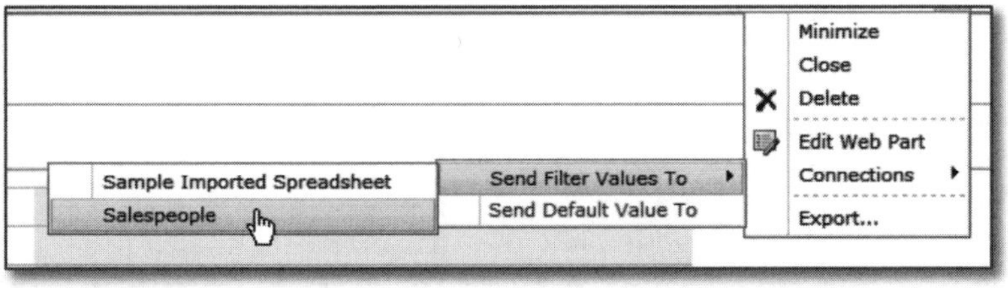

Illustration 32

The *Choose Connection – Webpage Dialogue* screen will display as shown in **Illustration 33** at right. Leave the default value of *Get Filter Values From* for the *Connection Type* and click the *Configure* button.

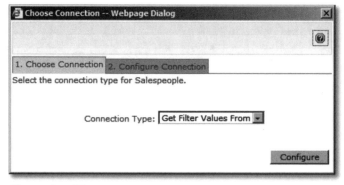

Illustration 33

The *Configure Connection – Webpage Dialogue* screen will display as shown in **Illustration 34** at right. The *Provider Field Name* will display "Current User". From the drop-down selection List for the *Consumer Field Name*, select "Sales Person Alias".

Illustration 34

As you can see in **Illustration 35** at right only the Salespeople record for the Current User (i.e. Ira Fuchs) now displays in the Salespeople Web Part.

Important Note – the *User Profile User name* attribute (and all other *User Profile Service* attributes) is case sensitive. The Sales Person alias "Ira H Fuchs" would not match the *User name* attribute "ira h fuchs" and no record would display in the Salespeople Web Part. As such, when creating user identity mapping Lists make sure that the alias values are created or entered with the correct case.

Illustration 35

Now go to the Web Part configuration menu for the imported spreadsheet List. Select *Connections*, choose the *Get Filter Values From* the drop-down option and then choose the *Salespeople* Web Part as shown in **Illustration 36** at right.

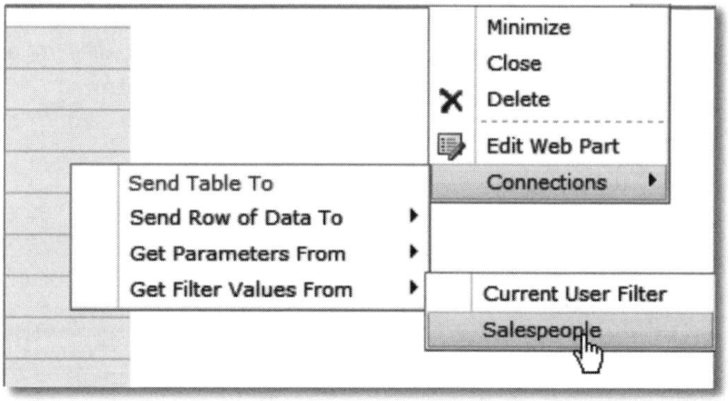

The *Configure Connection – Webpage* Dialogue screen will display as shown in **Illustration 37** at right. For the *Provider Field Name* select *Sales Person Name* from the drop-down selection. For the *Consumer Field Name* select *Salesperson* from the drop-down selection options.

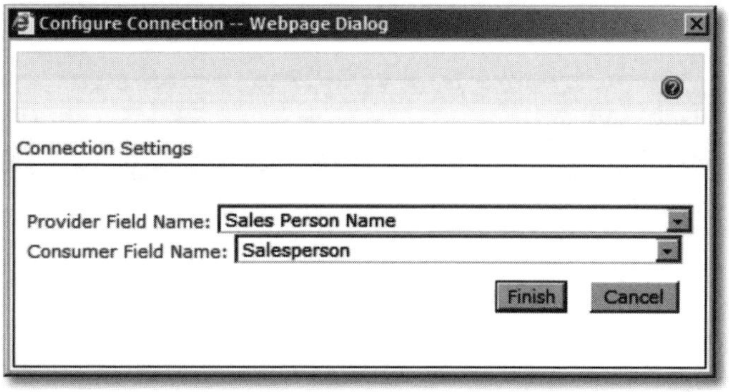

Illustration 36

Click the *Finish* button and voila, the imported spreadsheet Web Part now only displays the two records for the current logged in user as shown in **Illustration 38** below.

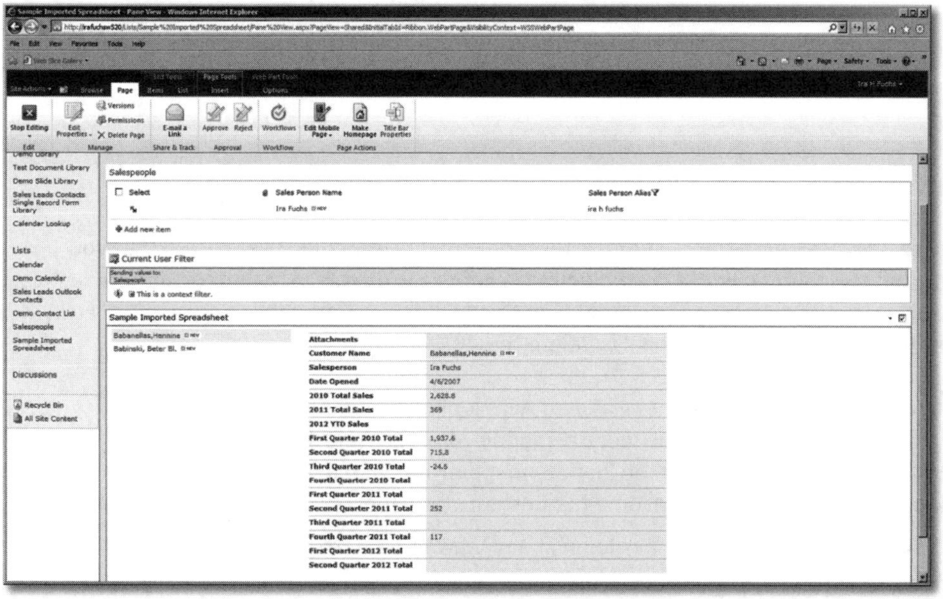

Illustration 37

Illustration 38

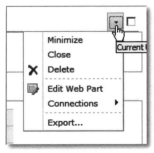

Illustration 39

Go back to the *Web Part configuration* menu for the *Salespeople* Web Part and select *Minimize* as shown in **Illustration 39** at left and click the *OK* button.

Click the *Stop Editing* button on the *Ribbon* menu. **Illustration 40** below shows you the completed result of this method of embedding a *Current User Filter* and a user identity mapping List on any List or Library Web Part Page! Pretty good and highly useful!

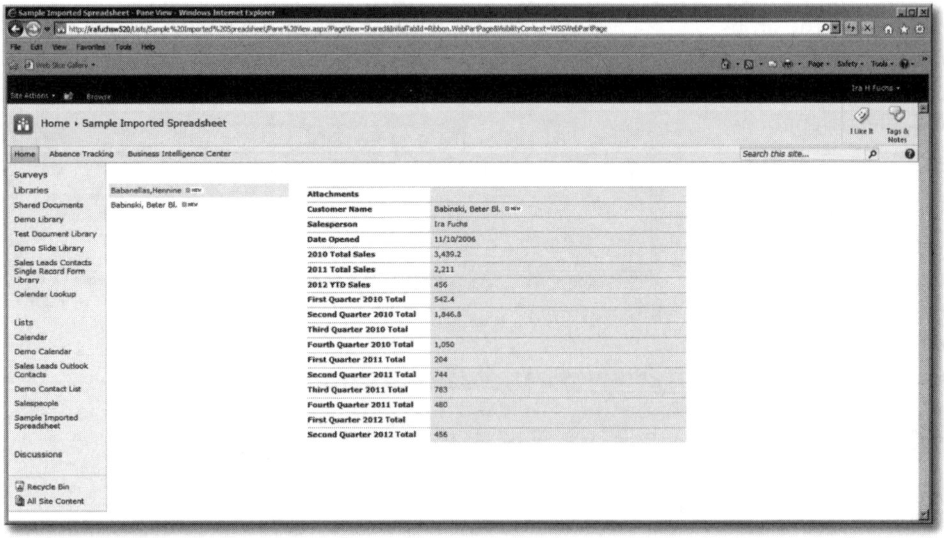

Illustration 40

You can log in to *SharePoint* with the credentials for the second Salespeople user record that you created to see that this method works. Two different records will display in the imported spreadsheet Web Part. Also note, you can set the *Pane View* to be the default view in either the *SharePoint Edit View* page or in *SharePoint Designer*; and optionally, delete the *All Items View*.

> **Note** — a variation of this method is to add an Alias look-up column to any List or Library that obtains the Alias value from the identity mapping List (i.e. Salespeople). Using this method you do not have to embed the identity mapping List web part onto the page. The look-up field would directly consume the Current User Filter value.

> **Note** — you do not have to display a column in any View in order to use it to send or receive filter values.

Using InfoPath Web Part Forms to Present Information Effectively and Enhance the Way SharePoint Pages Look.

InfoPath is one of *Microsoft's* most useful and valuable applications; and it is also one of its most underutilized and underappreciated. *InfoPath* has been part of the *Office* application suite since version 2003. It is a tool for creating data entry and information gathering forms. However, this is a simplistic description of what *InfoPath* is actually capable of and we are going to examine some of its capabilities in this chapter. As you will see *InfoPath* can access and submit information to and from any number of data sources; it can readily apply sophisticated functional logic to the information captured in the form as well as to the behavior of the form itself; and it can accommodate complex information structures handily.

Furthermore, *InfoPath* has been integrated into *SharePoint 2010* and *2013* in a number of ways. The most important integration point is through *SharePoint Forms Services*, which allows you to publish an *InfoPath* form to a *SharePoint Form Library* and then have that form render in a Web Browser. You can then place an *InfoPath Form Web Part* on any *SharePoint* page and render the published form on the page. The form is fully interactive and capable of behaving like any *InfoPath* Browser form.

In this chapter we are going to create three simple and easy *InfoPath* forms and publish them so that we can embed them in Web Parts on any *SharePoint* page. The purpose and value of these embedded forms is to provide a *SharePoint* user with a well-designed and configurable display of information as well as flexible ways of selecting subsets of information.

> **Important Note** – The techniques and functionality reviewed in this chapter are particularly important and useful to organizations that are already on *SharePoint 2013* or are planning to migrate to it, either online or on premise. This is because the visual Design edit mode for working with List and Data Views is no longer available in *SharePoint Designer 2013*. As a result, modifying and enhancing List, Library, and Data Views in *SharePoint 2013* is no longer an option in *SharePoint Designer 2013* unless you are capable of working directly with HTML and XSLT code. However, *InfoPath* is still fully supported in *SharePoint 2013* and all of the functionality described in this chapter provides an alternative, easy-to-use visual methodology for creating and enhancing List and Data Views for use on *SharePoint* pages.

The first *Web Part Form* we will create will be used to select and display information in a tabular format from the *Sales Leads Outlook Contacts ECT List* that we created earlier; however you can use any *SharePoint* List for this purpose. This *Web Part Form* will look like **Illustration 1** on the next page.

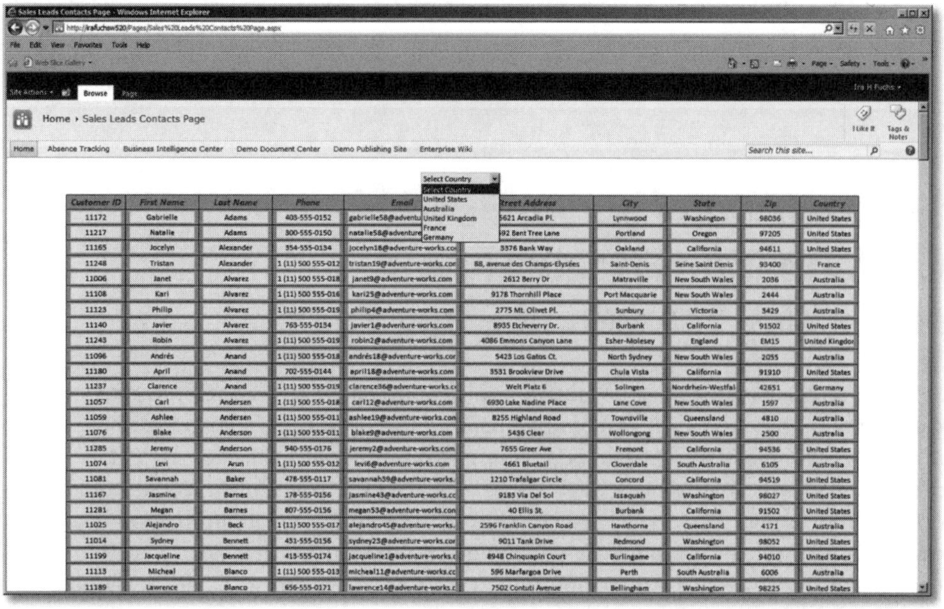

Illustration 1

The second *Web Part Form* will also access information from the *Sales Leads Outlook Contacts ECT List* but will display one record at a time. This *Web Part Form* will look like **Illustration 2** below.

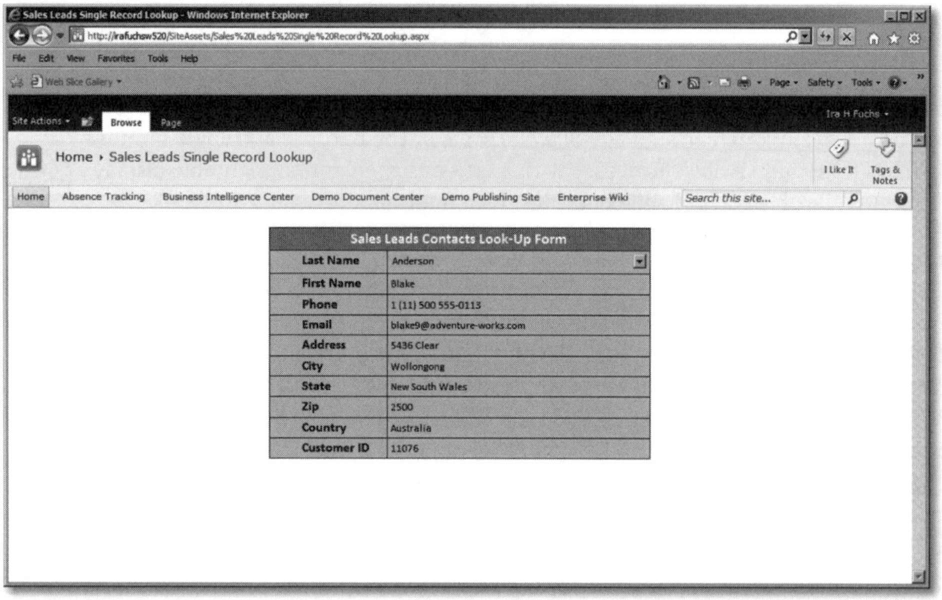

Illustration 2

The third *Web Part Form* will use the *Resource Reservation and Scheduling* calendar we created earlier to keep track of the calendar events for multiple people. A typical use case for this type of form is to provide a sales manager with a snap shot view of where salespeople are and what meetings they have on any given day. This *Web Part Form* will look like **Illustration 3** below.

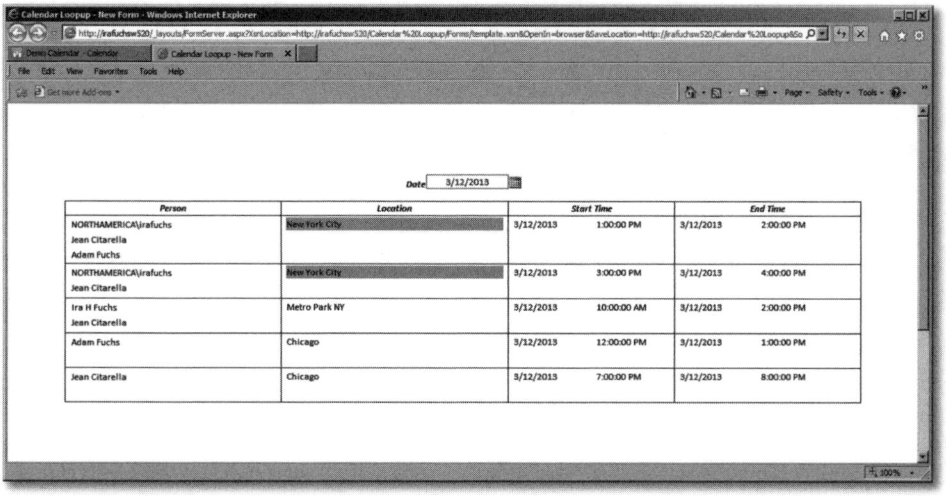

Illustration 3

Creating a Repeating Table InfoPath Web Part Form

So let's get started. The first thing we want to do is reference the fields in the *Sales Leads Outlook Contacts ECT List* that we created earlier, so open this List in *SharePoint* as shown in **Illustration 4** below.

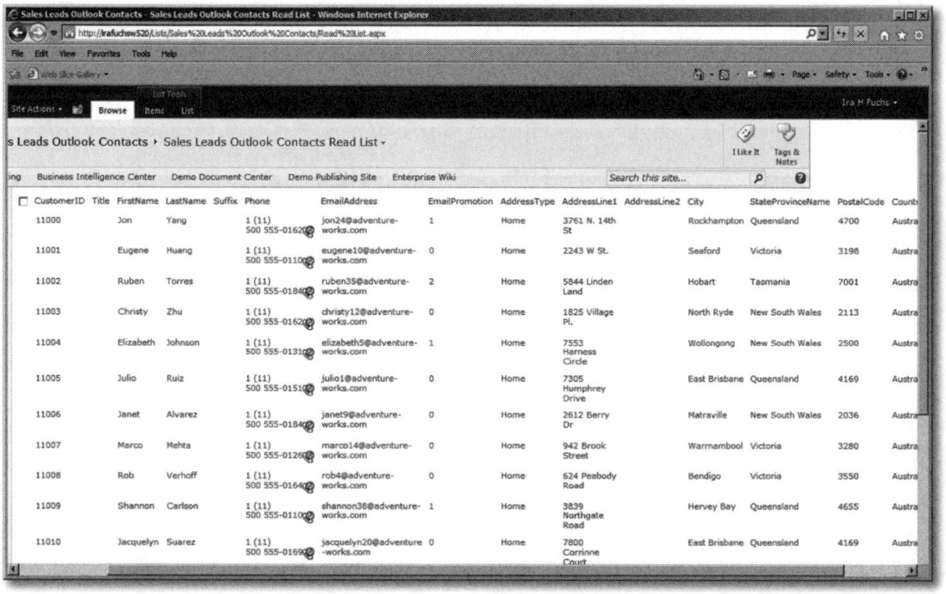

Illustration 4

Now open the *InfoPath* application. The *File New* menu page will open by default as shown in **Illustration 5** below.

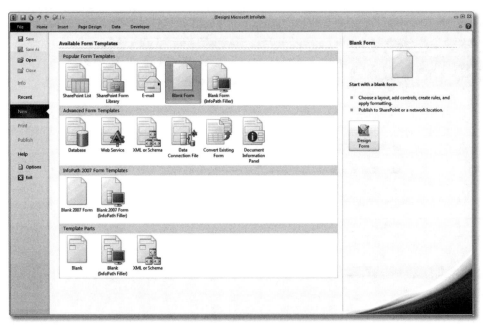

Illustration 5

Click on the *Blank Form* template and then the *Design Form* button. A new form will display as shown in **Illustration 6** below. The fundamental objects that comprise a form are layout tables, controls and fields. Layout tables provide a structured way to design the form as well as organize the placement of controls. Controls are the functional objects placed in the form that fields are bound to. Controls display or generate the values for the fields. The fields are the information set that the form generates when information is entered into or are generated by the controls.

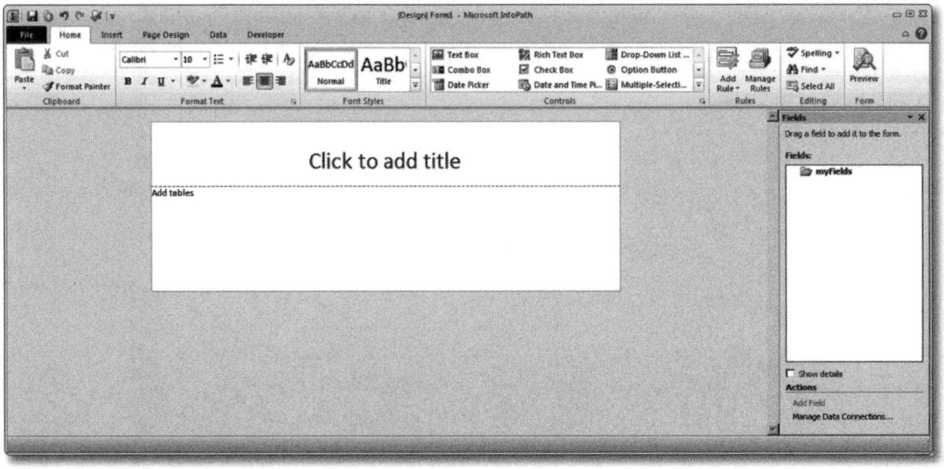

Illustration 6

The design surface will display a default table. Select this and remove it so that the design surface is empty. Now we are going to create a data source connection to the *Sales Leads Outlook Contacts ECT List*. Click on the *Data* tab of the *Ribbon* menu and double click on the *From SharePoint List* button. The first screen of the *Data Connection Wizard* will display. Enter the location of the *SharePoint* site that contains the *Sales Leads Outlook Contacts ECT List* as shown in **Illustration 7** below, and click *Next*.

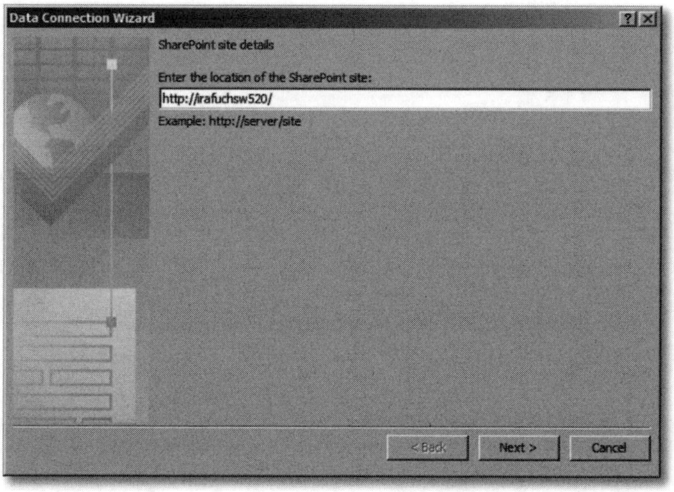

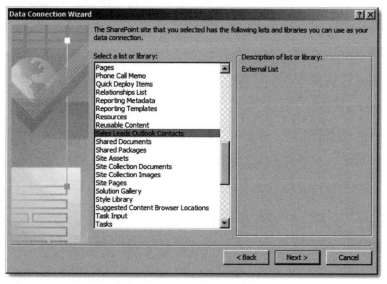

Illustration 7

The next dialogue screen of the *Data Connection Wizard* will display all the Lists and libraries on the *SharePoint* site. Scroll down and select the *Sales Leads Outlook Contacts ECT List* as shown in **Illustration 8** below.

Illustration 8

The next dialogue screen of the *Data Connection Wizard* will display the fields of the *Sales Leads Outlook Contacts ECT List* as shown in **Illustration 9** at right. Select *Customer ID, FirstName, LastName, Phone, EmailAddress, AddressLine1, City, StateProvinceName, PostalCode* and *CountryRegionName*. For *Sort by* select *LastName* and click the *Next* button.

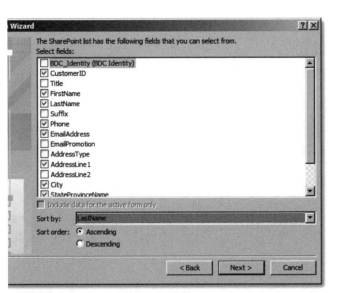

Illustration 9

The next screen of the *Data Connection Wizard* will display as shown in **Illustration 10** at right. On this screen you can select a check box to store data from the source offline. Leave the check box empty and click the *Next* button.

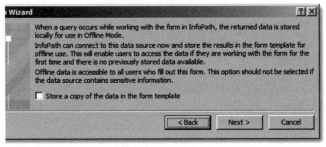

Illustration 10

On the final screen of the *Data Connection Wizard* as shown in **Illustration 11** at right you can use the List name for the name of the data connection or you can provide an alternative name. There is also a check box setting to automatically retrieve data when form is opened. This is checked by default. Leave this setting and click the *Finish* button.

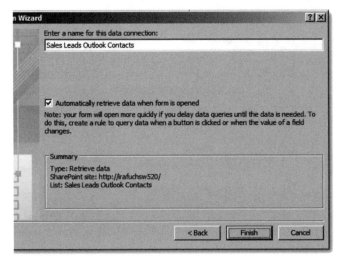

Illustration 11

The *Data Connection Wizard* will finish and you will be returned to the *InfoPath* form template. On the right of the *Fields:* drop-down selection List click on the *selection button* to display the *Sales Leads Outlook Contacts (Secondary)* data source. Note that two groups are displayed: *queryFields* and *dataFields*. Click on the expand box to the left of each group to expand the field nodes in each group as shown in **Illustration 12** at right.

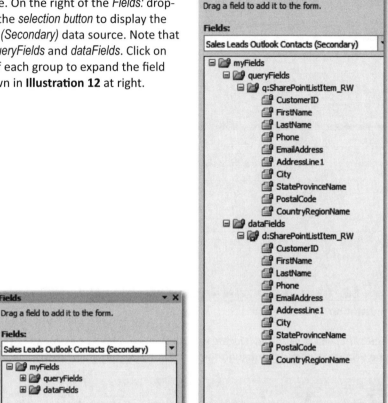

Illustration 12

The fields in the *queryFields* and *dataFields* groups are identical. What *InfoPath* is providing is a representation of the List for two different functions available in *InfoPath*. Using the *queryFields* in *InfoPath* provides the ability to execute a select query on the List for the purpose of returning a subset of the records in the List for display or to execute additional logic on the record subset. When using the *queryFields* in *InfoPath* you can read and write back to the values in the List. We will be setting the value of the *queryFields* to select a subset of records.

In the *dataFields* group, click on the group named *d:SharePointListItem_RW* that contains the field nodes as shown in **Illustration 13** at right.

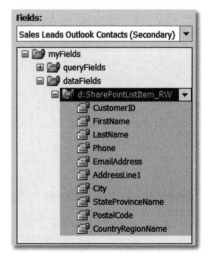

Illustration 13

Now drag the group to the design surface. You will be presented with three options: *Repeating Table, Repeating Section with Controls* and *Repeating Section* as shown in **Illustration 14** below.

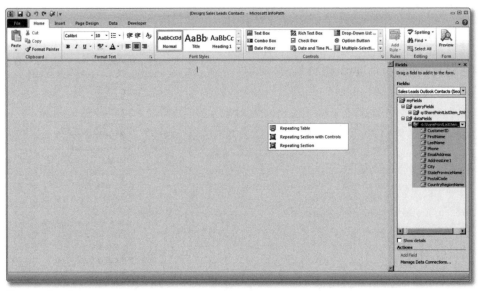

Illustration 14

Select *Repeating Table* and *InfoPath* will automatically lay out a repeating table containing the fields in the order that they are found in the data source as shown in **Illustration 15** below.

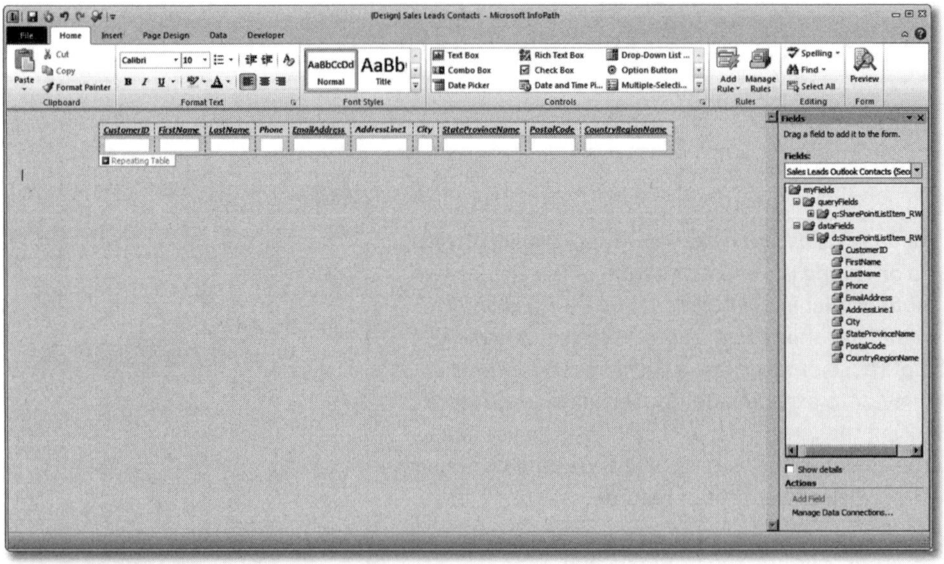

Illustration 15

Click on the *Preview* button on the far right of the *Ribbon* menu. The runtime representation of the form will begin to open and the *InfoPath Editor Security Notice* warning will display as shown in **Illustration 16** below. Click the *Yes* button.

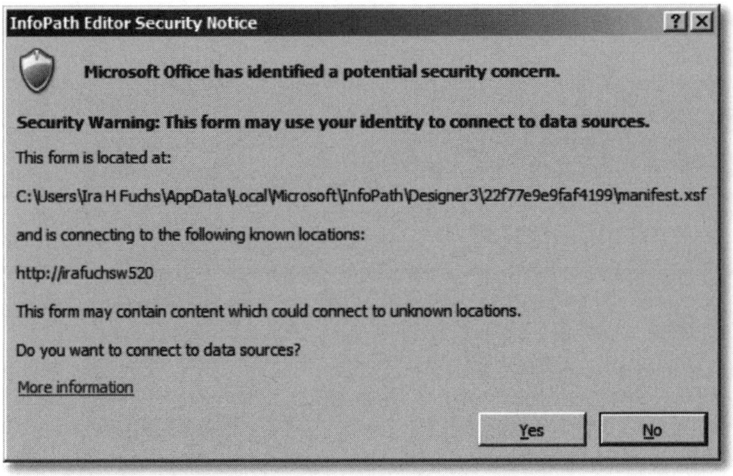

Illustration 16

The form preview displays the records in the List in the format of the form controls that were automatically laid out as shown in **Illustration 17** below. Note that the CustomerID field values display with a comma. We will change this when we restructure and redesign the table, which is our next step. Click on the *Close Preview* button to close the form preview.

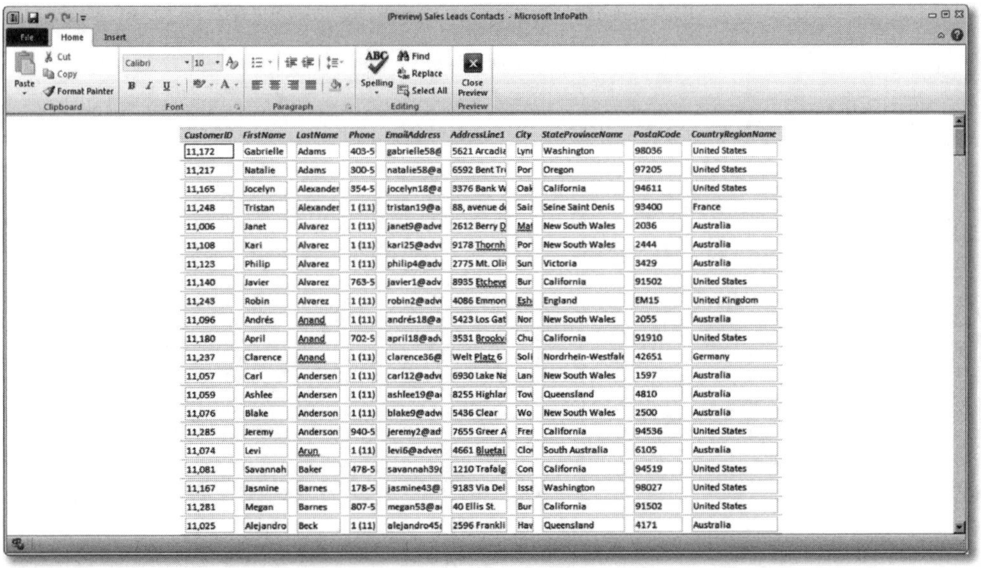

Illustration 17

Click on the *Repeating Table* control on the far left of the table and right-click. The floating text formatting menu and *Properties* menu will display as shown in **Illustration 18** below.

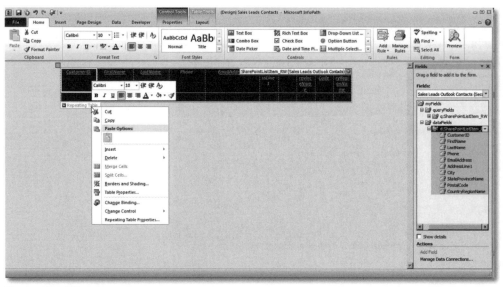

Illustration 18

Select the *Table Properties* option to display the *Tables Properties* dialogue screen as shown in **Illustration 19** below. Click on the *Column* tab.

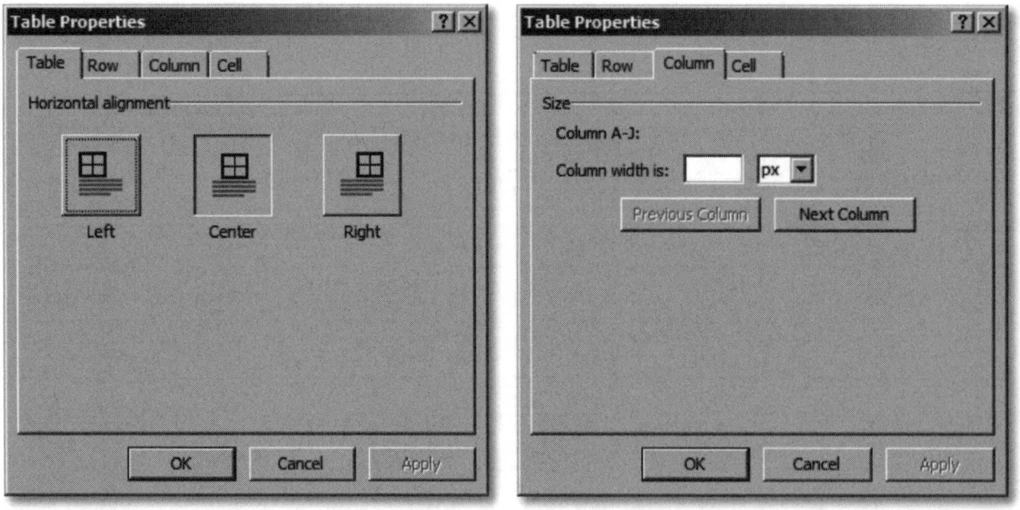

Illustration 19

The *Column width* setting will be displayed for Column A, the first column and that column will also be highlighted in the table as shown in **Illustration 20** below.

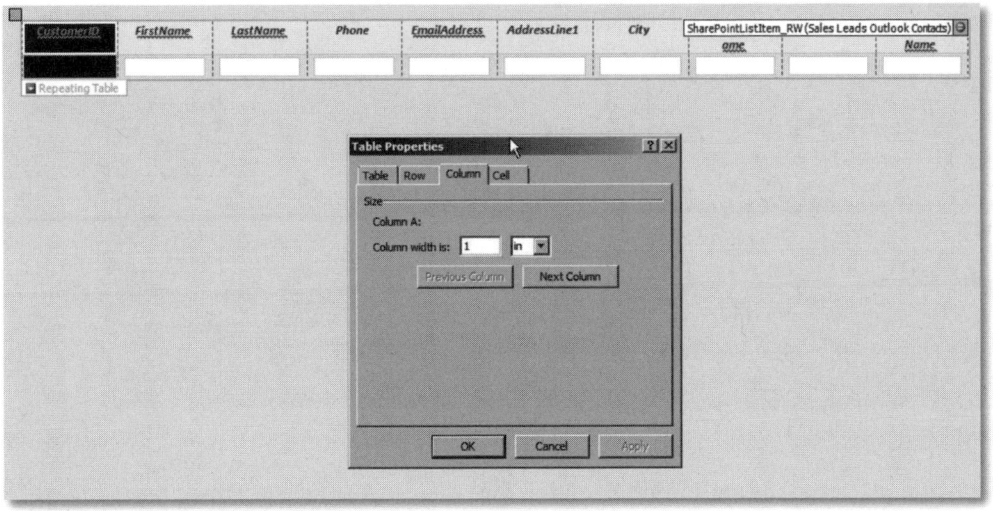

Illustration 20

Set the measurement value in the drop down selection box to "in" (inches). Set Column A's width to 1 inch. Click the Next Column button and set Column B's width to 1.25 inch. Set the width of columns C through H to the following values: C = 1.25 inch, D = 1.25 inch, E = 1.75 inch, F = 2 inch, G = 1.25 inch, H = 1.25 inch. Note that as you move back or forth to each column, that column is highlighted in the table and the change in width is shown immediately. You can adjust these values at any time using the *Table Properties* dialogue screen, from the *Layout Ribbon* menu or by manually dragging the vertical border of a column. Preview the form so that you can make any additional column width changes.

By default the text alignment is set to left for all the text box controls and you can change those individually for each text box control or you can shift-click to select multiple controls and change their formatting settings all at once.

You can also remove or rearrange any of the columns of the repeating table. Which field values and in what order you want them to display is entirely up to you.

Now change the name of the column headers to the following: *Customer ID, First Name, Last Name, Phone, Email, Street Address, City, State, Zip* and *Country*. Note that the column headers are center aligned and you can change any formatting attribute of these as well.

Select the entire repeating table and click the *Table Tools* Layout menu. Experiment with the visual display of the form using the *Shading and Borders* settings. Preview the form at any time to see the results of your settings.

Select the *Customer ID* text box control and right-click. Select the *Text Box Properties* option to display the dialogue screen for its properties as shown in **Illustration 21** on the next page. Click on the *Format* button on the *Data* tab. On the *Integer Format* dialogue screen de-select the check box for *Use a digit grouping symbol (,)*. Click *OK* and *OK* again. The *Customer ID* values will now display correctly.

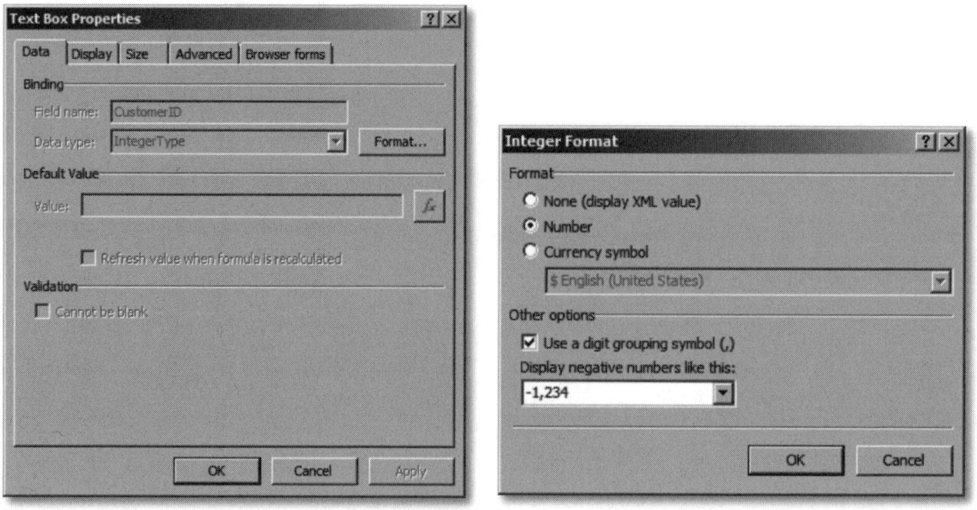

Illustration 21

With your cursor placed on the outside left border of the table hit your *Enter key* three times to add space in the form above the table. Now return to the *Fields* pane and select the *Main* data source from the *Fields* drop-down selection box as shown in **Illustration 22 left below**. The *Main* data source is the form's internal set of fields that will store information that is either entered manually, auto-populated, or generated by rules. As this is an empty form there are no fields yet except the *myFields* group that is the parent container for the dataset. If you drag controls onto the design surface *InfoPath* will automatically create generic fields named field1, field2 etc. You can also import an existing XML document or XML schema into *InfoPath* to be the *Main* data source but in most cases you will use *InfoPath's* schema creation facilities to build the internal dataset. Since we are not creating this form to gather or generate information but simply to display information from the ECT List we will only be creating a single Country field to store the names of the same countries in the ECT List to use as selection criteria.

Right click the *myFields* group and select the *Add* option in the drop-down menu as shown in **Illustration 22 right below**.

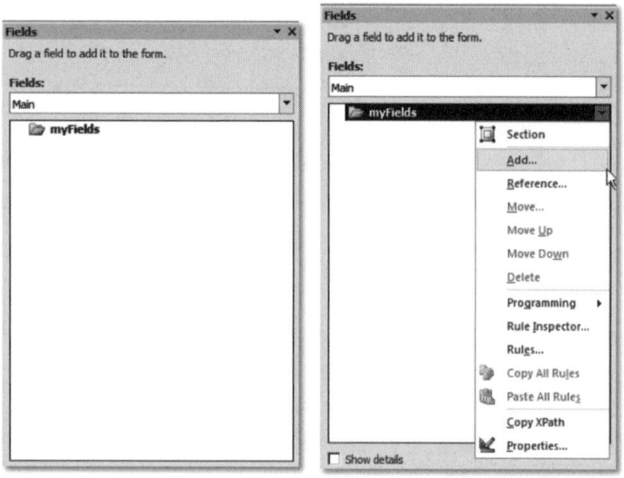

Illustration 22

The *Add Field or Group* dialogue screen will display as shown in **illustration 23 below left**. Enter "Country" in the *Name* field; leave *Field (element)* for the *Type*; and from the drop-down selection box for *Data type* select *Text*. Click *OK* and you will see that the *Country* field has been added to the dataset as shown in **Illustration 23 below right**.

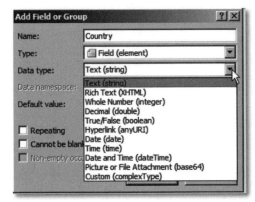 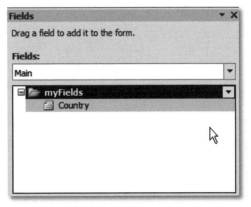

Illustration 23

Now place your cursor above the repeating table in the design suface and select the *Country* field in the *Fields* pane. Right click and select the *Drop-Down List Box* control option as shown in **Illustration 24** at right.

Illustration 24

A *Drop-Down List Box* control will appear on the design surface above the repeating table as shown in **Illustration 25** below.

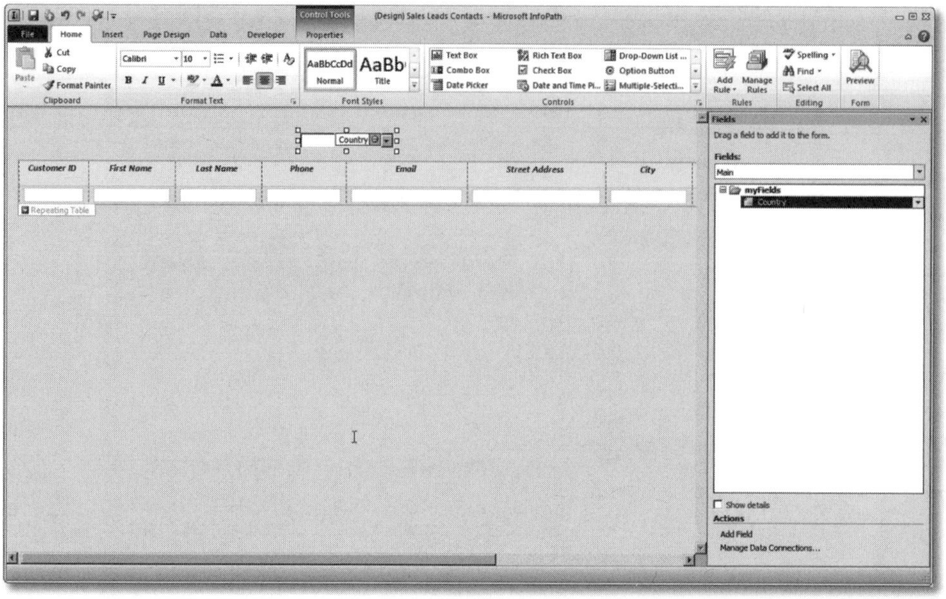

Illustration 25

Select this control and right click to display the options menu for the control. Select the *Drop-Down List Box Properties* option. Select the *Enter choices manually radio button* as shown in **Illustration 26 below left**. Now click the *Add* button to the right. The *Add Choice* entry screen will display as shown in **Illustration 26 below right** . Enter "United States" and click the *OK* button.

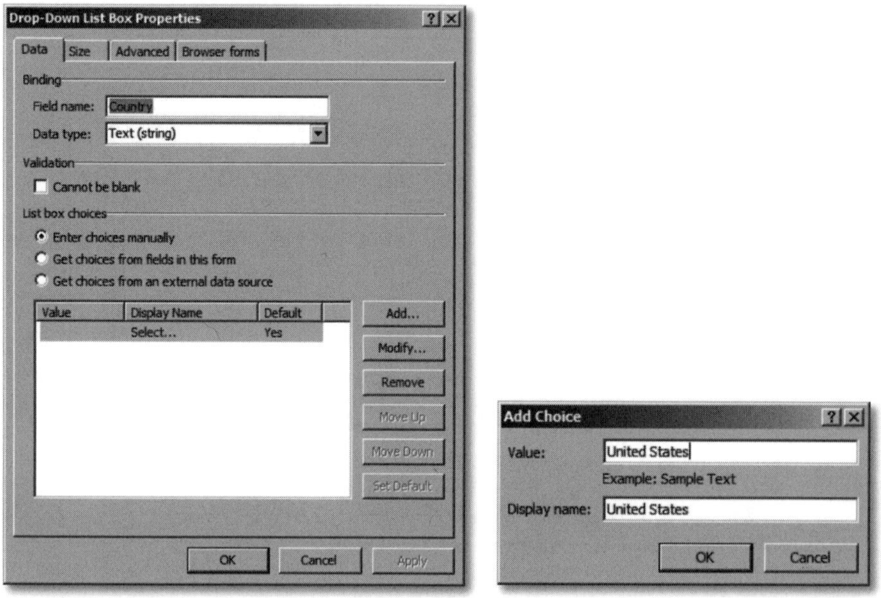

Illustration 26

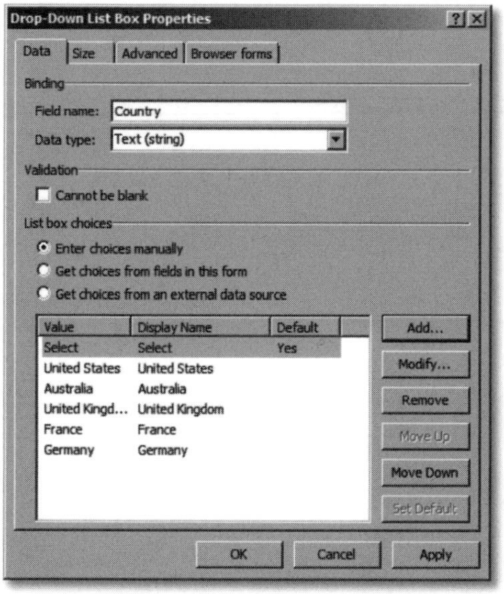

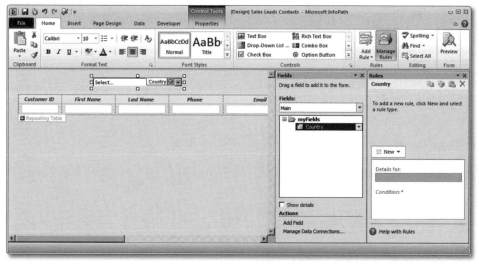

Now repeat this step to add values for Australia, United Kingdom, France and Germany. When you are done the *Drop-Down List Box Properties* dialogue screen will look like **Illustration 27** at left. If the *Select* option is not at the top of the List and the Default value, use the *Move Up* button to move it there and click the *Set Default* button as well.

Note that we could have also obtained the values for this control using an external data source such as a *SharePoint* List, XML file or database.

Illustration 27

Now we will add the rule logic to the *Country* field that will filter the records in the *Sales Leads Contacts ECT List* so that only the records for the *Country* picked in the *Drop-Down List Box* will display. Right click on the *Country* field in the *Fields* panel or the *Drop-Down List Box* control for *Country* and select *Rules*. The *Rules* panel will display as shown in **Illustration 28** below.

Illustration 28

Click the *New* button and select *Action*. A new *Rule 1* will be created as shown in **Illustration 29** below.

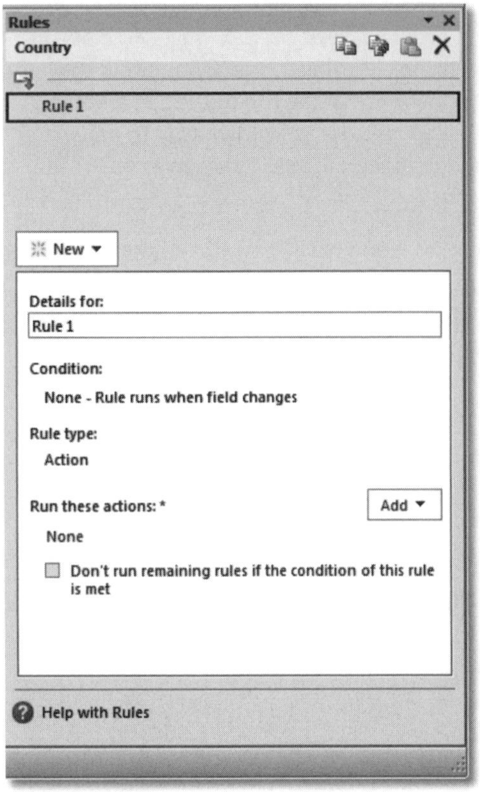

Illustration 29

In the *Details for* box change *Rule 1* to "Filter Country". Now click the *Add* button and select *Set a field's value*. The *Rule Details* dialogues screen will display as shown in **Illustration 30** below.

Illustration 30

Click on the *Field selection* button to display the *Select a Field or Group* dialogue screen. From the *Fields* drop-down selection box select the *Sales Leads Outlook Contacts (Secondary)* data source. Click the + sign to the left of the *queryFields* group to expand it; click the + sign to the left of the *q:SharePointListItem_RW* group to display the query options for the List. Select the *CountryRegionName* field. Your screen should look like **Illustration 31** below.

Illustration 31

Click *OK*. Now click the *Formula* button to the right of the *Value* field. The *Insert Formula* dialogue screen will display as shown in **Illustration 32 below left**. Click the *Insert Field or Group* button to display the *Select a Field or Group* dialogue screen. The *Main* data source will display by default and the Country field will be highlighted (because it is the only field available) as shown in **Illustration 32 below right**.

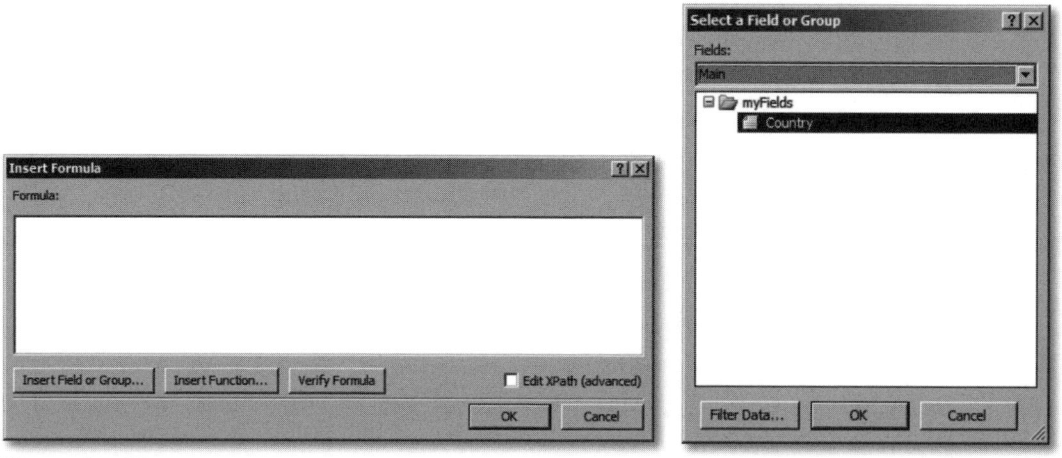

Illustration 32

Click *OK* and then *OK* again on the *Insert Formula* dialogue screen. The completed *Rule Details* dialogue screen will look like **Illustration 33** below.

Illustration 33

Click *OK*. On the *Rules* pane click the *Add* button for *Run these actions:* and select the *Query for data* action. The *Rule Details* dialogue screen for this action will display as shown in **Illustration 34** below. Click *OK*.

Illustration 34

The completed *Filter Country* rule set will look like **Illustration 35** below.

Illustration 35

The *Set a field's value* action takes the value selected in the *Drop-Down List Box* for Country and uses it to filter the records we want to display in the *Sales Leads Outlook Contacts ECT List*. The *Query using a data connection* action executes the display query for the filtered values. Note that we did not set any Condition criteria for when these actions should run; the default value of *None-Rule runs when field changes* is the condition under which we want the rule actions to execute. Click on the *File* tab of the *Ribbon* menu and then *Save*.

Now let's see what the results of this Rule are. Click the *Preview* button. The security notification screen will come up again; click *Yes*. The records for all the countries will display. From the *Drop-Down List Box* select the *United States*. Now only the records for the United States will display as shown in **Illustration 36** below. Select any of the other countries to see the results. Good Stuff!

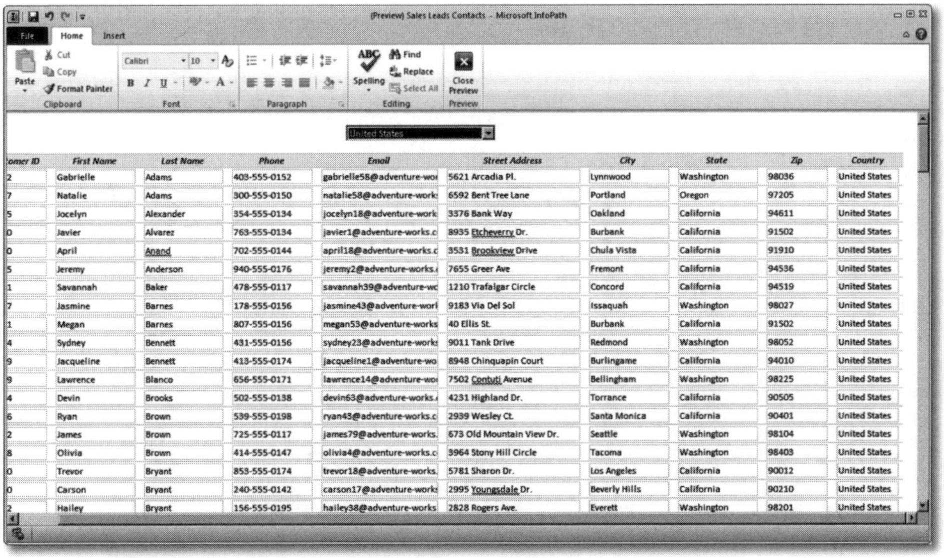

Illustration 36

Click the *Close Preview* button. Before we publish the form template to a *SharePoint* Form Library let's examine the various options available for enhancing the way the form can display information as well as the behavior of the form itself.

Let's start with the options for the overall form. Just like *SharePoint* Lists and libraries you can create multiple Views of a form. Each View can look completely different, display different (or duplicate) sets of information and controls, and have different rules and behavior.

Place your cursor on the design surface and right click, or from the *Page Design Properties* tab on the *Ribbon,* click on *Properties*. The *View Properties* dialogue screen will display. On the *General* settings tab as shown in **Illustration 37 below left** you can do the following things:

- Give a name to a View. The default View is named View 1 and you can change that here. When you create additional views you have the option to set which View becomes the default view and whether you want a View to be available to a user.

- Set a View to be Read-only. Displaying information while preventing it from being edited is a particularly useful capability for which there is no equivalent functionality in *SharePoint* views.

- Set a background color for the View or use a picture for the background. Again, there is no comparable out-of-the-box capability in *SharePoint* to do this.

- Set scroll bars to display. This feature is great for displaying tabular data in a *Web Part Form,* and once again, this capability is not available natively for a *SharePoint* List or Library View.

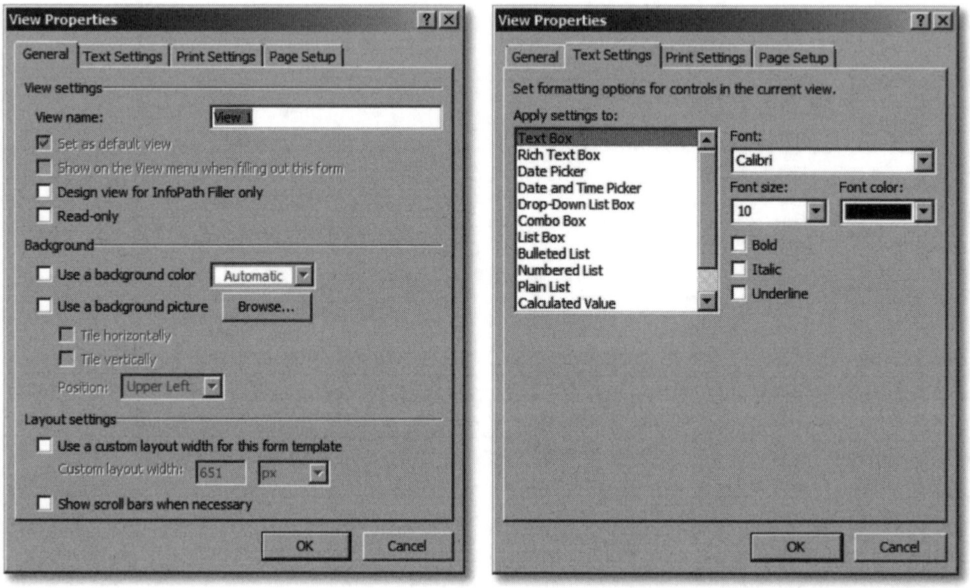

Illustration 37

On the *Text Settings* tab you can set default text attributes for a control. In this way a default setting is established for a control and you do not have to manually set the text properties for each instance of the use of that control.

There are two additional tabs, *Print Settings* and *Page Setup*. As these are not applicable to Web Part forms we are not going to review here.

Now click on the *Insert* tab on the *Ribbon,* where additional form design options are available as shown in **Illustration 38** on the next page. A number of pre-defined table formats can be placed on the design surface or use the *Custom Table* tool to create a matrix of rows and columns. In addition you can insert other design artifacts such as pictures and symbols.

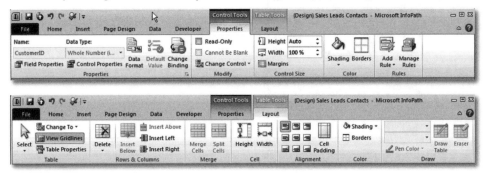

Illustration 38

Now click on the *Home* tab on the *Ribbon*. From here you can apply text format settings to any control, label or table. Click on any of the text box controls in the repeating table. The *Control Tools* and *Table Tools* menu options on the *Ribbon* will become available as shown in **Illustration 39** below. From these two menus you can set various layout attributes and properties. Note that you can also select multiple controls by holding down the *Ctrl key* while selecting and apply settings to the selected controls at once.

Illustration 39

Alternatively, if you right click on any control a drop down selection menu will display the formatting and other options. Let's modify the way the borders and shading of the repeating table display so that the actual *Web Part Form* looks better than the current preview. With the repeating table selected right click and select *Borders and Shading*. The *Borders and Shading* dialogue screen will display as shown in **Illustration 40** below.

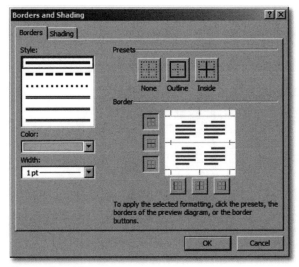

Illustration 40

The *Borders* tab will be selected by default. Click the *Color* drop down selection box and select the default black color. Leave the default Width of 1 pt. Click the *None* Presets button then click the *Outline* and the *Inside* button. Now click the *Shading* tab. Select the *Color* radio button and from the *Color* drop down selection box select any of the darker colors. Click *OK* on the *Borders and Shading* dialogue screen. Select any of the text box controls in the repeating table and add shading. With a *Text Box* control selected right click again and choose *Text Box Properties*. Click on the *Display* tab as shown in **Illustration 41** below and change the *Alignment*. Note also that you can make any individual control *Read-only*.

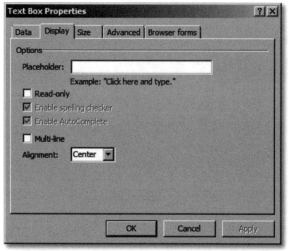

Illustration 41

Click the *Preview* button on the *Ribbon* again to see the changes that you have made. After you have added shading and center aligned all of the *Text Box Controls* your preview should look something like **Illustration 42** below. Not bad for just a few minutes of work! Certainly a lot better than your standard List view.

Customer ID	First Name	Last Name	Phone	Email	Street Address	City	State	Zip	Country
11172	Gabrielle	Adams	403-555-0152	gabrielle58@adventure-works.c	5621 Arcadia Pl.	Lynwood	Washington	98086	United States
11217	Natalie	Adams	500-555-0150	natalie58@adventure-works.cor	6592 Bent Tree Lane	Portland	Oregon	97205	United States
11165	Jocelyn	Alexander	354-555-0154	jocelyn18@adventure-works.cor	3276 Bank Way	Oakland	California	94611	United States
11248	Tristan	Alexander	1 (11) 500 555-012	tristan19@adventure-works.con	88, avenue des Champs-Elysées	Saint-Denis	Seine Saint Denis	93400	France
11006	Janet	Alvarez	1 (11) 500 555-018	janet9@adventure-works.com	2612 Berry Dr.	Matraville	New South Wales	2036	Australia
11108	Karl	Alverez	1 (11) 500 555-016	karl25@adventure-works.com	9178 Thornhill Place	Port Macquarie	New South Wales	2444	Australia
11123	Philip	Alvarez	1 (11) 500 555-019	philip4@adventure-works.com	2775 Mt. Olivet Pl.	Sunbury	Victoria	3429	Australia
11140	Javier	Alvarez	760-555-0134	javier1@adventure-works.com	8905 Etcheverry Dr.	Burbank	California	91502	United States
11243	Robin	Alvarez	1 (11) 500 555-019	robin2@adventure-works.com	4086 Emmons Canyon Lane	Esher-Molesey	England	EM15	United Kingdom
11096	Andrés	Anand	1 (11) 500 555-018	andrés18@adventure-works.cor	5423 Los Gatos Ct.	North Sydney	New South Wales	2055	Australia
11180	April	Anand	702-555-0144	april18@adventure-works.com	3531 Brookview Drive	Chula Vista	California	91910	United States
11237	Clarence	Anand	1 (11) 500 555-019	clarence36@adventure-works.cc	Welt Platz 6	Solingen	Nordrhein-Westfal	42651	Germany
11057	Carl	Andersen	1 (11) 500 555-018	carl12@adventure-works.com	6930 Lake Nadine Place	Lane Cove	New South Wales	1597	Australia
11059	Ashlee	Andersen	1 (11) 500 555-011	ashlee19@adventure-works.com	8255 Highland Road	Townsville	Queensland	4810	Australia
11076	Blake	Anderson	1 (11) 500 555-011	blake9@adventure-works.com	5456 Clear	Wollongong	New South Wales	2500	Australia
11285	Jeremy	Anderson	940-555-0176	jeremy2@adventure-works.com	7655 Greer Ave	Fremont	California	94536	United States
11074	Levi	Arun	1 (11) 500 555-012	levi6@adventure-works.com	4661 Bluetail	Cloverdale	South Australia	6105	Australia
11081	Savannah	Baker	478-555-0117	savannah39@adventure-works.	1210 Trafalgar Circle	Concord	California	94519	United States
11167	Jasmine	Barnes	178-555-0156	jasmine43@adventure-works.co	9183 Via Del Sol	Issaquah	Washington	98027	United States

Illustration 42

With *InfoPath* you have a great deal of granular flexibility in designing a form so that it displays information in almost any way that you want it to. Furthermore, as you will see shortly, we can use conditional formatting rules based on information criteria to highlight and/or hide selective information.

With this information you are now empowered to experiment with any and all of *InfoPath's* design capabilities that will enable you to present information effectively. As noted earlier, practically none of this layout and design functionality is available natively in *SharePoint* and even *SharePoint Designer's* facilities for modifying List views are not as simple and elegant to use as working with an *InfoPath* form.

> **Important Note** – *SharePoint Designer 2010* lets you edit a List or Library View in Design mode where you can apply many of the same formatting settings available in *InfoPath*. However, this Design mode is no longer available in *SharePoint Designer 2013* which is required for working with *SharePoint 2013*. Consequently, using *InfoPath Form Web Parts* in *SharePoint 2013* to design and display tabular information becomes even more compelling.

Before we publish the form to *SharePoint* we will want to remove the *InfoPath Ribbon* menu items from the form that allow a user to Save the form and execute other form functions. We only want this form to display information, not save it. Click on the *File Ribbon* menu option then click on the *Advanced Form Options* button. The *Form Options* screen will open displaying the Web Browser options page as shown in **Illustration 43** below. De-select the check box for *Show InfoPath commands in Ribbon or toolbar*, and then click the *OK* button.

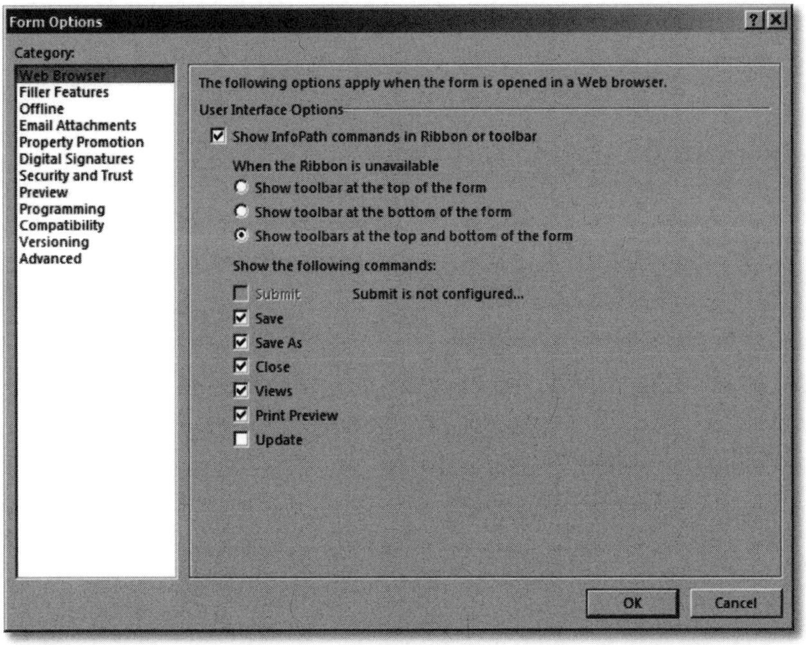

Illustration 43

We are now ready to publish the form to *SharePoint*. From the *File* tab on the *Ribbon* menu click the *Publish* button. The *Publish* options page will display as shown in **Illustration 44** below.

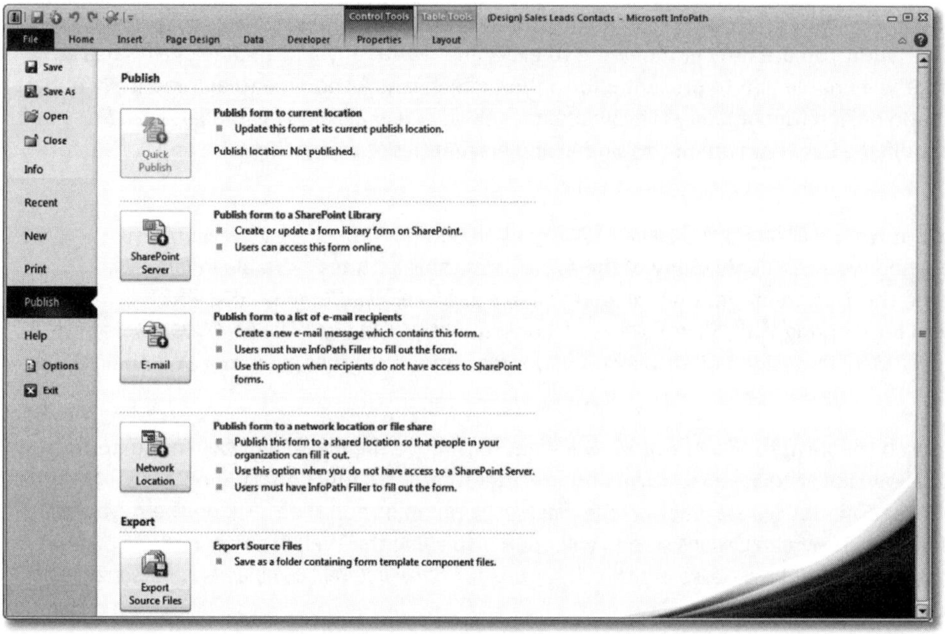

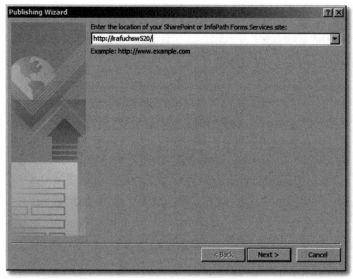

Illustration 44

Click the *Publish form to a SharePoint Library* button. The first page of the *Publishing Wizard* will display as shown in **Illustration 45** below.

Illustration 45

Enter the URL address of the site where you want to publish the form. Note that the site must be in a Site Collection that has the Enterprise Features activated. Click *Next* to display the next screen of the *Publishing Wizard* as shown in **Illustration 46** below.

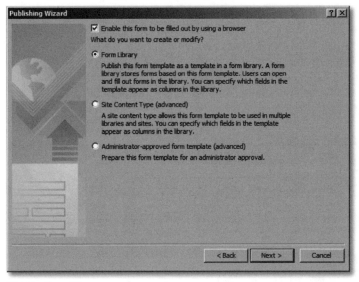

Illustration 46

Leave the default check box setting for *Enable the form to be filled out by using a browser* as well as the default selection for Form Library. Click *Next* again. The next screen of the *Publishing Wizard* gives you the option to create a new Form Library that will host the form template or Update the form template in an existing Form Library. Keep the selected default value of *Create a new form library* as shown in **Illustration 47** below.

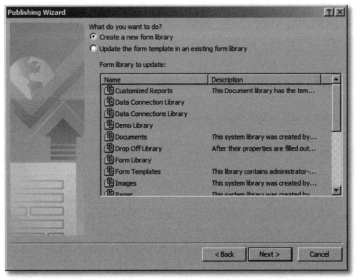

Illustration 47

Subsequently, when you make changes to the form you will re-publish it and on this screen you will choose the *Update the form template in an existing form Library* option. Click the *Next* button. On the following screen, as shown in **Illustration 48** below, you will enter a name for the Form Library that will be created to host the form template.

> **Note** – this Form Library provides no functional value other than providing a place for the form template to reside and allow *InfoPath Form Services* to access it in order to render it in a Web Part. As such there is no need for this Form Library to be accessible to anyone other than the person who supports the form. It is a good idea to provide a name for this Library that identifies its function and use the Description field to provide instructions not to delete the Library as shown in **Illustration 48** below.

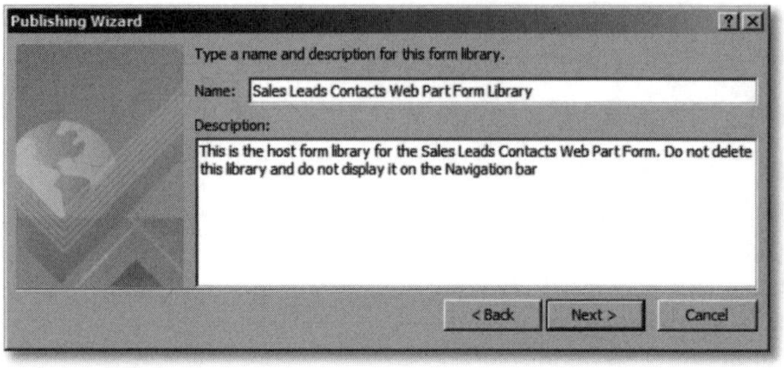

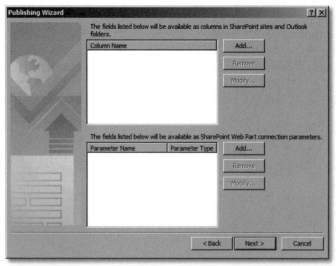

Illustration 48

Click the *Next* button again to go to the final *Publishing Wizard* screen as shown in **Illustration 49** below. In this screen you specify fields in the form that will populate the form Library's columns, or when used as a *Web Part Form*, those fields whose values will be exchanged among other Web Parts on a page in order to facilitate dynamic behavior. We are not using this Library for any functional purpose other than as a location where the form template is stored so we do not want to display any information in this Library. Also, there is only one field in the *Main* data source.

Illustration 49

Nonetheless, as this is a very important way in which *InfoPath* is integrated with *SharePoint* let's take a look at how these fields are selected and their settings. **Illustration 50 below left** shows the dialogue screen for selecting the fields that will display as columns. An *InfoPath* form can also be published as a *Content Type* and when this is done the promoted fields become *Site Columns*. **Illustration 50 below right** shows the dialogue screen for selecting the fields that will function as passed parameters among other Web Parts on a page.

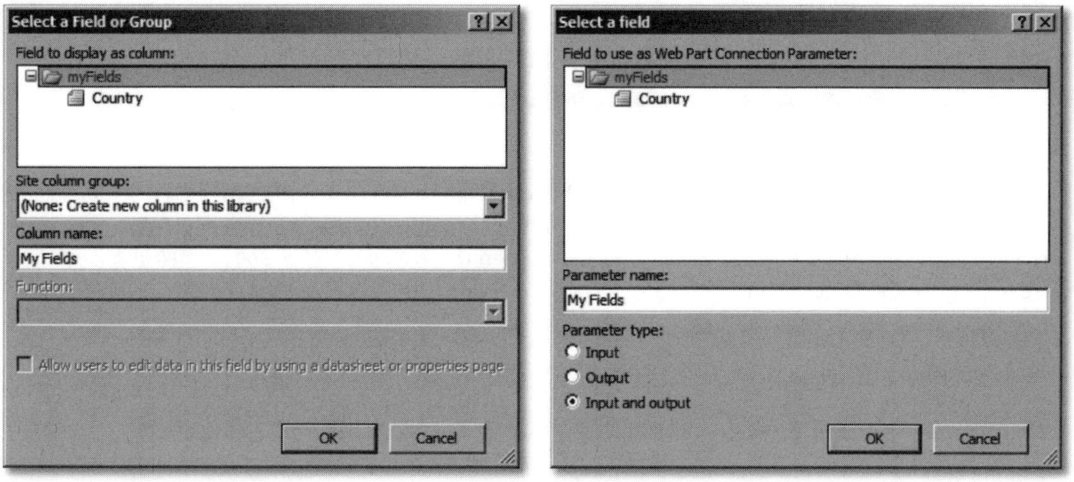

Illustration 50

Clicking *Next* brings you to the last page of the *Publishing Wizard* where you can confirm the settings or go back and change them as shown in **Illustration 51** below.

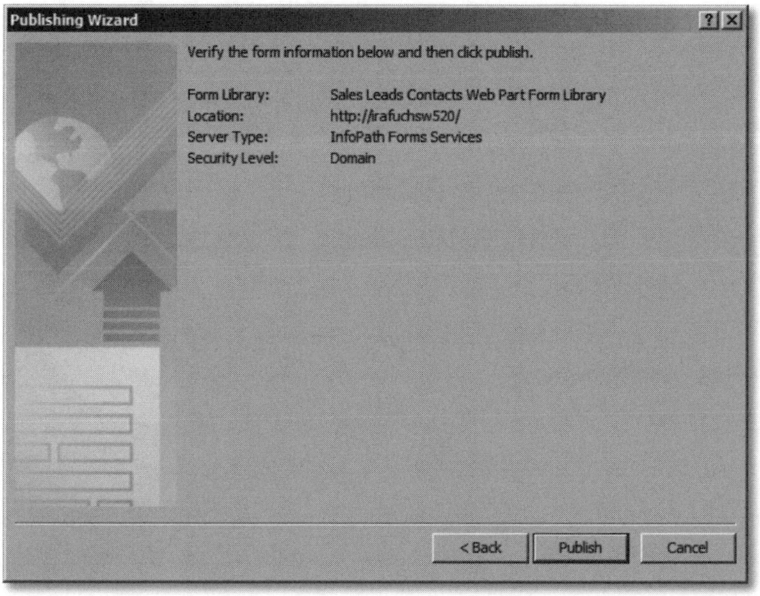

Illustration 51

Clicking the *Publish* button will commence the process of *InfoPath* communicating with the *SharePoint* site specified and creating the specified *SharePoint* artifacts. This process can take a while during which time *InfoPath* will display the status of the process as shown in **Illustration 52** below.

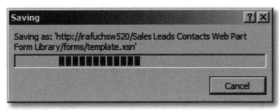

Illustration 52

When the process is complete you can click on the link to go to the Form Library which will look like **Illustration 53** below. Note that by default a link to the Library was created on the Quick Launch pane. You will want to go into the *Library Settings* page and then the *Title, description and navigation settings* page to remove the Quick Launch link.

Illustration 53

So now we are ready to create a page where we will place an *InfoPath form Web Part* and point the Web Part to the *Sales Leads Contacts Web Part* form.

You can create a new page in two ways. You can click on the *New Page* option on the *Site Actions* drop-down menu as shown in **Illustration 54 below left**. You will then be prompted for the name of the page which will be created in the *Pages Library* as shown in **Illustration 54 below right**.

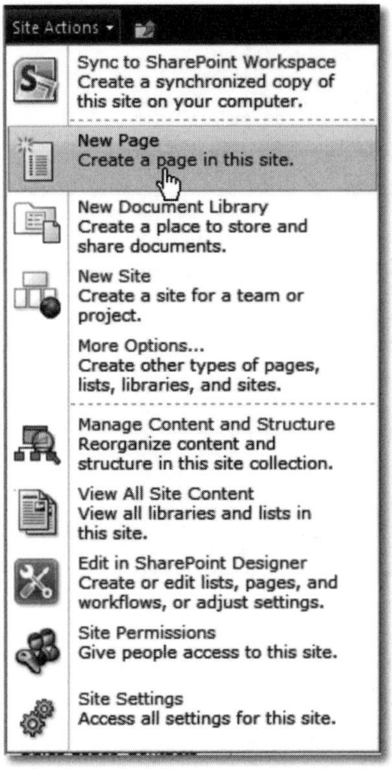

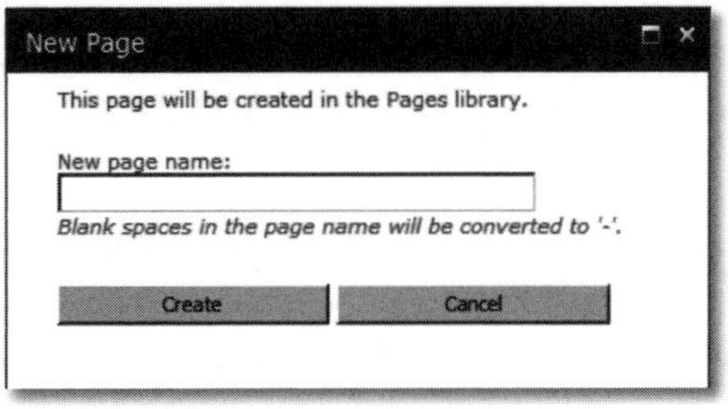

Illustration 54

Alternatively you can click on the *Site Actions More Options* link which will present you with the *Create* dialogue screen as shown in **Illustration 55** below. Click on the *Page* link on the left navigation pane and you will be presented with three page creation options: a standard *Page*, a *Publishing Page*, and a *Web Part Page*. Any one of these page will do but choose *Web Part Page* and click the *Create* button so that we can review the options available for this type of page.

Illustration 55

A new *Web Part Page* configuration screen will display as shown in **Illustration 56** below. Here you provide a name for the page, choose a layout and select the Library where you want to save the page. Clicking on each of the layout options will change the thumbnail view on the left. For this exercise pick *Full Page, Vertical.* Save the page in any convenient Library.

Illustration 56

You will now be brought to the new *Web Part Page.* Click on the *Ribbon Page* tab and then the *Edit Page* button. The *Web Part Page* will display in edit mode as shown in **Illustration 57** below.

Illustration 57

Click the *Add a Web Part* link on the Web Part zone. The options for inserting the numerous *SharePoint* Web Parts will display as shown in **Illustration 58** below. In the *Categories* section select *Forms*. Now select *InfoPath Form Web Part*.

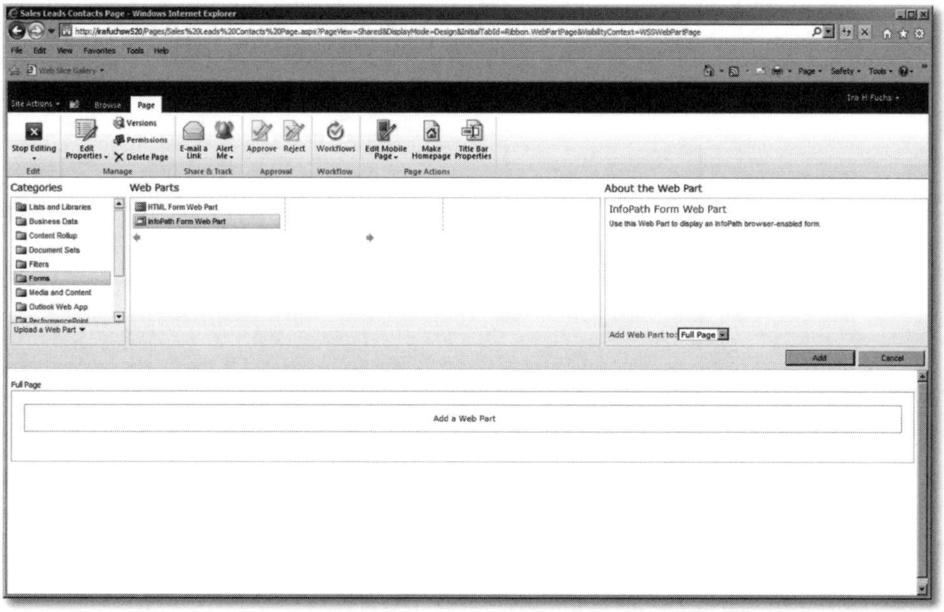

Illustration 58

The *InfoPath Form Web Part* control icon will appear in the *Web Part Zone* as shown in **Illustration 59** below. We now need to point the control to the form and configure the settings for the Web Part. The first time you do this you can click on the *Click here to open the tool pane* link to the right of the control icon. You will always be able to get to the *Web Part configuration* pane by clicking on the *Web Part* drop-down icon on the far right of the page and selecting *Edit Web Part* as shown in **Illustration 59** below.

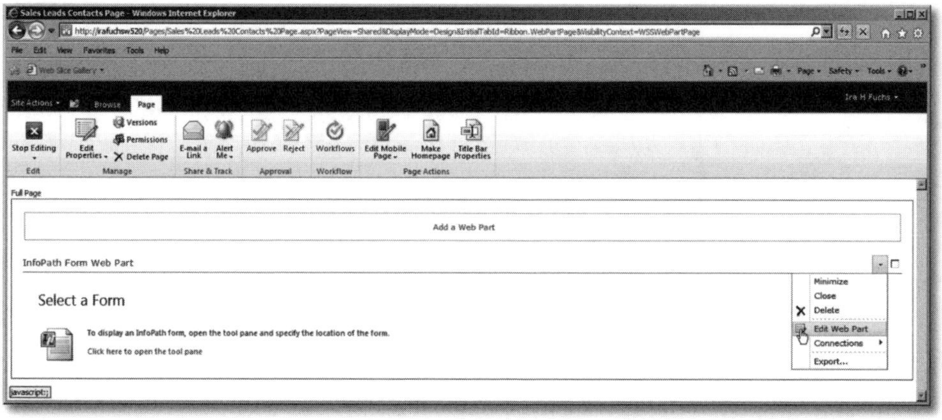

Illustration 59

The *Form Web Part Configuration* pane will display as shown in **Illustration 60** below. From the drop-down *List or Library* selection box select the *Sales Leads Contacts Web Part Form Library*. The *Content Type* will default to Form. Deselect the check box for *Show InfoPath Ribbon or toolbar*. You can use any *InfoPath View* to display in a Form Web Part; because our form only had one View, the default *View1* displays. Expand the *Appearance* section and remove the *Title* text; and from the drop-down selection box for *Chrome Type* select "None". We are now finished configuring the *Form Web Part* so click *OK* to save.

Use this Web Part to fill out an InfoPath form
that has been published to a SharePoint list or
document library.

List or Library:
| Sales Leads Contacts Web Part Form Libra ▾ |

Content Type:
| Form ▾ |

☑ Display a read-only form (lists only)

☐ Show InfoPath Ribbon or toolbar

☐ Send data to connected Web Parts when
page loads

Select the form view to display by default.

Views:
| View 1 (default) ▾ |

Select the action to perform after a form has
been submitted.

Submit Behavior:
| Leave the form open ▾ |

⊟ Appearance

Title
| |

Height
Should the Web Part have a fixed height?
○ Yes | | | Pixels ▾ |
◉ No. Adjust height to fit zone.

Width
Should the Web Part have a fixed width?
○ Yes | | | Pixels ▾ |
◉ No. Adjust width to fit zone.

Chrome State
○ Minimized
◉ Normal

Chrome Type
| None ▾ |

Illustration 60

Voila! There is our *Sales Leads Contact* form embedded on the page displaying the records from the ECT List and looking just like we designed it. Test the filter selection by selecting any country in the *Drop-Down List Box* control. The filtered display results will look like **Illustrations 61 and 62** on the next page.

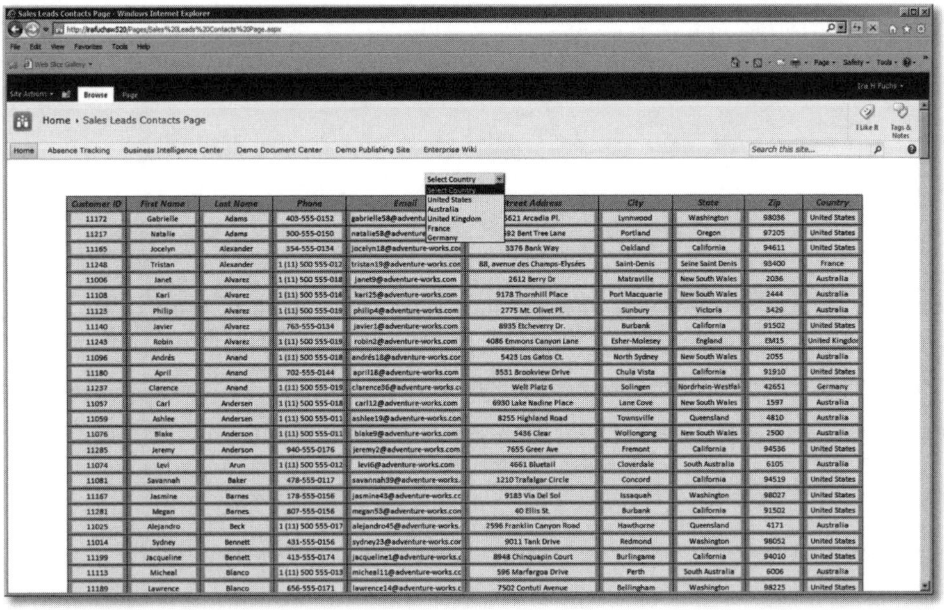

Illustration 61

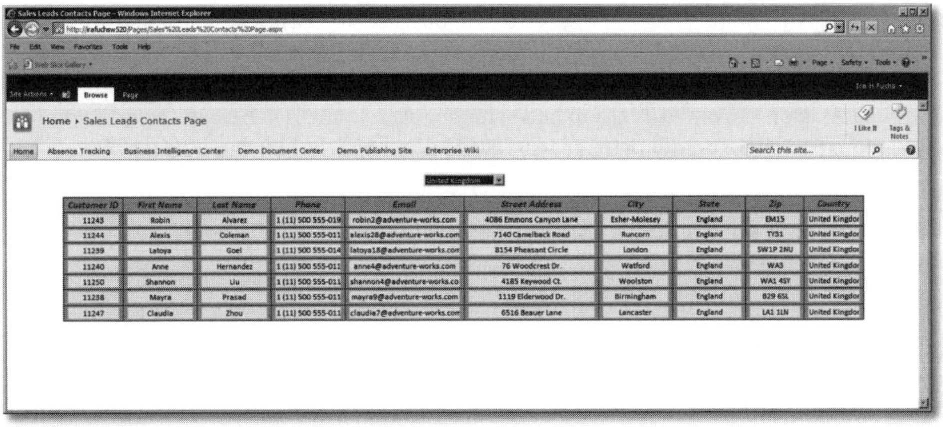

Illustration 62

All good! Now just to drive home the point that any *SharePoint* page, including Lists and Libraries, can host multiple Web Parts go to any List or Library in your site. From the *Site Actions* drop-down menu select *Edit Page*. You will see the editable Web Part structure of the page. From the *Page Tools* section of the *Ribbon* click *Insert*, then click *Web Part*. Select Forms and you will see you can insert an *InfoPath Form Web Part* on the same page that hosts the Web Part for the Library as shown in **Illustration 63** on the next page.

Using this ability to combine multiple *SharePoint* Web Parts on a page, and have them exchange information with each other, you can create sophisticated composite applications readily and easily.

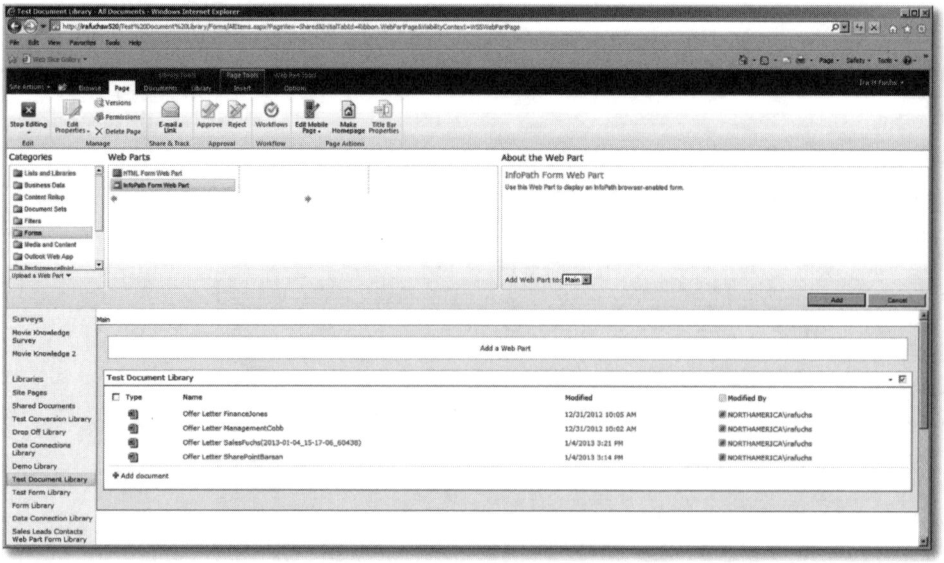

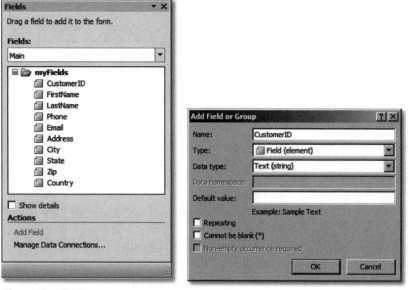

Illustration 63

Creating an InfoPath Web Part Form to Display a Single Record

Now we are going to create an *InfoPath Web Part Form* that will display one record at a time. Start a new blank form. Once again, create a *Data Connection* to the *Sales Leads Outlook Contacts* following the steps described on **pages 109 to 110**. When you are finished creating the *Data Connection* select the *myFields* group of the *Main* data source in the *Fields* pane. Add the fields shown in **Illustration 64 below left** by right clicking on the *myFields* group and selecting *Add*. In the *Add Field or Group* dialogue screen as shown in **Illustration 64 below right**, select *Field* for *Type* and *Text* for the *Data type* for each of the fields.

Illustration 64

In the first form that we created we placed a repeating table control on the design surface that was bound directly to the fields of the *Sales Leads Outlook Contacts List* secondary data source. A List usually contains multiple records and a repeating group (d:*SharePointListItem_RW*) is required to represent the presence of multiple List items in the data source schema. Consequently only an *InfoPath* control with repeating behavior (i.e. Repeating Table, Repeating Section with Controls, or just a Repeating Section) can be used to display the secondary List data source information directly as we did.

In order to display a single record from a *SharePoint* List we need to do so indirectly; or in other words, we need a mechanism to capture the information for a specific record from the secondary data source and then display it. That is the purpose of the fields that we just created in the *Main* data source. We will set the value of these fields to the corresponding values of a specific record in the *Sales Leads Outlook Contacts ECT List* and display that record using controls in the form.

So let's lay out the controls on the InfoPath design surface. Click the *Insert* tab on the *Ribbon* and then select *Custom Table*. The *Insert Table* visual tool will display as shown in **Illustration 65 below left.** Click the *Layout Table* option.

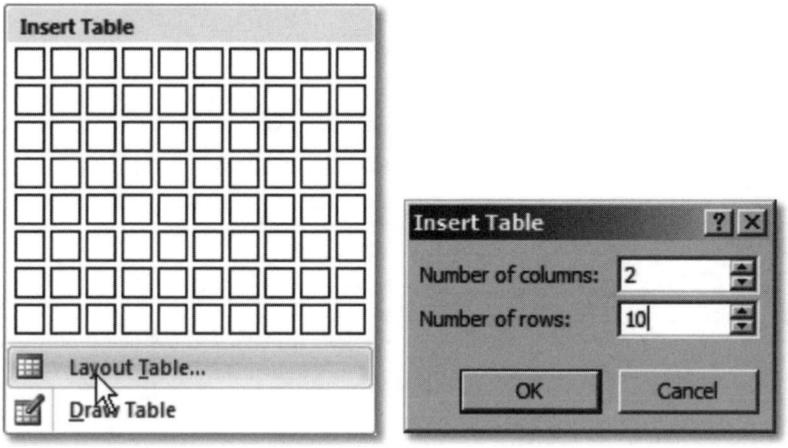

Illustration 65

A dialogue screen will open where you can indicate the number of rows and columns as shown in **Illustration 65 above right**. Enter 2 columns and 10 rows. The table shown in **Illustration 66** below will display. Place your cursor in row 1, column 1 and enter "Last Name".

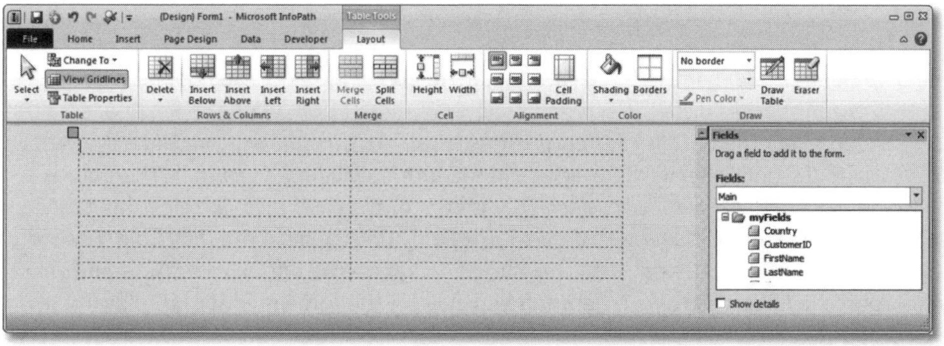

Illustration 66

Now place your cursor in row 1, column 2. Go to the *Fields* pane, select the *LastName* field, right click and then select the *Drop Down List Box Control* as shown in **Illustration 67** below.

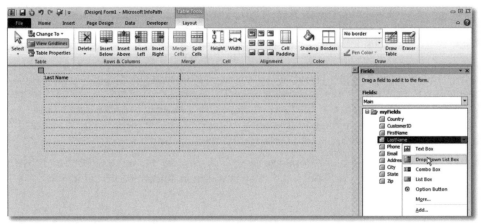

Illustration 67

The *Drop Down List Box* control will automatically be placed in row 1, column 2. Now add all the field labels to the rows in column 1 and repeat the step above to place *Text Box* controls in each of the corresponding rows of column 2. Your completed form will look like **Illustration 68** below.

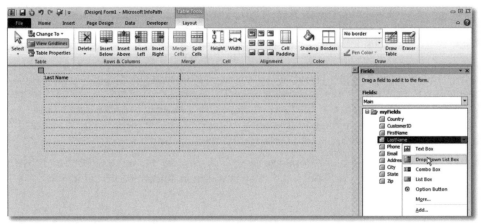

Illustration 68

Now select the *Drop-Down List Box* control for Last Name. Right click and select *Drop Down List Box Properties* to display the properties dialogue screen as shown in **Illustration 69** on the next page. In the List box choices section select the *Get choices from an external data source* radio button. Since the *Sales Leads Outlook Contacts* is the only external data source in the form it will default to that. The Entries selection will also default to the *d:SharePointListItem_RW* group for the *dataFields*. To select the *Last-Name* value to be written to the *LastName Main* data source field and display in the *Drop Down List Box* control use the selection button to the right. As you can see you have the option to capture one value for the *Main* data source field but display a different field value for the same record to display in the *Drop Down List Box* control.

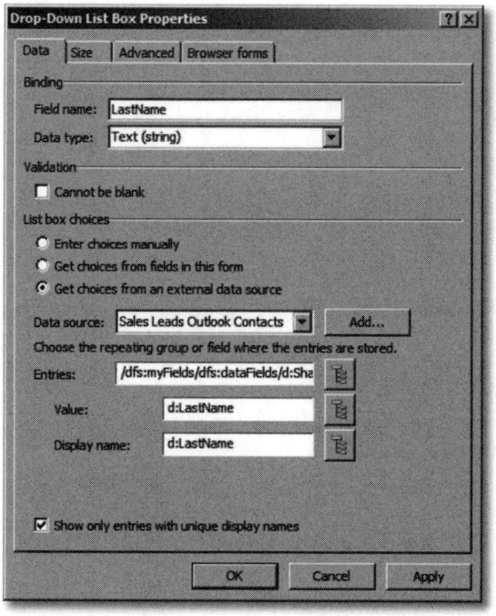

Illustration 69

Click the *OK* button. Now let's preview the form and see what the behavior for this control is. When you click on the *Drop Down List Box* control in the preview it should display all the last names from the *Sales Leads Outlook Contacts* as shown in **Illustration 70** below. Note that the last names are automatically sorted in alphabetical order.

Illustration 70

Close the preview. Now what we want to do is load the corresponding field values for the record found when a Last Name is selected in the *Drop Down List Box* control. Select the *LastName* field in the *Fields* pane, right click and select *Rules*, or from the *Control Tools Properties Ribbon* tab select *Add Rule* as shown in **Illustration 71** below. The *Rules* pane will display. Click the *New* button and select *Action*. Name the rule "Lookup by Last Name".

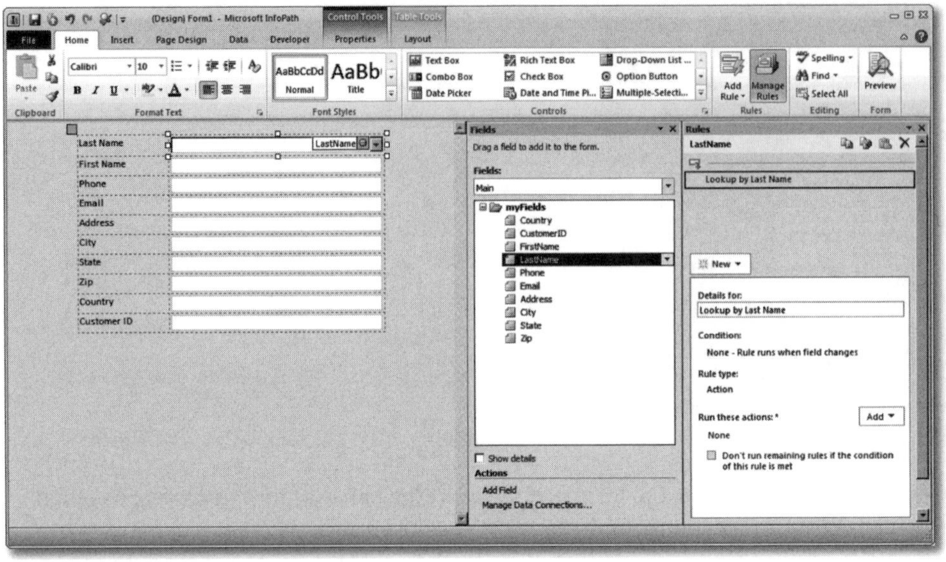

Illustration 71

Now click the *Add* button to the right of *Run these actions* and select *Set a field's value*. The *Rule Details* dialogue screen will display as shown in **Illustration 72** below.

Illustration 72

Click on the *Field* selection button and from the *Main* data source select the *FirstName* field. Now click on the *formula* button for the *Value* field. The *formula dialogue* screen will display as shown in **Illustration 73 below left**. Click the *Insert Field or Group* button to display the *Select a Field or Group* dialogue screen as shown in **Illustration 73 below right**. Select the *Sales Leads Outlook Contacts (Secondary)* data source and select *FirstName*. Do **not** click the *OK* button.

Illustration 73

Click the *Filter Data* button. The *Filter Data* dialogue screen will display as shown in **Illustration 74** below.

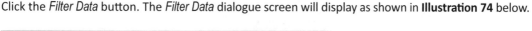

Illustration 74

Click the *Add* button. The *Specify Filter Conditions* dialogue screen will display as shown in **Illustration 75** below. By default the *FirstName* value from the *Sales Leads Outlook Contacts (Secondary)* data source will display in the first selection box. Click on the drop down selection icon and choose LastName, or choose *Select a field or group* to select *LastName* from the dialogue screen. Leave *is equal to* for the operator. In the second selection box choose *Select a field or group* and from the *Main* data source select *LastName*. Your completed *Specify Filter Conditions* dialogue screen will look like **Illustration 75** below.

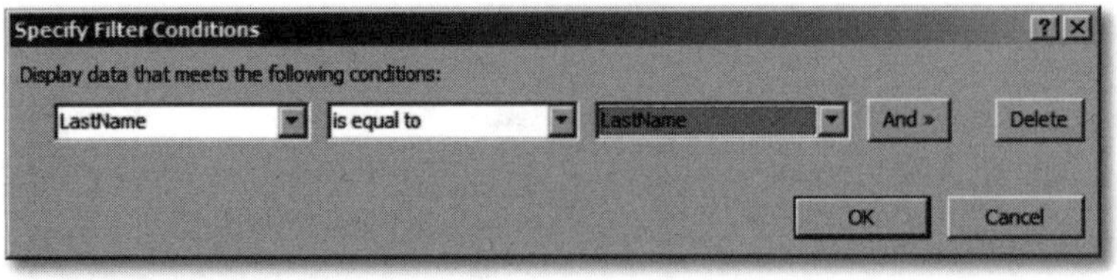

Specify Filter Conditions

Display data that meets the following conditions:

| LastName | is equal to | LastName | And » | Delete |

OK   Cancel

Illustration 75

Click *OK* back through all the dialogue screens. The completed *Rule Details* dialogue screen will look like **Illustration 76** below.

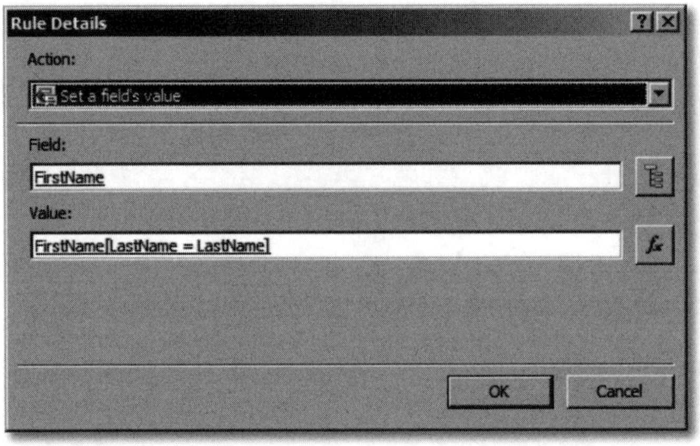

Rule Details

Action:

Set a field's value

Field:

FirstName

Value:

FirstName[LastName = LastName]

OK   Cancel

Illustration 76

Let's preview the form and see what this rule action does. From the *Last Name Drop Down List Box* control select any name and the corresponding First Name will display in its Text Box. Select any other Last Name and the First Name will change. We bound the rule to the *LastName* field because we wanted to use the default condition, to run when the value of the field changes, to trigger the rule action. The rule action copies the *FirstName* value from the *Sales Leads Outlook Contacts (Secondary)* data source to the *FirstName* field in the *Main* data source, for that record where the *LastName* value in the secondary data source matches the *LastName* value in the *Main* data source. The filter functions as a look-up.

Return to the *Rule* pane, select the *LastName* field to display the *Lookup by Last Name* rule and click the *Add* button to create another *Set a field's value* action. Repeat the same steps above for the Phone field and preview it to make sure you did it correctly. Then add a *Set a field's value* action for each of the remaining fields in the *Main* data source. When you are done your *Lookup by Last Name rule* should look like **Illustration 77** on the next page.

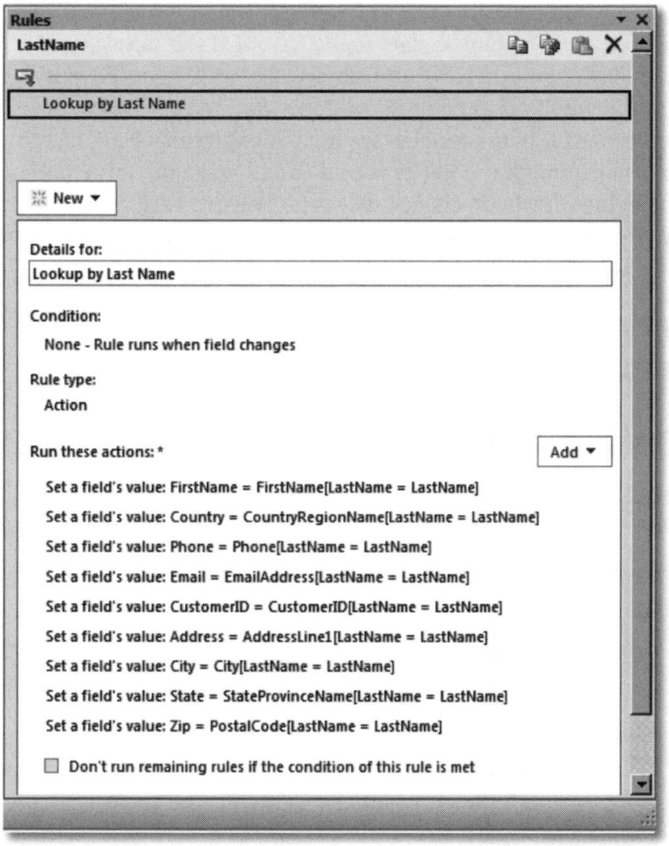

Illustration 77

The order of the *Set a field's value* actions does not affect the execution. The preview of the completed rule set will look like **Illustration 78** below.

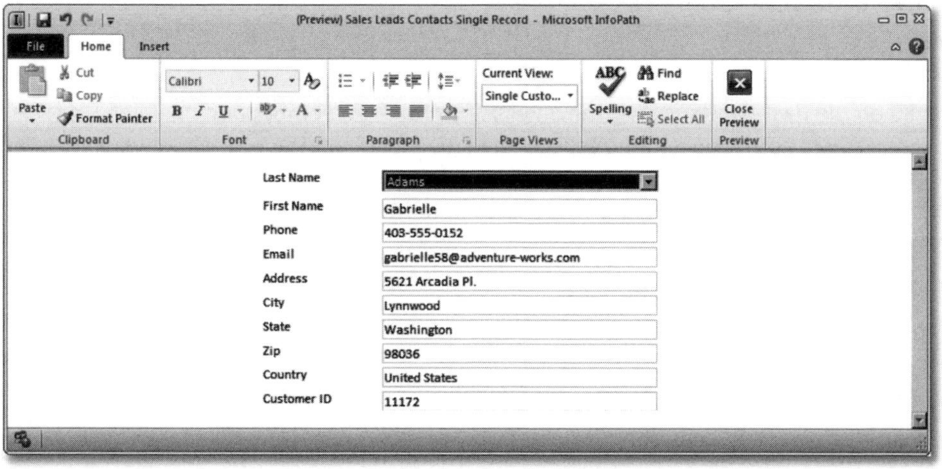

Illustration 78

We're done creating rule logic for this form. This is all the *InfoPath* rule logic that you need to display a single record from a secondary data source. At this point you are ready to repeat the same steps described on **pages 127 through 137** to publish the form to a Form Library; add an *InfoPath Form Web Part* to any *SharePoint* page and configure the Web Part to point to this form. Before you publish this form to *SharePoint* you might want to experiment with the various layout and design capabilities just to become more familiar with them. For example, one of the things you can do to make the form more user friendly is to display a Default Value in the *Drop Down List Box* that says "Select a Last Name". With this information the user knows exactly what to do. To set this value right-click on the *LastName* field and select *Properties*. Enter the text in the *Default Value* box as shown in **Illustration 79** below.

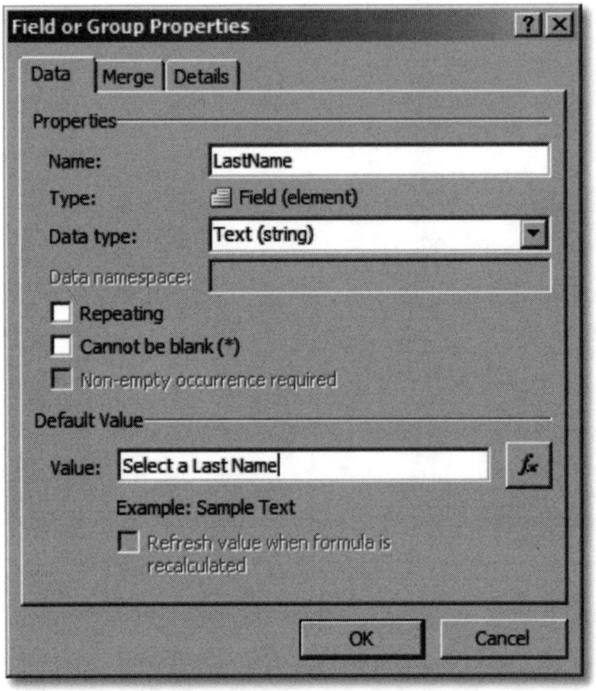

Illustration 79

In **Illustration 80** on the next page showing the *InfoPath Form Web Part* embedded on a page, an additional row was added at the top and the cells merged for a heading. The row labels were indented and made larger and bold, and background colors were added to the heading row and the field rows. The design choices made, including using a table to begin with, were completely arbitrary. You can design this form any way that you want.

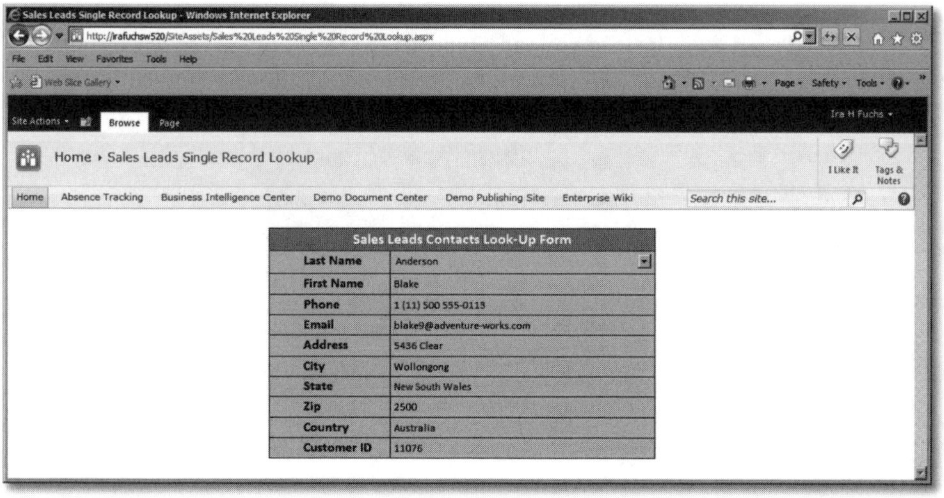

Illustration 80

Note – While we have disabled the ability to save information by not displaying the *Ribbon* menu for the *InfoPath Form Web Part*, you can also accomplish the same result by setting the View to be *Read-Only* from the *View Properties* dialogue screen as shown in **Illustration 81** below.

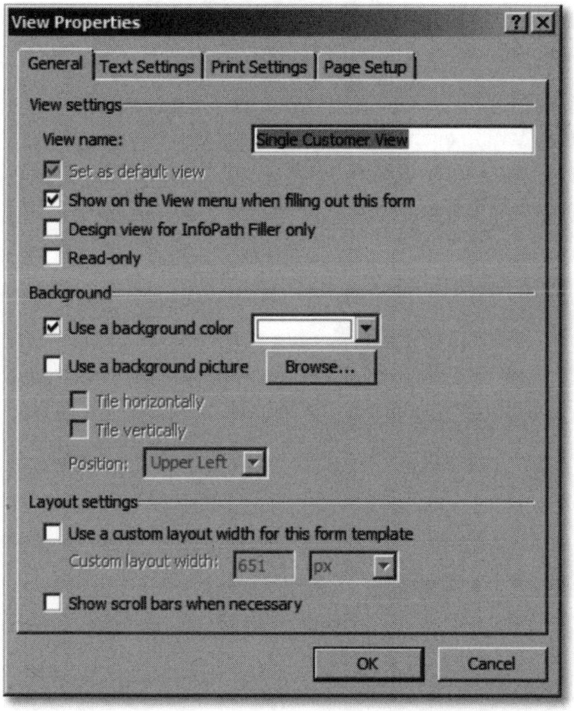

Illustration 81

Each time you make changes to the form and re-publish it, you do not have to go through the multiple steps of the *Publishing Wizard*. Instead you can simply go to the *File* tab which will display the Info page for the form. From there you can click on the *Quick Publish* button to re-publish the form in one step as shown in **Illustration 82** below.

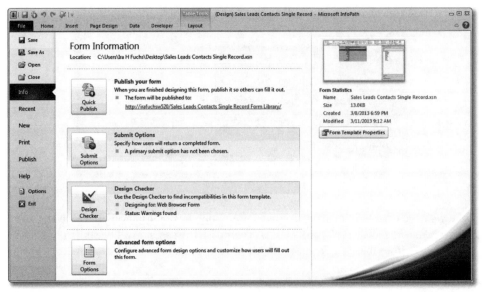

Illustration 82

You can always go through the full *Publishing Wizard* process at any time. One of the reasons you would want to do so is to promote field values that can be exchanged with other Web Parts on a page. Alternatively to do the same thing without going through the full publishing process you can click on the *Form Options* button as shown in **Illustration 82** above and select *Property Promotion*. In this dialogue screen, as shown in **Illustration 83** below you can specify the field-parameter values that will be available for exchange. You can then re-publish using the *Quick Publish* option.

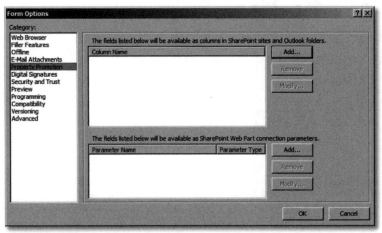

Illustration 83

Creating a Form Web Part to Track Events Created on the SharePoint Scheduling and Resource Reservation Calendar

Obviously, we are paying a good deal of attention to what can be accomplished with *InfoPath Form Web Parts*. It really is highly complementary to *SharePoint* and it doesn't take much effort to take advantage of it, as this exercise has demonstrated. So let's go on to another use case where an *InfoPath Form Web Part* provides a lot of value for a little bit of work.

Suppose you need to keep track of where people are and what they do at any given time, whether for a current, future or historical date. We demonstrated that the extended *SharePoint* scheduling and resource reservation calendar is a great facility for capturing the scheduled events of multiple people in an organization. What it doesn't do effectively though is provide a quick snapshot of all the scheduled events for those people on any given day; a tracking function that is required in many situations. Yes, you guessed it; InfoPath can handily address this requirement. So let's go to work and get it done.

Create a new blank form and add a data connection to the *SharePoint* scheduling and resource reservation calendar that we created earlier (in our example it is named Demo Calendar, but you may have used a different name). When you get to the field selection page of the *Data Connection Wizard*, select the fields shown in **Illustration 84** below.

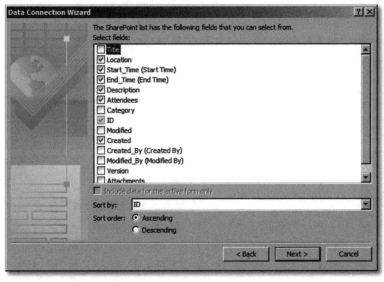

Illustration 84

When you get to the last page of the *Data Connection Wizard* where you give the data connection a name, make sure the check box for *Automatically retrieve data when form is opened* is selected as shown in **Illustration 85** at right.

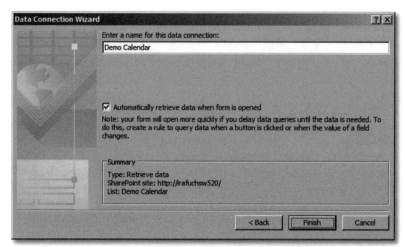

Illustration 85

As we did earlier go to the *Fields* pane, choose the *Calendar secondary data source* and select the *d:SharePointListItem_RW* group in the *dataFields* group, as shown in **Illustration 86** at right.

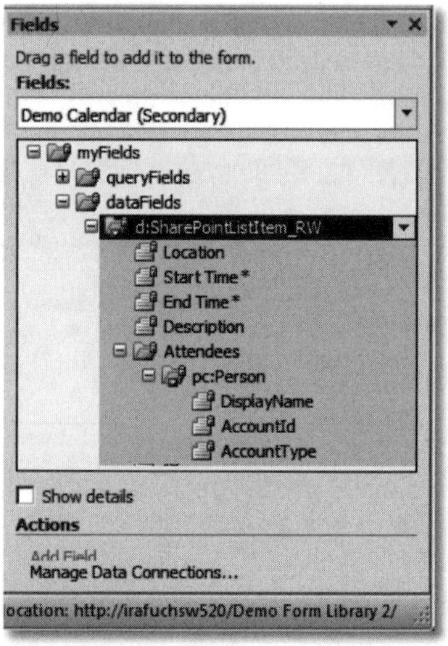

Drag the group to the design surface and select *Repeating Table*. The *Repeating Table* will look like **Illustration 87** below.

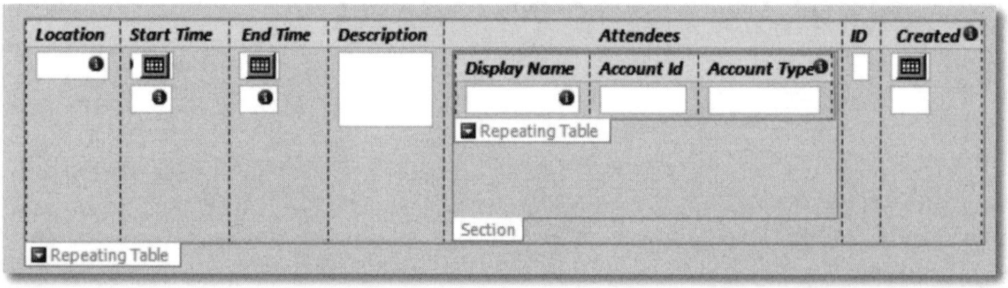

Illustration 86

Illustration 87

Now you need to rearrange the table so that it looks like **Illustration 88** below.

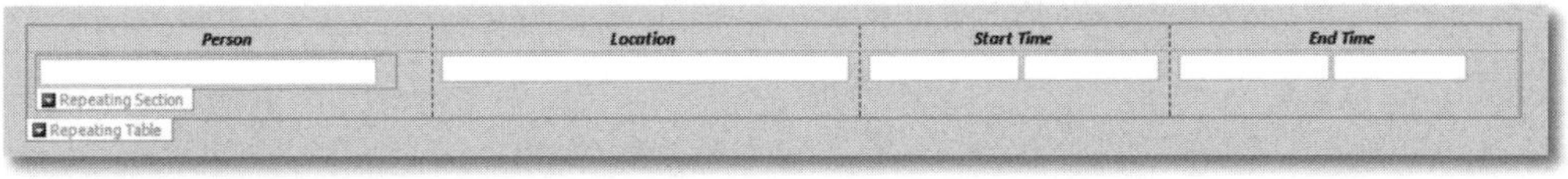

Illustration 88

You will do this by deleting the *Description, Account ID, Account Type, ID* and *Created* columns. Then you will cut and paste the remaining columns and rearrange their width. Finally you will change the Column name "Attendees" to "Person". If you make mistakes you can always add or remove columns and add or remove the Text Box controls for any field.

Note that the Start Time and End Time fields use two *Text Box* controls; the first is for the date and the second is for the time. Make sure that both of these *Text Box* controls are present as shown in **Illustration 88** above.

Now select the *myFields* group in the *Main* data source and add a field (element) as shown in **Illustration 89 below left**. Name it Date and select *Date (date)* for its *Data type*. For the *Default Value* field, click on the *formula* button and insert the *InfoPath today function*. The completed *Field or Group Properties* dialogue screen will look like **Illustration 89 below right**.

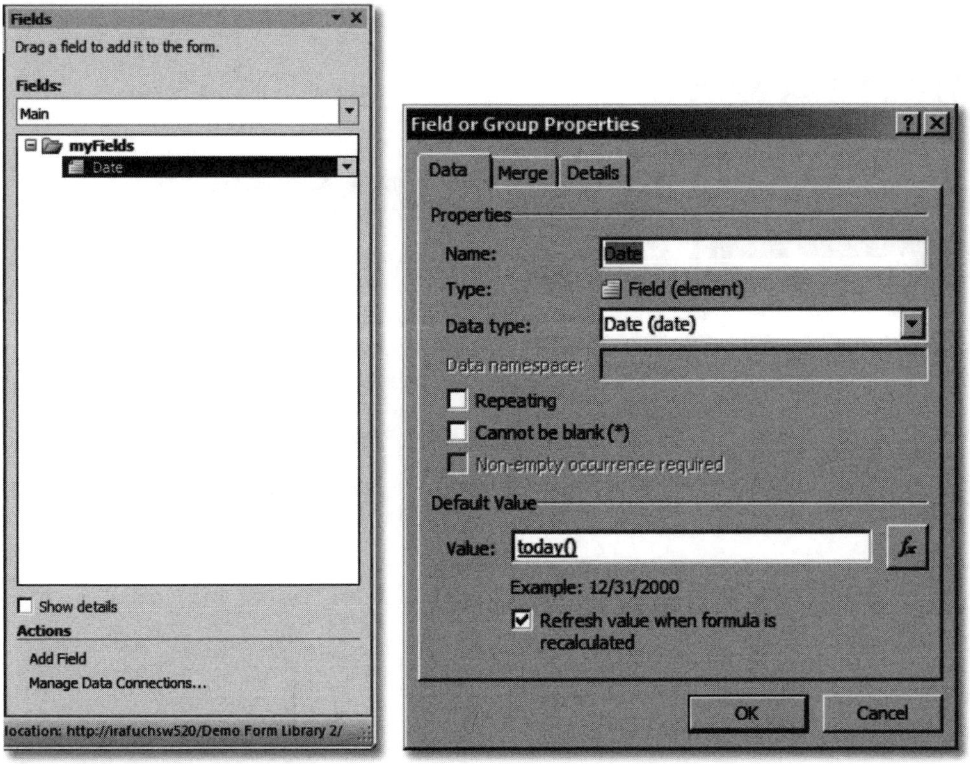

Illustration 89

Now drag the *Date* field to the design surface above the repeating table. A date picker control will be placed as shown in **Illustration 90** below.

Illustration 90

With the Date field still selected right click *Rules* to open the *Rules* pane. Click *New* and choose *Action*. Name the rule "Date Selection". Click the *Add* button and select *Set a fields value* to display the *Rule Details* dialogue screen. Click the *Field Selection* button and select the *Demo Calendar* secondary data source (or whatever name you gave it) and choose the *Start Time* field in the *q:SharePointListItem_RW* query group as shown in **Illustration 91 below left**. For the *Value field* select *Date* from the *Main* data source. Your completed *Rule Details* dialogue screen will look like **Illustration 91 below right**.

Recall that what we are doing with this rule action is filtering the calendar List to return only those records whose Start Time date values are the same as the Date value, which by default is the current date.

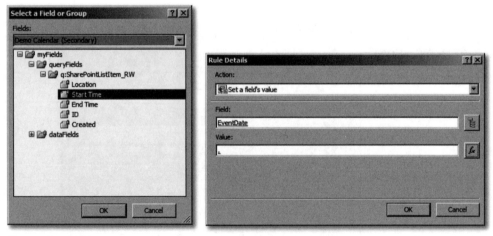

Illustration 91

Now add a *Query* action, which will default to the Demo Calendar. Your completed *Date Selection* rule will look like **Illustration 92** below.

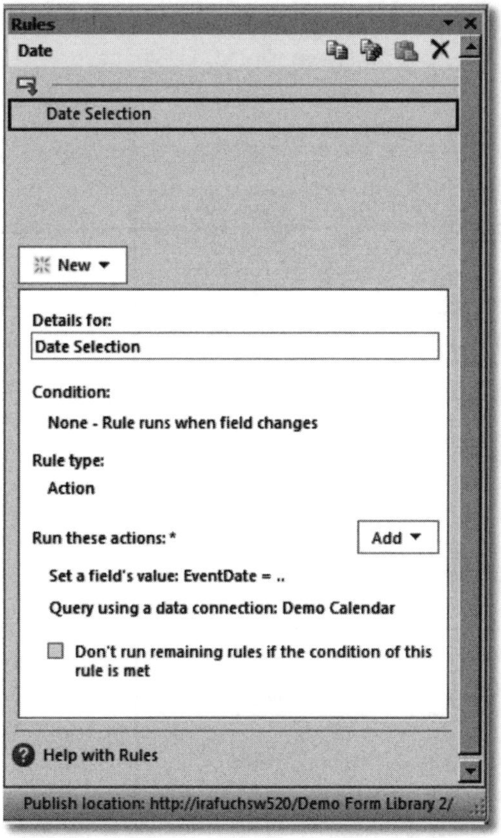

Illustration 92

Before you preview the form, return to the Demo Calendar and create some Schedule and Reservation events for the current date as well as some other dates, so that the preview will return data and we can test the date picker functionality. Make sure you enter values for the Location field.

Your preview will look like **Illustration 93** below. If there are no events for the current date you will only see the field titles. Click on the *date picker* control and select a date that you know contains events. Note that if multiple people are scheduled for the same event they will be displayed in the first column but the Location, Start Time and End Time will only display for the first person displayed. Also note that the *Text Box* field controls, as well as the *Repeating Section* control for Person have their own borders so the preview looks unnecessarily busy.

Date	3/12/2013					

Person	Location	Start Time		End Time	
NORTHAMERICA\irafuchs Jean Citarella Adam Fuchs	New York City	3/12/2013	1:00:00 PM	3/12/2013	2:00:00 PM
NORTHAMERICA\irafuchs Jean Citarella	New York City	3/12/2013	3:00:00 PM	3/12/2013	4:00:00 PM
Ira H Fuchs Jean Citarella	Metro Park NY	3/12/2013	10:00:00 AM	3/12/2013	2:00:00 PM
Adam Fuchs	Chicago	3/12/2013	12:00:00 PM	3/12/2013	1:00:00 PM

Illustration 93

If you remove the borders for each individual control and add *Outline* and *Inside* borders for the *Repeating Table* your preview will look like **Illustration 94** below which is cleaner.

Date	3/12/2013					

Person	Location	Start Time		End Time	
NORTHAMERICA\irafuchs Jean Citarella Adam Fuchs	New York City	3/12/2013	1:00:00 PM	3/12/2013	2:00:00 PM
NORTHAMERICA\irafuchs Jean Citarella	New York City	3/12/2013	3:00:00 PM	3/12/2013	4:00:00 PM
Ira H Fuchs Jean Citarella	Metro Park NY	3/12/2013	10:00:00 AM	3/12/2013	2:00:00 PM
Adam Fuchs	Chicago	3/12/2013	12:00:00 PM	3/12/2013	1:00:00 PM

Illustration 94

Let's do one more thing to demonstrate the versatility of using an *InfoPath Web Part Form* to display schedule events. Suppose we want to highlight any event that takes place in New York City. We can accomplish this using a *Formatting rule*. Click on the *Location* field or control and right click to select *Rules*. Click on the *New* button and choose *Formatting*. Change the rule name to "New York City".

Now click on the *Condition*. The first selection box will default to "Location" and the operator selection box will default to "is equal to". In the third selection box choose *Type text* and enter "New York City" as shown in Illustration 95 below.

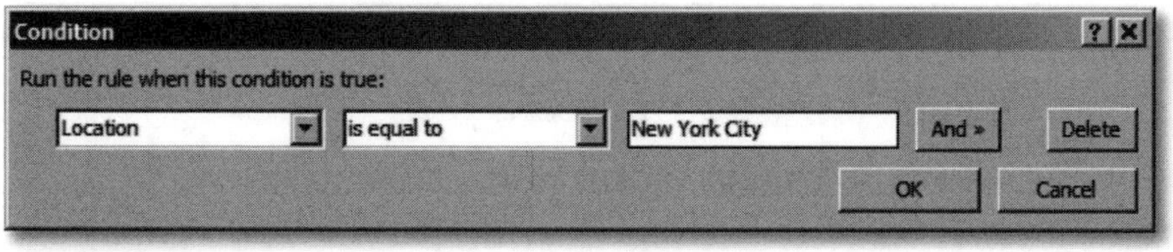

Illustration 95

For the formatting click on the *Fill icon* and select a fill background as shown in **Illustration 96** below.

Illustration 96

Go back to the Demo Calendar and create one or more Schedule and Reservation events for a date and set New York City for the location. Now preview the form; it should look like **Illustration 97** below with any instance of New York City as the location highlighted with a fill background.

| | Date | 3/12/2013 | | | | | |

Person	Location	Start Time		End Time	
NORTHAMERICA\irafuchs Jean Citarella Adam Fuchs	New York City	3/12/2013	1:00:00 PM	3/12/2013	2:00:00 PM
NORTHAMERICA\irafuchs Jean Citarella	New York City	3/12/2013	3:00:00 PM	3/12/2013	4:00:00 PM
Ira H Fuchs Jean Citarella	Metro Park NY	3/12/2013	10:00:00 AM	3/12/2013	2:00:00 PM
Adam Fuchs	Chicago	3/12/2013	12:00:00 PM	3/12/2013	1:00:00 PM
Jean Citarella	Chicago	3/12/2013	7:00:00 PM	3/12/2013	8:00:00 PM

Illustration 97

And now you have a simple and elegant way to track people's schedules and locations for any arbitrary date. Now repeat the steps itemized earlier to publish this form to a *SharePoint form Library* and then point to the form using an *InfoPath Form Web Part* control on any page.

As you can see from these three examples, *InfoPath* is a great tool for creating forms that allow the end user to select and display information on a *SharePoint page*. There are many additional capabilities and benefits that *InfoPath* forms bring to *SharePoint* that you can further investigate.

Creating Dynamic Catalogs that Use Managed Metadata to Filter and Search for Catalog Items and Other Really Useful List Functions

Catalogs are used to compile, organize and present structured and unstructured information for many different use cases and requirements. The most common type of catalog is the presentation of product offerings organized by category. Each catalog item typically contains a picture of the item, a detailed description of it, its model number, SKU, specifications, price, etc. Another type of catalog is the presentation of information about a team of people. This could be a sports team or a group of consultants within a specific discipline. In either case the team catalog would contain pictures, relevant textual and structured information such as date of birth, a curriculum vitae synopsis, etc. Yet another type of catalog is a general purpose bulletin board where upcoming events, items for sale, or real estate offered for rent or purchase are posted.

Whatever your catalog requirement or use case may be, you can generate flexible, dynamic catalogs with *SharePoint* easily and readily, as shown in **Illustration 1** below. In addition *SharePoint* provides the tools to automate the process of adding and deleting catalog items, and impose design standards so that the catalog has a consistent look and feel; all of which we will demonstrate in this chapter, and more!

Illustration 1

A catalog can easily contain hundreds or thousands of items so you will also want to implement a mechanism to filter and display only those items that are relevant to, or of interest to a viewer. To accomplish this we will implement a *Term Store* using *SharePoint's Managed Metadata* capabilities.

A Term Store is a hierarchical grouping of terms organized by logical classification. For example a *Term Set* for Geography would have a first level term hierarchy for the regions North America, South America, Europe and APAC. Each region would contain another hierarchical level for the names of the respective countries or states in each region. Once you create a Term Store you can then use the terms to define the column metadata for Content Types, List items and Library documents.

Managed Metadata facilitates the consistent classification and use of information in an organization which in turn helps facilities like a Search engine to return more precise results. In addition, you can turn on *Metadata Navigation and Filtering* on any *SharePoint* List or Library to filter and display items using *Managed Metadata Terms*, which can be seen in **Illustration 1** above. So the first thing we will do now is create a *Managed Metadata Term Store.*

A *Term Store* can be set up for an entire *SharePoint* farm through *SharePoint Central Administration* or for individual Site Collections. Assuming you have the permissions to do so, go to the *Site Settings* page for a Site Collection and select *Term store management* under *Site Administration*. The *Term Store Management Tool* page will display. If you are already using the *Managed Metadata Term Store*, then you will see existing *Term Sets* as shown in **Illustration 2** below. If not you will see a single root group node named "Site Collection – your Site collection's name". Right-clicking on this node will display a drop-down selection List with the option to create a *New Term Set*. Before you can do this you will need to assign one or more *Group Managers* and optionally *Contributors* to the top most group node.

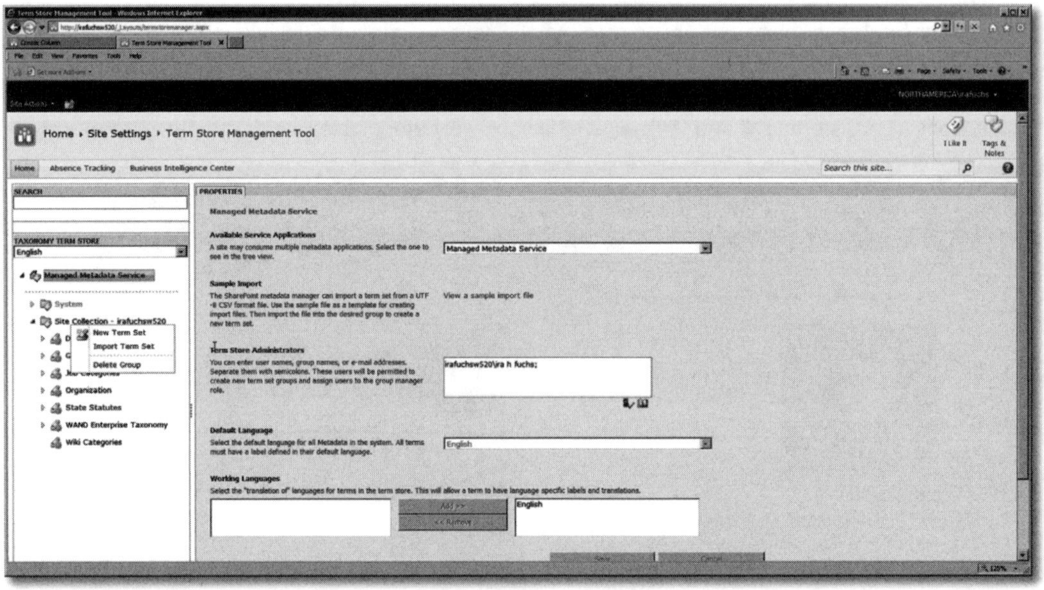

Illustration 2

Upon creating a new *Term Set* it will display in the hierarchy tree without a name. Click on it and give it a name, such as "Geography". Each *Term Set* has its own *Setting* page where you can specify specific attributes as shown in **Illustration 3** on the next page.

Right click on the *Term Set* in the hierarchy tree to display its drop-down selection options. Choose *Create Term*. Add the Terms "APAC", "EMEA", "North America" and "South America".

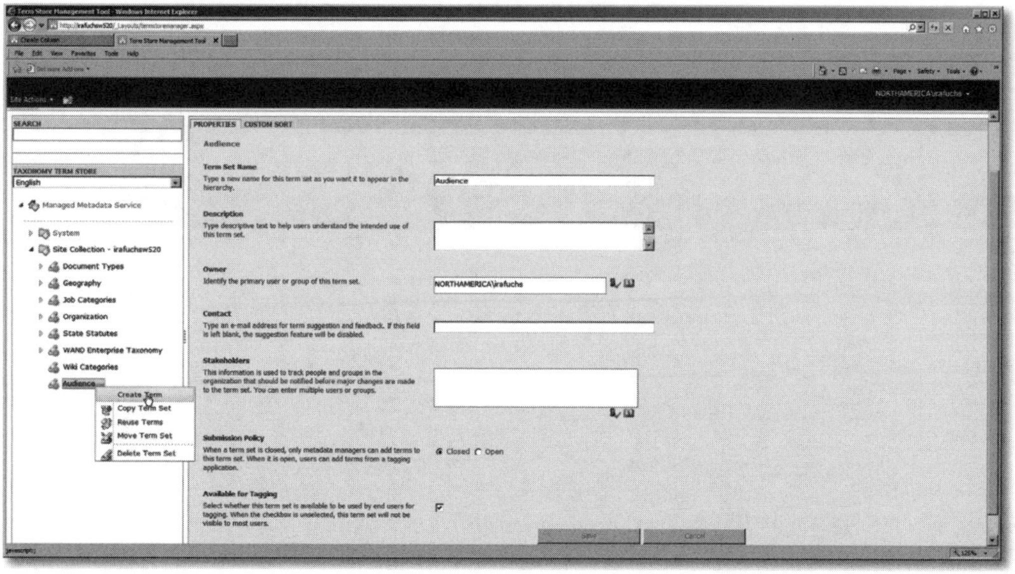

Illustration 3

Each term will also have a *Settings* page as shown in **Illustration 4** below.

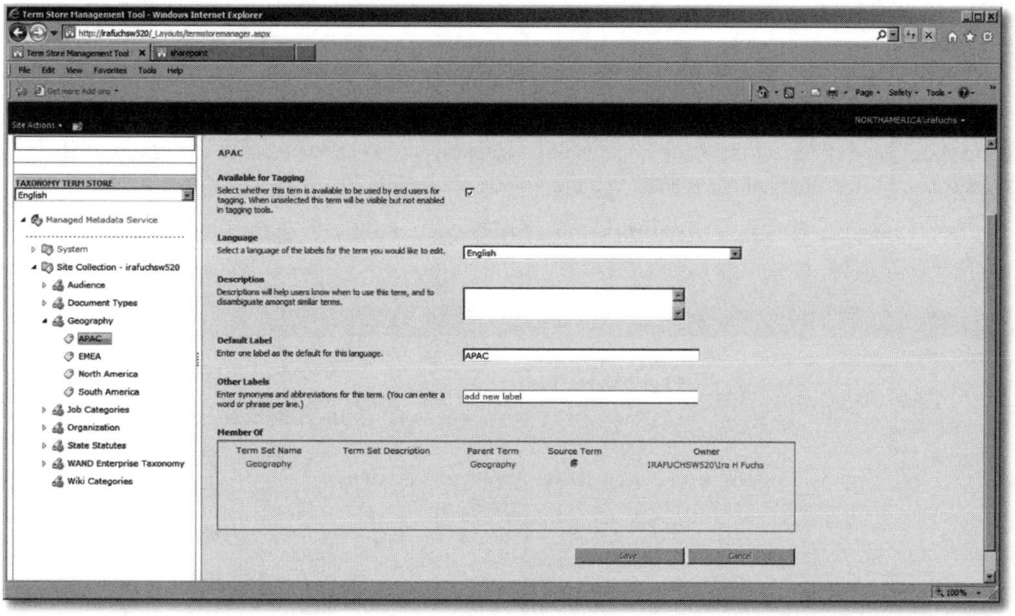

Illustration 4

Return to the top *Term Group* to add the *Term Set* for "Audience".

In the *Audience Term Set* add the following *Terms*: "Marketing", "Sales", "Support" and "Technical". Your *Term Store* will look something like **Illustration 5** below.

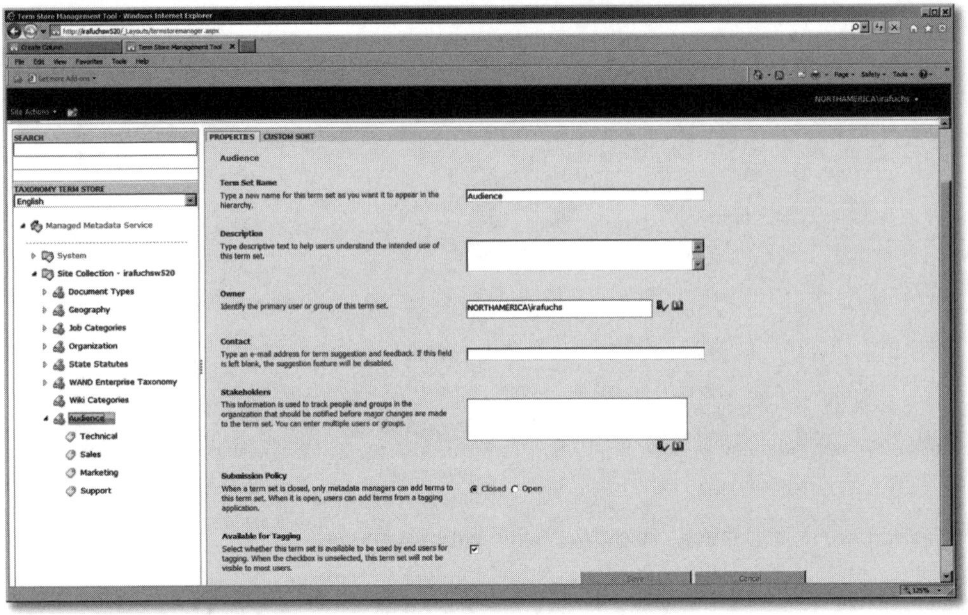

Illustration 5

You are now done creating a small but perfectly usable *Term Store* that is accessible from any Site in the *Site Collection*. Now go to the Site where you will be creating the *Catalog List* and click on *Site Actions* and then *Site Settings*. On the *Site Settings* page click on *Manage Site Features* found under the *Site Actions* section. The *Site Features Activation* page will display as shown in **Illustration 6** below.

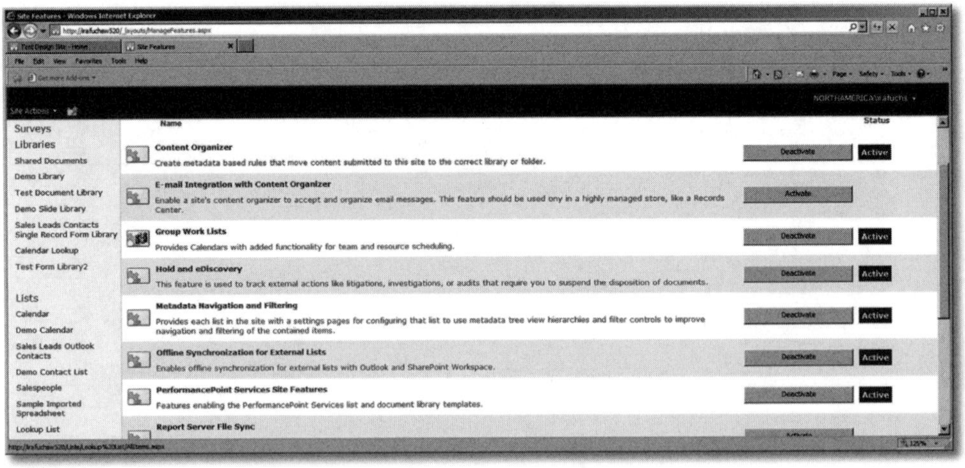

Illustration 6

Scroll down to the *Metadata Navigation and Filtering Feature* and click the *Activate* button. This feature will now be available for use in any List or Library on the Site.

From *SharePoint Designer* or the *SharePoint* user interface create a new custom List and name it Catalog. Go to its' *Settings* page and select *Versioning*. On the *Versioning Settings* page click the *Yes* radio button for *Require content approval for submitted items?* as shown in **Illustration 7** below.

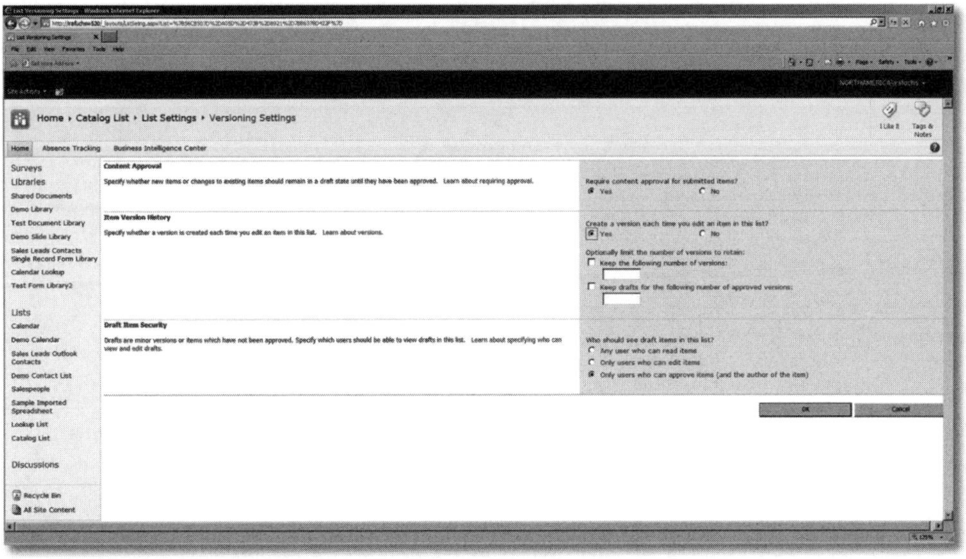

Illustration 7

Now create a new column named "Topic". Select the *radio* button for *Multiple Lines of Text* and enter "2" for the *Number of lines for editing* and select the *radio* button for *Enhanced rich text (Rich text with pictures, tables and hyperlinks)* as shown in **Illustration 8** below.

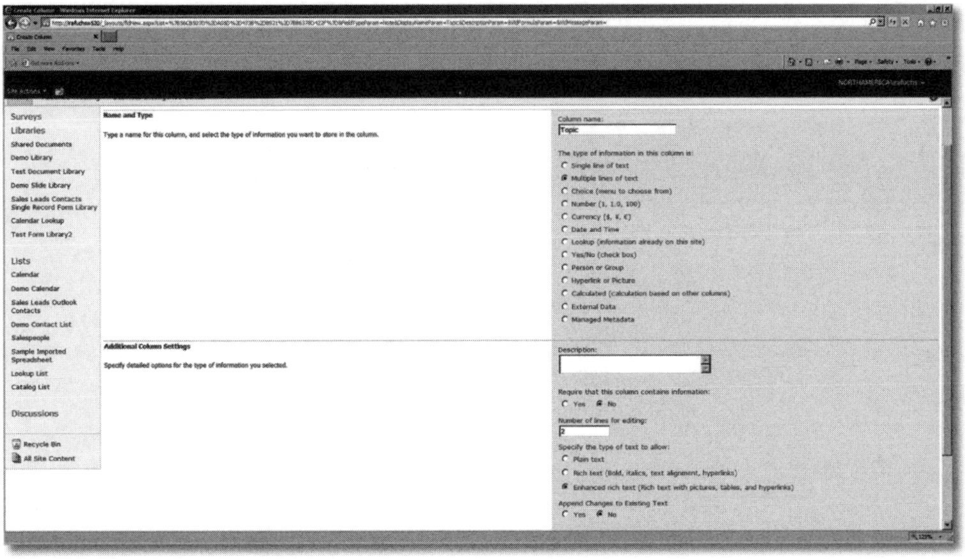

Illustration 8

Next, create another column with the name "Description". Again, select *Multiple Lines of Text* and enter "8" for the *Number of lines for editing* and select the *radio* button for *Enhanced rich text (Rich text with pictures, tables and hyperlinks)* as shown in **Illustration 9** below.

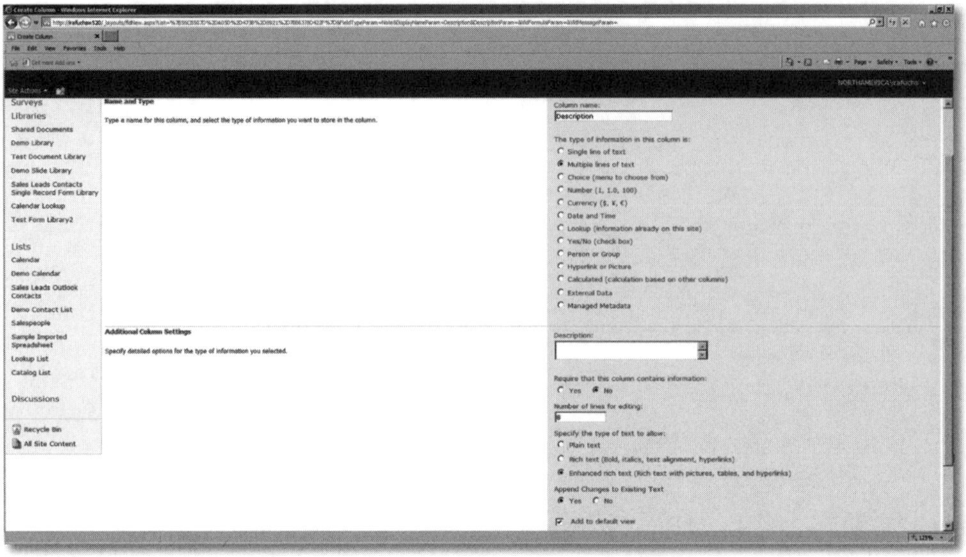

Illustration 9

Add one last column with *Multiple Lines of Text* named "Images" and enter "8" for the *Number of lines for editing*. Again, select the *radio* button for *Enhanced rich text (Rich text with pictures, tables and hyperlinks)*.

Now we will add Managed Metadata columns. Create a new column named "Geography". Select the *radio* button for *Managed Metadata*. The *Managed Metadata* selection box will display on the *Column Settings* page as shown in **Illustration 10** below. Select the *Geography Term Set* and click *OK*.

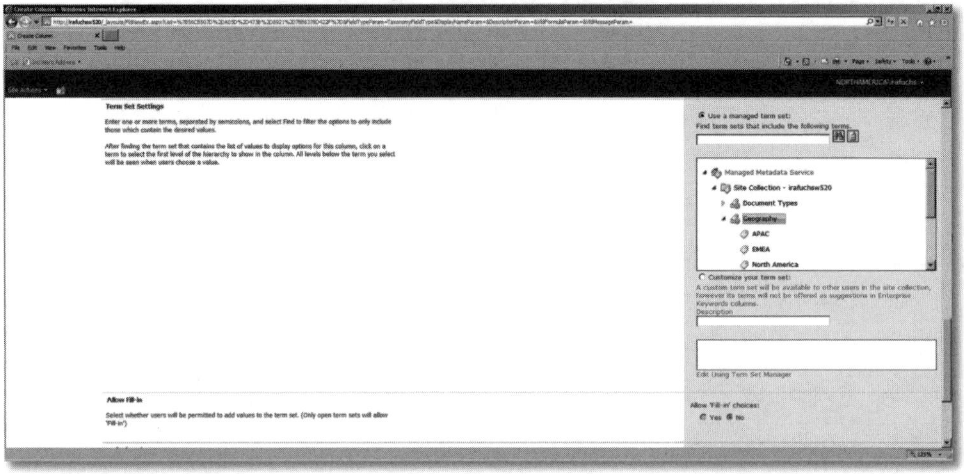

Illustration 10

Now create Managed Metadata columns for "Audience". When you are done your *List Settings* page should look like **Illustration 11** below.

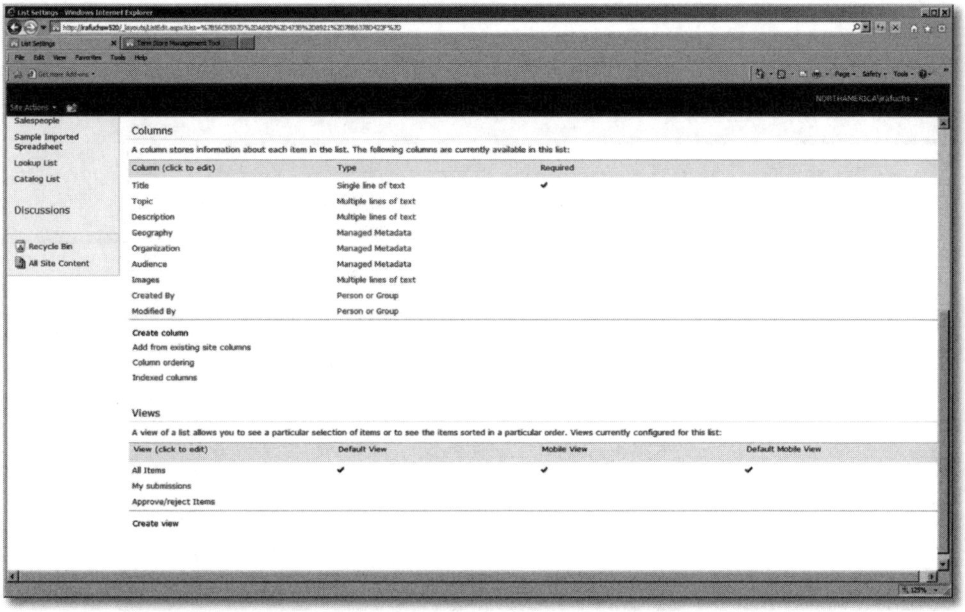

Illustration 11

The next thing we will do is create a new View that will display the List information in the catalog format shown in **Illustration 1** on **page 157**. From the *List tools Ribbon* menu select *Create View*. The *Create View* page will display as shown in **Illustration 12** below. Select the *Standard View* option.

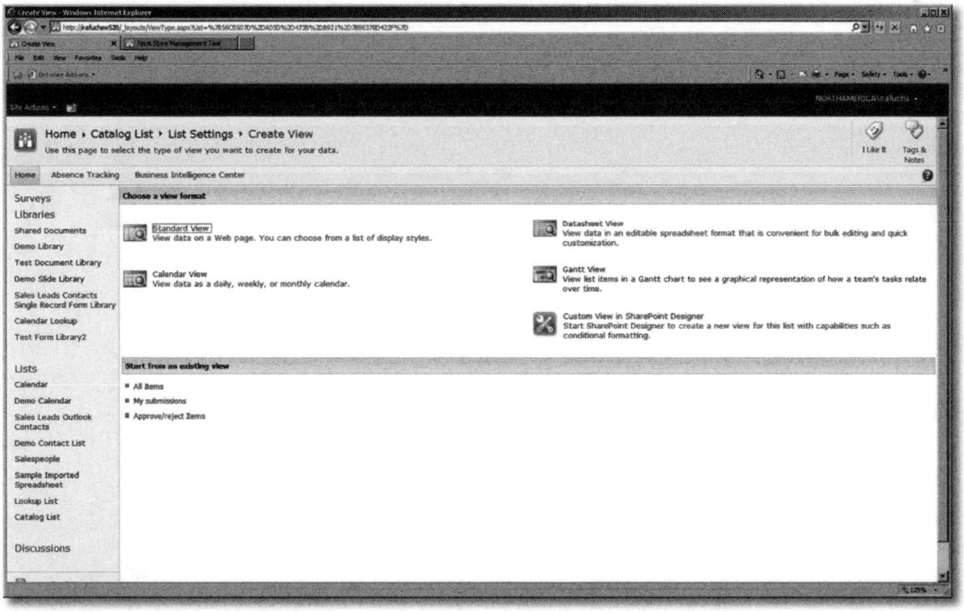

Illustration 12

Name the View "Catalog View". In the *Columns* section click the *Display* button for the *Topic, Description, Images, Geography, Audience and Title (linked to Item with edit menu)* columns and set their positions in this order as well. Your *View Settings* page will look like **Illustration 13** below.

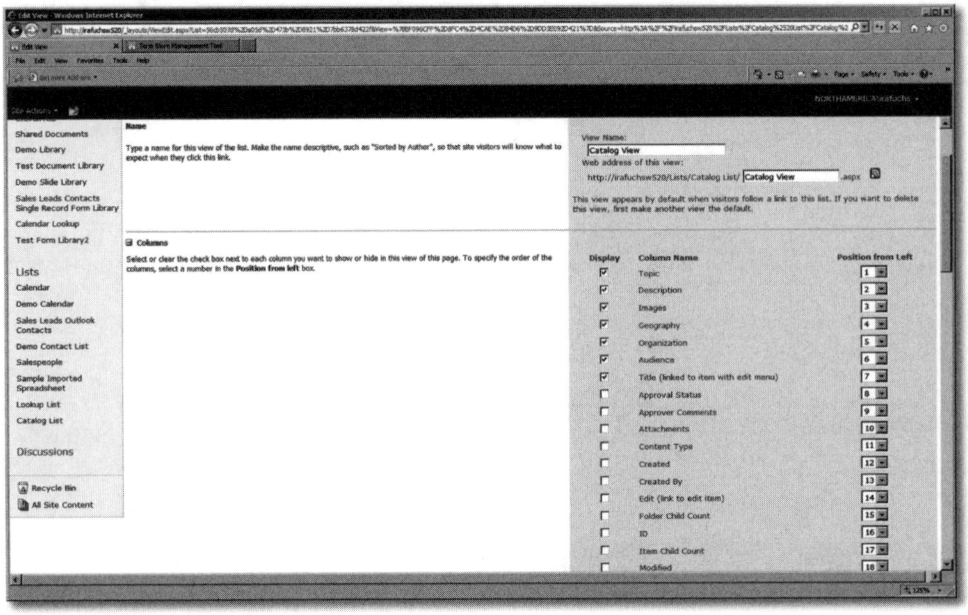

Illustration 13

Scroll down the *View Settings* page to the *Style* section and expand it to display the *View Style* option box. Select the *Boxed, no labels* option as shown in **Illustration 14** below.

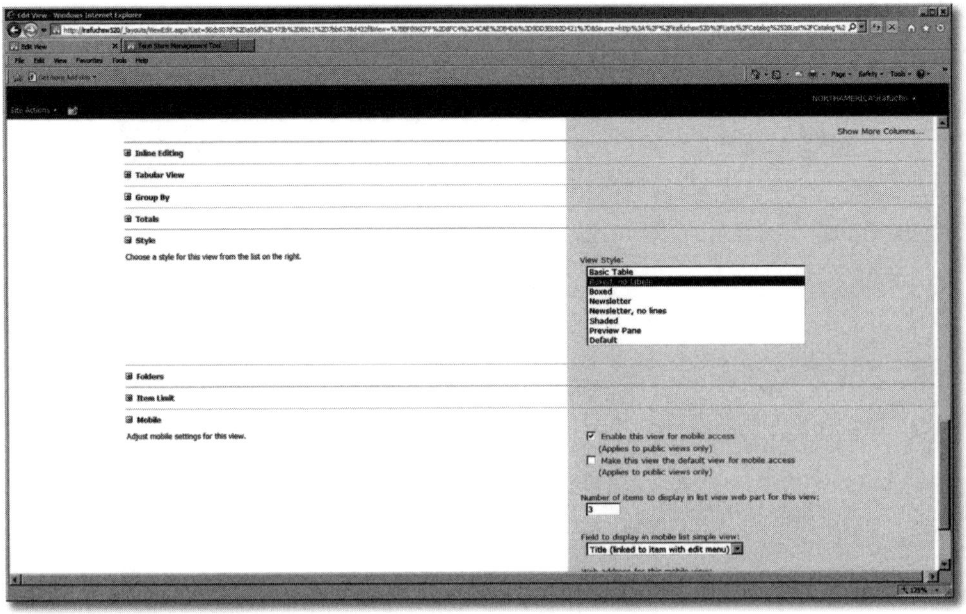

Illustration 14

Click *OK*. That's it! We are done creating and designing the *Catalog* List. Now it's time to create some catalog items in it. Select the *Items* tab on the *Ribbon* menu and click *New Item*. The *New Item* dialogue screen will display as shown in **Illustration 15** below.

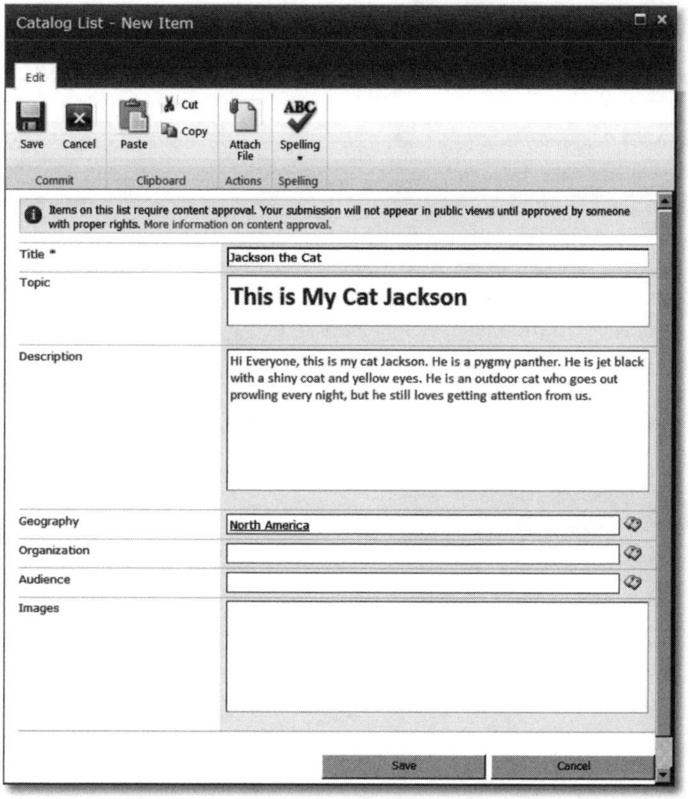

Illustration 15

When you place your cursor in the *Topic, Description* or *Images* fields the *Editing Tools Ribbon* menu will display as shown in **Illustration 16** below. The *Format Text* menu will display by default.

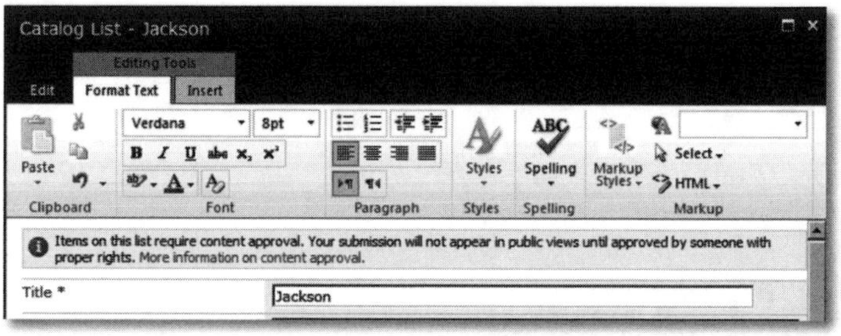

Illustration 16

Clicking the *Insert* tab will display the Insert menu option as shown in **Illustration 17** below.

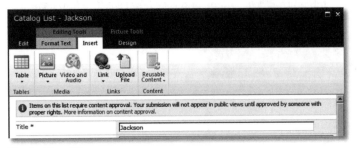

Illustration 17

Enter text into the fields for *Title, Topic* and *Description*. Because these are Rich Text fields you can format the text anyway that you like. Now click on the *Managed Metadata* selection icon on the right side of the *Geography* field as shown in **Illustration 15** on the previous page. The *Geography Term Set* selection box will display as shown in **Illustration 18** below. You can expand the hierarchy and click on a selection. With a selection highlighted click the *Select* button to choose it and then click the *OK* button.

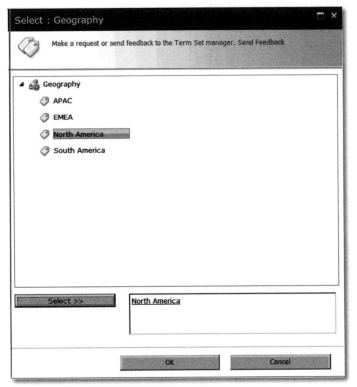

Illustration 18

Repeat this for the *Audience Managed Metadata* field. When you are finished your *New Item* dialogue screen will look like **Illustration 19** below. Place your cursor in the *Images* field and select the *Insert* tab from the *Ribbon* menu. Click the *Picture* button and from the drop-down selection options select *From Computer*.

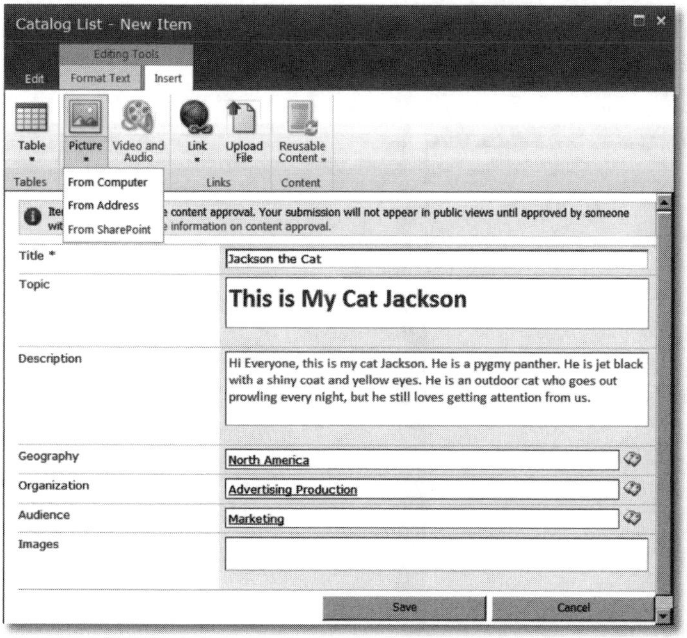

Illustration 19

The *Choose File to Upload* dialogue screen will display as shown in **Illustration 20** below and you can select an image from your computer. If you set the *filetype* dropdown selection option to *Pictures* it is easier to find images on your computer.

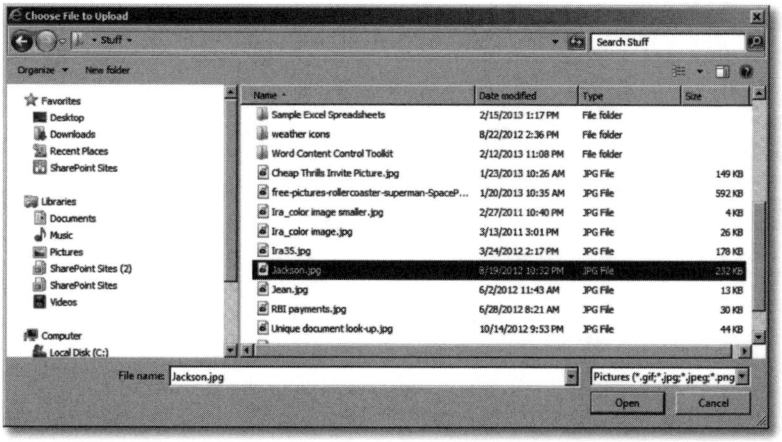

Illustration 20

After you have selected a picture from your computer you must select the *SharePoint* Library where the image will be uploaded and stored. The default Library is *Site Assets* but you can choose any Library that you wish, as shown in **Illustration 21** below.

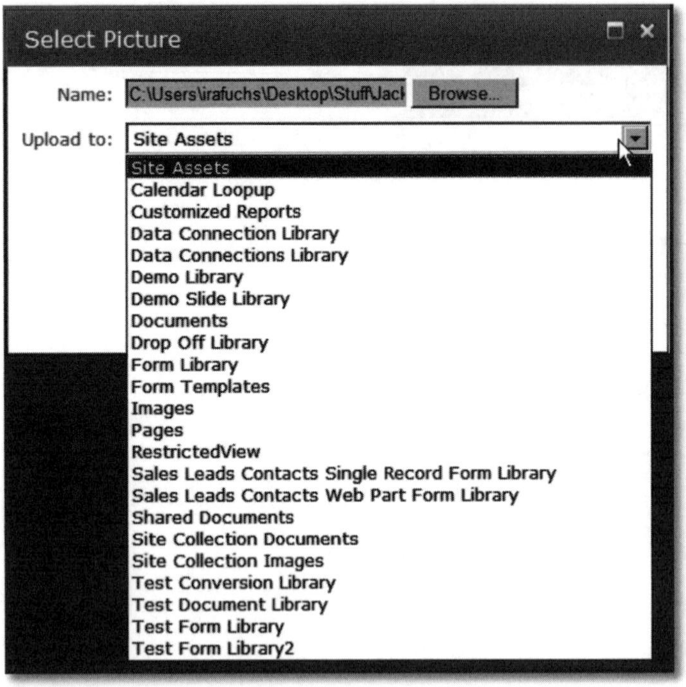

Illustration 21

You will then be prompted to save the picture to the Library as shown in **Illustration 22** below.

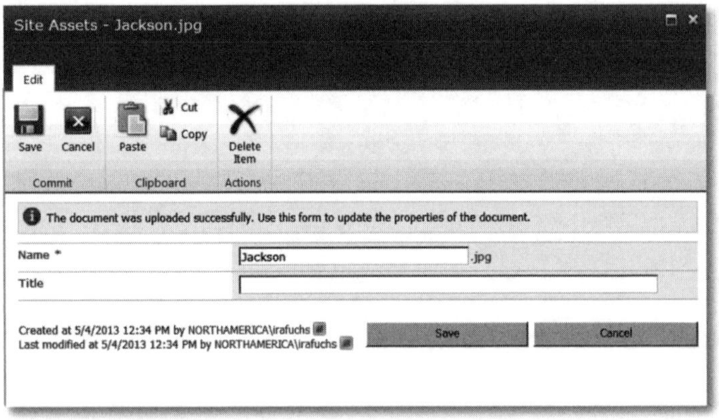

Illustration 22

The picture will display in the *Rich Text Box* control and the *Picture Tools Design* menu will be available in the *Ribbon* as shown in **Illustration 23** on the next page. You can simply grab the edges of the image and enlarge or reduce its size while maintaining its aspect ratio.

Illustration 23

Click *Save* and voila, you now have your first catalog item as shown in **Illustration 24** below. Note the *SharePoint* column headers at the top of the page which are not functional in this View. We will remove these shortly.

Illustration 24

Create some additional items and experiment with the *Rich Text* settings. The "box" for each List item will be added to the page in a left to right and down sequence as shown in **Illustration 25** below. If you want to restructure the order of the fields you can do this simply by returning to the *Edit View* page for the *Catalog View* — click the *List Ribbon* tab and then the *Modify View* button. Now change the display order of the columns.

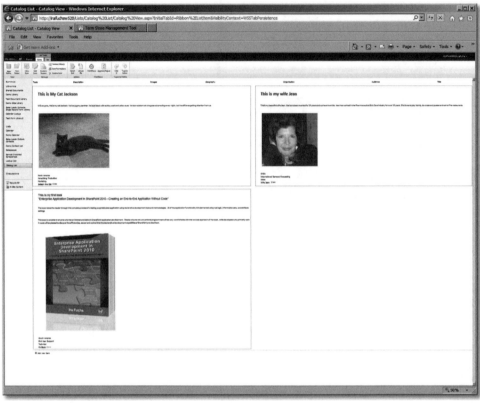

Illustration 25

Adding the Metadata Navigation Tools to the List

The reason why we created *Managed Metadata Term Sets* for Geography and Audience is to use their values to filter or search the Catalog List. In this step we will configure and add the *Metadata navigation tools* so that they display on the *Quick Launch* pane for the Catalog List. Click on the *List* tab of the *Ribbon* menu and then click on *List Settings*. From the *List Settings* page click on the *Metadata Navigation Settings* link under *General Settings*. The *Metadata Navigation Settings* dialogue screen will display as shown in **Illustration 26** on the next page.

In the *Configure Navigation Hierarchies* section select the *Geography* and *Audience Term Sets* from the *Available Hierarchy Fields* box and add them to the *Selected Hierarchy Fields* box. Repeat this in the *Configure Key Filters Section*. Your *Metadata Navigation Settings* page will look like **Illustration 26** below.

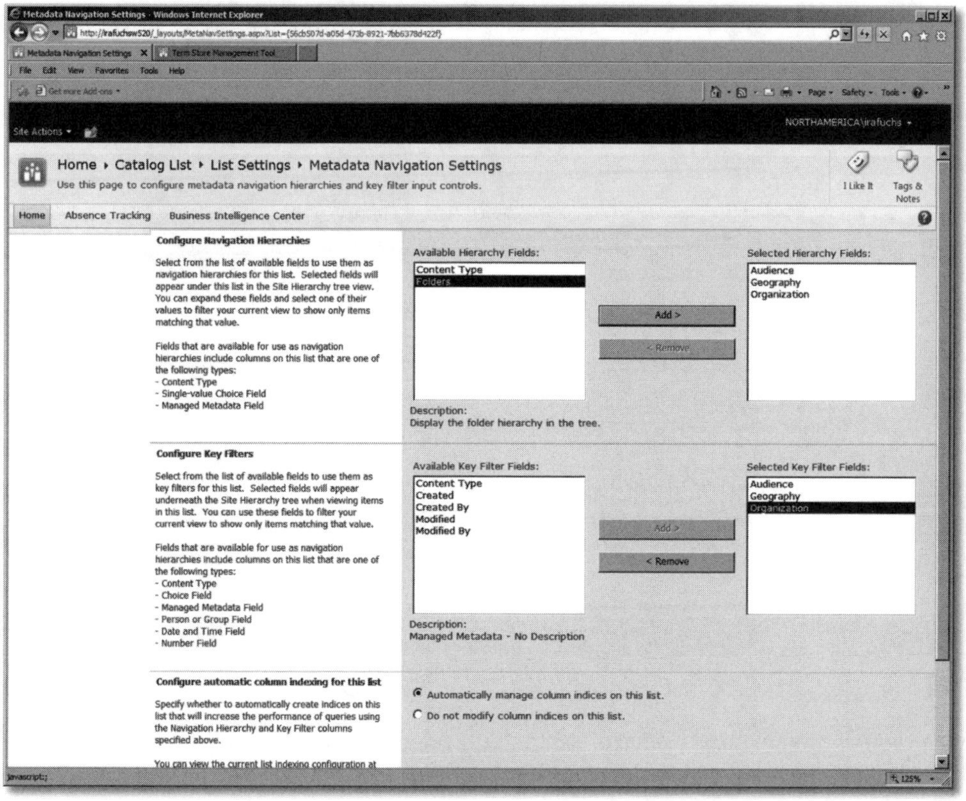

Illustration 26

Click the *OK* button when you are done. The *Terms Sets* and a *Key Filters Selection Tool* using the *Term Sets* are now displayed on the Quick Launch pane as shown in **Illustration 27** on the next page. Experiment by selecting different term values to see how the Catalog items display based upon the values selected.

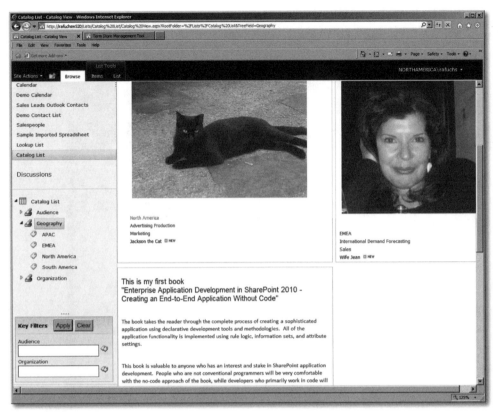

Illustration 27

Note that when you use the *Term Set Hierarchy* you can only select one term for each *Term Set*. When you use the *Key Filters* you can select multiple terms in each *Term Set* as shown in **Illustration 28** below. This provides a more granular level of selection.

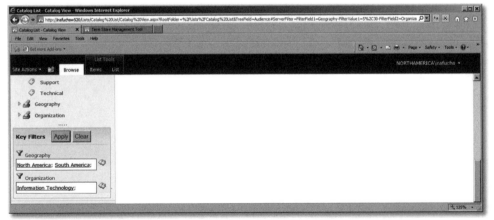

Illustration 28

We are done creating a Catalog List and making it easy to filter and select items using metadata navigation capabilities. Now we will further enhance the Catalog List using additional *SharePoint* capabilities.

Turning on Ratings for the Catalog List

The Ratings setting is available on any List or Library and it simply displays a List column with the image of five stars as shown in **Illustration 29** below. A user can hover their cursor over any number of the stars and then click to rate the item visually. A User Profile Service Timer Job captures the ratings picked by all users and averages them out. The average rating is displayed as a sequence of blue stars. When a user hovers over the blue stars their individual rating will be identified.

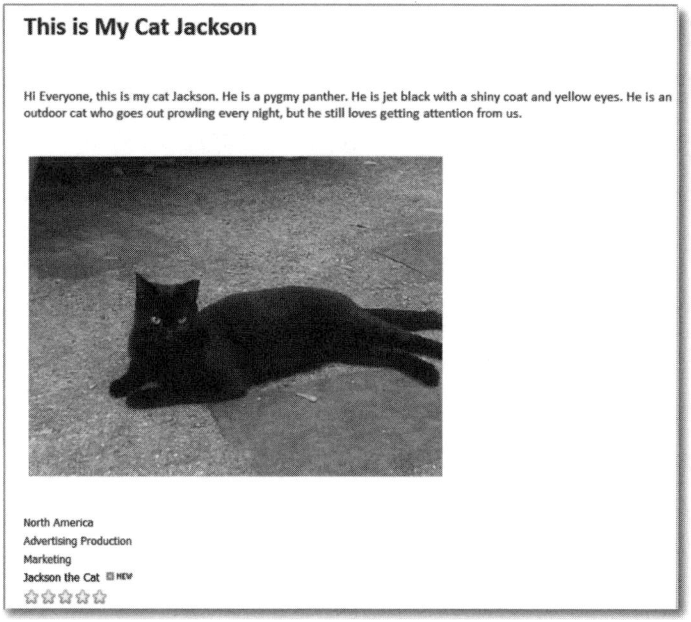

This is My Cat Jackson

Hi Everyone, this is my cat Jackson. He is a pygmy panther. He is jet black with a shiny coat and yellow eyes. He is an outdoor cat who goes out prowling every night, but he still loves getting attention from us.

North America
Advertising Production
Marketing
Jackson the Cat

Illustration 29

Removing the Column Headers from the Top of the Page

The *Boxed, no labels* Style that we applied to the List to create the Catalog View still displays column headers even if they are no longer functionally useful in this View as shown in **Illustration 30** below. Since this is inelegant and potentially confusing to users you will want to remove it.

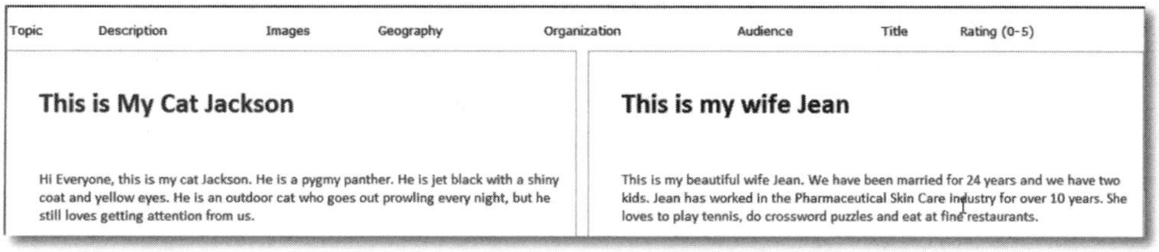

Topic	Description	Images	Geography	Organization	Audience	Title	Rating (0-5)

This is My Cat Jackson

Hi Everyone, this is my cat Jackson. He is jet black with a shiny coat and yellow eyes. He is an outdoor cat who goes out prowling every night, but he still loves getting attention from us.

This is my wife Jean

This is my beautiful wife Jean. We have been married for 24 years and we have two kids. Jean has worked in the Pharmaceutical Skin Care Industry for over 10 years. She loves to play tennis, do crossword puzzles and eat at fine restaurants.

Illustration 30

To do this we will modify the *Catalog View* of the List in *SharePoint Designer*.

> **Important Note** – You will not be able to do this in *SharePoint Designer 2013* because the Design mode editing capability was removed.

Open the Site containing the Catalog List in *SharePoint Designer*. Select *Lists and Libraries* from the *Navigation Site Objects Pane* and then click on the *Catalog List* in the main section. The *Summary Page* for the List will display as shown in **Illustration 31** below. In the *Views* section you will see the *Catalog View*. Double click on it.

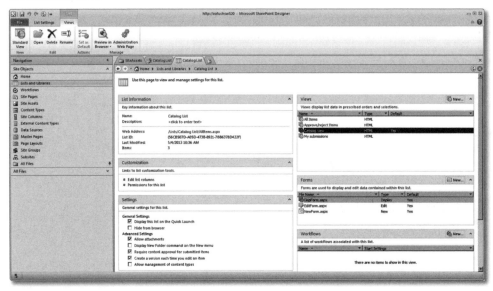

Illustration 31

SharePoint Designer will open the View in design mode. The column headings are embedded in a single row table as highlighted at the top of **Illustration 32** below.

Illustration 32

Select this table (***but only this table***) with your cursor and right-click. From the drop-down selection menu select *Delete* and then *Delete Table* as shown in **Illustration 33** on the next page. Make sure that you save the change by clicking *Save* from the *File* menu.

Illustration 33

Standardizing Text Formatting in Rich Text Fields

In many Catalog use cases the items in the List will be generated by multiple users. Consequently these users will have the capability to format the text in the Rich Text fields anyway they want. As a result the Catalog will quickly take on an ungainly and haphazard look that will make it unappealing to use. Fortunately there is a way to constrain the formatting applied by a user to a Rich Text field by defaulting to pre-defined settings. The pre-defined settings will override any text formatting applied by a user resulting in the Catalog having a consistent look and feel, while still being able to take advantage of flexible design choices.

This constraint is implemented by using the *Conditional Formatting* facility of *SharePoint Designer*.

> **Important Note** – You will not be able to do this in *SharePoint Designer 2013* because the Design mode editing capability was removed.

In *SharePoint Designer* open the *Catalog View* for the List and select the *Topic* field for any item. The *Topic* field will be highlighted for all the items that are displayed. Right-click to display the drop-down selection menu and choose *Conditional Formatting* as shown in **Illustration 34** below.

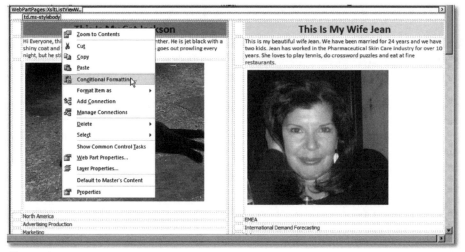

Illustration 34

Click *Conditional Formatting* from the *Ribbon* menu and choose *Format Selection* from the drop-down selection as shown in **Illustration 35** below.

Illustration 35

The *Condition Criteria* dialogue screen will display as shown in **Illustration 36** below. Here you can create multiple and/or conditional clauses based on field values to define a particular criteria. In this case the condition has a single criterion: The *Topic* field is *Not Null*, meaning that it will contain some text. Select the *Topic* field from the *Field Name* drop-down selection List and select the *Not Null* option from the *Comparison* down-down selection List. Now click on the *Set Style* button.

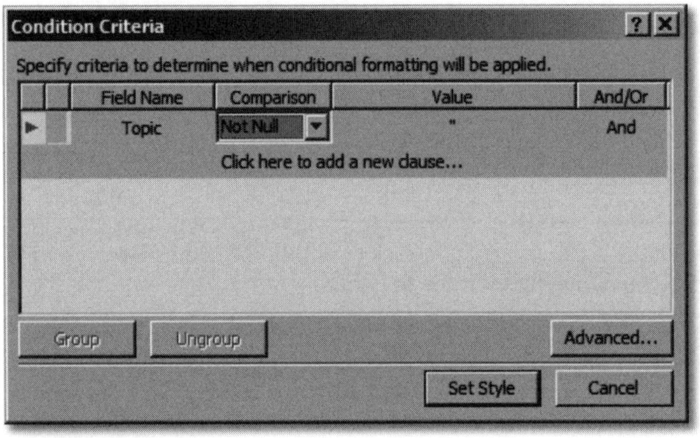

Illustration 36

The *Set Style/Modify Style* dialogue screen will display as shown in **Illustration 37** on the next page where multiple settings for a field can be set. Use the drop-down selection options to choose *Font Settings* as shown in **Illustration 37** on the next page. Note that there is a text-transform option. Select the *capitalize* option. No matter how the user enters text in the *Topic* field, the entered text will be displayed with each word capitalized.

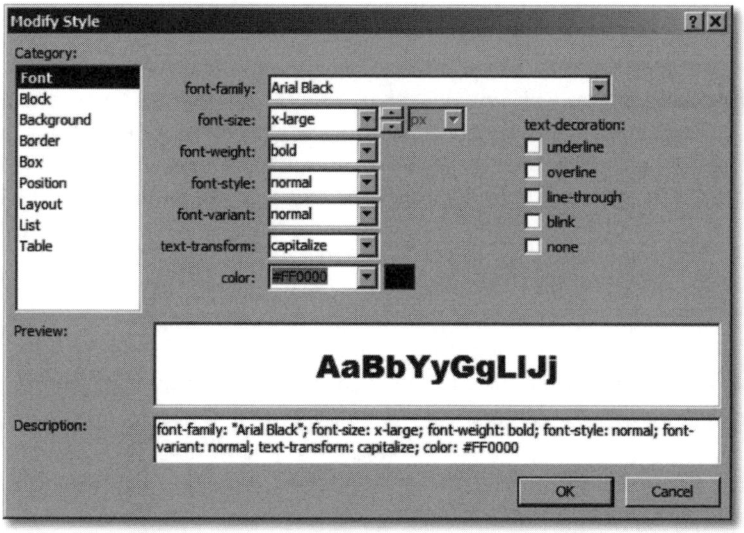

Illustration 37

Click *OK* when you are finished. Now test the effect of this Conditional Formatting by creating a new item in the Catalog List and display it in the Catalog View. In the Topic field use any combination of formatting attributes and then save. What you will see is that no matter what styling attributes you applied to the Topic field the text will default to the settings specified in Conditional Formatting. Repeat the steps above for applying conditional formatting to the Description field.

> **Note** – the conditional formatting settings will be applied to all new List items that are added, and in most cases will be applied to List items created before the conditional formatting settings were defined. However, sometimes the new default settings won't "take" on existing items. You will need to manually adjust those items.

To modify the conditional formatting settings click the *Conditional Formatting Ribbon* menu tab in *SharePoint Designer* and select *Show Taskpane*. The *Conditional Formatting* pane will display showing all your conditional formatting settings as shown in **Illustration 38** at right. Click on the drop-down selection icon on the right of a setting and select *Edit condition* or *Modify style* to make your changes.

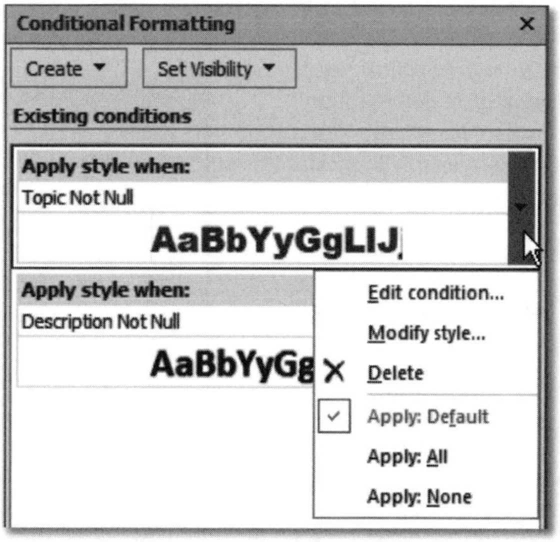

Illustration 38

Using the SharePoint Item Approval Function

Earlier in this chapter, when we created the Catalog List we set the *Require content approval for submitted items* setting to *Yes* on the *Versioning Settings* page. This setting enables a simple, lightweight approval process where each new item added becomes a minor version automatically and is only visible to the person who created it and any person who has the Approve permission assigned to them for the List. Once the item is approved it becomes a major version and is visible to anyone who has access to the List.

Illustration 39 below shows the Catalog List in the *All Items* View. Note that in this View the *Approval Status* column is visible. This column is automatically created when the *Require content approval for submitted items* setting is set to *Yes*. The status for an item that has not been approved is *Pending* and selecting it will make the *Approve/Reject* button on the *Ribbon* menu active or right-clicking on the item will display an *Approve/Reject* option on the drop-down selection menu as shown in **Illustration 39** below.

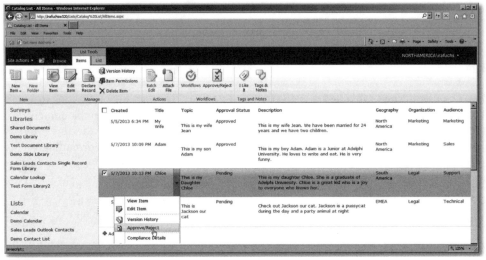

Illustration 39

Clicking on the *Approve/Reject* button or drop-down option will display the *Approve/Reject* dialogue screen as shown in **Illustration 40** at right, where the approver can approve or reject the item.

Note that the *Ribbon* button is greyed out when items that have been approved are selected, but the drop-down *Approve/Reject* option is always available. As such you can change the approval status of an item even when it has been previously approved.

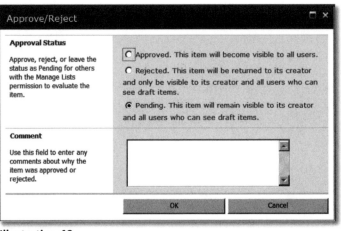

Illustration 40

Creating an Expiration Policy for an Item

In many catalog use cases the items are temporal; they have a freshness or lifetime period after which the items should expire and be removed from the catalog or updated. *SharePoint* provides the content management functionality, called an *Information Management Policy*, for automating an expiration process.

Information Management Policy settings can be applied to Content Types as well as Lists and libraries. By design, the best practice for working with *Information Management Policies* is to define them for Content Types and then instantiate those Content Types in a List or Library. While we could have created a "Catalog List Content Type" it is not a necessity to do so and instead we will demonstrate how to apply an *Information Management Policy* directly to the List.

In *SharePoint* go to the *List Settings* page for the *Catalog List* and click on *Information management policy settings*. The Information *Management Policy Settings* page as shown in **Illustration 41** below will display.

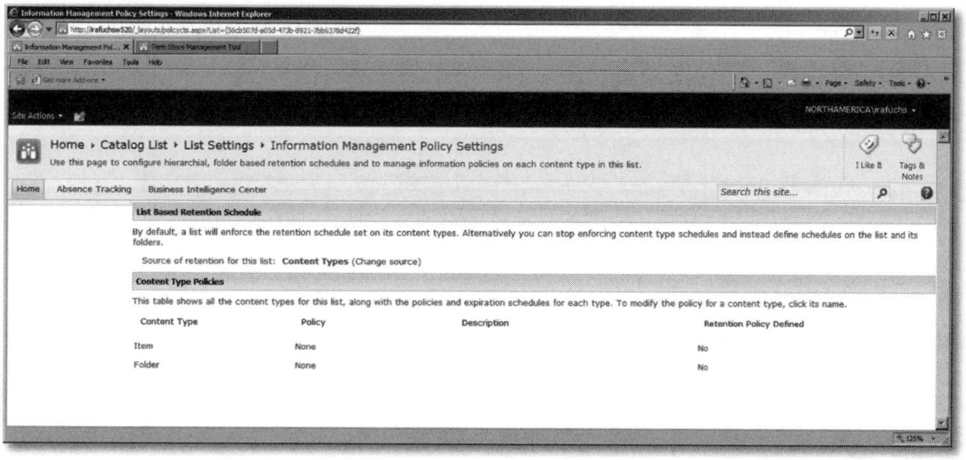

Illustration 41

The built-in Content Types for any generic *SharePoint* List are Item and Folder. And because retention scheduling is a function of an *Information Management Policy,* this page informs you that retention settings are typically defined and applied to those Content Types.

Click on the *(Change source or configure List schedule) link*. The *Edit Policy: List Based Retention Schedule* page will display as shown in **Illustration 42** below. By selecting the *Library and Folders radio* button for the *Source of Retention* setting you effectively change the default retention schedules defined for Content Types in the List or Library. Those will be overridden by the retention schedule defined directly for the List or Library, and a message indicating that you want to make this change will display as shown in **Illustration 42** below.

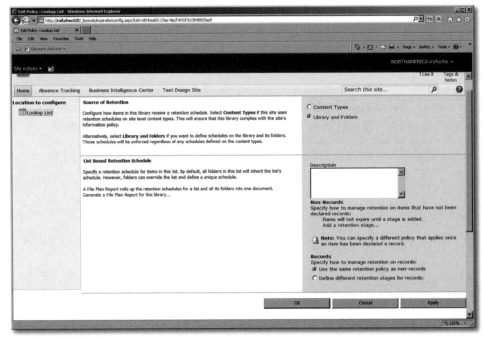

Illustration 42

Click the *OK* button on the message. The page will refresh displaying the *List Based Retention Schedule* section as shown in **Illustration 43** below.

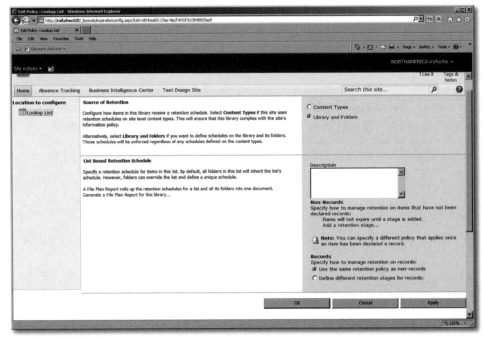

Illustration 43

Click the *Add a retention stage link* to bring up the *Stage properties* dialogue screen as shown in **Illustration 44** below. This is where you define a retention schedule for the List or Library items. A retention schedule is composed of one or more stages; and a stage is comprised of an *Event* and a corresponding *Action*.

The *Event* is a point in time defined from the time the item was Created, Modified or Defined as a Record, plus an additional duration of time specified in days, months or years. The *Actions* that can be triggered are displayed in **Illustration 44** below.

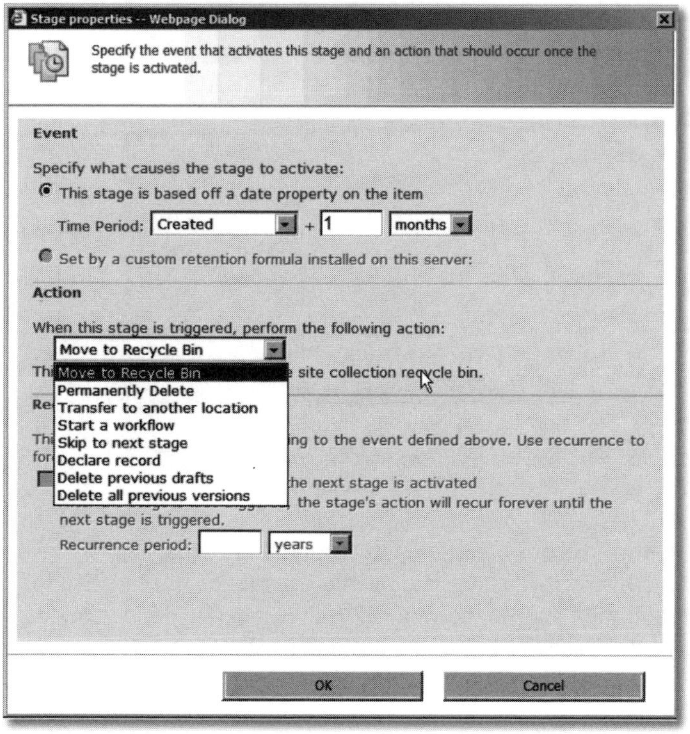

Illustration 44

The *Recurrence* setting will be available for those *Actions* where the item continues to exist, such as when the item is declared a record. Note that one of the *Action* options is to start a workflow, which can be defined in *SharePoint Designer* to incorporate more complex conditional criteria and execute multiple actions such as sending notification emails.

Select an *Action* and click the *OK* button. The stage will be saved as shown in **Illustration 45** on the next page. You can then create additional stages that comprise a sophisticated retention schedule.

Automated retention schedules for List and Library items are one of the truly useful content management capabilities of *SharePoint* and very simple to deploy. Using this capability you eliminate the need for any manual intervention in maintaining the freshness of a catalog.

Illustration 45

This concludes the exercise of using an out-of-the-box *SharePoint List View Style* setting to create a catalog that contains both structured and unstructured information. There are many use cases and scenarios for creating catalogs in an organization and you now have the knowledge to design and implement them quickly and effectively using *SharePoint,* and take advantage of the lifecycle management functions for List items that are also available out-of-the-box.

How to Create Custom Designed SharePoint Site Templates without Having to Modify SharePoint Master Pages, HTML Code or Style Sheets!

SharePoint is great for creating Web based Sites for collaboration, document management and no-code declarative applications. However, unless you are knowledgeable in working with the components of Web Page design, such as HTML and Cascading Style Sheets (CSS), it is not easy to change the look and feel of *SharePoint* Sites, or modify the way you can organize Web Parts on a Page. In his chapter we will demonstrate how to easily modify the design of *SharePoint* Pages and generate custom Site Templates, in order to address two different *SharePoint* use cases: creating Sites for casual publishing of content, and Sites for specific collaboration requirements.

> **Important Note** – The page layout and design techniques described in this chapter are only applicable to *SharePoint 2010* sites, because they utilize Design mode editing features only available in *SharePoint Designer 2010*. Unfortunately Design mode editing has been removed from *SharePoint Designer 2013*.

The first use case is the common requirement in organizations to publish Web content that simply contains formatted text, images, embedded documents, and links to other Pages or Sites. Typically, these Pages should, or need to adhere to some corporate design standards. The problem with using out-of-the box *SharePoint* templates for generic Web publishing, such as a Team Site, is the *SharePoint* artifacts that are generated (e.g. Welcome Page, Navigation Pane, Shared Library, Calendar, etc.) are not relevant to simple Page publishing requirements. **Illustration 1** below shows the standard Team Site template.

Illustration 1

Furthermore, the generic *SharePoint* Site branding is typically not appealing for generic Web publishing requirements and the effort to change the look and feel of *SharePoint* Pages is beyond the scope of most people's knowledge, or their desire to acquire that knowledge. **Illustration 2** below shows a Team Site Welcome Page in edit mode where Page content can be edited. It is typically not a good starting point for this type of casual Web publishing.

Illustration 2

Some readers might be asking "Why not use a Publishing Page for this purpose?" Publishing Pages are not useable for this purpose for the following reasons: Publishing Pages are only available if the Publishing Features are turned on for a Site Collection and underlying Sites, and this may not be the case for many organizations. Second, Publishing Pages are not editable in *SharePoint Designer*; only their underlying Publishing Page Layouts. Creating or modifying Publishing Page Layouts is not trivial. There is an entire process of creating the Content Types for the objects in a Page Layout and then creating Field Controls that are bound to those Content Types. Furthermore, Page Layouts must be edited in Advance Mode which provides access to Master Page elements. Access to this editing functionality should not be made available to most people, if anyone at all. **Illustration 3** below shows what a Page Layout file looks like in edit mode.

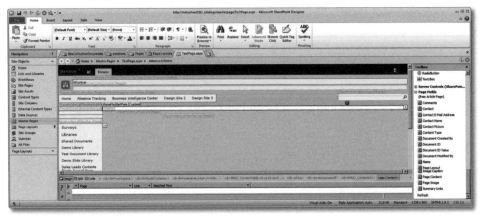

Illustration 3

What we want is a light-weight, safe, and easily accessible method to make Pages and Sites look like they were designed and can be flexibly modified.

The second use case is to create customized Site Templates for standard *SharePoint* collaboration functions. Often, organizations want to provision *SharePoint* Sites that only contain specific functional artifacts (Pages, Lists, Libraries, Web Parts) that also contain predefined content and are pre-configured as well (i.e. with Content Types and Views).

What will be demonstrated here is a technique for creating Pages and Sites that address both of these use cases. The methodology is straightforward; we will create a blank Site with a single Page. We will then use *SharePoint Designer's* Page layout capabilities to insert and arrange tables on the blank Page. We will continue working in *SharePoint Designer* to add images, shading and borders to areas of the Page, as well adding Content Editor Web Parts and Hyperlinks. We can also use the *SharePoint* user interface to add content to the Page and then return to *SharePoint Designer* to refine the layout of that content. We will then save multiple copies of the designed Page in the Site Pages Library. The replicated Pages can then be individually modified and linked together, and saved as a Site Template. The Sites generated from the Site Template provide a light-weight Web content publishing framework where different types of content can be easily added by end-users using the *SharePoint* user interface. All the initial design work only had to be done once.

For collaboration Sites, Lists and Libraries can be added to the initial Site Pages and these artifacts, including their content, can also be bundled up into a Site Template. After a new Site is generated from the Site template, *SharePoint* Web Parts and content can be flexibly added to the Pages using the *SharePoint* user interface. If design refinements are required for any of the new Pages they can be opened in *SharePoint Designer* for further modification.

Illustration 4 below shows a sample of a formatted generic Web content Page with a logo, border framing and an editable area in the center. Note that the *SharePoint Quick Launch* pane has been included.

Illustration 4

The same Page is displayed in **Illustration 5** on the next page but the *Quick Launch* pane has been removed. You have the option to remove this so that you have a pure and simple set of Pages that are not encumbered by *SharePoint* artifacts, but are nonetheless hosted within *SharePoint*.

Illustration 5

Illustration 6 below shows a Survey Page that contains a clip art image; a fully functional *InfoPath Form Web* Part with a background fill color that matches the background of the underlying Page; and a side bar in another color that contains a link to another Page. It took all of ten minutes to design and build this Page. Being able to utilize a variety of Page layout elements easily and quickly to achieve a more interesting and sophisticated Page design, without having to work with or modify the underlying Master Page, HTML or CSS, is a significant value provided by *SharePoint Designer*.

Illustration 6

Before we start the exercise of building a lightweight Web Publishing Site, let me say upfront that I do not do Page layout and design. I have not invested any significant time in finessing the aesthetics of the Pages that are constructed in this chapter. Consequently you might find the design to be less than sophisticated. However, this is not due to the technique employed or the capabilities available from the tool. It is certainly possible to design Pages to look any way you want them to.

So let's begin. Open an existing Site Collection or Site using the *SharePoint* user interface. From the *Site Actions* drop-down menu click on *New Site* and select the *Blank Site* Template as shown in **Illustration 7** below.

Illustration 7

Your blank Site will look like **Illustration 8** below. The only object on the Page is the Quick Launch pane containing the Headers for Libraries, Lists, and Discussions; as well as the *Recycle Bin* and *All Site Content* links and icons.

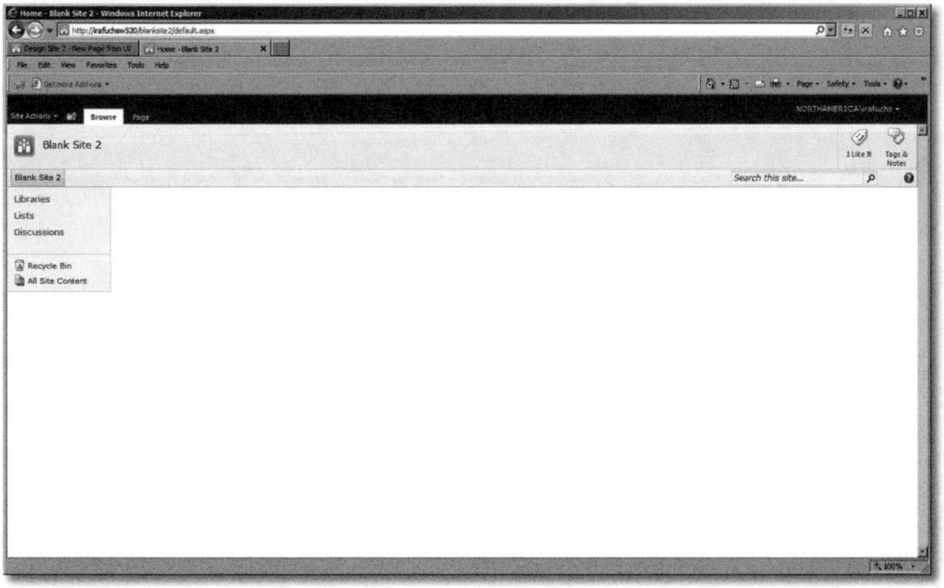

Illustration 8

Click on the *All Site Content* link to display the *All Site Content* Page as shown in **Illustration 9** below. As you can see there are no Lists or Libraries. When you create a Site from any of the other *SharePoint* Site templates a number of Lists and Libraries will automatically be created, including a *Site Pages* Library that contains the Home Page that you see when a Site is created.

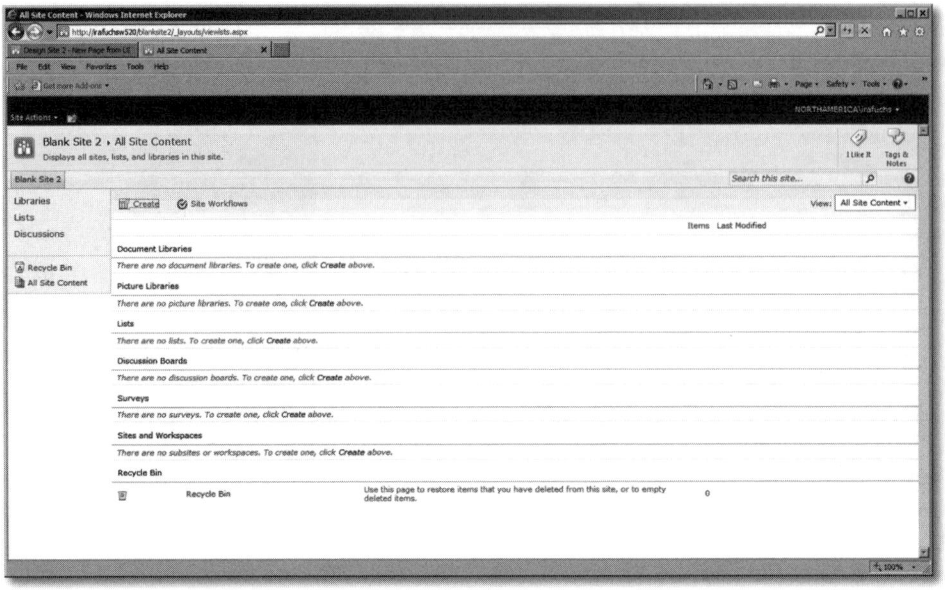

Illustration 9

Click the Create button on the *All Site Content* Page. Select *Page* from the *Selection Pane* and then select the Page option as shown in **Illustration 10** below.

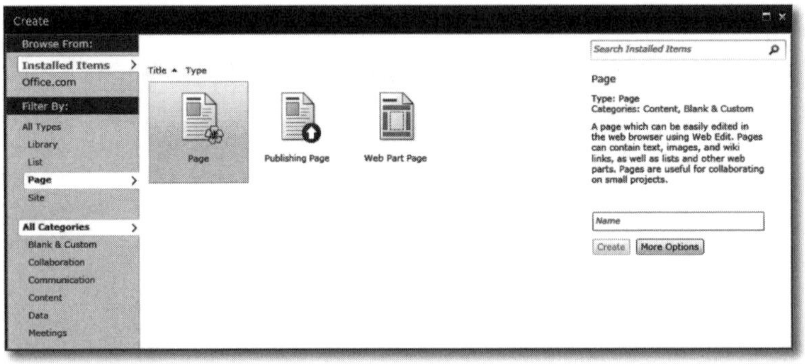

Illustration 10

> **Important Note** – You must select the **Page** option and not the *Web Part Page* or *Publishing Page* (which will display if the Publishing Feature has been turned on) options; neither of these Pages can be modified in *SharePoint Designer* in the manner that will be described shortly. Also, you **must create this initial Page** in *SharePoint*. If you create it using *SharePoint Designer* it will not contain the references to the *SharePoint Master Page* and other supporting format files. Later, we will save this Page multiple times in *SharePoint Designer* after it has been designed.

Note – When you create a Page for the first time in a Blank Site you will be informed that the Site Pages and Site Assets libraries will be created as well. All Pages in a Site are stored in a Site Pages Library and pictures are stored by default in the Site Assets Library, so these artifacts need to be created. The new Page will display and it will also be empty.

Now we are going to modify this Page using *SharePoint Designer*. Open the blank Site that you created in *SharePoint Designer* and select *Site Pages* in the *Navigation Site Objects* pane. You will see the Page as shown in **Illustration 11** below. Note that it was created as a *Wiki Page* Content Type.

Illustration 11

Select the *Page* and click the *Edit File* button on the *Ribbon* menu and choose *Edit File in Normal Mode*. The Page will open in the *SharePoint Designer Editor* as shown in **Illustration 12** below. Note that the only editable area is within the *PlaceHolderMain* area; all other parts of the Page are locked down and can't be edited.

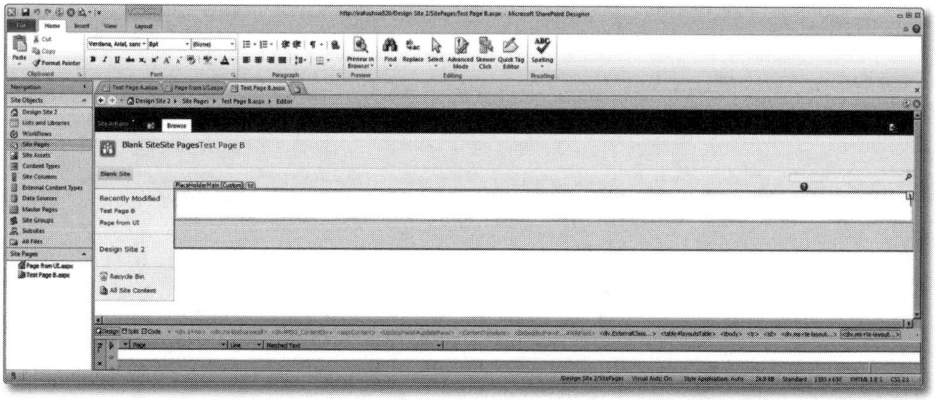

Illustration 12

Important Note – Do not choose *Edit File in Advanced Mode*. Doing so will make the attached Master Page template accessible for editing which will detach the Page from its Site definition. Modifying these elements will not change the actual Master Page definition but it will modify the applied instance of it for this Page. However, when that happens you cannot create a Site Template from this Site.

Place your cursor in the *PlaceHolderMain* area and press your *Enter* key twice to create some empty space at the top. Now select the *Insert* button from the *Ribbon* menu and choose *Table*. The table layout option will display; select one row and three columns as shown in **Illustration 13** below.

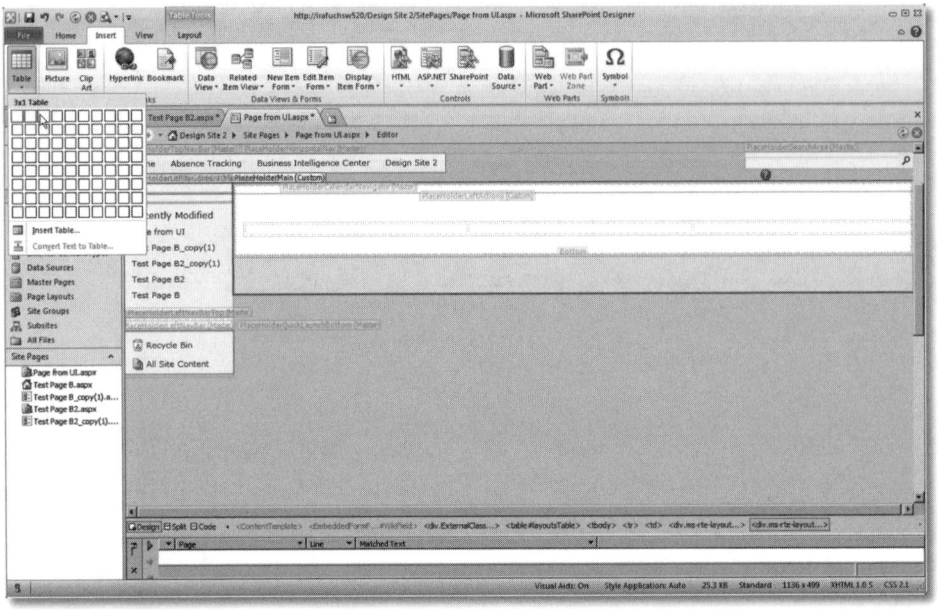

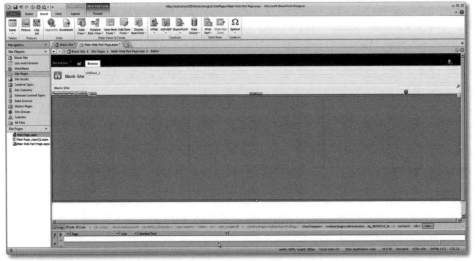

Illustration 13

A table will be inserted into the *PlaceHolderMain* area. Grab the bottom of the table and drag it down to enlarge the height of the row. Place your cursor in the first column and with your *Ctrl-key* pressed down select the second and third column. They will be highlighted as shown in **Illustration 14** below to indicate that they are all selected.

Illustration 14

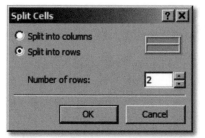

Illustration 15

Now click on the *Layout Ribbon* section and choose *Split Cells*. The *Split Cells* dialogue screen will display as shown in **Illustration 15** at left. Click on the *Split into rows radio button* and leave "2" for the *Number of rows*. Click *OK*.

Alternatively you can place your cursor anywhere in the table, right-click and choose Insert to add rows, columns or cells to the table as shown in **Illustration 16** at right.

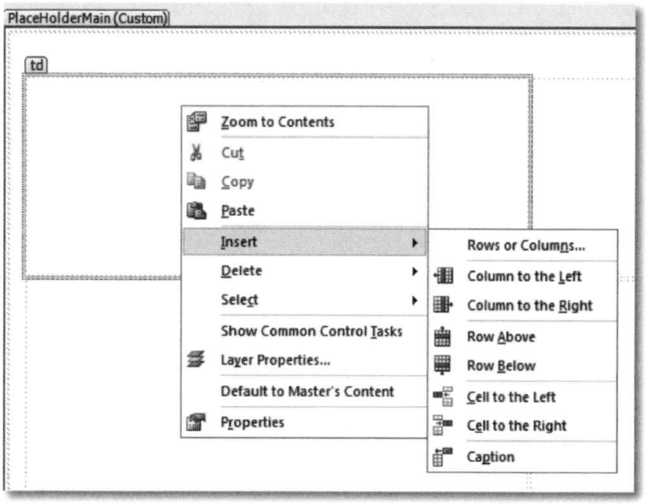

Illustration 16

Place your cursor in the top left cell. On the *Ribbon* menu select *Layout* and enter "200px" for the width. Do the same thing for the top right cell. Now the left and right columns are 200px each and the center column has absorbed the additional space as shown in **Illustration 17** below.

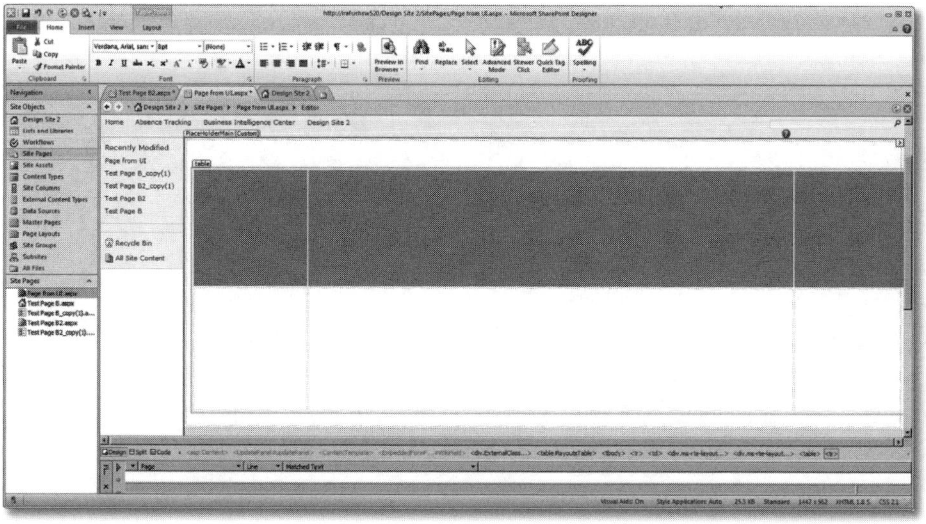

Illustration 17

You can also select the edges of any cell and drag them to adjust the size of rows and columns. Select the center column in both rows using your *Ctrl-key*. From the *Layout Ribbon* menu click *Merge Cells*; this will result in a single center column that spans both rows.

Position your cursor above this table and move it down by hitting your *Enter key*. Now insert another table above it that contains two rows and five columns. Adjust the height of the rows so they look like **Illustration 18** below.

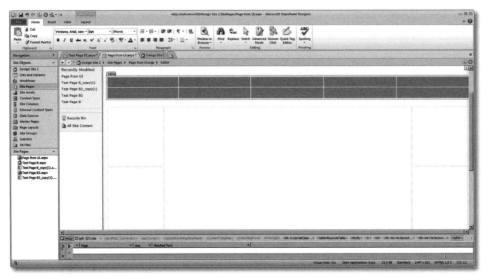

Illustration 18

Select the table icon at the top left corner of the new table to select the entire table, which will then be highlighted. Click on the *Shading Ribbon* button and select *More Fill Colors*. The *Color palette* will display, as shown in **Illustration 19 below left**, where you can select colors from a specific set. If you click on the *Custom* button the *Custom Color* specification dialogue screen will display as shown in **Illustration 19 below right**. From here you can define a set of reusable colors. You can create any color scheme to match an existing theme.

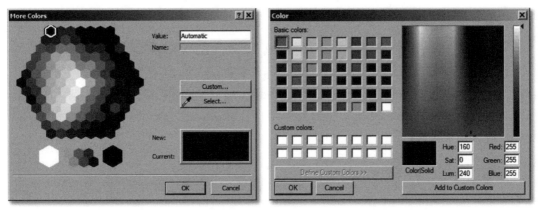

Illustration 19

Pick a color for the table shading. Your Page will look like **Illustration 20** below.

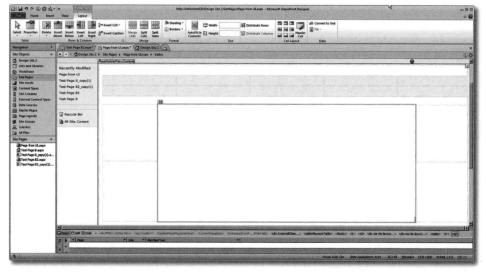

Illustration 20

With the new table still selected click on the *Properties Ribbon* menu button. The *Table Properties* dialogue screen will display as shown in **Illustration 21 below left**. From here you can modify any of the properties of the table. Now select any cell in the table and again click on the *Properties Ribbon* menu button. The *Cell Properties* dialogue screen will display as shown in **Illustration 21 below right**. These Properties dialogue screens are very useful for adjusting the size of a table or individual cells.

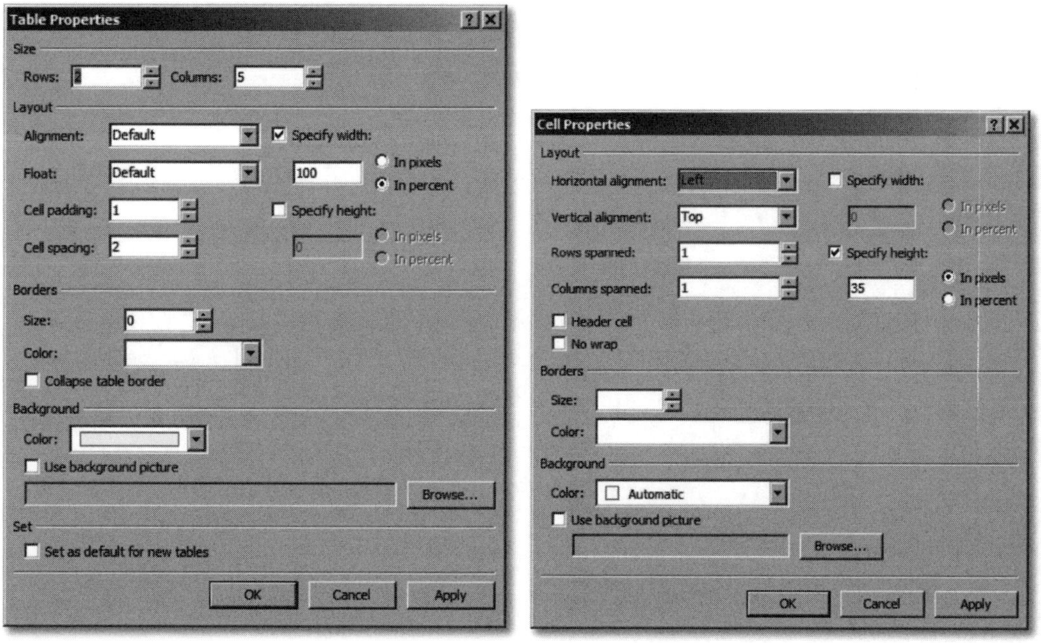

Illustration 21

Place your cursor in the top left cell of the table and click on the Insert tab of the *Table Tools Ribbon* menu. We are going to insert a Picture in this cell. Any picture that you have available on your computer will work. Pick a picture from the dialogue screen and click the *Open* button. An *Accessibility Properties* dialogue screen will display as shown in **Illustration 22** below. Entering an Alternate text value is optional and you can de-select the check box for *Show this prompt when inserting images*.

Illustration 22

Your picture will be inserted into the cell in its original size which will enlarge the host cell and compress all the other cells in the table as shown in **Illustration 23** below.

Illustration 23

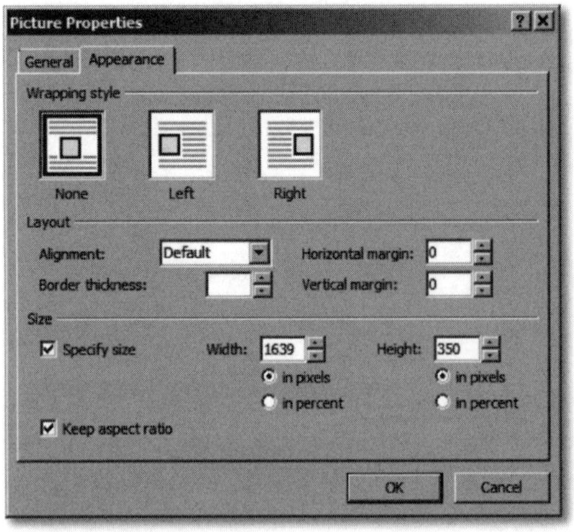

Right-click on the picture and select *Picture Properties*; the dialogue screen as shown in **Illustration 24** at left will display. Use the *Width* and *Height* specification boxes to resize the picture so that it fits comfortably in the original size of the cell. To maintain the aspect ratio of the image make sure the check box is checked.

Illustration 24

After you have resized the picture you will need to adjust the width of the four other columns in the table which were compressed to the right when the first column was expanded by the picture insertion as shown in **Illustration 25** below.

Illustration 25

The easiest way to do this is by grabbing the right border of the first cell and dragging it to the left. The four other columns will adjust their size automatically. You can also use the *Properties* dialogue box for both the *Table* and *Cells* to fine tune the height and depth of the tables and cells. Your layout should look like **Illustration 26** below.

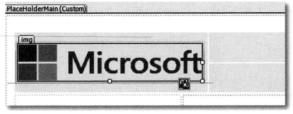

Illustration 26

Illustration 27

The *Microsoft* logo has a white background but I wanted the white area to be transparent so that the background table shading would be displayed within the logo as shown in **Illustration 27** at left.

The original picture was a JPEG file and that file format does not support transparency. However by right-clicking on the image the drop-down selection menu will present the option to *Change Picture File Type*. The dialogue screen allows you to change the file format. Select the *GIF radio button* and check *Transparent* as shown in **Illustration 28** below.

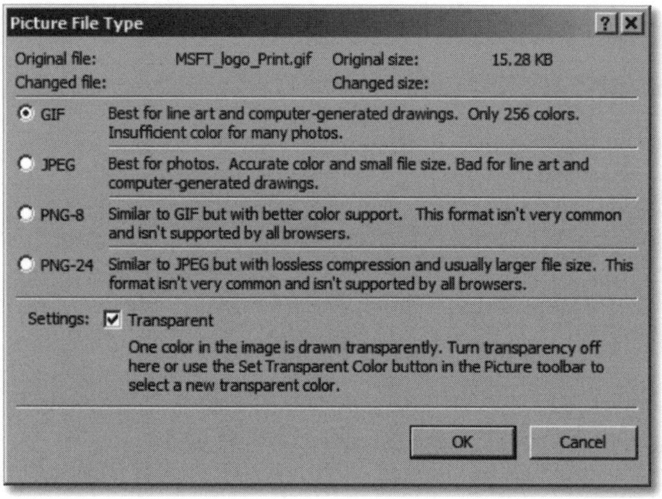

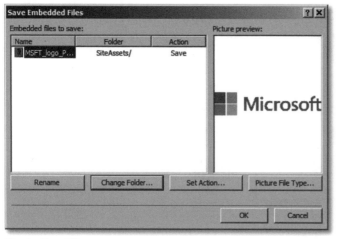

Illustration 28

The Format tab on the *Picture Tools* section of the *Ribbon* menu now displays a *Set Transparent Color* option as shown in **Illustration 29** below. Clicking on this button and then selecting the white area of the picture made it transparent.

Illustration 29

As you can see *SharePoint Designer* provides rich tooling for addressing most Page layout design requirements. Now *Save* the Page from the *File* menu. The *Save Embedded Files* dialogue screen will appear as shown in **Illustration 30** at left. Note that the picture will be saved to the default *SiteAssets* folder that was created. Click *OK*.

Illustration 30

Click *OK*. You will then be presented with the message shown in **Illustration 31** below. Click the *Yes* button.

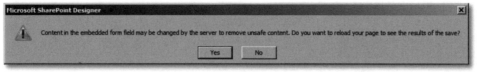

Illustration 31

We are Now Going to Deal with a Bug!!

That's right; our next order of business is to work around a bug in *SharePoint* and *SharePoint Designer*. The problem is that when you place a picture on a Page using *SharePoint Designer* and save the Page, *SharePoint* removes the visual representation of the picture but keeps a placeholder reference to the picture as shown in **Illustration 32** below.

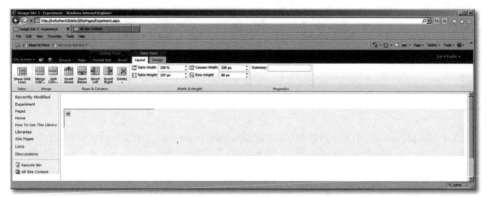

Illustration 32

Open the blank Site using *SharePoint* and click on the *Site Pages* link on the *Quick Launch* pane, then click on the *Page* that you are working with to open it. The table you created in *SharePoint Designer* will be visible due to the shading and placeholder for the picture as shown in **Illustration 33** below.

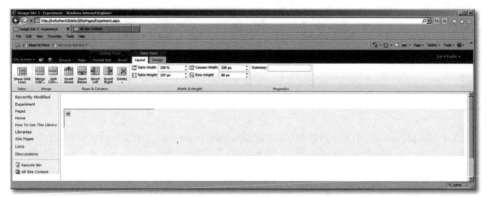

Illustration 33

Click on the *Page link* and then the *Edit Page* button. When you place your cursor anywhere in the table the *Table Tools Ribbon* menu tabs will display. Click the *Layout* button to display the layout options on the *Ribbon*. Click *Show Grid Lines* to display the row and column table cells you defined for the table as shown in **Illustration 34** below. Note that *SharePoint* provides tools that allow you to work with the Page layout as well but you don't have all the capabilities that *SharePoint Designer* has, such as the *Properties* dialogue screen for tables and cells.

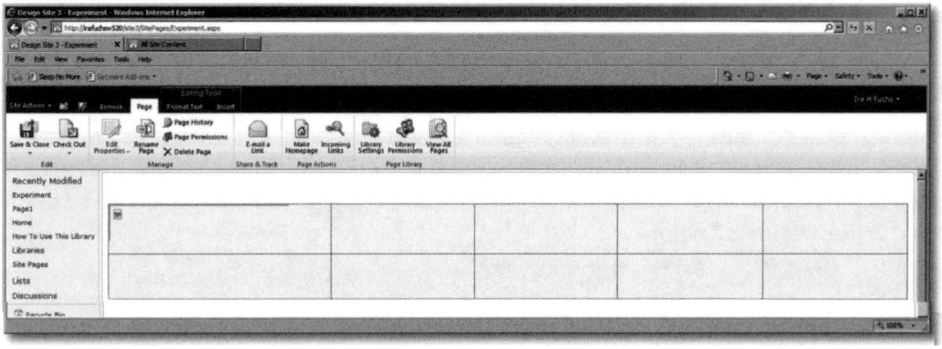

Illustration 34

Select the picture placeholder in the top left cell. The *Picture Tools* tab will display on the *Ribbon* menu. Delete the picture placeholder by right-clicking on it and selecting *Cut*. With your cursor in the same cell click the *Insert Ribbon* tab and click *Picture*. Choose from *Computer* for the location of the image. The *Select Picture* dialogue screen will display. Browse for the picture you inserted and select it. The picture with its original dimensions will be inserted as shown in **Illustration 35** below.

Illustration 35

Change the width of the picture from the *Picture Tools Design Ribbon* menu. The columns will automatically be adjusted as shown in **Illustration 36** below. Now Save & Close the Page.

   Important – if you don't save your changes, they won't be saved!

Return to the Page in *SharePoint Designer* and click the *Refresh* icon on top left or press your *F5* key. The table and the picture will be displayed as shown in **Illustration 36** below.

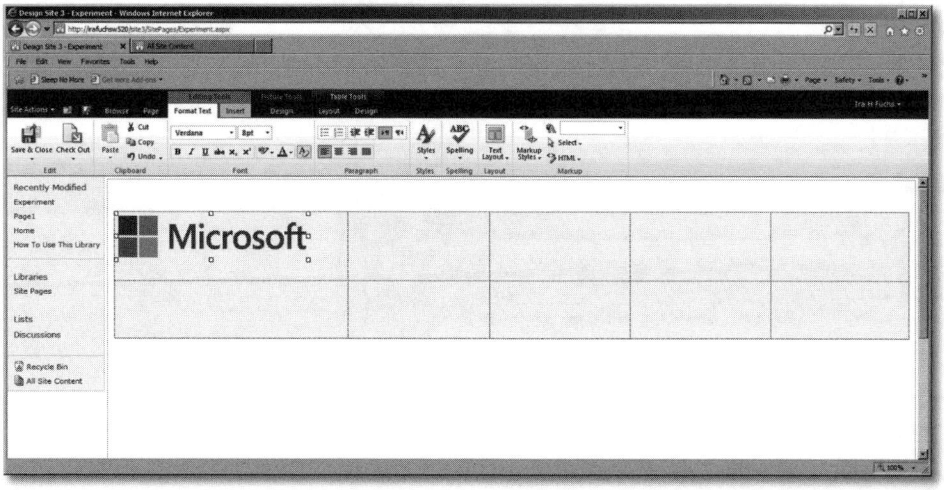

Illustration 36

Let's go on to design and layout the Page. Now we are going to insert and format hyperlinks in the cells of the top table. Select the cell in row 2 and column 2 as shown in **Illustration 37** below.

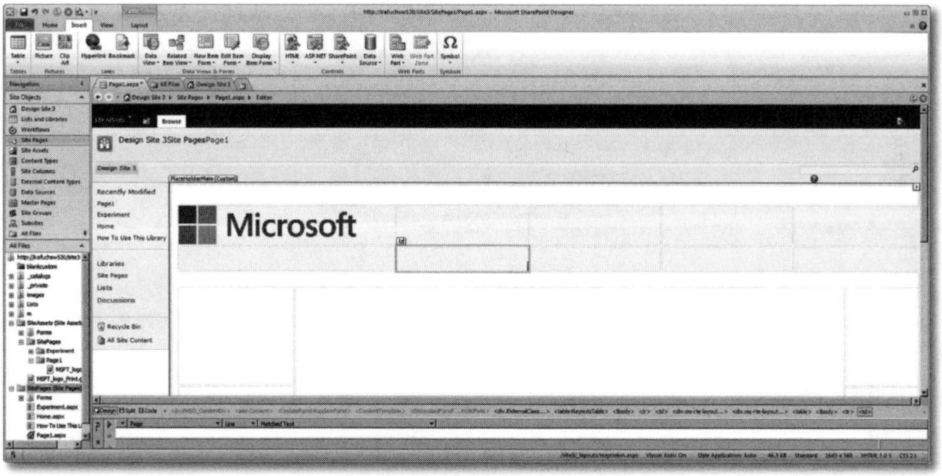

Illustration 37

From the *Insert Ribbon* tab click on *Hyperlink*. The *Insert Hyperlink* dialogue screen will display as shown in **Illustration 38** on the next page. *SharePoint Designer* provides rich tooling for creating links to practically any internal or external objects and places, as shown in **Illustration 38** on the next page.

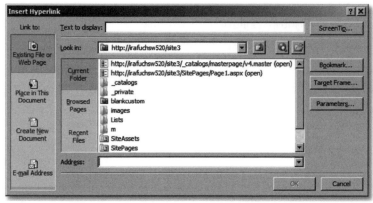

Illustration 38

Select the *Look* in drop-down selection box and you can access objects on your computer or select *Web Sites* as shown in **Illustration 39** below.

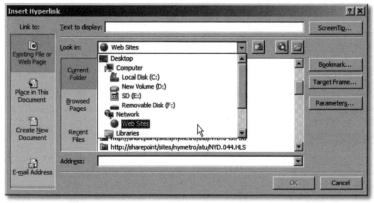

Illustration 39

Selecting this option will display the various *SharePoint* Sites you have accessed previously that are stored in the *Web Sites* cache as shown in **Illustration 40** below.

Illustration 40

Selecting the *Address* drop-down selection box will display a List of the Web Sites you have visited from your Browser cache as shown in **Illustration 41** below.

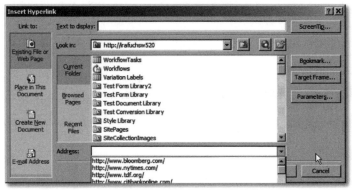

Illustration 41

We will create a *Hyperlink* that will open a new Browser Window to the New York Times for this exercise. You can just select the address or type it in. Enter "New York Times" for the *Text to display* as the hyperlink. Click on the *ScreenTip* button to enter a *ScreenTip* that will display when a user hovers over the link as shown in **Illustration 42** below.

Illustration 42

Click on the *Target Frame* button and select *New Window* as shown in **Illustration 43** below and click *OK*.

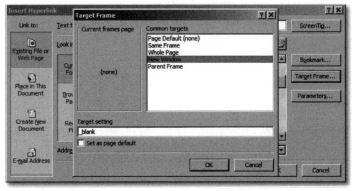

Illustration 43

Click *OK* on the *Insert Hyperlink* dialogue screen and you will see a hyperlink inserted in the target cell as shown in **Illustration 44** below. Note that once again the cell containing the link has been extended to the right. Grab the right border of the cell and drag it to the left and the cells to the right will adjust in width.

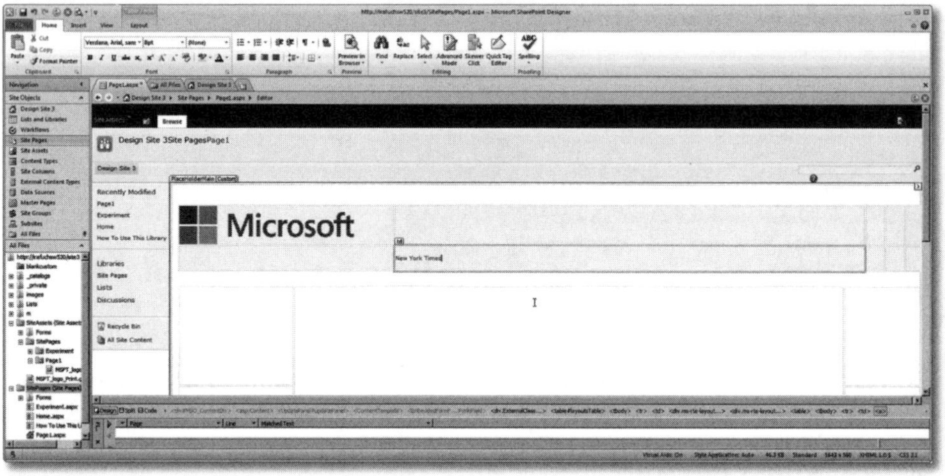

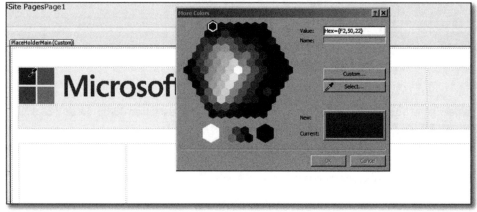

Illustration 44

Now highlight the *New York Times hyperlink text* and from the *Home* tab on the *Ribbon* menu choose a typeface and size, and center the text in the cell. Now we are going to do some interesting design work that is very useful for branding to a design standard. Click the *text color* drop-down selection tool and select the *More Colors* option. The *More Colors* selection tool will display as shown in **Illustration 45** below.

Illustration 45

Click the *Select* button. The *eyedropper* tool will display. Choose an area on the picture that you placed in the first cell. In the example here we are using a red square in the Microsoft logo as shown in **Illustration 45** above. Click *OK* to apply this color to the *Hyperlink Text*.

Now do the same for the text shading but pick another color in your picture. In this example we used an orange square in the logo. The hyperlink text will now look like **Illustration 46** below.

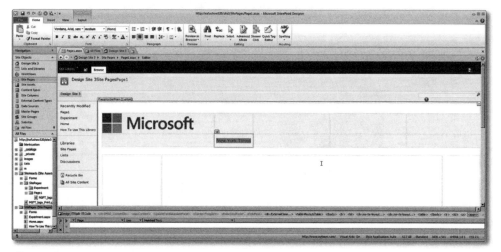

Illustration 46

Pretty cool! You can do this for any design object placed on the Page. In this manner you can easily match the design themes and elements already in use in your organization.

Open the Page in *SharePoint* (you can do this in *SharePoint Designer* by clicking the *Preview in Browser* button from the *Home* tab on the menu). Hover over the hyperlink to see the screen tip you entered for it as shown in **Illustration 47** below.

Illustration 47

Now click on the link. A new Browser window will open to the New York Times Page as shown in **Illustration 48** below.

Illustration 48

So far so good, everything is working. Let's return to *SharePoint Designer*. Create another hyperlink in the adjacent cell to the right for Bloomberg.com and use "Bloomberg" for the link text. Apply the same coloring and shading to the text as you did for the New York Times text. Your layout should look like **Illustration 49** below. Because we applied the color and shading to the text the link design is not visually consistent; the width of the shaded area is dependent on the number of text characters for the link.

Illustration 49

Remove the shading from the *text* of both links and use the *Custom color* technique described above to apply the shading to the *cells* containing the links. Your Page will look like **Illustration 50** below. This is a more visually consistent design.

Illustration 50

Note that as you create or use colors from the *Color Picker*, those colors become available to use for each type of Page object as *Recent Colors* in the drop-down selection menu for *Shading* or the coloring of other objects.

Now let's create another hyperlink and take a shortcut. Select the cell containing the New York Times link and copy it. Now place your cursor in the cell to the right of the Bloomberg link and paste it. The New York Times hyperlink with all of its design attributes is now duplicated on the Page as shown in **Illustration 51** below.

Illustration 51

Highlight the new *New York Times* hyperlink and click on the *Hyperlink Ribbon* menu button. The *Edit Hyperlink* dialogue screen will display as shown in **Illustration 52** below, where you can change the link.

Illustration 52

Notice on your *SharePoint Designer* Page, as can be seen in **Illustration 51** above, that although we centered the hyperlink texts in their respective cells, they don't look centered. Not to worry, this is also a bug but you don't have to do anything to work around it. Open the Page in *SharePoint* and the text will be perfectly centered as shown in **Illustration 53** below.

Illustration 53

SharePoint Designer makes this type of accessible Page design possible because of the excellent tools that it provides. The robust functionality of the *Insert Hyperlink* tool is a case in point. Compare the *SharePoint Designer* capabilities for this function with the facility for Inserting a Link in the *SharePoint* user interface as shown in **Illustration 54** below.

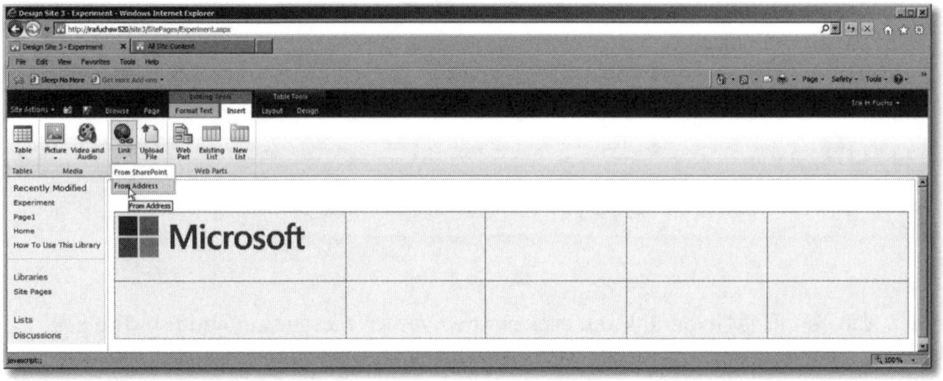

Illustration 54

The *Insert Hyperlink* dialogue screen as shown in **Illustration 55** below represents the total functionality available from within *SharePoint*.

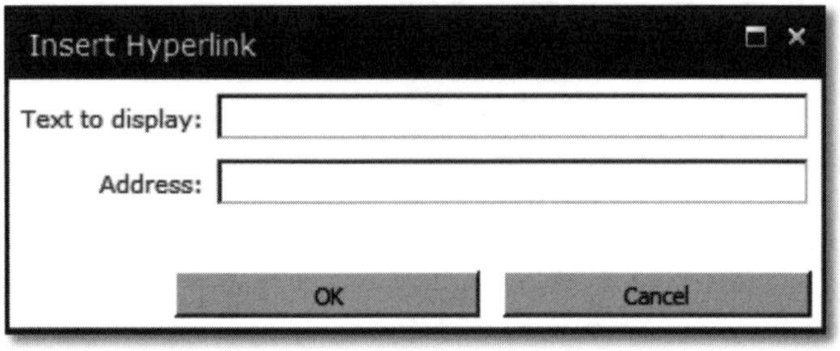

Illustration 55

Note that *SharePoint* natively provide the ability to inspect and modify hyperlinks that have been embedded using *SharePoint Designer* from the *Link Tools Ribbon* menu as shown in **Illustration 56** below.

Illustration 56

Return to *SharePoint Designer*. Using the *Ctrl-key*, select all the cells in the third column of the first table that we created, as shown in **Illustration 57** below.

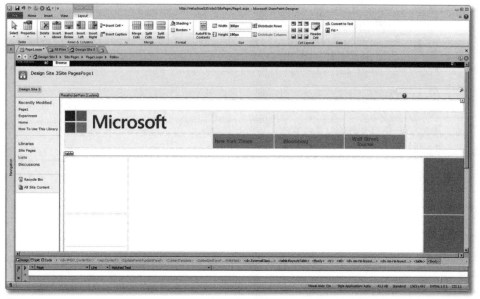

Illustration 57

Click the *Shading* button from the *Ribbon* and select a color from the drop-down menu or use the *More Colors* tool. Your Page should look like **Illustration 58** below.

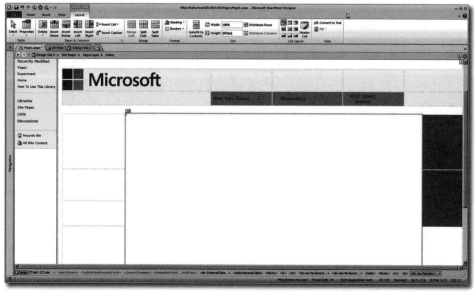

Illustration 58

Now select the bottom cell in the third column and right-click. Select *Insert* and then *Row Below* as shown in **Illustration 59** below.

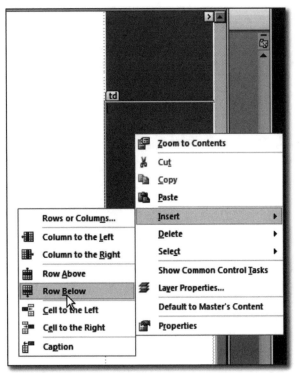

Illustration 59

An additional row will be added to the table and the same coloring that was applied to the third column cells will also be applied to the new cell in this column as shown in **Illustration 60** below.

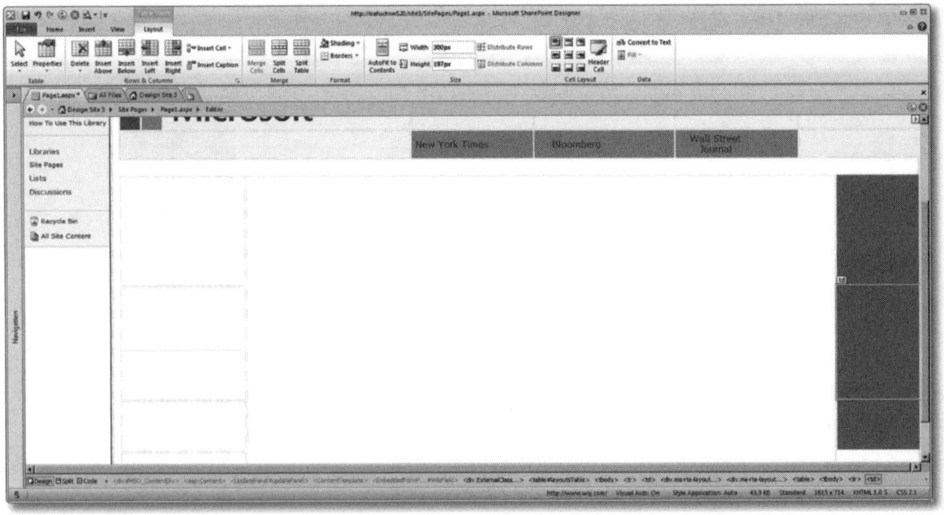

Illustration 60

Save your Page and preview it in the Browser as shown in **Illustration 61** below. Later we will remove the extra space above the top table and between the two tables. It should becoming apparent that it is possible to use this method to create a sophisticated layout.

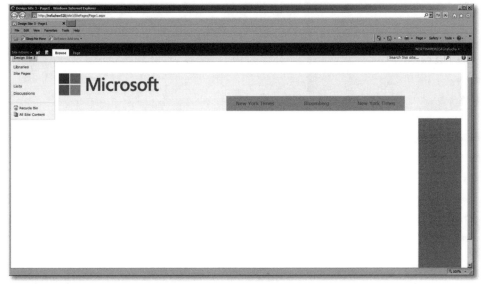

Illustration 61

The next thing we will add to the Page is a *Content Editor Web Part*. A *Content Editor Web Part* is the container where an end-user can manually enter or paste formatted text including tables, as well as insert images and hyperlinks. Select the cell in the middle column of the table as shown in **Illustration 62** below.

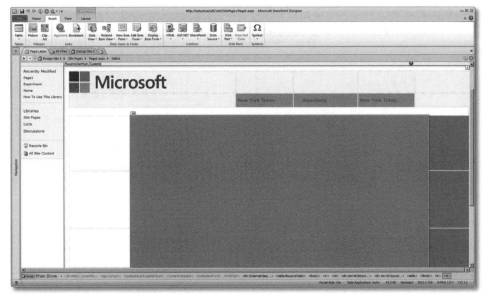

Illustration 62

From the *Table Tools Insert Tab* on the *Ribbon* menu click on *Web Part* to display the drop-down selection menu as shown in **Illustration 63** below.

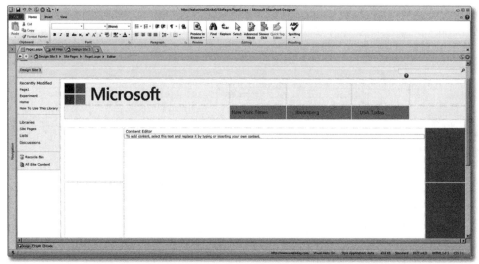

Illustration 63

Select the *Content Editor Web Part* which will be inserted in the selected cell as shown in **Illustration 64** below.

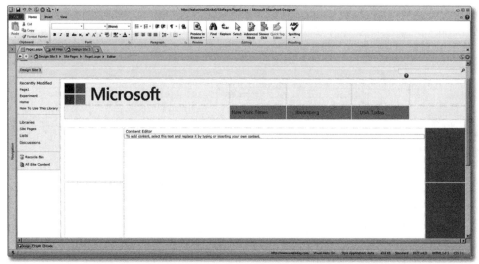

Illustration 64

Click on the editing area in the Content Editor and the *Ribbon* menu will display all the familiar text entry and formatting functions that are available in all of the *Microsoft Office* products. Expand the *Appearance* section of the *Web Part Configuration* pane as shown in **Illustration 69** below. Enter or paste text in the editing area.

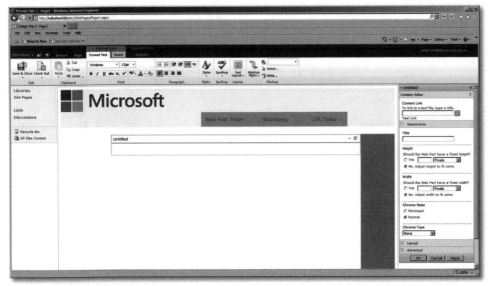

Illustration 69

In the *Configuration Pane* clear the *Title Box* and set the *Chrome Type* to None as shown in **Illustration 69** above. Click the *OK* button to close the *Configuration Pane*. Click the *Save & Close* button on the *Ribbon* menu. The effect of these two settings is to remove the "framing" of the *Content Editor* in Browse mode so that only the content displays as shown in **Illustration 70** below.

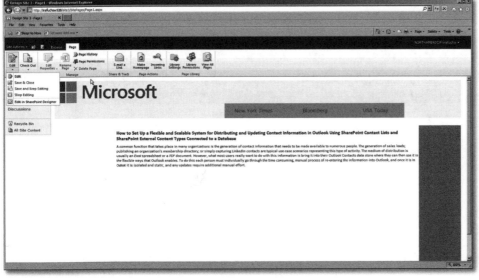

Illustration 70

Save the Page and preview it in a Browser window, which will look like **Illustration 65** below.

Illustration 65

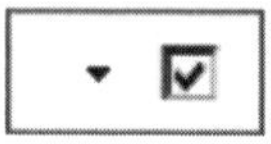

Select the *Web Part Configuration* drop-down icon on the top right corner of the Web Part as shown in **Illustration 66** here.

Illustration 66

Select the *Edit Web Part* option as shown in **Illustration 67** at left.

Illustration 67

The *Content Editor* is now in *Edit* mode and clicking on the content area allows a user to enter content. The *Web Part Configuration* pane will also display on the right side of the Page as shown in **Illustration 68** below.

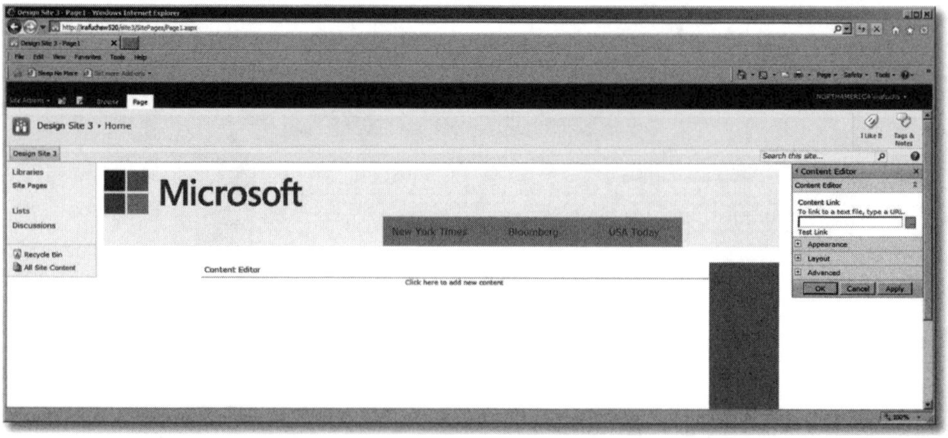

Illustration 68

Return to the Page in *SharePoint Designer* and click on the *Refresh* icon or your *F5* button. The refreshed Page will display the content you entered or inserted from the Browser as shown in **Illustration 71** below. When you click on the *Content Editor Web Part* the *Ribbon* menu will change to show the Web Part *Tools*. Click on the *Format* button and you will see that the settings for the *Title* and *Chrome* are available here as well as in the *Configuration Pane*.

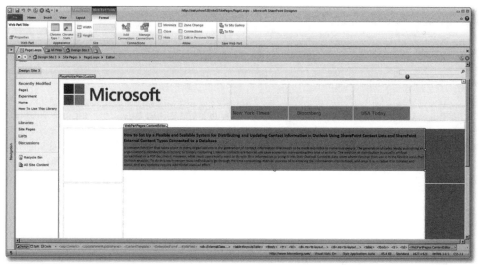

Illustration 71

Now that we have a Page with design elements (i.e. logos and shaded table cells that frame the Page), hyperlinks, and a Content Editor Web Part; all of which are embedded in multiple tables, it is a good time to review what our next steps will be in creating a Site Template. We will also discuss what artifacts can be embedded on a Page that will reproduce when a new Site is generated from the Site Template.

Our next step is to do a *Save As* of this Page multiple times with different names. The replicated Pages will all be stored in the Site Pages Library. Since the Pages are fully formatted with all the design elements we added, all a user needs to do is edit a Page and then reference it using a hyperlink, which we will do shortly. Optionally, we can link some of these Pages together before generating the Site Template, the effect of which will be that any Site generated from the template will automatically contain those links. Any of the replicated Pages in the Site Pages Library can be individually modified, and the Site Template will include these modifications. Furthermore once Sites are instantiated from the Site Template, the Pages in the Site Pages Library of those Sites can be modified as well using *SharePoint Designer* or the *SharePoint* user interface.

As was seen when we inserted the *Content Editor Web Part*, it is possible to place *SharePoint* Web Parts into cells of a table, thus facilitating flexible Page layouts. It is not necessary to use *Web Part Pages* to deploy Web Parts, and Web Part Pages cannot be modified in the ways demonstrated here.

Important Note – Not all Web Parts placed on a Page are included in a generated Site Template. When this happens a Site that is created from the Site Template will not contain the Web Part at all, or there will be a placeholder for the Web Part as there was for the picture that we placed earlier. An indication that a Web Part may be dropped is the message shown in **Illustration 72** below when a Site is saved.

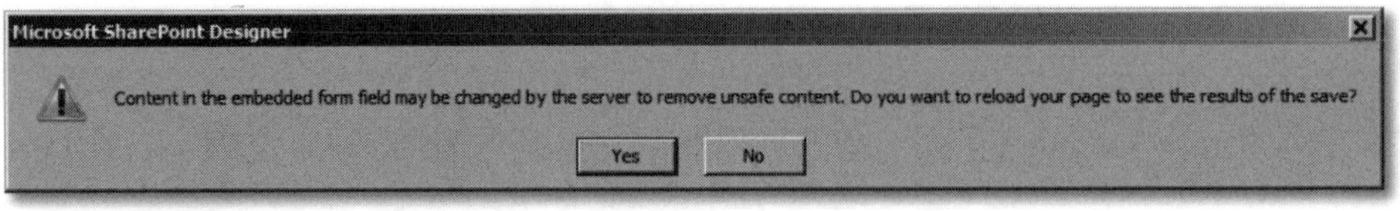

Illustration 72

From testing a partial set of Web Parts it appears that most will make it into the Site Template, and in in turn will be replicated in a new Site generated from the Site Template. **Illustration 73** below shows multiple Web Parts (Content Editor, Summary Links, Table of Contents, User Profile Filter, a List saved as a Global Web Part, Page Viewer, Content Query, Silver Light, Note Board and Media Web Part) placed in cells in a table.

Note – In the next chapter we will demonstrate how to create a Global Web Part from a List or Library.

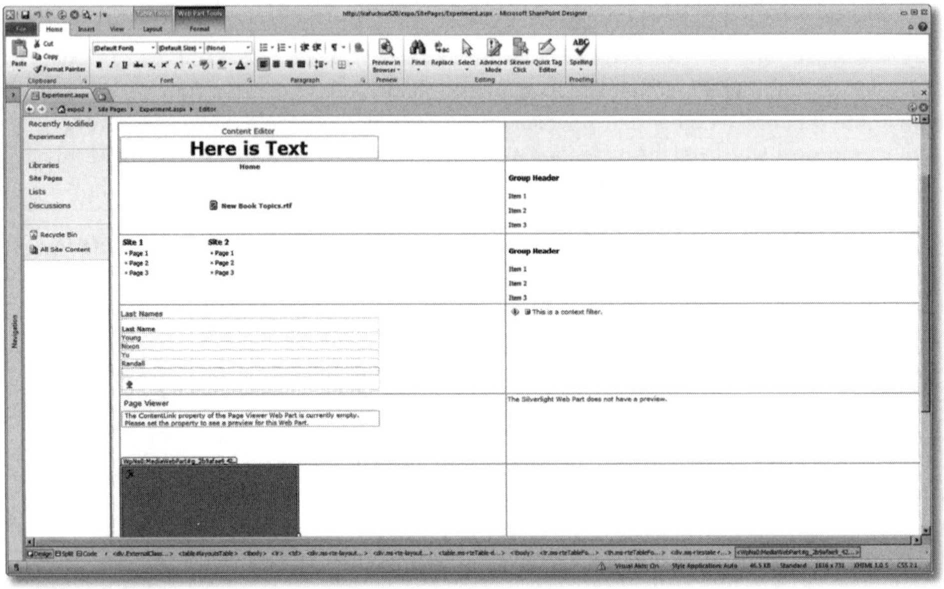

Illustration 73

A Site Template was generated from the blank Site containing this Page. In turn another Site was created from the Site Template. **Illustration 74** on the next page shows this Page in *SharePoint* from the new Site.

Illustration 74

> **Note** – although some Web Parts may not be included in the generation of a Site Template they will still work in the original Site. Furthermore these Web Parts can be added manually to a Site generated from a Site Template and they will also work just fine.

All of the Web Parts placed on the original Page display and work with the exception of the *User Profile Filter* and the *Note Board*. There is also a *Wiki hyperlink* ([[Home]]) and an embedded document (*New Book Topics.rtf*) on this Page as well, as shown in **Illustration 75** below.

Illustration 75

These objects can only be inserted from the *SharePoint* user interface. We will review how to use the *Wiki Page* editing capabilities of *SharePoint* Pages shortly. The embedded document was placed on the Page using the *Upload File Ribbon* menu button as shown in **Illustration 75** above.

Return to *SharePoint Designer* and select Site Pages from the *Navigation Site Objects* pane. You will see three Pages in this folder as shown in **Illustration 76** below. "Page1", which we created; a "Home" Page and a Page named "How to Use This Library". These two additional Pages were created by *SharePoint* when the *Site Pages* and *Site Assets* libraries were instantiated when Page1 was created. These additional Pages can be deleted later.

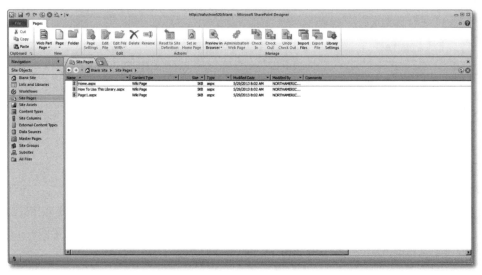

Illustration 76

We want to make a copy of Page1, so copy and paste it back to the *Site Pages* Library. You will see a Page named *Page1_copy(1)*. Open this file in the *SharePoint Designer* Page editor as shown in **Illustration 77** below.

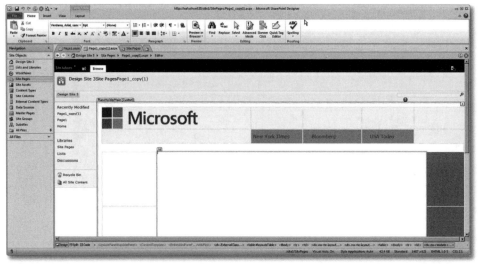

Illustration 77

Unfortunately, due to another "bug" the copied Page is missing the *Content Editor Web Part* that was inserted in the original. We want complete fidelity in the copied Pages so this method of copying won't work. The method of copying that will reproduce all the elements on a Page is to do a *Save As*. So open Page1 in the editor and from the *File* menu click *Save As*. The *Save As* dialogue screen will display as shown in **Illustration 78** below.

Illustration 78

Name the new file "Page2" and click the *Save* button. Open Page2 in the editor and you will see that the *Content Editor Web Part* is present as shown in **Illustration 79** below.

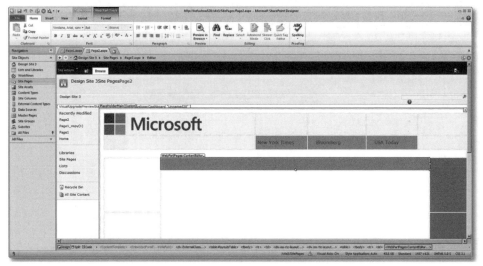

Illustration 79

Preview Page2 in a Browser. It appears that the *Content Editor Web Part* is not on the Page as shown in **Illustration 80** below. It is present but not visible because we configured it not to have a *Title* or display its *Chrome* in Browse mode.

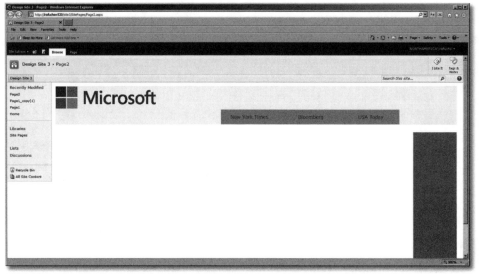

Illustration 80

Click on *Edit Page* from the *Site Actions* drop-down menu and place your cursor in the middle of the Page. The *Content Editor Web Part* will display. To enter or copy text and other objects click on the *Edit Web Part icon* on the right of the Web Part as shown in **Illustration 81** below.

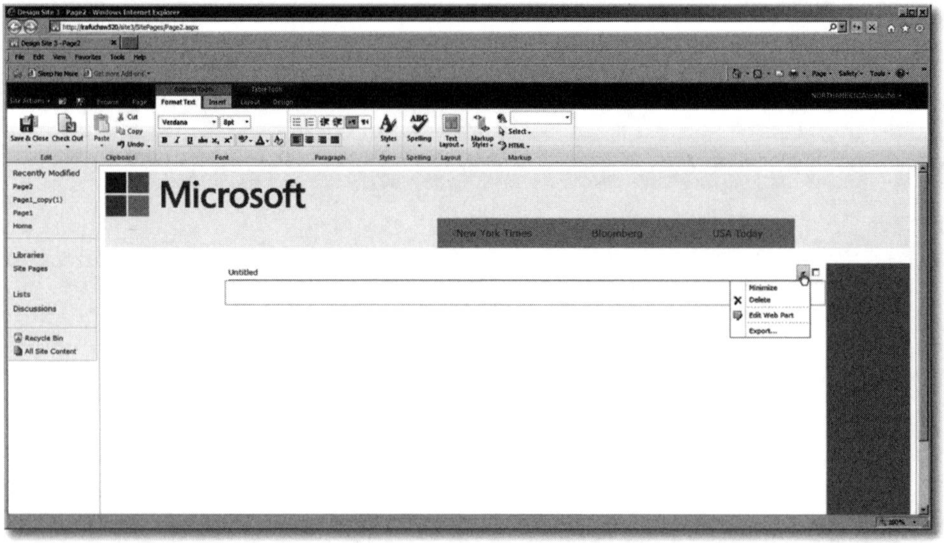

Illustration 81

Returning to *SharePoint Designer,* use *Save As* to make two more copies of Page1 and name them Page3 and Page4. Return to the *Site Pages* Library. Select *Page1* and click the Set as *Home Page Ribbon* button; the "Home" icon will now be displayed to the left of Page1. Select the two additional Pages created by *SharePoint* and delete them so that only Pages 1 to 4 remain in the *Site Pages* Library as shown in **Illustration 82** below.

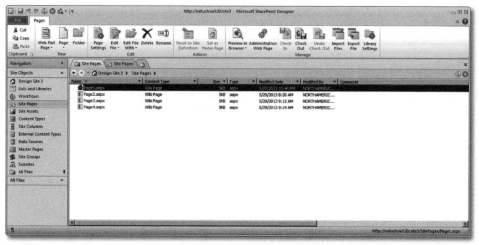

Illustration 82

Open Page1 in the *Editor* and select the first hyperlink for the New York Times (or whatever Page you linked to); then click the *Hyperlink* button on the *Ribbon* menu to open the *Edit Hyperlink* dialogue screen as shown in **Illustration 83** below.

Illustration 83

We are going to change this hyperlink so that it will link to Page2. Change the Text to display to "Page 2" and modify the *ScreenTip* to reflect the same. In the *Look in* drop-down selection box choose *SitePages*. In the *SitePages* folder you will see Pages 1 through 4 as well as a reference to the underlying Master Page.

Note – If you click on any of the Pages displayed, such as Page1.aspx, the *Address box* will display "Page1.aspx". If you save the link as is, it will not work correctly because "Page1. aspx" is not a valid address. You must enter the address using the format */Site3/SitePages/ Page2.aspx*, or *http://irafuchsw520/Site3/SitePages/Page2.aspx* as shown in **Illustration 84** below.

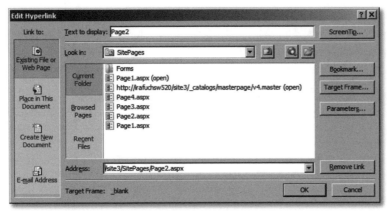

Illustration 84

Now modify the two other hyperlinks on the Page so they link to Page3 and Page4 respectively. You can click on the drop-down selection box for *Address* to select and modify a previously entered address so that you do not have to enter it manually as shown in **Illustration 85** below.

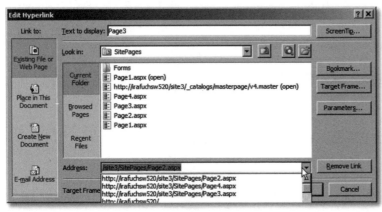

Illustration 85

Save the Page and preview it in your Browser to see that the hyperlinks work. The default *Target Frame* behavior for a hyperlink is to open the linked Page in a new Browser window. You can change the *Target Frame* behavior by clicking on the *Target Frame* button to select a different target frame as shown in **Illustration 86** on the next page.

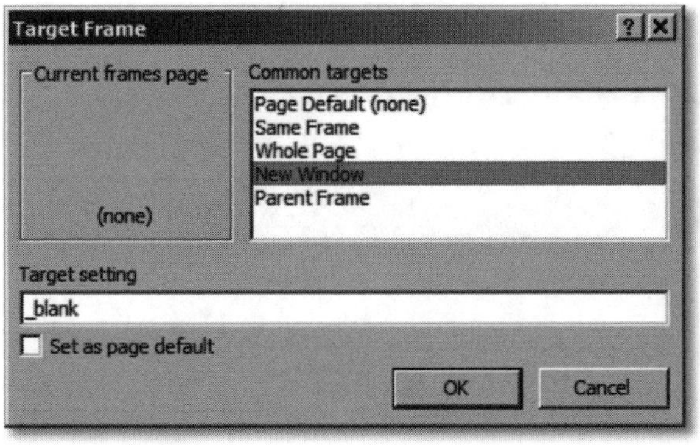

Illustration 86

Now open Page2 in Edit mode and change the hyperlinks to reference Page1, Page3 and Page4. Save it and then change the links on Page3 to reference Page1, Page2 and Page4. Finally, do the same on Page4 using Page1, Page2 and Page3 for the reference links. Remember to change the Screen Tips as well. Save your changes and then preview Page1 in a Browser to see that the hyperlinks work.

You now have a basic four-page Web Site that can be used as is for publishing content. We arbitrarily created four pages and linked them together, but this could just as easily have been accomplished with one page. If we had not linked the pages together they will still be included in the Site Template. The Site Pages included in the template can be linked together at any time in the same manner, or in other ways, as we will demonstrate shortly.

For now, let's generate a Site Template from this Site to see how it works. Click on the *Site icon* on the *Navigation Site Objects* pane in *SharePoint Designer* as shown in **Illustration 87** below. From this Page you can generate a Site Template by clicking on the *Save as Template* button.

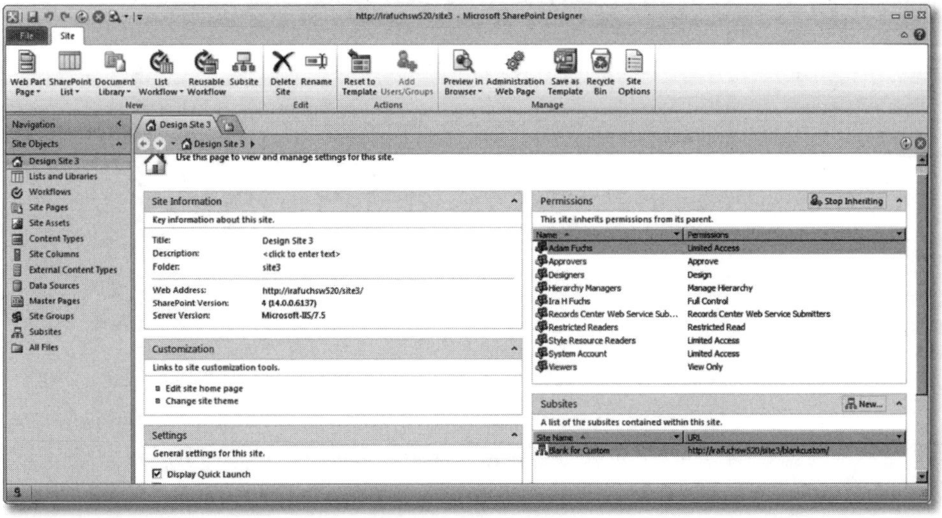

Illustration 87

Alternatively, in the *SharePoint* user interface you can go to the *Site Settings* page for the Site and under the *Site Actions* section click on *Save Site as template* as shown in **Illustration 88** below.

Illustration 88

In either case the *Save as Template Page* will display as shown in **Illustration 89** below. Enter a *File name* and a *Template name* and check the *Include Content* check box. Click the *OK* button.

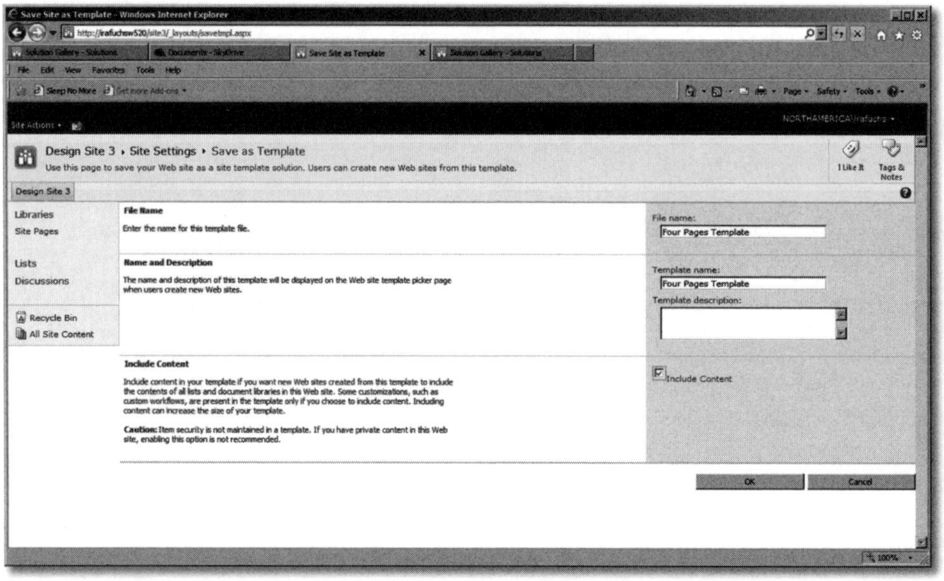

Illustration 89

In a few minutes a Page will display informing you that the Site Template was created with a link to the *Solutions Gallery* at the Site Collection level where the Site Templates are stored. Click on the *Solutions Gallery* Link to open the *Solutions Page* where you will see the Site Template was installed on the Site Collection as a Solution, and automatically activated as shown in **Illustration 90** below.

> **Note** – A Site Template Solution must be activated to be available as a Site creation option. You can deactivate and activate Solutions at any time.

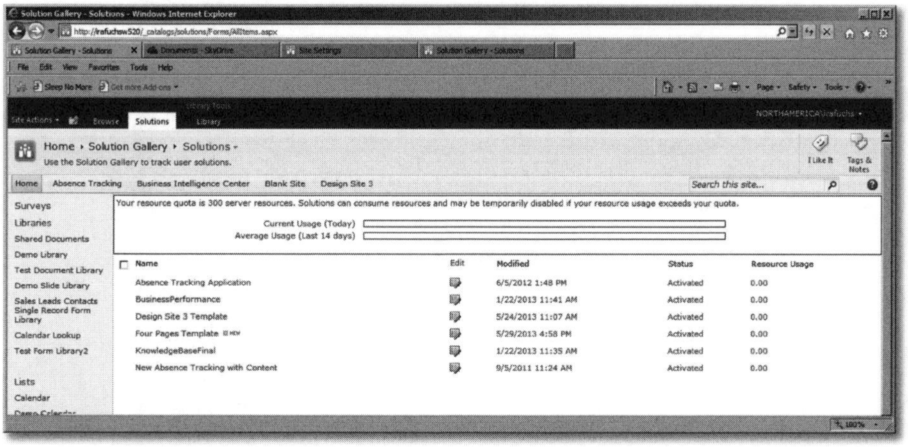

Illustration 90

Now let's create a new Site from this Site Template. From the *Site Actions* drop-down menu select *New Site*. The *Create* Silverlight dialogue screen will display (if Silverlight is running on your Site) as shown in **Illustration 91** below. Scroll down to the bottom of the Site options and you will see the named Site Template that you just saved. Select it and enter a name for the Site you want to create and its URL address. The new Site name does not have to use the Site Template name.

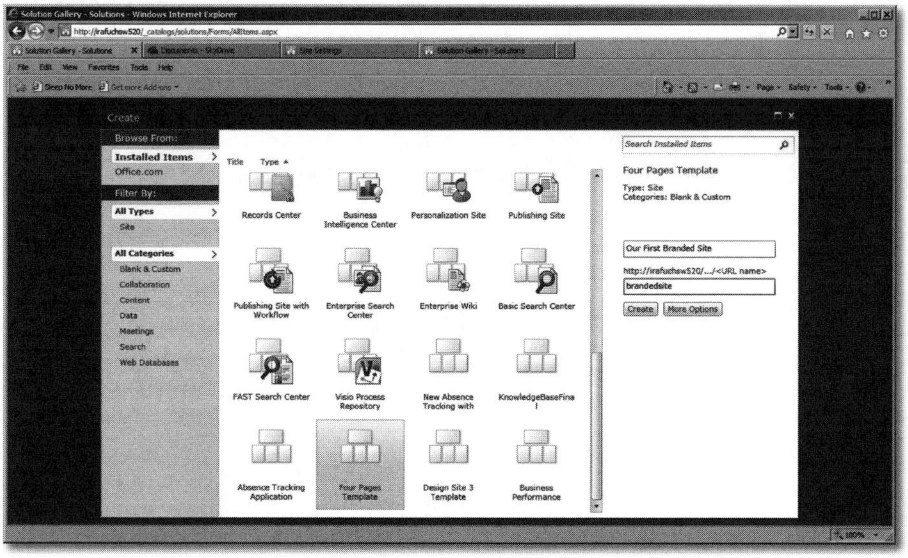

Illustration 91

A Processing screen will display while the Site is being created and when it is complete the new Site will open in a Browser as shown in **Illustration 92** below.

There you have it! You now have a reusable custom designed Site. It behaves just like any Site and can be edited by clicking on *Edit Page* from the *Site Actions* Page. Click on the *Edit Page* link and place your cursor in the center of the *Page*.

Something is wrong! The *Content Editor Web Part* is missing from Page1.

Illustration 92

Click on the links to the other Pages in the Site and check if the *Content Editor Web Part* is present on those Pages by clicking *Edit Page* on each. In this particular instance the *Content Editor Web Part* was included on Pages 2, 3 and 4 as can be seen in **Illustration 93** below but not on Page 1.

Illustration 93

If you are experienced in working with *SharePoint* this type of anomalous behavior is not surprising. *SharePoint* is a complex product and these types of issues show up regularly. The fix in this case was changing the home Page from Page 1 to Page 2 (and reversing their names) and then removing the Content Editor Web Part from Page 1 and inserting it again. The Site Template subsequently created with this modification generated new Sites with the Content Editor Web Part present on all Pages.

> **Note** – Changing the names of the Pages in turn requires changing the hyperlinks on the Pages and this type of dumb re-work is the most frustrating part of the process. Notwithstanding the effort to create a fix, *SharePoint Designer* at least eliminates some of the tedious work involved in implementing the fix: every time you change the name of a Page *SharePoint Designer* will automatically update the hyperlinks on all of the referenced Pages. Not only does it change the hyperlink addresses but it changes the names of the link on each Page as well, as shown by the message screen in **Illustration 94** below that displays when you change a Page's name.

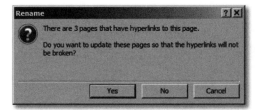

Illustration 94

It is very likely that you will be confronted with this type of anomalous behavior regularly and it is part and parcel of working with *SharePoint*. Fortunately it is very easy to generate Site Templates and create Sites from those templates, which you will do frequently if you are interested in creating a library of custom Site Templates that contain different features and functions. Conversely it is also easy to delete Sites (from either the *SharePoint Site Settings* Page or in *SharePoint Designer,* as well as the *Site Template Solutions*. To delete *Site Template Solutions* go to the *Solutions Gallery* from the *Site Collection Site Settings* Page. Select the Solution you wish to delete and click on the *Deactivate Ribbon* button as shown in **Illustration 95** below.

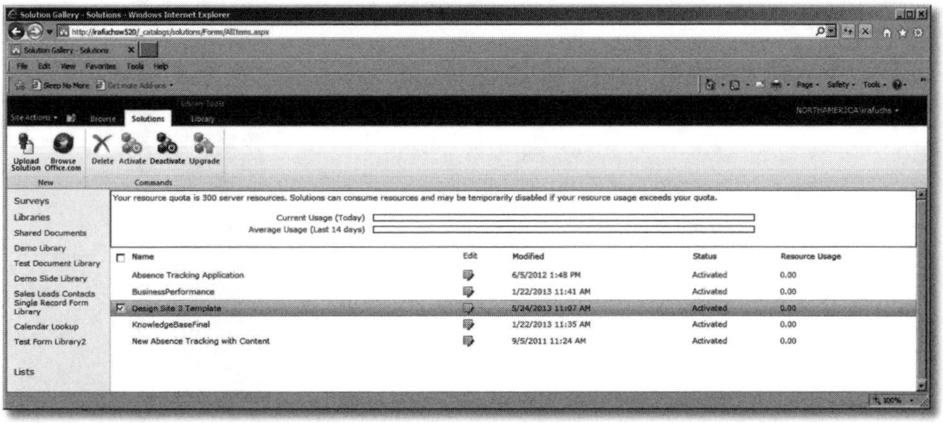

Illustration 95

The *Deactivate Solutions* dialogue screen will display. Click the *Deactivate* button again to confirm that you want to deactivate the Solution as shown in **Illustration 96** below.

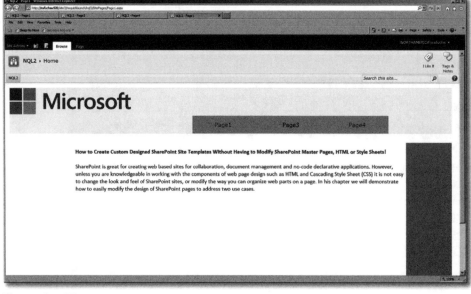

Illustration 96

Click the *Close* button. On the *Solutions* Page select the *Solution* again and click the *Delete Ribbon* menu to delete it.

Eliminating the Display of the Quick Launch Pane from a Page or Site

The next thing we want to do is create a version of this Site that does not display the *Quick Launch* pane as shown in **Illustration 97** below. This provides users with a simple, stripped-down page layout, unencumbered by extraneous *SharePoint* artifacts which are not relevant to generating and delivering Web based content.

Illustration 97

The first step in accomplishing this is to create another Site from the existing Site Template (the one that was fixed to contain the Content Edit Web Part on Page1). Name the Site "No Quick Launch Design", which will look just like your original Site as shown in **Illustration 98** below.

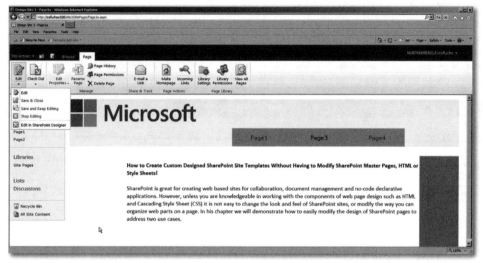

Illustration 98

We are going to continue working directly in the *SharePoint* user interface in order to point out some of the design and content generation options available to end-users without access to *SharePoint Designer*. Open the Page in *edit* mode by clicking on the *Page Ribbon* button and then click the *Edit* button. Place your cursor on the Page and click on the *Layout* button that displays. Click the *Show Grid Lines* button to display the table you we originally placed on the Page as shown in **Illustration 99** below.

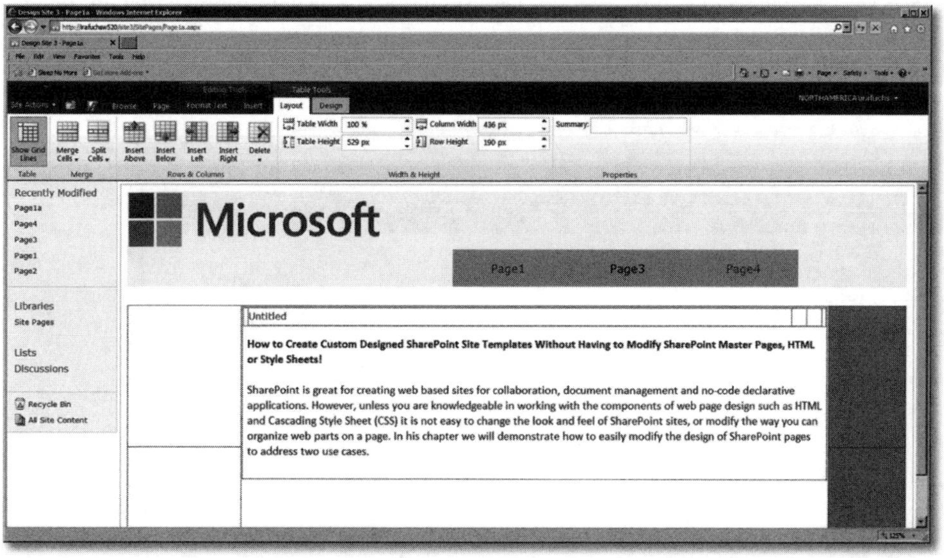

Illustration 99

The *Ribbon* menu provides options for adding or deleting rows and columns, and modifying cells. Scroll down the Page and place your cursor in the lower left cell of the table. Click the *Insert* button on the *Ribbon* and select *Web Part*. The *Web Part Insert* menu will display as shown in **Illustration 100** below. Any Web Part can be placed in any cell. Using a flexible table matrix for inserting Web Parts provides a more versatile end-user design experience than using *Web Part Pages*. Select the *Media and Content Category* folder; select *Content Editor* and click the *Add* button.

Illustration 100

The *Content Editor Web Part* will be inserted. Select the *Web Part Configuration* drop-down icon on the top right corner of the Web Part and click the *Edit Web Part* option. Click the *Click here to add new content link* on the *Content Editor Web Part* as shown in in **Illustration 101** below.

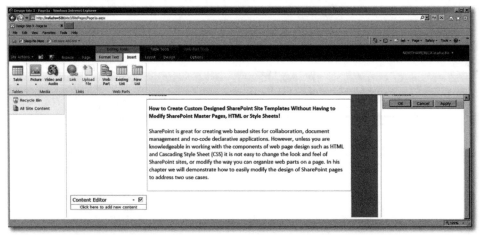

Illustration 101

The *Editing Tools* tab of the *Ribbon* menu will display as shown in **Illustration 102** below.

Illustration 102

Click the *HTML* button on the top right of the *Ribbon* menu and select *Edit HTML Source* as shown in **Illustration 103** below.

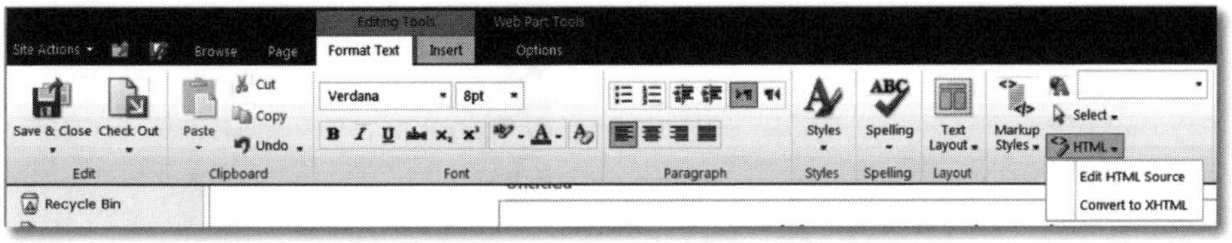

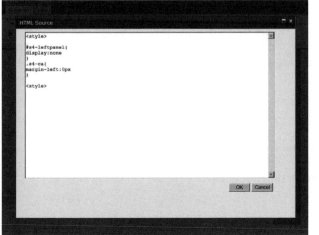

Illustration 103

The *HTML Source Editor* will display as shown in **Illustration 104** below.

Enter the following HTML code into this editor box as shown in **Illustration 104** below:

<style>

#s4-leftpanel{
display:none
}
.s4-ca{
margin-left:0px
}

<style>

Illustration 104

Click *OK* and the Quick Launch pane will disappear as shown in **Illustration 105** below. In addition to displaying content, the *Content Editor Web Part* also functions as a container for HTML and JavaScript code that can modify the rendering of *SharePoint* Pages in a Browser. In the *Content Editor Configuration* pane clear the *Title Text* box and set the *Chrome Type* to "None" to hide the Web Part. Click *OK* to close the *Configuration* pane. Finally, select the *Minimize* setting for the *Content Editor Web Part* as shown in the image below. This essentially hides it on the Page.

Illustration 105

Now add a *Content Editor Web Part* with this *HTML code* on the other three Pages. You now have a light-weight content publishing Site that contains consistent design elements and eliminates unnecessary *SharePoint* artifacts. We placed active hyperlinks on all the Pages in this Site in order to demonstrate the *Hyperlink* functionality of *SharePoint Designer*. However, in most cases people will only need a single Page to publish their content. It's simple enough to create a Site from a Site Template, remove the hyperlinks and use that Site or create a new Site Template from that one. The additional Pages will be there in case they are needed and links can be added to any Page at any time, which now brings us to a review of *SharePoint's* Wiki Page functionality.

SharePoint Wiki Page Functionality

Open any of the Pages in edit mode and place your cursor in any cell. Enter double left brackets '[[' and *SharePoint* will display a type-ahead like prompt identifying the various artifacts that are available to link to in the Site as shown in **Illustration 106** on the next page.

Illustration 106

The prompts display Pages, Lists, Libraries and Views. If the Lists or Libraries contain other artifacts or content a *forward slash* will be present indicating that they contain other artifacts or content. Selecting a List (which we will discuss shortly) containing Views will then identify those Views as shown in **Illustration 107** below.

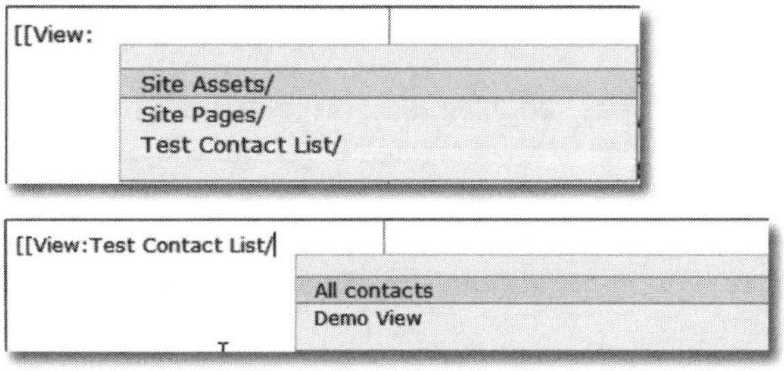

[[View:	
Site Assets/	
Site Pages/	
Test Contact List/	

[[View:Test Contact List/	
All contacts	
Demo View	

Illustration 107

Once the final artifact or content to create a link to is identified add two right brackets "]]" to complete the link reference as shown in **Illustration 108** below.

Illustration 108

Save and Close the Page to exit edit mode and you will see the new link, as shown in **Illustration 109** below. In *edit mode* you can format the links with any of the Text formatting functions available on the *Ribbon*. If you edit a link in *SharePoint Designer* you have additional formatting options as well.

Illustration 109

This Wiki page functionality provides an additional way in which to connect artifacts in a Site together simply and easily.

> **Note** - When you type arbitrary text between left and right double brackets (i.e. [[This is a New Page Link]]), the Wiki convention creates a new link to a yet created Page that will be named with the text entered in the brackets. The link's dotted underline indicates the Page has not yet been created. Clicking on the link will display a prompt to create the new Page, however the new Page will be a ***standard SharePoint Page without the layout elements*** that the other Pages have.

Web Page Publishing and Management Options

Creating a Site where the Pages are not necessarily connected to each other provides the opportunity to use one or more Pages for separate, independent publishing requirements. For example you can just name a Page "Bob's Page" for Bob to publish some content. Another Page would be named "Jill's Page, for Jill's content. As a result, you do not have to create multiple Sites, just duplicate the Pages in a Site and name them appropriately. One of the benefits of this is that Pages in a Site Pages Library have the same behavior as any List or Library object; you can use *SharePoint's* versioning facilities to require approval of the Page; it can have its own permissions; and you can apply a policy that auto-matically enforces retention and expiration of the Page.

Creating Designed Lists and Libraries in a Site for Specific Collaboration Purposes

Now we will address the second use case of creating designed Sites that incorporate *SharePoint* artifacts for specific collaboration purposes, such Lists, libraries and Web Parts. We have already demonstrated that *SharePoint* generic Pages with embedded Web Parts will reproduce correctly in most cases from a Site Template. However, Lists and libraries are based on *Web Part Pages* and these cannot be structured, edited and modified as we did with generic Pages. So now you have a design consistency challenge: if you want to implement the same design standards in a Site that will include Lists and libraries, how do you accomplish that so when a user moves from a designed Page to a List or Library Page they don't have an inconsistent visual experience.

There is a simple and elegant way to incorporate custom design elements from a generic Page into a Web Part Page: by placing a Content Editor Web Part onto a List or Library Page and copying the design elements from a Page opened in *SharePoint Designer* into the Content Editor Web Part. **Illustration 110** below displays a standard *SharePoint* List Page containing the same table that we created earlier in *SharePoint Designer*.

Illustration 110

Illustration 111 below shows the List in *edit mode* from the *SharePoint* user interface with the grid lines exposed. The table cells, pictures and links are fully accessible, as are the *Ribbon* menu options for working with all of the objects on the Page. All that needed to be done was to select the table from a Page opened in *SharePoint Designer,* copy it, and then paste it into the *Content Editor Web Part* from the *SharePoint* user interface in edit mode.

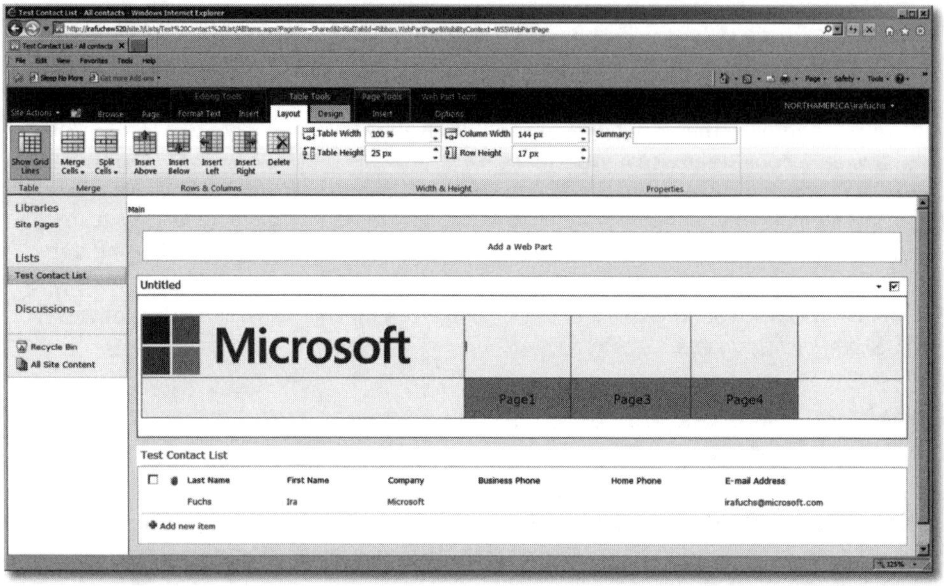

Illustration 111

Optionally, you can use *SharePoint Designer* to edit the objects embedded in a Content Editor Web Part that has been placed on a List or Library Page by editing the Views for a List or Library. All of *SharePoint Designer's* enhanced editing capabilities are available for modifying the content embedded in the Content Editor Web Part as shown in **Illustration 112** below.

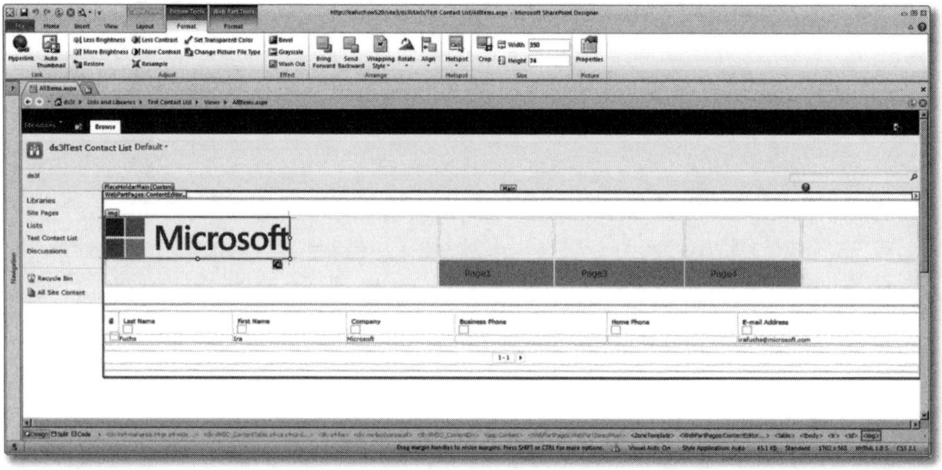

Illustration 112

The question that you might have at seeing this is "What happens if a user creates a new View of the List or Library? As can be seen in **Illustration 113** below additional Views were created for this List, and happily, the additional Views only modify the Web part that contains the List data but does not affect any other Web Parts on the host Page. Consequently any additional Views created for a List or Library will also incorporate the added custom design elements.

Illustration 113

Lists and libraries modified in this way will also reproduce correctly in Sites generated from a Site Template. The work that needs to be done upfront is to create designed Site Templates that incorporate the same List and Library artifacts found in an out-of-the box *SharePoint* Site Template and substitute these modified templates for the originals. One of the significant benefits of doing this is that you can also incorporate object behavior; such as applying versioning, content types and policies to Lists and Libraries. Doing so implements the substantial value-added functionality that is available from *SharePoint*, but not implemented by default in out-of-the box *SharePoint* Site Templates.

> **Important Note** – List Templates generated from a List modified in this way **will not** incorporate the additional Web Parts embedded on the Page.

Selectively Display Artifacts on the Quick Launch Pane

The Quick Launch Pane is meant to aide navigation to artifacts within a Site. Its use without modification however presents two issues: one, it becomes cluttered as links are added to it, and two, not all links are relevant to users of the Site and their presence, as well as the presence of the artifacts themselves, becomes confusing. There are a number of flexible ways in which to modify what artifacts are displayed on the Quick Launch pane as well as the Site links displayed on the Site Tabs as shown in **Illustration 114** on the next page.

Illustration 114

At the Site Collection level you can use the *Site collection navigation* Page as shown in **Illustration 115** below, which is found under *Site Collection Administration*, to completely turn off Quick Launch and Site Tab navigation for all Sites in the Site Collection. Every Site created in the Site Collection will only display its own tab. The Quick Launch is not hidden entirely as we were able to do earlier, the Recycle Bin and All Site Content links will still display.

> **Note** – you can turn off the display and use of the Recycle Bin for an entire Site Collection through its Settings Page under Site Collection Administration.

If the *Security Trimming* and *Audience Trimming* settings are checked then artifacts will be seen on the Quick Launch pane by users only if they have the permissions to access those artifacts or are members of an Audience that can access them.

Illustration 115

A more fined grain approach to managing displayed Quick Launch artifacts and Site Tab links are the use of the settings on the *Navigation Settings* Page for each Site, as shown in **Illustration 116 and 117** below. This Page is accessed from the *Site Settings* Page, and provides the ability to configure the Sites displayed on the Site Tab as well as edit, delete, add and restructure the artifacts that are displayed on the Quick Launch Pane.

Illustration 116

Illustration 117

A detailed view of the editing options, which change based on the artifact selected, is shown in **Illustration 118** below.

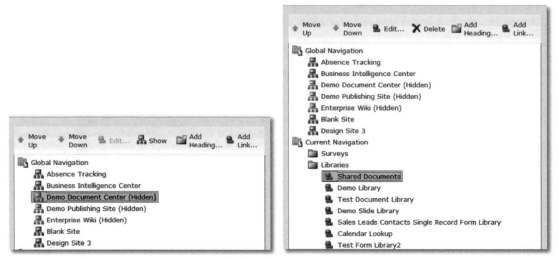

Illustration 118

These navigation settings can also be incorporated into a Site Template and inherited by any Site created from the Site Template. In this manner you can design Site Templates that only provide the specific functionality to address a particular purpose, and contain only those artifacts that support that purpose; much in the same way we created a simple light-weight content publishing Site earlier.

While *SharePoint* provides a wealth of features and functions, sometimes the best way to make sure that they are utilized and deployed most effectively is to avoid provisioning Sites that are not configured for a specific purpose and lack well defined lifecycle management settings and policies. A more purposeful and specific design and configuration of Site Templates can make the experience of using *SharePoint* better for the end user while advancing its adoption in functionally useful ways.

So there you have it – a fairly versatile and easy way to customize Pages and Site Templates along design standards and functional requirements. With a nominal amount of experimentation you should now be able to "institutionalize" the way *SharePoint* looks and works within your organization for the benefit and pleasure of all stakeholders.

Why SharePoint Designer is Your Best Friend

By now you are well aware of how useful and necessary *SharePoint Designer* is for creating *SharePoint* application artifacts such as workflows and External Content Types. In this last chapter we will be reviewing a variety of additional features and functions that *SharePoint Designer* provides in support of applications but, also enhance the experience of working with *SharePoint* in general. If you are responsible for creating, configuring and managing *SharePoint* artifacts than *SharePoint Designer* is your best friend because it will substantially improve the experience and efficiency of creating, configuring and managing those artifacts from a Site Collection level down to a List column.

The very first thing about *SharePoint Designer* that makes it your best friend is the fact that you can work with multiple artifacts and objects simultaneously. Creating and configuring artifacts using the *SharePoint* interface is a painfully linear experience where you must click back and forth through multiple pages to access settings and other functions. The experience in *SharePoint Designer* is markedly non-linear; you can access any artifact and its respective settings or functionality using the *Navigation Site Objects* pane in conjunction with the *Ribbon* menus as shown in **Illustration 1** below.

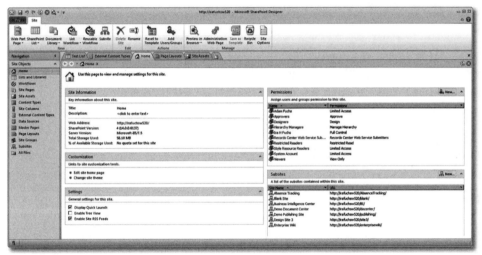

Illustration 1

Furthermore, you can keep multiple artifacts and functions open simultaneously and move between any of them with a single mouse-click. **Illustration 2** below shows multiple Tabs open indicating the simultaneous working access to a List, an External Content Type, a Site Collection Summary Page, the Page Layouts Library and the Site Assets Library. The Ribbon menu will also change its functional context whenever you select a different Tab.

Illustration 2

In addition, when a Tab or artifact is selected, bread crumb navigation provides you with the ability to move up and down the hierarchy of objects or functions for the Tab or artifact in focus; right-clicking on any artifact also presents its' relevant functions and related objects, as shown in **Illustration 3** below.

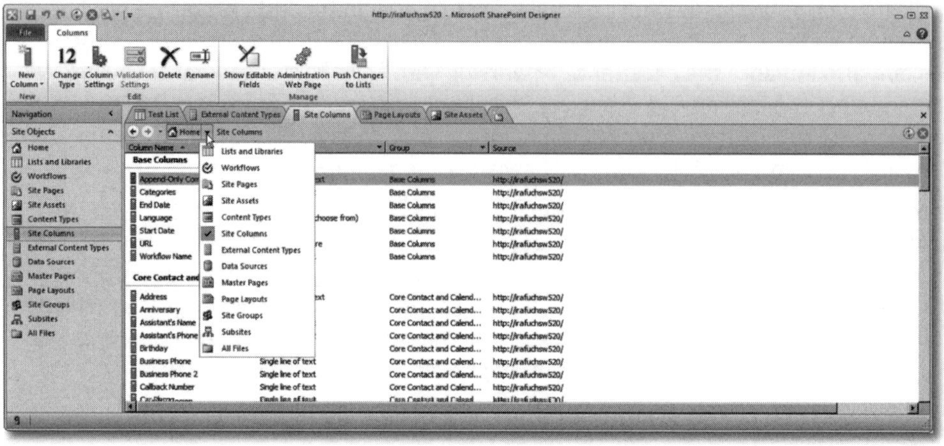

Illustration 3

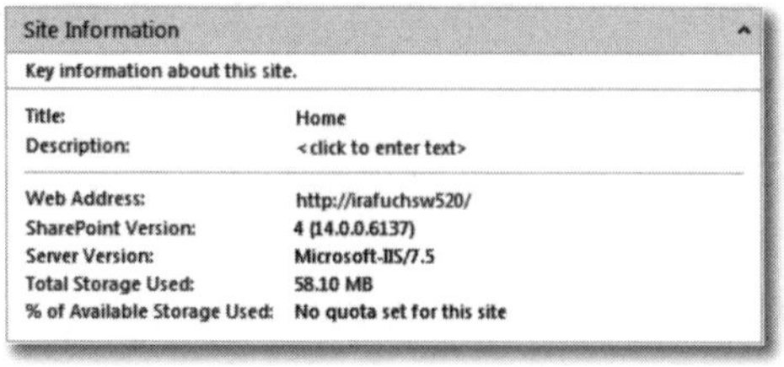

Illustration 4

Every artifact has a *Summary Page* that provides a snapshot of its most important settings. **Illustration 4** at left shows a section of the Summary Page for a Site Collection.

Illustration 5 below shows the full *Summary Page* for a Site Collection showing the Permissions and SubSites on the right.

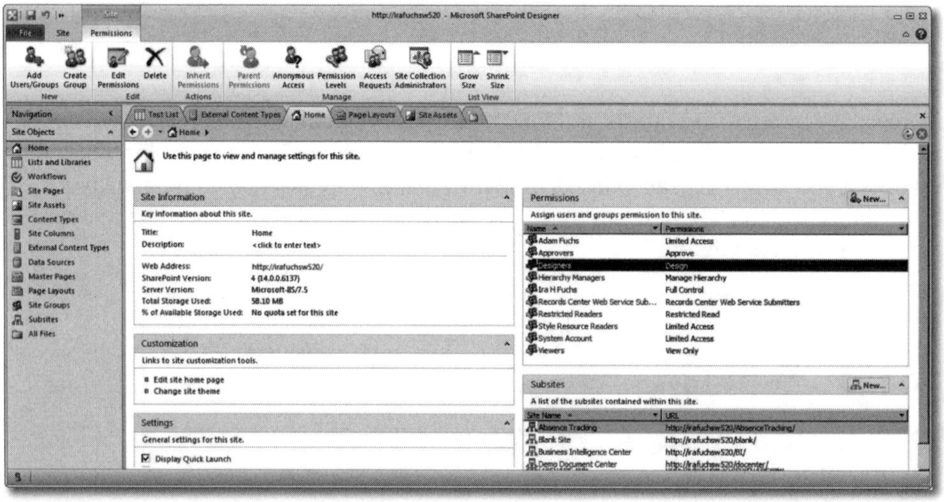

Illustration 5

The Settings dialogue screens open in context and are straightforward and snappy to work with as shown in **Illustration 6** below.

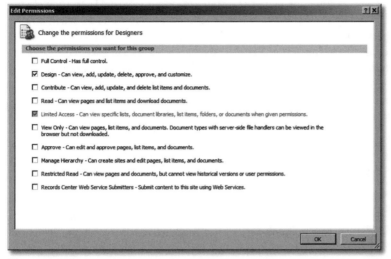

Illustration 6

The experience of opening a Site from *SharePoint Designer* is shown in **Illustration 7** below. *SharePoint Designer* maintains a cache of all the Sites that have been accessed and presents them clearly. This is very helpful if you work with many Site Collections and Sites; you don't have to guess where the Sites are or their URL addresses.

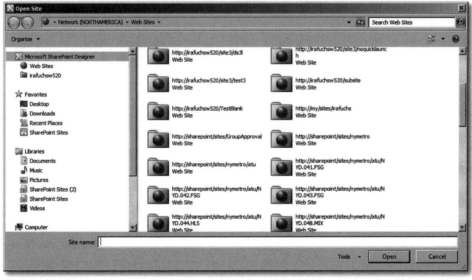

Illustration 7

Illustration 8 below shows how *SharePoint Designer* presents the inventory of Lists and Libraries in a Site when the Lists and Libraries Navigation pane icon is selected. Note that External Lists are included and the number of items in a List or Library is also presented. The number of items is a particularly useful piece of information when you need to ascertain whether List and libraries in a Site are being utilized or if attention needs to be paid to the size of a List or Library. The access to this information is not available directly in *SharePoint*. Right-clicking on the *Column Headings* displays a drop-down selection menu for both arranging and grouping List and Library artifacts by their attributes, further facilitating an immediate grasp of their characteristics. From the Lists and Libraries Object Navigation screen you can create and delete Lists and libraries as well.

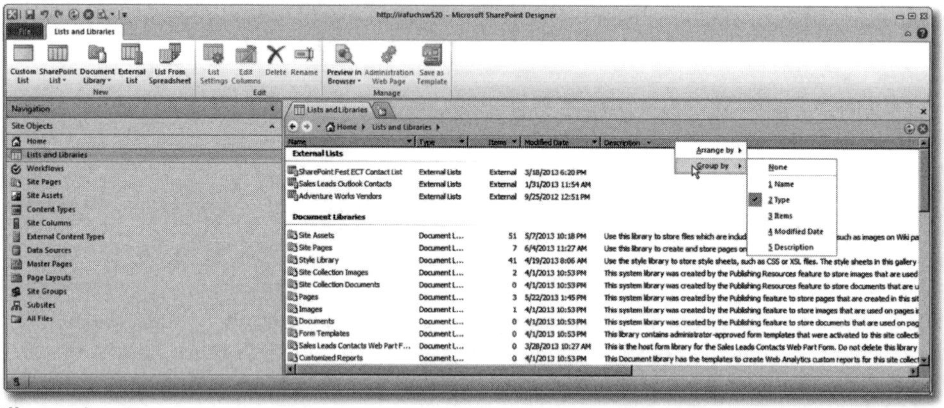

Illustration 8

Clicking on a List or Library will display its *Summary Page* as shown in **Illustration 9** below and this is where a great deal of useful information and functions are made available in a concise and elegant manner.

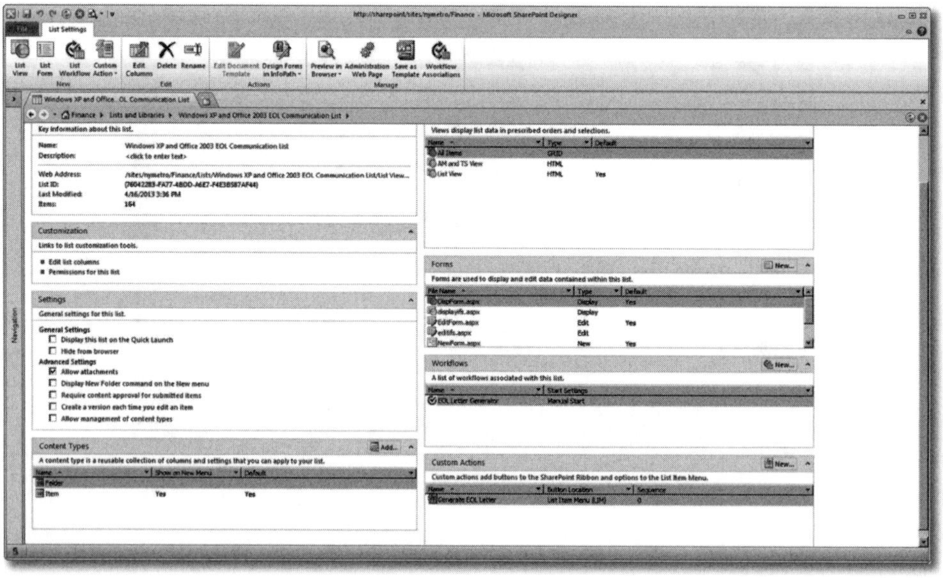

Illustration 9

Illustration 10 below shows an enlarged image of the left side of a List or Library Summary Page which displays the most commonly accessed settings for Lists and libraries. In the *SharePoint* user interface you would need to open and close multiple pages to get to these settings.

List Information ^

Key information about this list.

Name:	Test Document Library
Description:	<click to enter text>

Web Address:	/Test Document Library/Forms/AllItems.aspx
List ID:	{185859F2-C93D-47CF-8A6F-1A87F56E86A8}
Last Modified:	5/15/2013 3:47 PM
Items:	11

Customization ^

Links to list customization tools.

▣ Edit list columns
▣ Permissions for this list

Settings ^

General settings for this list.

General Settings
☑ Display this list on the Quick Launch
☐ Hide from browser
Advanced Settings
☑ Display New Folder command on the New menu
☐ Require content approval for submitted items
☐ Create a version each time you edit an item
☑ Allow management of content types
Document Template URL: /Test Document Library/Forms/template.dotx

Illustration 10

Note the *Hide from browser* check box setting. This is only available through *SharePoint Designer*. In building *SharePoint* applications there are two use cases where you will want to hide Lists and libraries. The first is where information is accessed programmatically (e.g. by a workflow or a look-up in a form) but should not be directly accessible by users. The second is the case, described in an earlier chapter, when a form template is published to a Library and the Library provides no additional functionality other than as the location where Form Services accesses the template. Hiding the form Library prevents people from inadvertently deleting it or changing it in any way.

> **Note** – Hiding a List or Library will also hide it from *SharePoint Designer* and it will not show up when you select the List and Libraries Navigation Object. However, the hidden List or Library is visible when you expand the *All Files Object Folder* as shown in **Illustration 11** on the next page. Clicking on the hidden List or Library here will open its Summary Page where you can deselect the *Hide from browser* checkbox.

This brings us to a review of the *All Files* hierarchy of objects and artifacts. Click on the *All Files Folder* on the *Navigation Site Objects* pane and then click on the *Pin icon* on the right of the *All Files Folder* so that it is pointing down as shown in **Illustration 11 below left**. The *All Files* hierarchy of objects and artifacts provides access to nearly everything in the *SharePoint* Content Database for a Site Collection or Site. **Illustration 11 below left** shows the *All Files* hierarchy for a Site Collection while **Illustration 11 below right** shows the *All Files* hierarchy for a Subsite. At the Site Collection level you have access to all Site Collection artifacts, objects, **as well as content!**

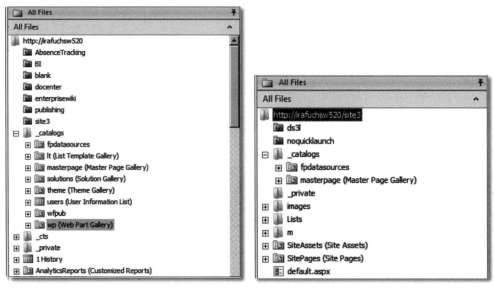

Illustration 11

If you have access to a Site Collection expand the *_catalogs* folder as shown in **Illustration 11 above left**. You will see the libraries for the various Site Collection artifacts and objects. Expand and double click on the *wp (Web Part Gallery)* folder in the Navigation pane. The inventory of Web Parts will display below the folder in the navigation pane as well as in the main display area as shown in **Illustration 12** below.

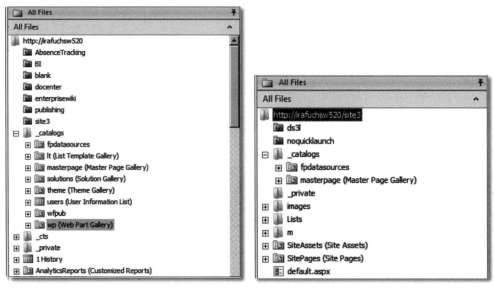

Illustration 12

From this screen you can delete, rename and copy a Web Part as well as import and export Web Parts. We will be examining the enhanced capabilities for importing information into any Library from *SharePoint Designer* shortly.

Scroll further down the *All Files Library* nodes in the *Navigation Site Objects* pane. Now expand and double-click on a Library. The document contents of the Library will be displayed in the N*avigation Site Objects* pane as shown in **Illustration 13** at right.

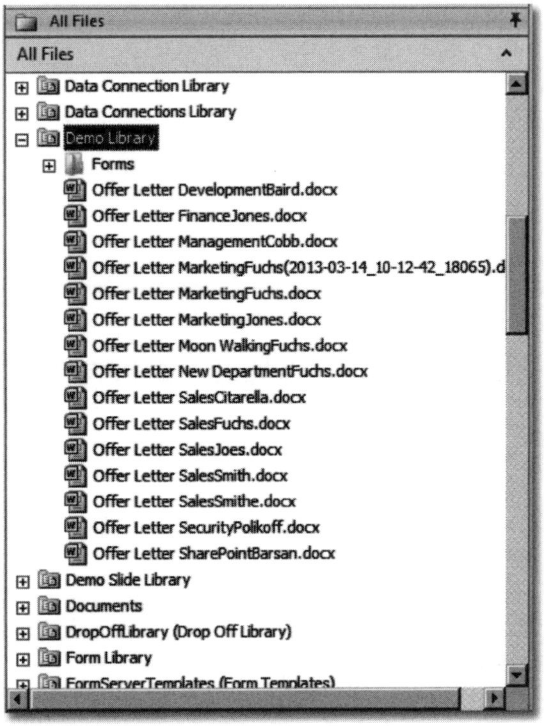

In addition, the contents of the Library will display and be accessible from the main display area with the documents' attributes, including the size of each file as shown in **Illustration 14** below. The documents can be opened in their respective applications directly from within *SharePoint Designer*.

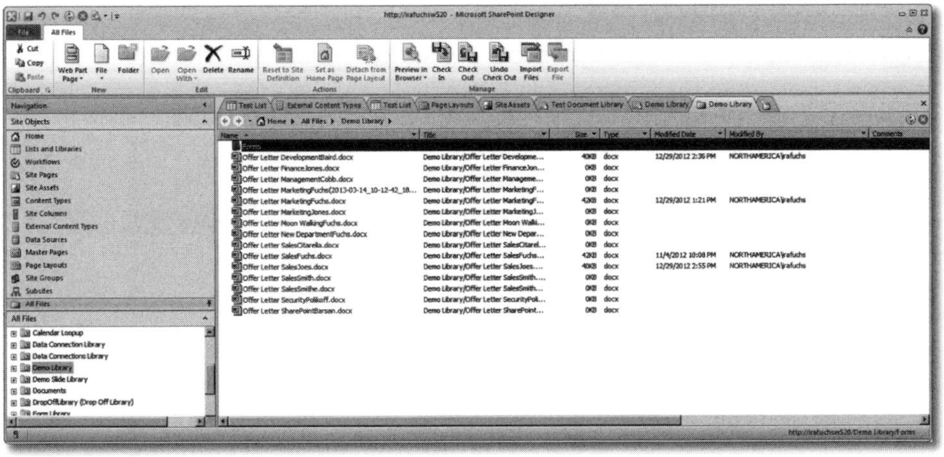

Illustration 13

Illustration 14

Not only that, but you can copy one or multiple documents from one Library to another! Simply select the files you want using your Shift-key or Ctrl-key to make multiple selections, right-click and select Copy from the drop-down selection menu. Now go to another Library in the All Files Folder, double-click on it to display its contents in the main display area. Place your cursor anywhere in the main display area, right-click and select Paste from the drop-down selection menu. This is a really valuable Site management capability.

From a Site management perspective the ability to access the content in Libraries directly from within *SharePoint Designer* is very useful when you need to determine why a Site Collection or Site is approaching its storage limit. Being able to quickly click from one Library to another and inspect their contents will provide an immediate indication of which libraries are populated with files that are very large, and rarely accessed. Furthermore you can also inspect a document's version history, as shown in **Illustration 15** below, which will often indicate if a Library is being overrun by multiple versions. The ability to inspect content quickly and efficiently in multiple libraries is indispensable for determining where there is inefficiency and waste in a *SharePoint* Site.

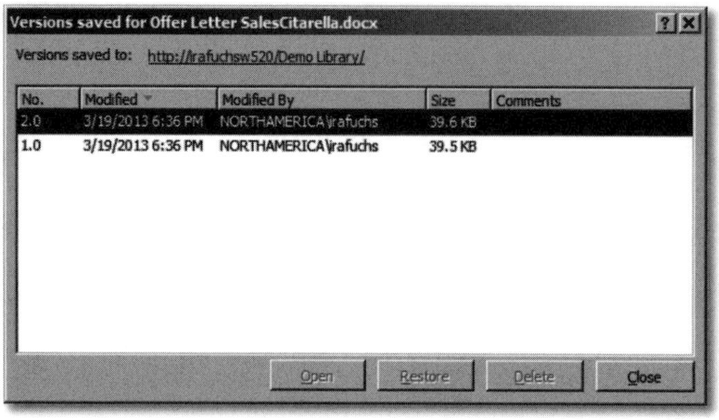

Illustration 15

In addition, you can also determine immediately, from a visual check mark cue, which files have been checked-out for an inappropriate period of time and check them back in as shown in **Illustration 16** below.

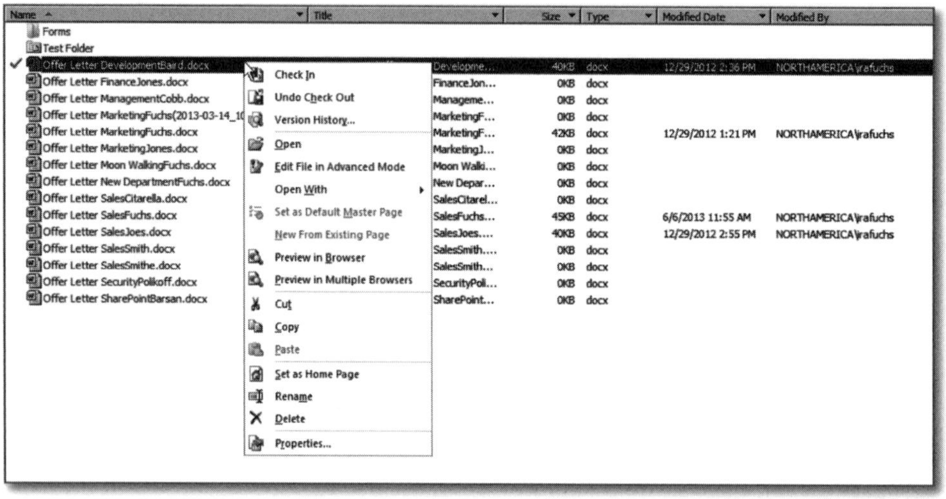

Illustration 16

Perhaps the most valuable file handling capability available through *SharePoint Designer* from a document management perspective is its efficient file and folder import facility as shown in **Illustration 17** on the next page. You can select multiple individual files, and even better, you can import a folder of files directly into a Library. Compare this capability with the Upload Multiple Documents functionality in *SharePoint*; it is substantially more efficient.

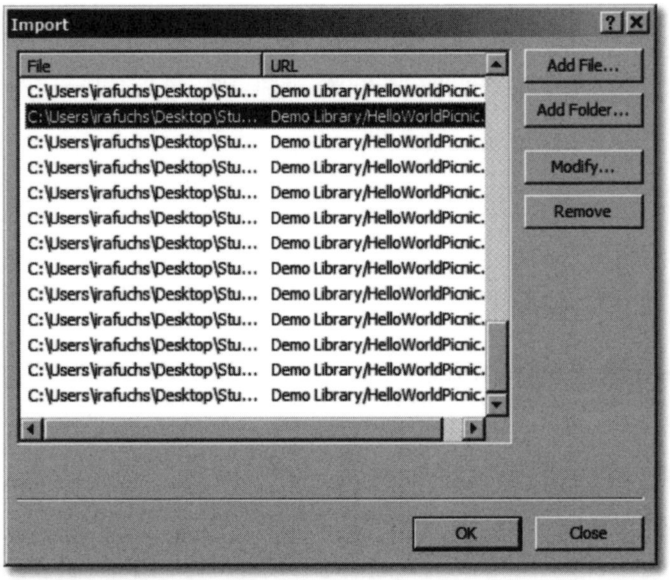

Illustration 17

Click on the *List and Libraries* folder on the *Site Objects Navigation* pane and then click on any List or Library to display its *Summary Page*. On the bottom right you will find the *Custom Actions* section. Click on the *New* button to open the *Create Custom Action* dialogue screen as shown in **Illustration 18** below.

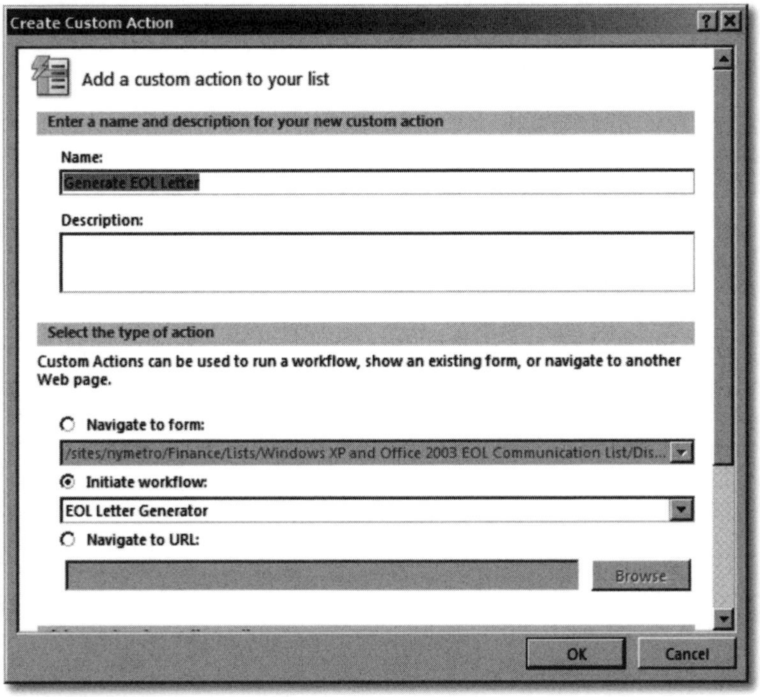

Illustration 18

Creating Custom Actions are another capability that is only available from *SharePoint Designer*. Custom Actions are displayed in the drop-down selection menu that is displayed when you right-click on any List or Library item as shown in **Illustration 19** at left.

Illustration 19

There are three Custom Actions that can be defined:

Navigate to a form – you can choose any of the forms that are either pre-defined or custom created for a List or Library.

Initiate workflow – which allows you to select a workflow that has been previously associated to the List or Library

Navigate to a URL – you can specify any URL, anywhere. This provides the ability to execute any application functionality that can be invoked by a URL address.

As was demonstrated in previous chapters, *SharePoint Designer* also allows you to visually modify List, Library and Data Views that have been defined in *SharePoint* as shown in **Illustration 20** below.

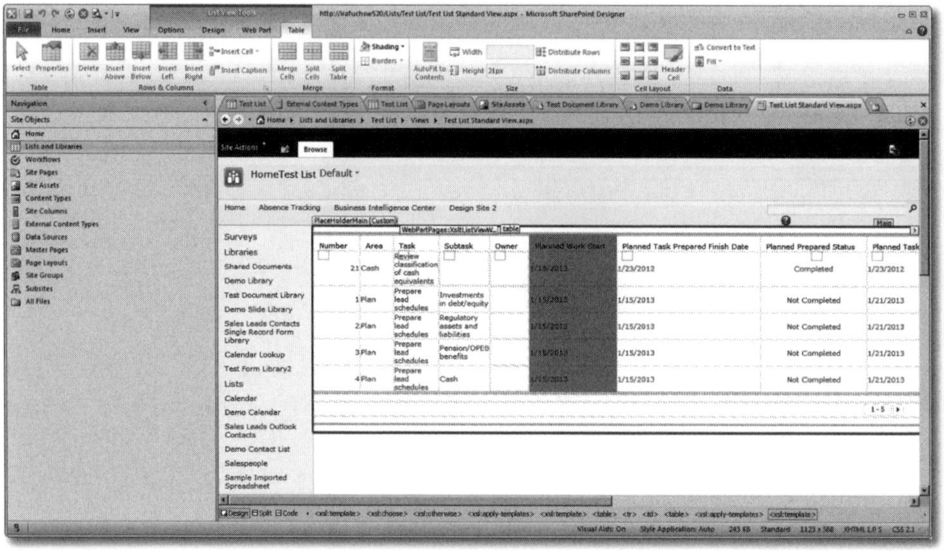

Illustration 20

Note – Design mode for editing List, Library and Data Views is no longer supported in *SharePoint 2013*, so this capability is not available.

A quick review of three functions available from the *Options Tab* of the *List View Tools Ribbon* menu, as shown in **Illustration 21** below, will identify additional *SharePoint Designer* capabilities that are not commonly known, yet are significant in the functional value that they can provide.

Illustration 21

Click on the *Filter* button to open the *Filter Criteria* dialogue screen as shown in **Illustration 22** below. As with the native *SharePoint* filter function for any given View, you can create any number of criteria clauses using And/Or conditional joins. However, when you click on the drop-down selection List for *Field Name* you will see that there are many more fields to choose from than what is available from the *SharePoint Edit View* page.

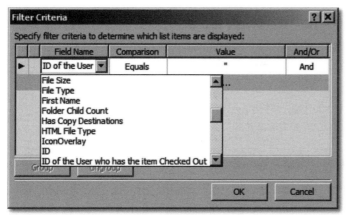

Illustration 22

Furthermore, the *Comparison Value* options are also expanded, including the option to *Create* a new parameter as indicated in **Illustration 23** below.

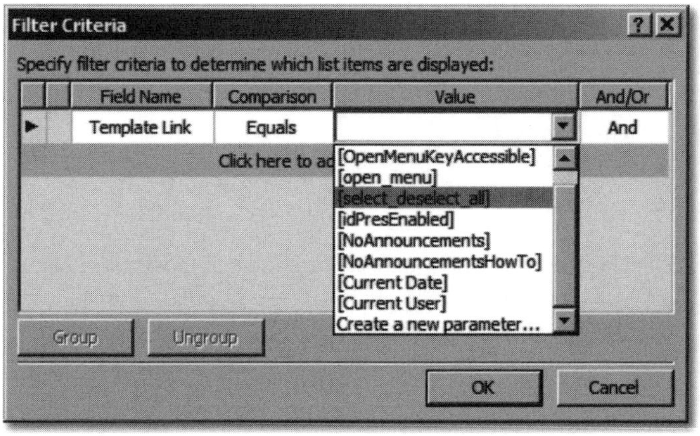

Illustration 23

Click on the *Create a new parameter* option from the *Filter Value* drop-down selection box or click on the *Parameters Ribbon* button to open the *Data View Parameters* dialogue screen as shown in **Illustration 24** below.

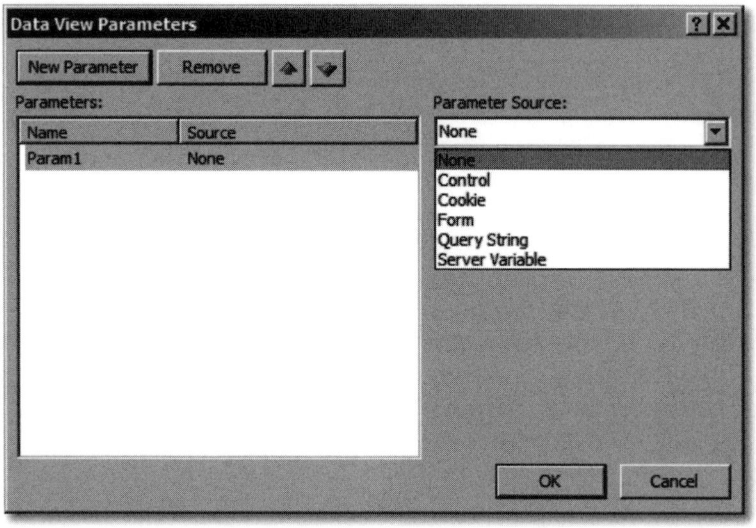

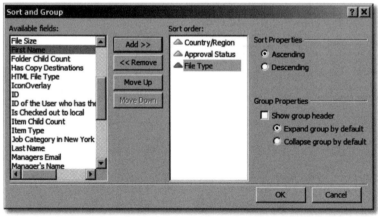

Illustration 24

Here you can define a *Parameter value* that is derived from another *Source* for use in a *Filter* or a *Formula*. Click on the *Sort & Group Ribbon* button to display the *Sort and Group* dialogue screen as shown in **Illustration 25** below.

Illustration 25

Click on the *Insert Formula Ribbon* button to display the *Insert Formula Editor*, as shown in **Illustration 26** on the next page, which can be used to populate the values of a field column, or manipulate the values in an existing column. The *Editor* provides the ability to visually generate complex *XPath* expressions comprised of any combination of fields, objects, functions and parameters. The *XPath* expression results are then displayed in the *Preview* section of the *Editor*.

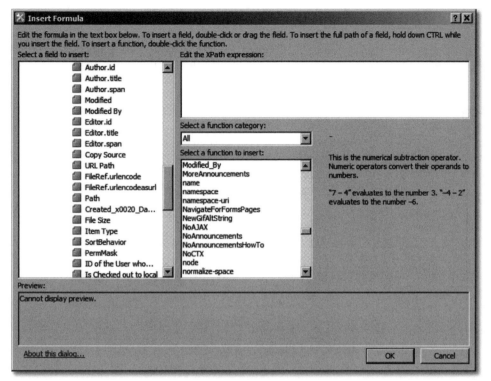

Illustration 26

Illustration 27 below shows the additional *List View Tools* that display on the *Ribbon* menu for the *Design, Web Part and Table Tabs*. These tools, in conjunction with the settings available from the *SharePoint Edit View* page, allow you to design and present information in *SharePoint* in ways that are significantly more useable and functionally useful than the standard default presentation of *SharePoint* Lists and Library information.

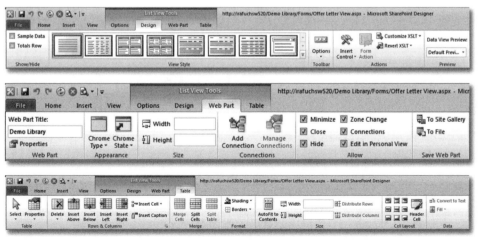

Illustration 27

A feature available from the *Web Part Tab* of the *List View Tools Ribbon* menu that is particularly worth examining is the ability to create a *Global Web Part* from any List or Library. A *Global Web Part* is a Web Part that is stored in the *Site Collection Web Part Gallery* and can be inserted onto any page in any Site of that Site Collection. When you create a List or Library in a *SharePoint* Site that List or Library becomes available as a Local Web Part that can be inserted on any page within the Site that it was created. Suppose however that you create and design a List in any given Site that may also be useful to other people or groups in an organization, such as the *Catalog List* we created in an earlier chapter. However it may not be appropriate to give them access to the Site where the List resides. The solution is to create a *Global Web Part* from the local version. This is accomplished by opening a *List View* in *Share-Point Designer* as shown in **Illustration 28** below for the *Catalog List*.

Illustration 28

Note – Design mode for editing List, Library and Data Views is no longer supported in *SharePoint* 2013, however this function is still available on the *SharePoint Designer* 2013 *Ribbon* menu in Code mode as shown in **Illustration 29** below.

Illustration 29

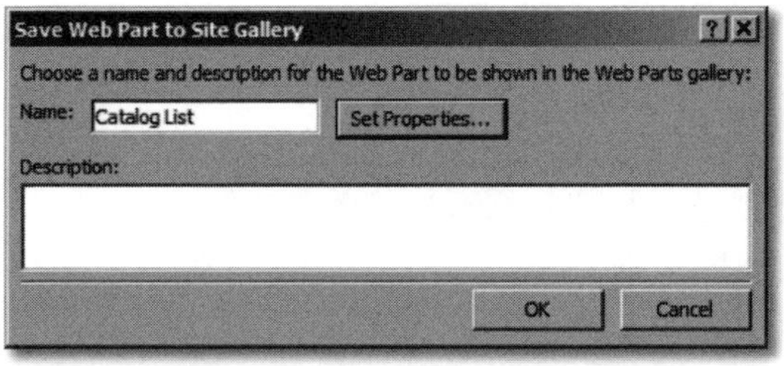

Illustration 30

Place your cursor anywhere in the *Web Part* area of the page and select the *Web Part Tab* of the *List View Tools Ribbon* menu. Now click on *To Site Gallery* to open the *Save Web Part to Site Gallery* dialogue screen as shown in **Illustration 30** at left.

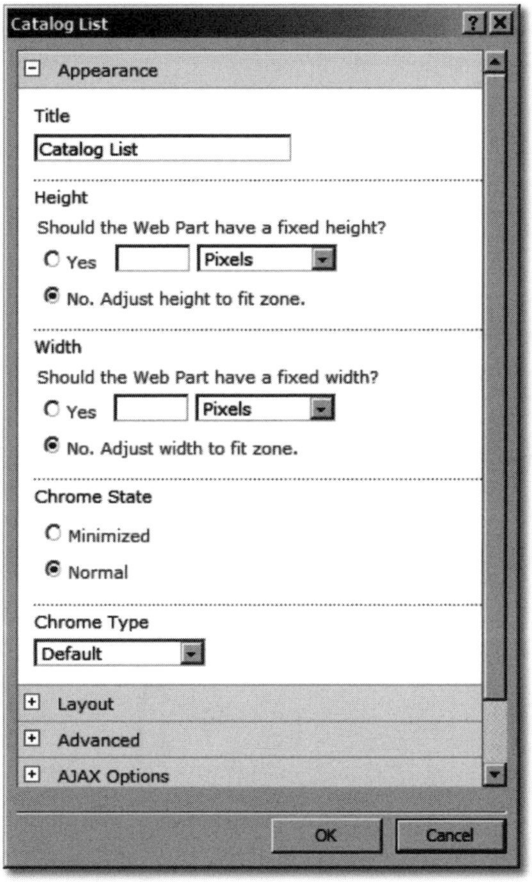

Illustration 31

If you click on the *Set Properties* button the *Web Part configuration* pane will display as shown in **Illustration 31** at left where you change or remove the *Title*, specify the *Chrome Type*, and specify the size of the Web Part.

When you click the *OK* button on the *Save Web Part to Site Gallery* dialogue screen, the prompt shown in **Illustration 32** below will display. Click *Yes*.

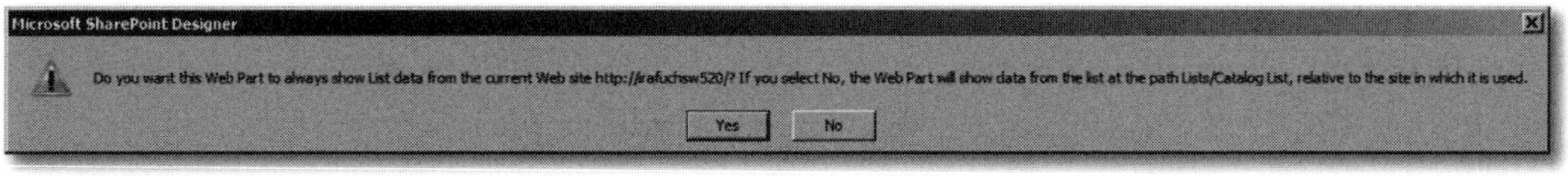

Illustration 32

Now, from any Site in the Site Collection open any Page, Web Part Page, List or Library in *edit mode* and insert a Web Part. Scroll down the *Categories* group and select the *Miscellaneous* folder; you will see the new Global Web Part in that folder as shown in **Illustration 33** below.

Illustration 33

Insert the Web Part and you will see that the View for the List or Library will be embedded in a Web Part Zone, Table cell, or directly on a page as shown in **Illustration 34** below.

Illustration 34

Our final area of review will be *Data Sources* in *SharePoint Designer*. Again, this is a set of valuable tools and functionality that is only available from *SharePoint Designer*. Click on the *Data Sources Folder* on the *Site Objects Navigation* pane. You will see all the Lists, Libraries and External Content Types created in your Site as shown in **Illustration 35** below.

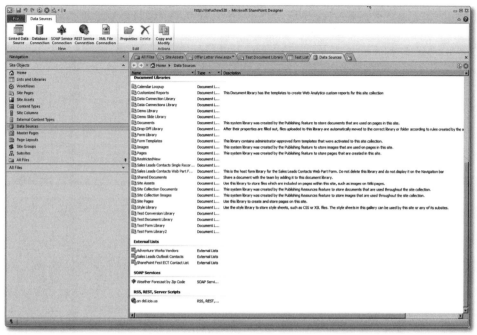

Illustration 35

Every List and Library is a Data Source. As we demonstrated using a *SharePoint* List as a *Secondary Data Source* in an *InfoPath* form, the List schema is represented as both query and data fields thus allowing *InfoPath* to filter and display selective records. In addition to Lists and Libraries, *SharePoint Designer* provides the capabilities to create a number of different Data Sources as indicated by **Illustration 36** below of the *Data Sources Ribbon* menu.

Illustration 36

The *SOAP (Simple Object Access Protocol) Service Connection* allows you to access the operations and data of an application that has been published as a Web Service. Web Services are an industry standard methodology of exposing application operations and data so that they can be accessed remotely through the Web. To use the *SOAP Service Connection* you need the URL address link of a WSDL (Web Services Description Language) file for an application such as:

http://wsf.cdyne.com/WeatherWS/Weather.asmx?WSDL

Clicking on this link will bring you to the WSDL file which is an XML description of the operations and data available from the application as shown in **Illustration 37** on the next page.

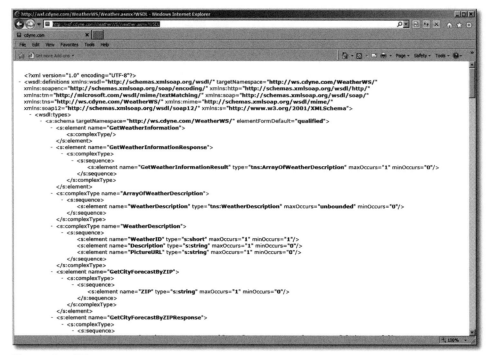

Illustration 37

Illustration 38

Click on the *SOAP Service Connection Ribbon* button to open the *Data Source Properties* dialogue screen as shown in **Illustration 38** at left. The *Source Tab* will be selected by default. Copy and paste the URL address for the WSDL above into the *Service description location* box and click on the *Reconnect* button to connect with the Web Service.

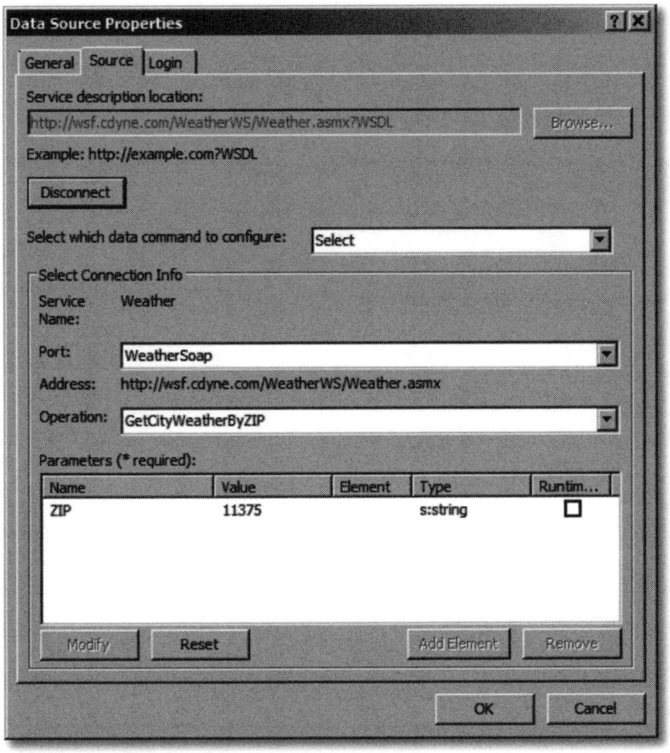

Illustration 39

The drop-down selection box for *Select which data command to configure* will become available; leave the default *Select* option. For the *Port* drop-down selection, leave the *WeatherSoap* option. In the *Operation* drop-down selection box choose *GetCityWeatherByZip*, and select the *Zip Parameter*. The completed dialogue screen will look like **Illustration 39** at left.

Click *OK* to finish. The *Data Source* main screen will now show a section for SOAP Services with a Weather Forecast by Zip Code item.

Now let's use this Data Source. Open any Page or Web Part Page and place your cursor in any editable area. Select the *Insert Tab* of the *Ribbon* menu and click on the *Data View* drop-down selection menu. Scroll down to the *Weather Forecast by Zip Code Web Services Data Source* and select it as shown in **Illustration 40** below.

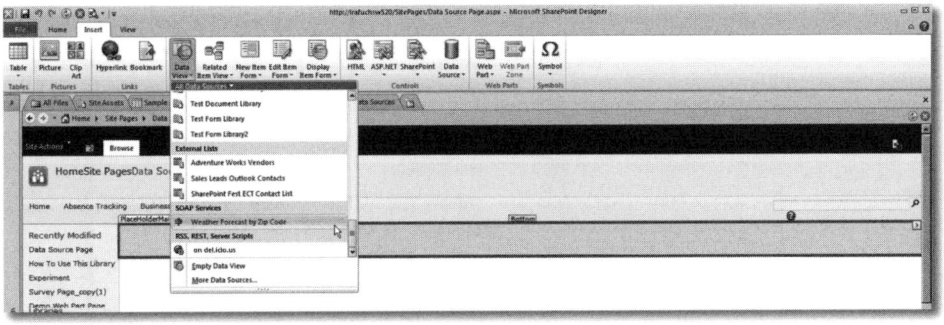

Illustration 40

Note – **do not** select the *Weather Forecast by Zip Code Web Services* from the *Data Sources* drop-down selection menu. This will not allow you to insert and work with the actual Data Source. You must first insert a *Data View*.

The *Data Source Details* pane will display on the right side of the screen as shown in **Illustration 41** below, showing the run-time query response for the fields and respective values returned for the Zip Code submitted as the parameter. A Web Part containing a *two-column, five row Table* is inserted on the page displaying the labels and respective values for the first five fields of the *Web Service Data Source*.

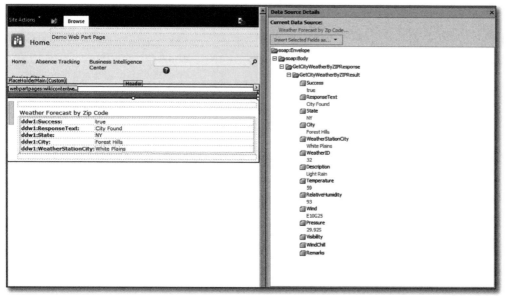

Illustration 41

You can edit and modify the *Table* any way you wish. In **Illustration 42** below two additional rows were added. Place your cursor in any *Table cell* and right click on any of the fields or values; a drop-down menu box will display showing the automatic insertion option as shown in **Illustration 42** below. You can choose and arrange any fields and values for display on your page, and you can apply any text and Table design attributes as well.

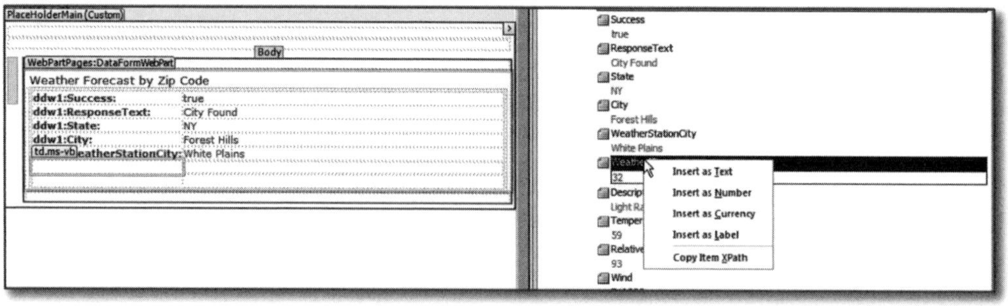

Illustration 42

Note – remove the "ddw1" prefix from the labels displayed in the first column. Once you have designed the Web Part to display the information you want save the page and preview it in a Browser. The Web Part will look like **Illustration 43** below.

Weather Forecast by Zip Code

City	Forest Hills
Weather Station	White Plains
Description	Light Rain
Temperature	59
Relative Humidity	93

Illustration 43

Is this not fantastic? This is a great feature that allows you to incorporate information on *SharePoint* Pages from any application that is exposed as a Web Service. And it was quick and easy to do!

Note – the *REST Service Connection* works the same way as the *SOAP Service Connection* but uses the *Representational State Transfer (REST)* protocol which is an alternative and widely used remote access API.

Now let's investigate the *Linked Data Source*, which is a *SharePoint Designer* tool for combining and displaying the information from multiple data sources in versatile ways. With the *Data Sources Navigation Site Object* selected click on the *Linked Data Source Ribbon* button. The *Data Source Properties* dialogue screen will display as shown in **Illustration 44** below with the *Source Tab* selected by default. Use the *General Tab* to provide a name for the *Data Source*.

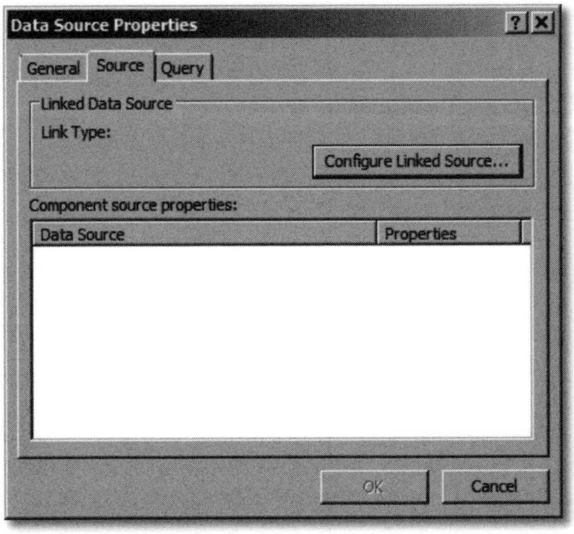

Illustration 44

Click the *Configure Linked Source* button and the *Link Data Sources Wizard* will display as shown in **Illustration 45 below left**. Here you can select the *Data Sources* that will provide the information that you want to combine. Note that as shown in **Illustration 45 below right** you can link any *Data Source* created in *SharePoint Designer*.

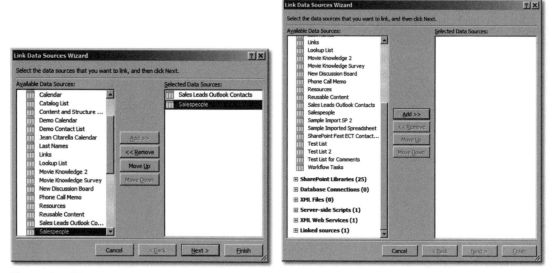

Illustration 45

The purpose in most cases for linking Data Sources is to combine and display related information, such as the Customers managed by a Salesperson. Consequently the Data Sources should contain a common field that provides the "related join" for the Sources, although it is not necessary if you want to display information from multiple Data Sources that are not related.

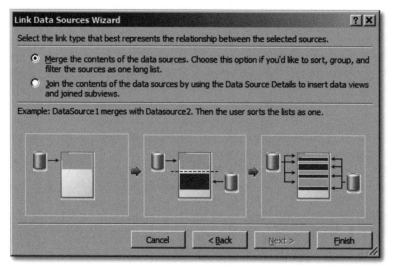

Click the *Next* button after you have selected the Data Sources. The next *Wizard* screen will allow you to specify how you want to display the joined information; either as a single List of columns or in a Master/Detail format, as shown in **Illustration 46** at left.

Illustration 46

Clicking the *Finish* button will return you to the *Data Source Properties* dialogue screen where the selected Data Sources will now be displayed as shown in **Illustration 47 below left**. Click on the *Properties Edit* link for a Data Source to display the *Query configuration* Tab as shown in **Illustration 47 below right**.

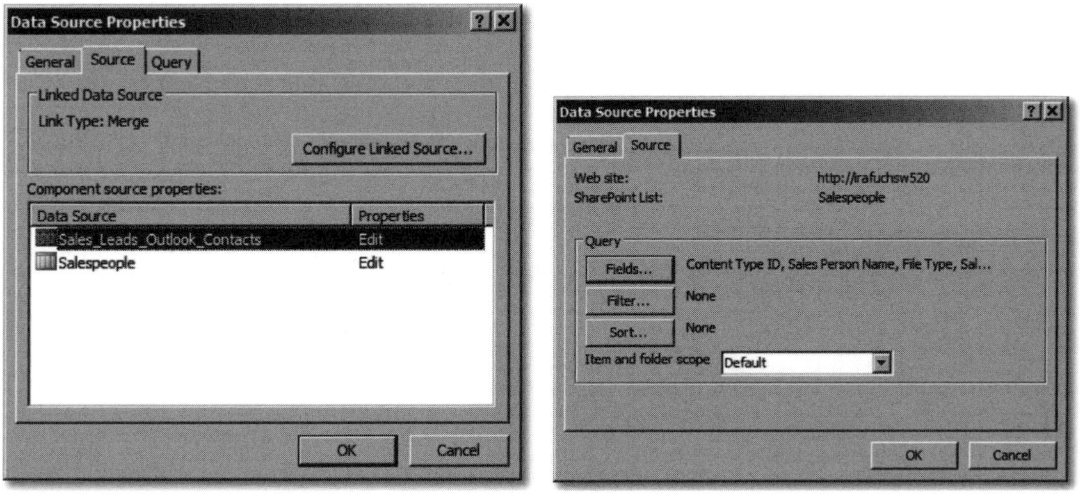

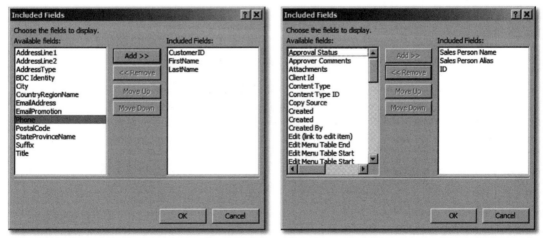

Illustration 47

Here is where you specify the fields from the respective Data Sources that you want to display. The *Included Fields* dialogue screen displays the *Available fields* from a Data Source from which you can select the ones you wish to use. You can also configure multiple field *Filter and Sort* settings from here. **Illustration 48 below left and right** shows the respective fields selected from the two linked Data Sources.

Illustration 48

This concludes creating and configuring a *Linked Data Source*. Now let's see how it works. Just as we did for the *Soap Services Connection Data Source* open any Page or Web Part Page and place your cursor in any editable area. Select the *Insert Tab* of the *Ribbon* menu and click on the *Data View* drop-down selection menu. Scroll down to the *Linked Data Source* you created and select it. The *Data Source Details* pane will display on the right side of the screen showing a schema of the selected combined fields from the linked Data Sources. A *List Web Part* containing the field names as column headers and rows of values for the respective records in the combined Data Source will display as shown in **Illustration 49** below.

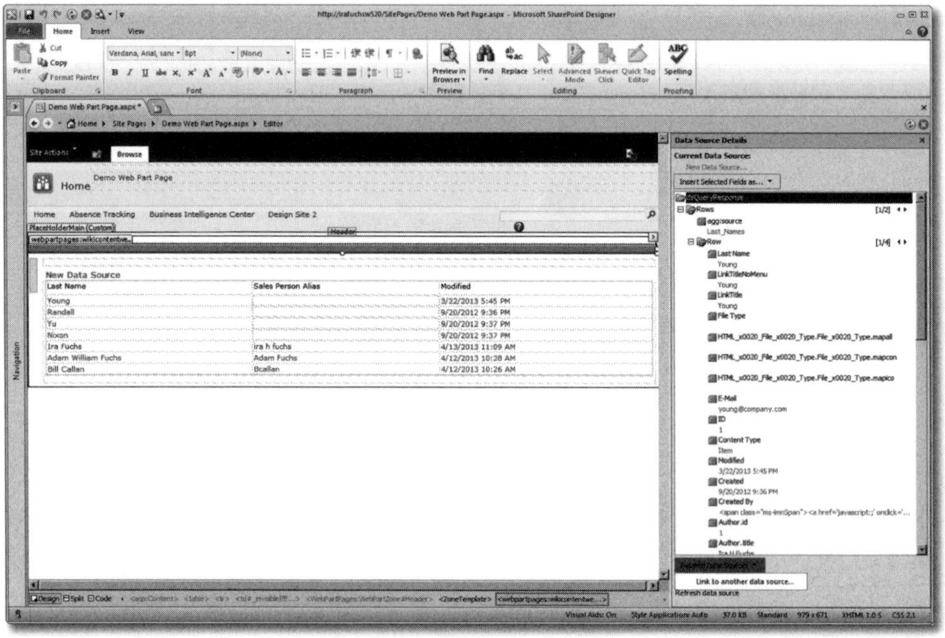

Illustration 49

As with any Tabular formatted Web Part you can edit and modify the Table any way you wish.

The last Data Source in our review is the *Copy and Modify Data Source*. This function does exactly what its name indicates: it allows you to copy an existing Data Source and create a new, modified version. But there is actually more to it than just that. When you want to present List or Library information in multiple ways you create Views. However every View is accessible to anyone who has access permissions to the List and you don't always want that. In addition, having too many Views can become confusing. When you *Copy and Modify a List or Library Data Source* you are essentially creating an artifact that behaves like a View but without having to physically instantiate the View in the List or Library.

Select any List or Library in the *Data Source Library* and click on the *Copy and Modify Button*. The *Data Source Properties* dialogue screen will display as shown in **Illustration 50 left** on the next page. Name the new Data Source from the *General Tab* and then click on the *Fields* button from the *Source Tab* to display the *Included Fields* dialogue screen, the same screen we saw working with the *Linked Data Source* as shown in **Illustration 50 right** on the next page.

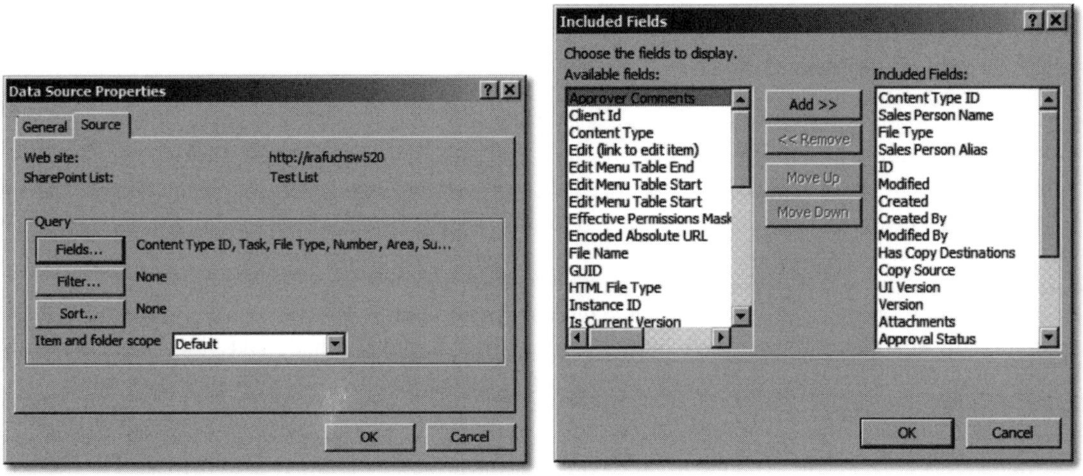

Illustration 50

Click the *Filter* button to display the *Filter Criteria* dialogue screen as shown in **Illustration 51 below left** where you can create any number of conditional filter clauses. Click on the *Sort* button to display the *Sort* dialogue screen where you can create an arbitrary number of Sort columns as shown in **Illustration 51 below right**.

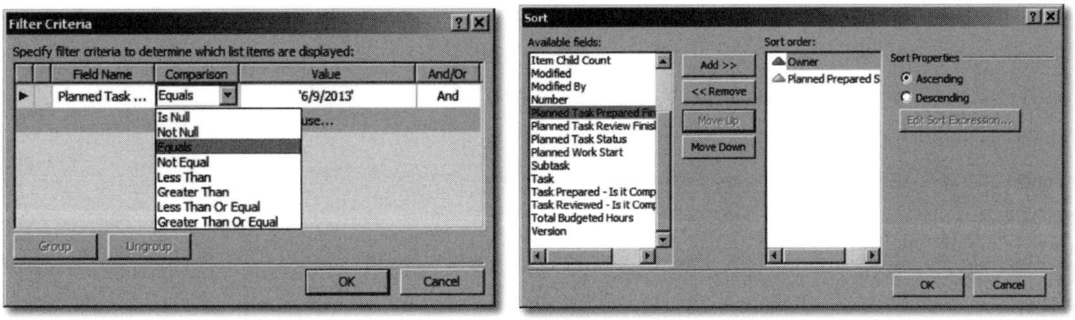

Illustration 51

Once you have created the new Data Source you can insert it as a *Data View* on any Page or Web Part Page where it behaves just like a Web Part. However, you can assign user and group permissions to the host Page for the new Data Source that are different than the permissions for the List or Library that the new Data Source was copied from, thus modifying access to a "View" of a List or Library.

Data Sources are one of the hidden gems of functionality in *SharePoint Designer* that expand the opportunities of what you can accomplish in *SharePoint*.

This concludes our overview of *SharePoint Designer*. If you were not previously conversant in all the goodness that is in *SharePoint Designer*, hopefully you now have a profound appreciation of the many ways it complements and enhances *SharePoint* and makes it significantly easier to work with, manage and extend.

Afterword

Certainly one of the great things about SharePoint is that there is always something new and exciting to learn. Every time I learn something new and useful about SharePoint I really do get a thrill, and I feel further empowered to provide value to people who work with and use SharePoint. Nothing pleases me more than knowing that the practical knowledge that I have shared with fellow SharePoint practitioners is being applied every day to address real-world needs. I hope that you have derived significant value from the information in this book and you apply it effectively and often.

If you enjoyed this book and you would like to discover more about what the art-of-the possible is with InfoPath, SharePoint Designer workflows, and overall SharePoint functionality, please consider my first book **Enterprise Application Development in SharePoint 2010 – Creating an End-to-End Application without Code.**

Please feel free to share your thoughts, comments and ideas about this book. My email is ira@ihfpublishing.com and you can also find me on Linked-In.

Index